THE

LIFE AND TIMES

OF

HANNIBAL HAMLIN

KENNIKAT PRESS SCHOLARLY REPRINTS

Dr. Ralph Adams Brown, Senior Editor

Series in
AMERICAN HISTORY AND CULTURE
IN THE NINETEENTH CENTURY
Under the General Editorial Supervision of
Dr. Martin L. Fausold
Professor of History, State University of New York

Hannibal Hamlin

THE

LIFE AND TIMES

OF

HANNIBAL HAMLIN

BY HIS GRANDSON

CHARLES EUGENE HAMLIN

———

ILLUSTRATED

Volume I

AUTHOR'S PREFACE

In offering "The Life and Times of Hannibal Hamlin" to the public, I beg to make a brief explanation. This volume represents three years' work on my part, in which time I have received valuable assistance from many sources. For the personal narrative I am chiefly indebted to my father, General Charles Hamlin, my grandfather's right-hand man for many years. He gathered material for the purpose of writing the biography, but was prevented on account of public and business duties. He also rendered me invaluable aid in consultation, while the manuscript was being written. I also acknowledge important help received from John G. Nicolay, Josiah H. Drummond, Noah Brooks, Henry L. Dawes, Albert E. H. Johnson, John Conness, Frank B. Fay, and others, in preparing the chapter which demonstrates Lincoln's desire for the renomination of the ticket of Lincoln and Hamlin in 1864. I would add that my own investigations into this subject cover a period of seven years, during which time I consulted and corresponded with many surviving delegates to the Union Convention of 1864. The genealogical record was obtained mostly from the comprehensive "Life of the Hamlins," by H. Franklin Andrews, of Iowa; also from the researches of Professor Charles E. Hamlin, of Harvard University; James H. Hamlen, of Portland, Maine, and William Hamlyn, of Buckfastleigh, England.

The chief feature of Hannibal Hamlin's career is his anti-slavery record. This is the principal story of the biography, and it includes a substantial account of the rise and fall of the slave party in Maine, as well as in the nation. In dealing with the struggles of the anti-slavery men in Maine, one invaluable authority was my grandfather's private correspondence, which included fully ten thousand letters, and nearly half of which related to this picturesque phase of Maine politics.

C. E. H.

BANGOR, MAINE, January 24, 1899.

CONTENTS

CHAPTER I

ANCESTRY OF THE HAMLIN FAMILY

CHAPTER II

BIRTH AND BIRTHPLACE OF HANNIBAL HAMLIN

CHAPTER III

BOYHOOD AND EDUCATION

CHAPTER IV

FARMER, PRINTER, AND LAW STUDENT

CHAPTER V

HANNIBAL HAMLIN AS A LAWYER

CHAPTER VI

HAMLIN IN THE LEGISLATURE

CHAPTER VII

ELECTED TO CONGRESS

CHAPTER VIII

WORK OF THE TWENTY-EIGHTH CONGRESS

CHAPTER IX

MR. HAMLIN AS A REFORMER

CHAPTER X

THE ANNEXATION OF TEXAS

CHAPTER XI

MR. HAMLIN ON DUELING

CHAPTER XII

THE PARTITION OF OREGON

CHAPTER XIII

THE MEXICAN WAR

CHAPTER XIV

DEFEATED FOR THE SENATE

CHAPTER XV

THE WILMOT PROVISO

CHAPTER XVI

THE CONSPIRACY AGAINST OREGON

CHAPTER XVII

ELECTED TO THE SENATE

CHAPTER XVIII

MR. HAMLIN IN THE SENATE

CHAPTER XIX

THE COMPROMISES OF 1850

CHAPTER XX

MR. HAMLIN'S WORK IN THE SENATE

CHAPTER XXI

HAMLIN'S HARDEST CONTEST WITH THE SLAVE POWER

CHAPTER XXII

PRESIDENTIAL CAMPAIGN OF 1852

CHAPTER XXIII

THE PIERCE ADMINISTRATION

CHAPTER XXIV

MR. HAMLIN LEAVES THE DEMOCRACY

CHAPTER XXV

HAMLIN A FATHER OF THE REPUBLICAN PARTY

CHAPTER XXVI

GOVERNOR AND SENATOR

CHAPTER XXVII

LINCOLN AND HAMLIN

CHAPTER XXVIII

ELECTION OF LINCOLN AND HAMLIN

CHAPTER XXIX

MR. LINCOLN AND MR. HAMLIN MEET

CHAPTER XXX

FORMATION OF THE CONFEDERACY

CHAPTER XXXI

THE SLAVEHOLDERS' REBELLION

CHAPTER XXXII

FIRST YEARS OF THE REBELLION

CHAPTER XXXIII

EMANCIPATION OF THE SLAVES

CHAPTER XLI

MINISTER TO SPAIN

CHAPTER XLII

THE LAST YEARS

LIST OF ILLUSTRATIONS

THE LIFE AND TIMES

OF

HANNIBAL HAMLIN

CHAPTER I

ANCESTRY OF THE HAMLIN FAMILY

THE Hamlins are believed to have been Teutonic tribes, clans, or nations of people who lived along the banks of the rivers and lakes in the far-off ages of old Germany. The name Hamlin is probably of locative origin, being derived from the old Saxon words "ham" and "lin" or "lyna," which mean home and pool. Hence, etymologists hold that a "hamlin" or "hamlyn" was "the home by the pool," and that the Hamlin or Hamlyn was the person who lived by the pool. A circumstance that appears to bear out this theory is the fact that Hamlins are now living in the ancient town of Hamelin, in Hanover, at the confluence of the rivers Hamel and Weser, which is the town made famous in the legend of "The Pied Piper of Hamelin," by Robert Browning. There are other seats in Germany whose names seem also to uphold the theory concerning the origin of the name of Hamlin, and to indicate that the Hamlins were spoken of as a distinctive tribe, clan, or nation, as the Highlanders of Scotland, for example, are spoken of in distinction from other branches of the Scottish race. Many surnames were derived in this way, and when Germany emerged from barbarism, Hamlin became a family name. Bearers of this name gradually found their way into other countries, and now the Hamlins are an immense representative family in Germany, France, England, Canada, and the United States of America. There are various ways of spelling the name, — Hamlin, Hamlyn, Hamblin, Hamblen, Hamline, Hamlyne. In early times members of a family often spelled their common name differently, and this accounts for the various ways in which this surname is now written. In the United States it is generally spelled Hamlin ; in England, Hamlyn ; in France it is Hamelin, — the name of the distinguished admiral who commanded a fleet in the Crimean war, and that also borne by many Huguenot families.

The American Hamlins are descended from the English branch of their race, whose origin is clearly proved by the old Norman and English chronicles. The first authentic records of individual Hamlins were made by William the Conqueror, in his "Battle Abbey Roll" and "Domesday Book." When he planned his invasion of England to take the throne from Harold, he gathered his army for embarkation at Dives, France, in 1066. He assembled an army of about sixty thousand knights and soldiers, who were of the flower of Norman, French, and German arms. Before the departure William had a roll made of his knightly companions, who were about five hundred in number, and placed it in the old cathedral in Dives, where it may be seen to-day. On this roll is inscribed the name of Hamlin de Balon, the first Hamlin to appear in authentic records. After the battle of Hastings, William, to commemorate his victory over the English, built the Battle Abbey on the field of his triumph, and to perpetuate the names of his knightly companions who fought under his banner he had a second roll made, which he caused to be placed in Battle Abbey. This roll, it is supposed, was removed to Cowdray House, near Midhurst, and lost when that ancient seat was destroyed by fire in 1793. But fortunately many copies of the original record were taken and safely preserved. While some of these copies are obviously incorrect, having had names added to them, yet the name of Hamelin de Balon appears on all, and on some without descriptive title.

English authorities [1] hold that some names on the "Battle Abbey Roll" represent families, and if this theory be true the name Hamelin, in this instance, stands for several men of that name. There are no trustworthy records that show how many Hamlins were among the Normans at Hastings; but there is convincing evidence that there were at least two knights among William's companions, and many among the soldiers. When William set about completing his subjugation of England he had the "Domesday Book" written in two volumes, in 1086, which is the authoritative record of his division of land among his trusted companions. In this are the names of Hamelin, Sire de Balon, and Hamelin, sometimes spoken of, and published, as Hamelinus.[2] In old English chronicles, such as land patents and other documentary evidence reproduced by Worthy, the English historian, there are other records which show that after the battle of Hastings large tracts of land in various parts of England, mostly in Cornwall and Devonshire, were apportioned in small allotments to other Hamlins, who, it is thought, came from Germany; but this is not pertinent to the narrative which is confined to the ancestors of the American branch of the Hamlin family, and is, therefore, of no special interest to these pages.

---

[1] Charles Worthy's history of *The Suburbs of Exeter.*
[2] In the *Domesday Book* it is spelled Hamelin. See illustration.

CORNWALL.

Hamelin holds of the Earl, Cariorgel. Edwin held it in the time of King Edward, and was taxed for one ferling; the arable land is 3 carucates: there are 2 ploughs, and 4 bordarii, and 6 acres of wood, and 100 acres of pasture: formerly it was worth 15 shillings, now 10 shillings.

Hamelin holds of the Earl Moidelton; Alwin held it in S. R. E., and was taxed for two hides and a half; nevertheless there are five hides: the arable land is 20 carucates: there are 9 ploughs and 7 bond servants, and 14 villaines, and 20 bordarii, and 6 acres of wood, and 100 acres of pasture: formerly it was worth 60 shillings, now 50 s.

The same Hamelin holds Serge. Aluuin held it in S. R. E., and was taxed for 1 hide and a half, nevertheless there are 3 hides: the arable land is 15 carucates: there are 6 ploughs, and 8 villaines, and 12 bordarii, and 10 acres of wood, and 30 acres of pasture: formerly it was worth 40 shillings, now 30 s.

EXTRACTS FROM THE DOMESDAY BOOK, Vol. I, folio 1, 2, 3, *et seq.* Page VII of fac simile, showing some of the land holdings of Hamelin, the Norman. The fac simile was made by Sir Henry James, Colonel of Engineers and Director of the Ordnance Survey Office, Southampton, England, and presented by him to Vice-President Hamlin, 1863.

Hamelin, Sire de Balon, was a man of some distinction as implied by his title, which means that he was the lord of Balon, a town in France. He was also "the son of a great Norman chieftain, Dieu de Baladun or Balure," as noted in Coxe's "Monmouthshire." It is suggested by Worthy that Hamelin, Sire de Balon, and Hamelin or Hamelinus were related, possibly brothers, but while this is not susceptible of documentary proof there seems to be moral evidence that there was a relationship between the two knights, in the similarity of their names, nationality, rank, and crossing of fortunes. William's confidence in the two Hamlins is proof of their Norman origin, for when he subjected the English people to his severe process of subjugation by compelling them to accept Norman lords, officers, speech, ways, and customs, he placed only Normans on guard. William ordered the Sire de Balon to take command of the territory of Ober-went, in Monmouthshire, where he built the castle of Bergavenny, at the king's command, and ruled there over his subjects until his death. To the other Hamelin, William, or his half-brother Robert, the Earl of Montaigne, gave twenty-two manors of land in Cornwall and Devonshire. In Devonshire Hamelin, according to the "Domesday Book," had the lordship over Hamistone, which is now called Broadhempstone, and also Alwington, under the Earl of Montaigne, a circumstance that indicates that he sustained close relations with Robert. The Sire de Balon died childless at about the end of the reign of William Rufus, and bequeathed his estate to Brian, the son of his sister Lucy. Brian settled the property on his cousin, Walter of Gloucester, then High Constable of England. Walter's son was created Earl of Hereford, but his male line became extinct. One of his daughters became the wife of Sir William Braose, and their descendant, Eva, married William de Cantilupe. He succeeded Hamelin in the lordship of Broadhempstone, a fact which might have been simply a curious coincidence, or yet might have been due to the relationship existing between the houses of the two Hamlins.

Hamelin most probably came to Cornwall in the immediate train of the Earl of Montaigne, and there founded the family from which the American Hamlins are descended. He was in command of a large body of men and exercised much power in Cornwall, but besides these facts not much of interest is known of him. He had a numerous progeny; and the name Hamlin frequently occurs in the early records of Cornwall in ways which show that the Hamlins of that time were large landholders and held high social positions. It is a fact at least worthy of mention, that from the time the Phœnicians discovered Cornwall and worked its tin mines, up to the present, Hannibal [1] was a favorite Christian name among the people of

[1] Hannibal means "favor of Baal."

Cornwall. But most of the descendants of Hamelin eventually migrated to Devonshire, and the main branch of the English Hamlins is, therefore, chiefly identified with its history. To-day they are one of the representative families of Devonshire; and it is due to their energy that the woolen business, the staple industry of the old county, still flourishes in the valley of the Dart.

Many other Hamlins also settled in Leicestershire, Warwickshire, Worcestershire, Oxfordshire, Gloucestershire, and Rutland after the battle of Hastings, and came into possession of large land interests. It is possible that they entered William's army from the town of Hamelin, which is but twenty miles from Hanover. But this is conjecture, although the fact that they became landowners simultaneously in various counties after Hastings would seem to be moral evidence that they rendered William services. From the Norman period the records of certain counties of England bear testimony to the numbers and political and social position of the Hamlins. Thus a Hamelin, a descendant of Hamelin, was Reeve of Launceston in 1207. In 1260 Sir William Hamlyn was member of Parliament from Totnes. Sir John Hamelin was a conspicuous representative of the descendants of Hamelinus in the early part of the fourteenth century, and his effigy may now be seen in the old church at Wymondham. Under Edward the Fourth, William Hamelin was sheriff of the counties of Leicester and Lincoln. Geoffry Hamlin also had a commission to protect the Black Prince in Gascony. In 1468 John Hamlyn was mayor of Exeter; in 1499 Nicolas held the same office, and Henry Hamlyn in 1526 and 1538. James Hamlyn, of Cloverly, was created baronet in 1795. But the list is too long to be extended further beyond the beginning of the Hamlins' history in the New World.

The pioneer Pilgrims, who came to this continent in 1620, as a result of religious persecutions, were followed by a second group of English men and women who shared their convictions. The men were mostly graduates of Cambridge, and held about the same social status as Cromwell, Hampden, and Prynne.[1] It was a remarkable body of men and women; they voluntarily gave up comfortable homes and good social positions in England in exchange for a hazardous life in a wilderness. James Hamlin, of Devonshire, was one of this number. Not much is known about him, but his acts tell their own story. He was the son of Giles Hamlin, of Devonshire, and a brother of Thomas Hamlin, of London, who had the privilege of inscribing himself "gentleman." James is the ancestor of the larger part of the Hamlin race in this Republic. He made a voyage to Cape Cod unaccompanied by his family, and there made a home for them at

[1] John Fiske's *American Political Ideas.*

Barnstable. He then returned to England, and in 1639 brought back his wife and several children. A numerous progeny was also sprung from Captain Giles Hamlin, who immigrated to Middletown, Conn., in 1650. It is supposed that James and Giles were brothers, but their relationship, like the connection between Sire de Balon and Hamelinus, was never determined. At the time Giles came to this country, Lewis Hamelin, of France, settled in Canada and established the Hamlin family of that part of the continent.

Cape Cod was a bleak and desolate spot when James Hamlin and his companions took up their life there. The country was flat and sandy, and the soil was hardly capable of cultivation. The land was apportioned among the settlers, and after much toil they founded the ancient and historical town of Barnstable, and James Hamlin was one of the thirteen incorporators. The land that he received was called Hamlin's Plains, and his house remained standing for many years after his death. Hamlin was also a friend and a follower of the famous Pilgrim preacher, John Lothrop, who managed to supply the needs of the church at Barnstable for years, in addition to his duties at Scituate. Hamlin is supposed to have come to this country in the same ship with Lothrop. In 1690 James Hamlin died, full of years, — he must have been fully eighty, — leaving a good name and a large family of children, most of whom were born at Barnstable. Five sons are supposed to have survived their father; and an amusing tradition has been handed down concerning them that illustrates the indifference people of this period showed about their family name. It is said, and the story appears well borne out by facts, that when James made his will and spelled his surname Hamlin, his sons agreed that each should spell it differently.

When the Pilgrims settled in Massachusetts the Indians were disposed to be friendly. There were five hundred or more living around the neighborhood of Cape Cod, and they gave the people of Barnstable no trouble. But as the English began to get a foothold, to multiply and extend their interests, the Indians became alarmed and jealous. The old story of a weaker people retiring before a stronger people was repeated. The Indian was wronged by the freebooters of all nations that ravaged these shores, but he was never destined to be civilized. He was a passing phase, a picturesque figure in the human family. Contact with Anglo-Saxon civilization shivered and finally broke him. While the Indian was shamefully treated in many respects by the whites, his cruelty and treachery towards his own race must not be forgotten. He had noble qualities, but at the same time he had also the nature of a savage. To the honor of the Pilgrims it must be recorded that their treatment of the Indian was in the main generous and humane, albeit they were guilty of some high-handed acts. The conflict between the Pilgrims and the Indians, in the Narragansett war, was precipitated by Philip to check the advance of the English, not to retaliate on them for any acts of cruelty or oppression.

Philip, king of the Wampanoags, was a great warrior, the Vercingetorix of his people. In 1675 he formed the tribes of New England into a league to exterminate the English. It was war to the knife, and the English, calling their best fighters, prepared to break the Indians' power in New England. The Narragansett war was a period of terrible tension and suffering for the English; an experience with a new kind of warfare, lurking foes and ambuscades, with one brilliant battle which, judged by results, should be ranked among the great battles in history. The English decided that to put the war to an end they would have to find Philip and strike him an unexpected blow. Philip was in camp in a large swamp, where the town of Kingston, R. I., is now located. In the bitterest of December weather, the English, over a thousand strong, marched all one day and night through forests and swamps to Pattyswamscott. Over four hundred of their number were overcome by the piercing cold, but the remainder of the English pressed on. They had the bull-dog stuff their kinsmen showed at Waterloo and their descendants exhibited at Little Round Top. They completely surprised Philip, and routed him after a desperate battle of six hours. Seven hundred warriors were killed, and probably over three hundred died from their wounds. Philip was killed not long after. The battle of Pattyswamscott destroyed all hopes the Indians had of success in that part of New England, and they gradually withdrew until forced out completely by the French and Indian wars. The importance of the victory at Pattyswamscott was recognized by the Massachusetts General Court in 1685, in grants of lands to the soldiers and their survivors. Among those who received land were Bartholomew and Eleazer Hamlin, sons of James, who marched in Captain Gorham's company. In his company of one hundred men, thirty were killed, including Captain Gorham, and forty were wounded. The land the Hamlins received is now the site of the town of Gorham, Maine, but it does not appear that they ever claimed it.

The French and Indian wars followed, and in this struggle between the English and the French for the supremacy of this continent, the seeds of American nationality were sown. The colonies had little in common up to this time. New York was settled by the Dutch, who had no love for the Pilgrims and Puritans of New England. Pennsylvania was settled by the Quakers, who were disliked by their neighbors. The Southern Cavaliers were, moreover, a race by themselves. But a common interest drew the colonies together in the five

French and Indian wars. The success of the French would mean that the country would be Catholicized, and so Pilgrim, Puritan, Knickerbocker, and Cavalier fought for their religious independence side by side until the fall of Quebec, which is now ranked as the greatest event in the history of this continent since its discovery. Many Hamlins fought in the French and Indian wars. Among the descendants of James was Gersham Hamlin, who is supposed to have fallen by the side of Wolfe at Quebec, or in a battle fought by the Earl of Loudon. Seth Hamlin, of Barnstable, was a lieutenant. Jacob, another kinsman, of the Cape Cod family, and who was one of the first of his race to come to Maine, was one of the pioneers of Gorham who held the fort of that town against the assaults of the Pequakets and their allies. He was afterwards a prominent business man of Gorham. It is among the records of that old town that he gave a negro slave his freedom.

The Hamlins continued to live in and around Barnstable a long time as an unbroken family, and their numbers rapidly increased. They are spoken of in the history and chronicles of Cape Cod as good citizens, church-going and patriotic people. James, the second son of the ancestor, was the father of ten children. His third son, Eleazer, through whom the descent of interest to this biography is preserved, was in turn the father of seven children. It was probably his son Benjamin who maintained the line, although the historians and genealogists do not agree on this point, since there were several Benjamin Hamlins at this time. His wife bore him eight children, the seventh of whom was Eleazer, the grandfather of Hannibal Hamlin, and a man of prominence in revolutionary times. He was born about 1737, and at an early age struck out for himself. He settled in Pembroke, Mass., where he became a large farmer, and married Lydia Bonney, who bore him eleven children. She died, and he married a widow named Bryant, who presented him with six more children, so that when the war of independence broke out Eleazer Hamlin had a family of seventeen children and a large farm to take care of; but he was a sturdy patriot, and his services in the Revolution are interesting and worthy of commemoration.

Eleazer Hamlin is described as a large, powerful, and energetic man, with a kindly disposition and decidedly independent and original nature. He was well educated considering his opportunities, and had strong common sense and a shrewd knowledge of men. While he supported the church, it is quite evident that he had his own ideas about Puritanism and thoroughly enjoyed life. One amusing illustration of his originality is his attack on the nomenclature that had been handed down and preserved with a clannish-like tenacity in the Hamlin family for many generations. In the annals of the grim Cape Cod

era of his family Eleazer Hamlin found an array of Biblical and sym-
bolical names like Job, Thankful, Experience, Desire, Elkanah, Be-
thias, Melanthiah, Mehetable, Shobal, Ichabod, Deliverance, Content,
Zaccheus, Hopestill, Tobiatha, and Elnathan.   He made a departure
in the matter of nomenclature after a false start.   He was well read
on the history of war, and being a great admirer of Scipio Africanus,
he named one of his eldest sons for that Roman general.   But everybody insisted on calling the lad Africa.   This gave Hamlin a hint, and
he called his son in honor of the continent of that name, and children
that followed Africa were named America, Europe, and Asia.   Twin
sons were finally born, and these received the names of Hannibal and
Cyrus, in honor of the Carthaginian and Persian generals.

A story is told of Eleazer Hamlin's love of fun.   One day he
ordered two of his boys to do some work on his farm.   Presently he
heard them shouting with laughter, and proceeded to investigate the
cause.   A stream of water with high banks ran through his farm.   On
one of the banks were the boys, and a short distance away was a large
ram, that belonged on the farm.   The boys had a red handkerchief,
and when they waved it the ram would rush at them, full tilt ; then
the boys would drop quickly on the ground, and the ram, carried on
by his weight, would go flying into the stream below.   At first Hamlin
was incensed at this disobedience of his orders.   In stentorian tones
he shouted, "Boys, what are you 'kiveering' around here for ? Be-
gone about your business, sirs !"   While the crestfallen lads were
slinking off to their work, their father stood on the bank, meditating
on the ram and wondering if he enjoyed the boy's fun as much as
would appear.   There seemed but one way to find out, and that was
to make a test himself.   He took out his own red handkerchief and
signaled to the ram, who accepted the challenge and started for his
master.   But, alas for Mr. Hamlin ; he was too heavy to move as
quickly as his sons ; the ram struck him fair and square in the back.
The ram and Eleazer went over the bank together, unable to stop
themselves.   The boys, hearing the ram charge, ran up on the scene
just in time to see their astonished parent throw up a veritable geyser
as he struck the water full force.   The boys shrieked with laughter,
and one of them shouted : "Oh, father, what are you 'kiveering'
around here for ?"   Mr. Hamlin was at first disposed to resent this,
but his sense of humor led him to see the affair in its right light.
He joined his sons in their laugh, and told the story himself.

But the real stuff in Eleazer Hamlin was revealed in the war of
independence.   He was one of the first to favor separation ; his home
was the centre for the yeomanry of Pembroke.   There they heard
the latest news of the growing troubles between the colonies and the
mother country, — the appointment of mercenary colonial governors,

the selfish exactions of the London merchants, the preëmption of trade in certain articles between the colonies, compulsory trade with England alone, taxation without representation, and the obstinate refusal of George the Third to listen to true English demands for fair play. The climax of oppression was reached when British soldiers were stationed in Boston to enforce obnoxious laws. Patriots began to arm themselves ; minute men prepared for action. The night Paul Revere spread the alarm, Eleazer Hamlin, his two elder sons, Africa and Asia, and his son-in-law, Seth Phillips, marched in Captain Hatch's company, Eleazer as a lieutenant, to Scituate, and remained there eleven days ready for duty. Pitcairn's attack on Lexington and Concord aroused the country ; minute men poured in from all sides, troops were formed. Eleazer Hamlin was appointed captain in a Massachusetts regiment in command of General Durant, in May, 1775. Africa and Asia, aged seventeen and sixteen respectively, and Phillips, served in Captain Hamlin's company, and with him marched into Cambridge on July 3, to join the army of fifteen thousand men assembled there to receive Washington as their commander.

The Hamlins were in Washington's command, and therefore saw a great deal of him. Africa, who served to the close of the war, kept a diary,[1] in which he recorded much of personal interest about Washington, Knox, Lafayette, Pulaski, Rochambeau, Hamilton, and other leaders of the Continental army. It is said to have been a voluminous record, and after the war was widely read throughout Massachusetts by old soldiers to whom Africa loaned it. Unfortunately the diary was not returned after Africa Hamlin's death, and no trace of it can be found. But family tradition respecting this diary and the views the Revolutionary Hamlins held of Washington tend to represent him as a man of a more human nature, of warmer affections and more passionate disposition, than he is represented by the statuesque pictures drawn of him in the last century. Washington's personality was an immense factor in his success. He had to face the most difficult undertaking that ever confronted an American soldier and leader. Only a minority of the American people openly advocated separation from the mother country at the outbreak of the war. The majority thought that armed resistance would bring Parliament to its senses, if Pitt, Fox, Burke, and other fair-minded English statesmen could not. The American Tories and Washington's personal bitter enemies, like Charles Lee, who tried to betray him on the battlefield, were difficulties that only a Titan could overcome. But Washington bound his men to him with hooks of steel, and, half starved, half frozen at times, always inadequately armed, they followed him wherever he led. Personal affection as well as patriotism must have

[1] See *My Life and Times*, autobiography of the Rev. Dr. Cyrus Hamlin.

played a great part in keeping Washington's men together under his flag in all their long trials.

The three Hamlins fought in the disastrous battle of Long Island, — Eleazer being the fifth line captain in Colonel Bailey's 23d regiment of foot, Clinton's brigade, — which Washington's strategy saved from becoming a rout by withdrawing at night. They served in the New Jersey campaign, — at Trenton and Princeton, — which Frederick the Great pronounced to Washington's credit as "the most brilliant campaign of the century." Captain Hamlin at this time, to his great regret, had to return home; his wife had fallen ill, and she died shortly afterwards. With a family of fourteen or fifteen children, and a large farm to take care of, the situation peremptorily demanded Captain Hamlin's presence at home. An official report regarding certain of Captain Hamlin's acts commends his work, and speaks of his "gallant bearing as an officer" and "his fair fame as a gentleman." When he tendered his resignation Washington gave him several hundred dollars in Continental money as a token of his personal regard, the gift signifying more than the money itself. Africa and Asia remained in the army, and were joined by their brother America, whose name was subsequently abbreviated to Merrick, and who was a powerful dare-devil young fellow of seventeen, and as good a shot as his brothers.

One very serious obstacle Washington had to contend with was the short terms for which men were enlisted. Men would enlist for a few months and return home satisfied that they had done their duty. Africa Hamlin, who had the best military record of his family, refused to take advantage of the short term of service, and reënlisted every time his term expired. He was thus continuously in the field nearly seven years, with the exception of one furlough of a fortnight. Entering the army as a lad, Africa was promoted to be a corporal when he was nineteen, a sergeant-major when he was twenty-one, and on January 1, 1781, he was commissioned an ensign, carrying the Continental banner when Cornwallis was enmeshed at Yorktown, the most crushing defeat the British arms ever received. He appears to have been a quiet, modest man, and well regarded by his superior officers. An amusing incident is told that illustrates the young ensign's modesty. He was invited by Washington to a state dinner, and unluckily upset a dish of gravy. To quote his quaint words: "The circumstance covered me with so much confusion that I withdrew, and did not accept any more invitations to these grand occasions." Another circumstance establishes his status among his brother officers. Africa Hamlin was one of the officers of the Continental army who assembled at Newburg, N. Y., and founded the Society of the Cincinnati.

When Eleazer Hamlin returned to Pembroke, he entered the state militia, and was appointed major, by which title he was known the rest of his life. His second wife having died, Major Hamlin married again, and his courtship is still a choice story in the annals of the town of Harvard, where he carried on a large farm and potash works. He made the acquaintance of Mistress Grace Fletcher, a snug, cosy woman, a relative of Daniel Webster's wife, and who owned a little tavern on a farm in Westford. Mistress Fletcher was noted in the neighborhood for her amiability and palatable flip. Major Hamlin called for a glass one day, and, as he was smacking his lips over it, remarked, "Monstrous fine flip, Mistress Fletcher." The next day the major strode into the tavern and called for another glass of that "monstrous fine flip." The third day the major made his appearance in his best clothes. With a gallant bow he said : "And now I have come for the fine woman who brews the monstrous fine flip." He married her. Their farms made a handsome property, and Major Hamlin thus became one of the largest landowners in that part of the State.

After the war was over, the Massachusetts General Court gave Major Hamlin and his sons some grants of land in the District of Maine in return for their services. Major Hamlin visited his land, and wrote a sarcastic letter to the General Court, advising it to return the land to its original inhabitants, who happened to be bears. But Africa, Merrick, Eleazer, Jr., Cyrus, and Hannibal decided to push their way into Maine, and cultivate their fortunes there. Africa married Susannah Stone, of Groton, and settled where the town of Waterford is now located. He was one of the incorporators of the town, and held various positions of trust in its government. He was Waterford's first town clerk. He was also appointed colonel in the state militia, and was thereafter known by that title. Hannibal and Merrick also settled in Waterford. A story is still told in Waterford of his jovial, dare-devil disposition. One day while walking through Hamlin's grant, as his father's land was still called, Merrick met one of the original inhabitants face to face. The bear rushed at Merrick, and having only the arms that nature gave him, he put them to good use. In the words of a quaint and humorous chronicler of the times, "Merrick pelted the bear with stones into a pit, and thereby obtained a juicy bear-steak." Another venturesome son of Eleazer Hamlin was George, who was born during the war of independence. He, too, had fighting blood. Hannibal Hamlin's father told him that George went to Russia, entered the army of the Czar, and was an officer in the later Napoleonic campaigns. But nothing more definite was known of him.

The only one of the four brothers who did not settle in Waterford was Dr. Cyrus Hamlin, the father of Hannibal Hamlin. He and his twin Hannibal were born at Harvard on July 11, 1769. Cyrus pur-

sued a course of study for several terms at the Medical School of
Harvard College, and, as was customary at that time, finished his
preparation for the practice of his profession in the office of an experienced physician, without taking a degree. He probably resembled
his interesting father more closely than any other of Eleazer's sons.
He was of commanding size, standing six feet in height, and in his
prime weighing over two hundred pounds. His cheeks had a ruddy
tint and his eyes were blue ; but his thickly grown, jet-black hair and
bushy eyebrows gave a dark tone to his general appearance. He had
his father's kindly and large-hearted disposition and a strong and well
balanced mind. He had a shrewd knowledge of men ; he knew how
to make friends. He loved a good dinner ; he could tell a story in
capital style. His air of good-fellowship drew people to him. He
was a good scholar and ranked well as a physician.

Coming to Maine, Dr. Hamlin heard that a physician was needed
in the town of Livermore, not far from Waterford, in Oxford County,
which had been founded by Deacon Elijah Livermore, who had come
to Maine from Watertown, Mass., — a picturesque pioneer and a man
of uncommon force of individuality and integrity of character. It was
the custom in some parts of New England for towns to elect their
physicians, and Livermore prepared to do this. Deacon Livermore
practically ruled the town, and it appears had decided on a physician
already when Dr. Hamlin came on the scene. By a curious coincidence both physicians had fallen in love with Deacon Livermore's
daughter Anna. She favored Dr. Hamlin, and that spurred him on
to greater efforts. The deacon, however, stood by his own man, and,
to his amazement, Dr. Hamlin carried the election. But when the
deacon grasped the situation, and understood that Dr. Hamlin was
the choice of his daughter's heart, he gracefully acquiesced, celebrated the wedding in good old-fashioned style, and pushed his son-
in-law's fortunes with zeal. Through his influence Dr. Hamlin was
appointed clerk of the courts of Oxford County, when it was formed
in 1805, which position and that of probate judge and sheriff he held
a great many years.

This union between the Hamlins and Livermores was a happy one
in many ways. The Livermores were one of the first families to
settle in New England, and some of its representatives are among
New England's ablest men. The most distinguished Livermore of
this period was Samuel Livermore, of Holderness, N. H., and the
brother of Dr. Hamlin's father-in-law. He was a member of the Continental Congress, for many years United States senator, president
pro tempore of the Senate two sessions, and finally chief justice of
New Hampshire. He was a man of great ability, and his sound judgment, learning, and coolness gave him weight in the inner councils of

DR. CYRUS HAMLIN.

ANNA LIVERMORE HAMLIN.

Congress in shaping legislation. His brother Elijah might have distinguished himself had he entered public life, for he had the ability. A descendant of his, George Livermore, the antiquarian, of Cambridge, Mass., possessed some of these qualities, although he never sought a public career. His writings [1] on the slavery question greatly impressed Abraham Lincoln, and show that he was one of the safe, sagacious, and far-seeing advisers whom great men call to their aid, and of whom the public at the time heard little. It is an interesting fact that Hannibal Hamlin and George Livermore so closely resembled each other in their features that they might have passed for brothers.

Anna Livermore, on her mother's side, also inherited the best of New England blood. Her mother was Hannah Clark, whose ancestor, Hugh Clark, was a Pilgrim, and settled in Massachusetts contemporaneously with James Hamlin and the pioneer Livermore. His great-grandson, Captain John Clark, of Waltham, was the father of Mrs. Livermore. He was a man of prominence, and a near kinsman of Jonas Clark, the famous patriotic minister of Lexington. He was a great power in the days of '75. Edward Everett said of him: " He was of a class of citizens who rendered services second to none in enlightening and animating the popular mind on the great question at issue." The night of Paul Revere's ride, John Hancock and Samuel Adams came to him and asked him if the people of Lexington would fight. He replied: "I have trained them for this very hour; they will fight, and, if need be, die, too, under the shadow of the house of God." On the next day, April 19, the first blood of the American Revolution was shed in Lexington within a few rods of Clark's house. The men who gave up their lives were among Jonas Clark's parishioners. When the old patriot saw their bodies, he said: "From this day will be dated the liberty of the world."

Anna Livermore Hamlin's rounded character and womanly disposition shone in her eyes. She was patient and devoted, always energetic, yet not given to talking. She had New England's religious and domestic ideals and was loyal to them, but she influenced by gentle example and sweet suasion, and she had great persistence. Hannibal inherited some of his best qualities from his mother. During the earlier years of their married life Dr. Hamlin and his wife made their home in Livermore, where several of their children were born, — Elijah, Vesta, and Anna. At the same time the Washburn

[1] He wrote an *Historical Research*, respecting the opinions of the founders of the republic on negroes as slaves, as citizens, and as soldiers. President Lincoln read this book, and sent Livermore the pen with which he wrote the Emancipation Proclamation.

family lived in Livermore, where the Washburn brothers were all born, and grew up with the young Hamlins as playmates until they removed to Paris Hill.   With the exception of the Fields, no American brothers have surpassed the Washburns in attaining collective and individual distinction.   Elihu B. was the "Father of the House" and United States minister to France; Israel was once a leading member of the House and Maine's war governor ; Cadwallader was a major-general in the Union army and a member of the House; Charles was a successful diplomat and editor, and William D., the youngest, has been a member of the Senate.

In 1805 Paris Hill became the shire town of Oxford County, and Dr. Hamlin removed to the Hill.   At this time the court used to sit in the old Baptist meeting-house, and was called together by the beating of a drum, the drummer standing at the northwest corner of the church.

CHAPTER II

PARIS HILL stands near the Androscoggin Valley. It is an eminence that rises by steady degrees to a commanding height. A panoramic scene of great beauty rolls away on all sides of the Hill. The valley stretches on both sides, broken by forests and villages, to ranges of hills and mountains that nearly encompass the Hill within a neighborly distance. The foothills of the White Mountains are discernible to the west, and on a clear summer day the eye can see the summits of the mountains faintly shimmering in the hazy distance. There is a calm, tranquil atmosphere about the scene that comes from the restful and protecting mountains which tower up majestically around the Hill. The air is vitalizing. The little village that nestles on the summit of the Hill is a veritable home in the heart of nature. When the sun sets a pretty legend is recalled of an Indian who, standing on the Hill centuries ago one evening, as the sun was sinking and filling the landscape with its rays, exclaimed in his tongue: "'T is the smile of the Creator." No more poetic or more appropriate description has yet been given to the scene around Paris Hill. It is one of the loveliest scenes of nature in all New England.

At the foot of the Hill lies South Paris. On the east are Buckfield and Hebron. On the west are Norway and Waterford, and not many miles off is Fryeburg, where Daniel Webster once kept school. Many a homelike settlement is to be found throughout the valley. Scores of pretty trout brooks wend their way through the woods. Once game abounded ; once the red man built his wigwam in this region. The warlike Pequakets ruled for years, and many a story of the bloody war of extermination which raged between the English settlers and the Indians has been handed down, and is told to-day around the firesides of Paris Hill. One, which introduces a figure of personal interest, — the Princess Mollyockett, daughter of Paugus, the chief of the Pequakets, — is the battle of Lovewell's Pond. The English settlers of Maine found after nearly half a century of irregular warfare that with the Jesuit lurking around the scene it was impossible to make a peace with the Indians that they would keep. After a series of frightful massacres in 1724, Captain John Lovewell, one of Maine's bravest sons, determined to drive the Pequakets out of Maine. With only forty-six men Lovewell penetrated to the Pequaket village, which was where Fryeburg now stands, and gave battle a whole day to a superior number of Indians. English bravery and tactics won. Paugus was killed, and having lost their leader, the Pequakets sullenly withdrew to Canada, and the Indian power in Maine was forever broken. Before the battle Paugus buried his treasure in a mountain within sight of Paris Hill. Mollyockett was the sole survivor of Lovewell's battle who knew the treasure's hiding-place. A fire that swept over the mountain destroyed Mollyockett's landmarks, and for years she haunted the place, searching for her lost treasure. She lived to be fully one hundred years old, and when the Hamlins came to Paris Hill she looked like a veritable Meg Merrilies of the woods. But she was a kindly old creature, as the Hamlins had good reason to believe, and as will appear later.

Paris Hill was a very homelike little village, peopled by pioneer families of Maine. Emery, Carter, Rawson, Parris, Stowell, Ryerson, Cummings, Hubbard, were among the familiar names of the day, and some of them are still represented in the families of the Hill. There was an unusually large number of talented and cultivated people living on the Hill, and the life of the place was exceptionally pleasant and neighborlike. The college element was large for a town of this size; Harvard, Bowdoin, Dartmouth, Brown, Waterville, and Union were all represented at Paris Hill during this and subsequent periods. During Dr. Hamlin's early life at Paris Hill, a group of men lived there who exerted no little influence in shaping the course of Maine in her opening year of statehood. First was Enoch Lincoln, one of Maine's early governors and representatives in Congress. Another was Albion K. Parris, five times governor of the State and also a United States senator. A third was Judge Stephen A. Emery, Hannibal Hamlin's father-in-law. He was a man of scholarly mind, pure character, and serene disposition. Although his tastes disinclined him to active participation in politics, yet his sound judgment and knowledge of political principles were sought by the Republican-Democratic party of Maine. Twice he was attorney-general of the State and for many years was judge of the probate and district courts. Two sons of Judge Emery, who inherited political and musical tastes from him, were George F. Emery, who was editor of the "Boston Post" for many years, and now a citizen of Portland; and Stephen A. Emery, of Boston, who was one of the most useful and widely respected scholars of music New England has yet produced.

Dr. Hamlin built a fine colonial mansion on top of the Hill, and cleared a large farm in the immediate vicinity of his house. His home became a social and political centre. Enoch Lincoln lived at Dr. Hamlin's house for many years. In front of the Hamlin house

BIRTHPLACE OF HANNIBAL HAMLIN.

was the village common, and the young people of the town found the doctor's home an attractive place.   Dr. Hamlin acquired a considerable reputation throughout the county as a specialist in children's diseases.   It is related on Paris Hill that children instinctively recognized him as their natural friend.   He was eventually appointed sheriff of Oxford County, and in accordance with the requirements of the time wore during the session of court a dress-sword, cocked hat, blue coat, and brass buttons; but in spite of these insignia of office and his imposing size, the children of the town would follow him around, climb all over him when they found him sitting in his porch, and make him tell them stories.   Yet he was very dignified in the performance of his duties, adhering strictly to the ideas of the Federal party, to which he belonged.   He had also strong ideas of his duties to his own children and brought them up accustomed to work. His wife was a perfect helpmate and very active; in fact, she had the athletic nature for which the pioneer mothers of New England were noted, and yet it never seemed incompatible with her serene character, quiet and loving disposition.   It rather illustrated her courage and sense of duty.   One story is told on Paris Hill to-day about Mrs. Hamlin's pluck.   Among Mr. Hamlin's duties as sheriff was keeping the jail, which stood near his house.   One day the prisoners, led by a turbulent scamp, knowing that Dr. Hamlin was not at home, endeavored to force their way out of prison.   Mrs. Hamlin, hearing the noise, rushed on the scene.   The jail door had been partially forced open, and the ringleader was trying to push himself through the opening.   Mrs. Hamlin instantly seized the man by the throat, choked him into submission, and thrusting him into the corridor fastened the door tight.   In connection with this incident, to illustrate his mother's agility, Hannibal Hamlin used to tell his sons how he had often seen her place her hand on the back of a horse and without any assistance leap from the ground into the saddle.

Another view of the life and influences of Paris Hill is seen through the preacher of the village, Elder James Hooper.   He was a quaint old Puritan, albeit he held certain worldly ideas and eccentric notions; but he was the personification of conscientiousness and adhered to his radical views with iron-like tenacity, nor did he hesitate to differ from his church when he thought it was wrong.   He preached twice every Sunday at the old Baptist church, and was noted not for long sermons, but for short, pithy, and original discourses.   Indeed, brevity was one of his hobbies.   Once a long-winded visiting minister, who had been announced to preach twice at Elder Hooper's church, bored the congregation to the point of slumber in the morning service. When he had at last closed, Elder Hooper electrified his drowsy parishioners by rising and saying in his peculiar, snappy way: "There will be preaching in this church this afternoon, because I myself will preach." If the elder saw a rainstorm approaching when he was in the midst of a sermon, he would dismiss his congregation at once, telling the men that it was "better to get the hay in than to listen to any sermon." The elder had no patience with "new-fangled notions." When women's rights were being discussed at Paris Hill, Elder Hooper, in the pulpit, announced his opposition, and in this unique sentence gave his reasons: "Men and dogs roam abroad; women and cats should stay at home."

When the Temperance Union began its national crusade, Parson Hooper stormed at it in his original way. "God sent rum to us, and therefore it is a blessing if we know how to use it," he used to argue. By way of illustration, the elder said: "I gave my two boys rum and molasses this morning. Did it hurt them? No; you ought to have seen their eyes shine." Now Dr. Hamlin not only sympathized with the temperance movement, — for there was a great deal of drinking in Maine, — but also circulated a pledge and would allow no liquor in his house. This offended Elder Hooper, and for a long time he refused to visit Dr. Hamlin's house. But in spite of his eccentricities Elder Hooper accomplished a good work and was very much respected and beloved by his parishioners. His real goodness of heart was illustrated in the fact that the two sons mentioned were both adopted by him, although he barely eked out a living by preaching.

In the summer of 1809 there were five children in Dr. Hamlin's family, — Elijah, Eliza, Anne, Vesta, and Cyrus. On August 27 a sixth child, a boy, was born. About this time Dr. Hamlin and his twin brother Hannibal, of Waterford, had promised each other that if each should become the father of another son he would name the child after his brother. Dr. Hamlin, therefore, christened this son Hannibal Hamlin, and subsequently Hannibal Hamlin, of Waterford, had occasion to name a son Cyrus. This is how Hannibal Hamlin, the statesman, and the Rev. Dr. Cyrus Hamlin, the famous American missionary to Turkey and the founder of Robert College, received their respective names. It is an odd coincidence that both boys were sickly and puny infants. Hannibal's life, indeed, hung by a thread; but a somewhat dramatic incident occurred which probably turned the scales in favor of the child. As Mrs. Hamlin was sitting in her doorway one day, rocking her feeble infant, old Mollyockett, the Indian princess, appeared. She looked at the child very intently for a short time, and then said with great earnestness to Mrs. Hamlin: "You give papoose milk warm from cow, or he die." As the infant's lack of vitality baffled Dr. Hamlin's skill, he and his wife tried the remedy suggested by Mollyockett. The result was instantly favorable; the child thrived with great rapidity, and was soon a lusty, healthy boy. He rarely knew ill health again.

A few years after Hannibal's birth one more child, a daughter, named Hannah, was born to Dr. Hamlin and his wife.   Thus they had a household of seven children.   Elijah, the oldest son, resembled his father in build, looks, and disposition, although his complexion was of the swarthy type.   He was a natural scholar and wit, — the college-mate, friend, and correspondent[1] of Dr. Samuel G. Howe.   He was a student at Brown University when Hannibal began to go to school, and thus Hannibal was thrown into closer relations with his brother Cyrus at the time a boy craves sympathy and advice from an older brother.   Cyrus was of a sweet, sedate nature, and pure character.   Probably the premonition of an oncoming fatal disease, consumption, matured him far beyond his years.   He devoted himself to his young brother, taught him how to farm, and through gentle tact and kindness exercised more influence over him than any one else save Hannibal's mother.   To the end of his life Hannibal Hamlin never spoke of his brother Cyrus without emotion, or paying him an affectionate tribute.   Cyrus was to Hannibal Hamlin what Ezekiel Webster was to his great brother Daniel.   Hannibal's older sister, Vesta, resembled him somewhat in the gentler qualities of his nature and habits of thought, and was a sympathetic companion.   Anna was a quiet, affectionate sister; Hannah, the arch and merry pet of the family.   Eliza, the eldest daughter, was in some respects a remarkable woman.   She possessed great executive ability, and for years was famous as the schoolmistress of Paris Hill, and one of the best botanists in the State.   She might have attained prominence in other departments of life if she had lived where her gifts would have had fuller scope.

As a child Hannibal Hamlin evinced a sturdy, independent nature. He was very affectionate and not a little mischievous.   His vitality was extraordinary when he was old enough to play out of doors and take care of himself.   He bubbled over with fun and good-nature. There was no malice in his pranks, his mother said, but they were the result of an overflowing nature.   Hannibal Hamlin's first recollection of his childhood days was when he was three years old.   The war of 1812 had broken out, and he saw a company of soldiers march away from Paris Hill.   The red nodding plumes and shining accoutrements of the soldiers made a picture in his mind that never faded out. When the veterans of the war returned home, they had many stories to tell about the battles.   Hannibal, who was a boy of seven or eight by this time, was deeply interested in the battle of New Orleans, and thenceforth Andrew Jackson was one of his greatest heroes.

Hannibal's aggressive nature was illustrated about this time by an

[1] Elijah Hamlin discovered Mt. Mica, the famous tourmaline deposit near Paris Hill, now owned by his son, Dr. Augustus C. Hamlin, of Bangor.

incident told by his cousin, Cyrus Hamlin. In jumping over a fence one day Hannibal fell and broke his arm. His father was away from home and another doctor set the injured member. A few days later it was discovered that the bones had not been set right. The same doctor, without a word of warning, seized the arm and snapped the partially joined bones apart. Instantly Hannibal, doubling up his other fist, struck the bungling physician a sound thump on the end of his nose. It was a vigorous blow for a youngster of his years, and at first the doctor thought something had been broken. But after finding Hannibal had only drawn blood, the doctor spluttered: "Well, young man, I won't touch you again unless you are strapped down."

Hannibal attended the village school at Paris Hill. This was an excellent school for its time. Judge Emery, who led his class at Bowdoin, Governor Lincoln, who was a Harvard man, and Dr. Hamlin were on the town committee, and took a pride in maintaining a school of high standard. Hannibal, therefore, had a good schooling in his childhood. But while he was regarded as a bright boy in school, he was not a model pupil as far as rank and prizes were concerned. He seemed to learn with perfect ease, and never forgot what he learned. Too full of life and activity to be kept down at his books, he wanted to be out of doors. What he shone best in was athletic sports. He seemed to have been a leader among the boys of his age at Paris Hill, from the time he came among them to the time he left them. He was especially fond of round ball, — from which our national game of baseball was evoluted, — wrestling, running, and jumping. He was very loyal to his friends, and always had a crowd of boys around him. He was very fond of pets. He particularly liked horses and dogs; in fact, there never was a time in his life when he did not have a dog.

Hannibal Hamlin's individuality as a boy was so pronounced and his traits so clearly defined that old friends of his who survived him remembered him perfectly as he was when a lad of fifteen or sixteen, playing among them at Paris Hill. One description of him at this age says: "Han, as we always called him, was an unusually large boy for his age. He was as tall, straight, supple, and dark as a young Indian. He was very warm-hearted, affectionate, and magnetic; his big black eyes twinkled with fun and life. Han was always our leader, and yet he never appeared to put himself forward; it was natural for us to wait to see what Han was going to do, and then follow him. Sometimes we would get into a boyish scrape, but Han always stuck by us; he would go where we would. He never bragged what he was going to do, or had done, but he would go ahead and do it, and say nothing. He was perfectly natural and honest; no one ever thought of questioning his word." In connection with this,

Cyrus Hamlin, who often came over from Waterford to visit his cousins at Paris Hill, wrote: "In running, jumping, and wrestling Hannibal could beat us all. And it was easy for us to be beaten, because Hannibal was so fair-minded. There was an absence in him of any disposition to exult over a fallen foe. As a boy, Hannibal was as fair-minded, honest, and incorruptible as he was when a man. The boy was father to the man."

When Hannibal grew older his fondness for out-of-door life developed into his ruling passion. He was a born Nimrod, fisherman, and farmer. Bears, deer, rabbits, squirrels, partridges, and trout abounded around Paris Hill. About this time a story was told of an adventure a couple of little children had within a mile of the Hill. When they were walking along the main road one of them stopped and exclaimed to the other, "Oh, see that funny brown cow without any horns. Let's go play with her." They started to play with their new bovine curiosity, but fortunately the bear had business in another direction, and did not wait for the children. Hannibal used to scour the mountains and neighboring country for game and fish. He became a crack shot and a true fisherman. He seemed to find trout brooks by intuition, and eventually cared more for fishing than for hunting. When once he found a trout brook in an out-of-the-way place, he kept his secret to himself and one or two of his cronies. Years afterwards he would go back to Paris Hill to drink in the vitalizing air, and to fish. People around the Hill said that he could still find his secret trout brook, and no one else could.

As a result of his vigorous out-of-door life, Hannibal was an uncommonly powerful lad when he was sixteen or seventeen years old. Looked up to by his companions as their champion, Hannibal learned at this time what fame was. His reputation as an athlete spread. In those days wrestling was a favorite athletic sport, and a match between village champions was a great event. In a neighboring district lived a young blacksmith who was a champion wrestler. He challenged Hannibal to a match, each to strip to the waist and wrestle barefooted. Hannibal accepted, and the common in front of Dr. Hamlin's house was chosen as the place. There was great excitement among Hannibal's friends, and a good-sized crowd gathered on the scene of the struggle. As the blacksmith appeared, his advantage in size, weight, and strength was very apparent, and Hannibal's friends were discouraged. The blacksmith was very confident, but it was his confidence that beat him. Swinging his powerful arms around in fanciful feints to awe Hannibal, the blacksmith began to brag: "If I ketch a holt on yer, I won't let yer tech me." As the blacksmith said this he made a sweep of his arms that exposed him. Hannibal was not awed by this demonstration, but quick as a flash darted on the blacksmith, and grabbing him around the waist thumped him so hard on the ground that he saw stars. There was a great shout from the excited Paris Hill boys, and they danced and hugged each other for joy. The crestfallen blacksmith slowly arose, and said, "Anyhow, he ain't a scientific wrestler." There was another shout, and Hiram Hubbard retorted, "Han has n't got any use for science when he can beat it in his own way." The blacksmith was satisfied, and the match was over almost before it began. No more champions disputed Hannibal's supremacy. This match was long a favorite story at Paris Hill, and generally when a story of another match was told, it was closed with the remark, "But you ought to have seen Han Hamlin throw that blacksmith." [1]

Hannibal was a born politician, and showed a strong interest in politics when a young lad. He thought out political questions for himself and acted for himself. A circumstance happened when Hannibal was about seventeen that contributed to the formation of his political principles, and also demonstrates the lad's perfect independence and habit of self-reliance. Dr. Hamlin was a loyal Federalist in his early days, and on the death of the Federal party he became an ardent Whig. Elijah was also a Whig, and he and his father regularly read the "Portland Gazette," the Whig organ of the State, and as Hannibal was the youngest he had to wait his turn. Dr. Hamlin also subscribed for the "Eastern Argus," a leading Democratic newspaper of the day, and while waiting for the "Gazette" the boy fell into the habit of reading the "Argus." Finding that it expressed the same faith in Democracy that he had, Hannibal came to prefer the "Argus," and before his father realized it Hannibal had become a pronounced Democrat, and a warm partisan of the doctrines of Jefferson and Jackson.

Dr. Hamlin was too liberal a man to interfere with his son's convictions, and as he was a good politician himself he probably foresaw the rising ascendency of the Republican-Democratic party in Maine. He was a close listener to what his boys had to say on political subjects, and sometimes gave them good advice. Hannibal then, as

[1] One who was a chum of Hannibal Hamlin in boyhood days tells me that Hamlin even then was distinguished for great strength of body. On one occasion, when, clustered in the village grocery, a number of Paris youths tried one by one to lift a pig of lead, Hannibal was the only one who succeeded in raising it above his head. From the night of the lead-lifting incident, when Hamlin probably was twenty years old, my informant did not see the strong lad until he saw him standing under a certain tree in Paris, addressing his fellow-townsmen. The strong lad was then Vice-President of the United States. The tree, by the way, Hamlin himself had planted. My informant, while on a visit to Paris about two weeks ago, visited the tree, which is now "six feet round," and as vigorous as was once its celebrated planter. — *Boston Globe*, July 12, 1891.

afterwards, was an intense partisan in principles, and would argue with great vehemence.   One night he and Elijah had a heated discussion.   Dr. Hamlin, who had been a quiet listener, interrupted Hannibal with a hearty laugh and a fatherly pat on the back: "Hannibal, my son, live a little longer, live a little longer, before you enter politics, and you will know more."   Hannibal accepted his father's advice and all that it implied.   He and Elijah thereupon agreed that they would never again discuss politics while differing from each other, and that, finally, they would never allow political principles or affiliations to cause the slightest difference in their brotherly relations.   The boys shook hands on this agreement in a manly way, and although they even had to oppose each other in years to come, as the candidates of their respective parties, kept their word until they were released by the formation of the Republican party.

CHAPTER III

BOYHOOD AND EDUCATION

DOCTOR HAMLIN believed in the advantages of a college education. He had been a student at the medical school of Harvard College, and in 1813 was one of the incorporators of Waterville College, now called Colby. He had sent Elijah to Brown University, and intended to give Hannibal also a college course. Accordingly, when Hannibal was about seventeen he began to prepare himself to enter Brown or Waterville. He went to Hebron, and some of the pleasantest days of his life were passed as a student at the historic academy in that town. Hannibal developed a fondness for the classics, and was quick at mathematics, but he showed a marked preference for history and biography, which he followed closely both in his school and leisure hours. The boys at Hebron came to lean on him as the boys at Paris Hill had. His leadership at Hebron was revealed in an amusing frolic, which, by the way, had much to do with determining young Hamlin's choice of his profession.

The husking party was a popular institution among the farmers of Maine in those days. If a farmer had corn to husk, he invited his neighbors to help him, and in return for their assistance he provided a bounteous supply of the good things of the table; and, as the temperance sentiment of the State was still lax, old Medford and Jamaica rum were too often accompanying features of this old-time custom. To the young men the husking party was particularly attractive, because when a lucky husker found a red ear, the fashion of the day gave him the privilege of kissing any girl in the company, and thus the once famous couplet was originated : —

> "I would not husk for cows or steers:
> I 'd only husk to get red ears."

It is hardly necessary to add that the boys at Hebron Academy always accepted invitations to husking parties. But there was one thing in connection with these occasions that young Hamlin and his associates did not like, and that was the free use of liquor. At one memorable party an elderly man drank too much rum, and made himself particularly obnoxious. The schoolboys resented his behavior by pelting him with hard ears of corn, and rolling him round on the floor of the barn.   The old man left the scene of his discomfiture sore in body and mind.   The boys thought the affair had ended with the sobering-up of their victim, and the news the next morning that a warrant was out for their arrest, on the charge of assault and battery, came like a clap of thunder from the clear sky.   But they did not think of employing a lawyer; they turned to Hannibal Hamlin in their trouble.   They knew that he was in the habit of following trials with great interest, and at once concluded that he had picked up enough knowledge of the law which, together with his shrewdness and alertness, would enable him successfully to champion their cause. In a body the boys marched to the house of the local justice of the peace, where their trial was to take place.   He was a pompous old gentleman, with great ideas of dignity, but little knowledge of the law, or much natural ability.   The proceedings were opened with solemnity in the justice's kitchen packed with people, when the justice's ridiculous pomp and ceremony were interrupted by the collapse of the floor.   The court, the boys, the kitchen utensils, a closet of crockery, and the family cat were precipitated in a mass into the cellar. Above the uproar rose the laments of the justice bewailing the loss of his china and furniture.   Nobody was hurt, and the boys tumbled out of the ruins in a state of hilarity, arguing and predicting among themselves that the case against them could not stand any better than the justice's floor.

The trial was presently resumed in the academy, and Hannibal was placed on the witness stand.   As he appeared before the court, confident, smiling, and his big, black eyes twinkling with fun, his companions pressed around him, buzzing and whispering, " Give it to him, Hannie ; give it to him," — remarks that somewhat disconcerted his honor.   He called for order, and then with a frown asked Hannibal : —

" Did you throw any ear of corn at the plaintiff ? "

" No, sir," replied Hannibal, with a twinkle in his eye, " I did not throw any ear of corn at the plaintiff."

" Do you swear you did not ? "

" I swear I did not," answered the boy.

For a moment the court looked grave, and then asked, " Did you see anybody else throw any ear of corn at the plaintiff ? "

" That," replied Hannibal with perfect coolness, " is a question which I cannot answer, and which your honor has no right to ask me."

Then for fully five minutes Hannibal went on to cite law points in support of his position, all the time employing technical terms which were so much Greek to the justice, until that discomfited and completely crestfallen individual, greatly confused, and amidst loud laughter, discharged Hamlin, and fined a number of the boys a dollar each, and then quickly adjourned the court.[1]

This incident turned young Hamlin's attention to the law as a desirable profession; but while he was thinking of his college course and legal studies, his plans were upset by the sad news that his brother Cyrus was in failing health, and that he would have to return home and give up his college education that Cyrus might be relieved from his duties on the farm, to give all attention to his health. Hannibal had enjoyed less than a year's study at Hebron, but in that time he had practically fitted himself for entering college, although the requirements for admission to college at that time were not of the high standard of later days. He had read his Cæsar, Virgil, and some orations of Cicero, besides a little Greek, and had mastered algebra and plain geometry. This was practically all the education he obtained under the supervision of experienced instructors; but he was always a friend and supporter of the American college, and regretted that he had been deprived of its benefit.

The Hamlins' home circle was now broken. Elijah, the eldest son, had married Eliza Choate, a relative of the Ipswich family of that name, and was practicing law at Columbia, Maine. Cyrus entered the Maine Medical School, to become a doctor. Vesta was engaged to Dr. Job Holmes, whom she soon married, and removed to Calais, Maine. This left Hannibal the only son at home, and his duties were, therefore, largely increased. He accepted the situation manfully, and he had compensation in the thought that in giving up cherished ambitions he was making some returns to a brother who had done so much for him. Subsequent events made it exceedingly fortunate both for the family and Hannibal that he returned home. Cyrus had made him an excellent farmer, and he could make every inch of tillable soil on the farm yield produce. Finally, Governor Lincoln was still living at the Hamlin homestead, and Hannibal had the advantage of his friendship and counsel, which proved to be of value.

The relations between Enoch Lincoln and Hannibal Hamlin in the latter's student days are interesting. Lincoln was sprung from the famous Lincoln family of Hingham, Massachusetts, from which the Emancipator was descended, and possessed some of the marked characteristics of the noblest representative of his race. His father was General Levi Lincoln, and his brother was Levi Lincoln, Jr., both of whom succeeded to the gubernatorial chair of Massachusetts. Enoch Lincoln was born in Worcester in 1788, was a student at Harvard for several years, and after reading law with his brother, removed to Fryeburg, Maine. The people of Paris Hill saw a good deal of Lincoln, and formed a high opinion of him. Dr. Hamlin probably

[1] Carroll's *Twelve Americans*, p. 119.

met Lincoln during the sessions of the court at Paris Hill, and with others suggested to him that he take up his residence at that place, and represent the district in Congress when Maine should become a State. In 1819 Lincoln came to Paris Hill, and lived at Dr. Hamlin's home until 1826. When Maine became a State, in 1820, Lincoln was elected to Congress, and held his seat until 1825, when he resigned it to become governor. His popularity in Maine may be seen from the fact that he was chosen governor of the State three times by an almost unanimous vote.

Lincoln was active in public affairs when the controversy of the admission of Missouri as a slave State severely agitated the country. He got a glimpse of the menacing spirit of the slave power, and it filled him with foreboding. He brooded over slavery and the probable consequences that would follow its perpetuation. He was not a man of action in the full sense of the word. His tastes ran to literature; he was a scholar and poet. Slavery oppressed him as a moral wrong, and he denounced it. Dr. Hamlin was a sympathetic listener. Thus Hannibal Hamlin grew up in a strong anti-slavery atmosphere, and at the start imbibed the right practical ideas about the institution which he expressed in action as an anti-slavery leader. In connection with this it is interesting to recall some of Lincoln's words when he became governor, and which were formal expressions of his conversations at the Hamlins'. In one of his state papers to the legislature of Maine, in speaking of the slaves he said : " But they are men, and no plea of private advantage or public policy can justify their enslavement, or palliate the enormities committed in stealing them from their native country, subduing them to obedience, and working them, as though they were beasts in human form. It is idle to talk of legal restraints upon men whose crimes are witnessed only by accomplices or suffer-ers, of the former of whom the testimony would be evasive through interest and corruption, of the latter excluded by law. Indeed, when you have given power, you will legislate in vain about its exercise, and if you tolerate servitude, you cannot separate from it the horror of barbarous tyranny."

This was more than an acute warning and true prophecy ; it was a judgment on the fugitive slave law that was enacted more than a quarter of a century after the grass had grown over the grave of the one who uttered it.

Lincoln also spoke with the vision of a prophet of old when he wrote these lines in his poem, " The Village," — a picture of New England life that was widely read in Maine in his day : —

> " No slave is now, nor ever shall be here.
> O'er slavery's plague, ye happy freemen pause,
> And learn to love your country and its laws.

. . . .

Avenging justice follows after crime,
And sure o'ertaken in the lapse of time.
Oppressed humanity its chains will spurn,
And meanest slaves upon their tyrants turn."

Lincoln was but thirty-seven years old when he became governor
of Maine, and died at the close of his last term, at the age of forty.
His too pronounced artistic ability prevented him from attaining the
prominence that should have been his by virtue of his talents, honor,
and heart. His early death was a great loss to the State, and the
people sincerely mourned him.

Governor Lincoln had at this time one of the best private libraries
in the State of Maine. Books were then scarce and valuable. The
fact that Lincoln was not only generous in lending his treasures, but
also sought to encourage his boyish friends in reading, is another
proof of his high qualities. He gave Hannibal and his cousin Cyrus
of Waterford access to his library, and together the ambitious lads
read and studied the biographies of many a famous man. Hannibal's
studies were conducted under difficulties that, however hard they may
appear, operated in the end to spur him on to greater efforts. His
duties on the farm kept him busy a large part of the day, and made
him all the more eager to return to his books when he had the time.
He had to rise at five o'clock, milk half a dozen cows, and care for
other cattle before going to the farm. There he was busy enough
until sundown. After his work was done, he had to milk the cows
again and take care of the cattle for the night. It was usually seven
o'clock before his time was his own, but he was young, vigorous, and
ambitious. He read and studied every night he could spare as late as
his strength would permit.

The evenings young Hamlin spent in this way were of more practical benefit to him than all the time he had spent in school on the
study of Latin and Greek and other subjects required for the admission to college. Practically it was a year's study of character and of
the acquirement of information that was of solid use to him in beginning his political career. In connection with this a circumstance of
importance should be emphasized. He always spoke with great affection of his mother's influence over him in shaping his life, and one
thing in particular should be considered in this respect in the effect
it had on Hamlin's moral and mental development. Mrs. Hamlin
was very devout and exceedingly conscientious in observing her
religious duties to her children. She always insisted, in her quiet
way, on one thing, that while her children lived at her home, they
should twice a day memorize and recite at the family prayers passages
from the Bible. Hannibal Hamlin strictly complied with his mother's

wishes for more than a dozen years.   He had a deep religious nature that expressed itself in acts rather than words; his belief in the existence of the Supreme Being was always as strong as that in his own existence.   In addition to the moral influence the Bible exerted over him, it also offered him mental discipline, and was a source of strength to him in temporal affairs.   In after life some of his most effective arguments were rested on Biblical teachings, and often his terse, brief sentences were of Biblical style.

The line of reading which Hamlin liked best was American biography and history.   The life of Washington made the deepest impression on him.   Through Colonel Africa Hamlin his relatives knew more about Washington as a man than books told of him.   The more Hannibal learned of Washington, — the man whose generalship won the country its independence, whose statesmanship kept it in the right path, whose patriotism and unselfish nature prompted him to lay down power when he was most powerful, — the more the lad admired him.   Throughout all his life Hannibal Hamlin believed Washington to have been the greatest of all Americans.

The life of Jefferson appealed to the lad with great force.   He felt that Jefferson was a man to whom the common people could turn with perfect safety.   He was in sympathy with them; he could fathom their aspirations before any other leader, and guide them in the right direction.   Jefferson at this time had been long enough removed from the scene for the country to contemplate his services without partisan feelings.   His purchase of the Louisiana territory in the face of the fiercest opposition was now being thoroughly understood and appreciated, in the importance of its influence on the destiny of the country.   It converted the United States from a small seaboard nation into an empire stretching from the Atlantic to the Pacific.   Emigration to the West was now strong; a new national life sprang up, and Jefferson's fame was brightened for the new generation.

Dr. Cyrus Hamlin, in his reminiscences of these days, told an interesting story how he and his cousin Hannibal read Las Casas' Life of Napoleon together, and talked it over.   At this time the feeling against Great Britain, caused by the war of 1812, was still intense, and the two lads particularly enjoyed reading the great Corsican's life because he thrashed the Britishers, and also because Bonaparte and his army seemed to be bayoneted exemplars of Republican ideas. " Every soldier of France carries a field marshal's baton in his knapsack,"᾽ was a genuine American sentiment, and Napoleon's recognition of bravery and merit as a basis for promotion, rather than birth, glorified him in the eyes of ardent American boys.   Hannibal had his boyish dream of being a soldier; in fact, he even induced Governor

Lincoln, the last year he was in Congress, to promise him a cadetship at West Point. Whether the appointment was actually made is not known, but it is certain that Hanibal could have been a cadet, and was preparing to leave home, when his mother asked him for her sake to give up his ambitions to enter the army. Hannibal believed that he ought to yield to his mother, and did so, to her great happiness. This was the last favor Mr. Lincoln rendered this young friend. When he was elected governor of Maine he removed to Augusta, where he died.

Hamlin resumed his plodding life on his father's farm with undecided ideas as to the profession he should follow. He still cherished hopes of being able to pursue a college course after his brother Cyrus had been provided for, and thought of earning money to pay his own way. Perhaps to give Hannibal an opportunity to make a little money, and also to let him see some more of the world before making up his mind about a profession, Dr. Hamlin decided to send his son to Boston for a few months. Hannibal found employment as a clerk in a small fruit store. That which made the greatest impression on him at this time was the theatre. Dr. Hamlin was fond of acting, and his home at Paris Hill was the theatre for the ambitious Thespian Club of the Hill. There were jolly times at his house. Elijah Hamlin was the star actor of the Hill at first, and Hannibal about this time succeeded to his brother's histrionic mantle. Coming to Boston in 1827, he found the old Boston Theatre a place of great interest. Wallack, the elder, Edmund Kean, William Charles McCready, Edwin Forrest, William A. Conway, Junius Brutus Booth; Charles Matthews, senior, and other great actors, were appearing at the Boston Theatre at this time. The lad was carried away with the scenes before him, and was seized with the desire to become an actor. But before making any move he decided to consult his parents. Dr. Hamlin was too broad a man to entertain prejudice against acting as a profession, and he regarded the drama as an educator as well as a means of amusement; but he knew his high-spirited son would in all probability lead an unhappy life on the stage, and he believed Hannibal would have a career in politics. All this he pointed out in a tactful letter. The closing sentence, separated from the rest of the text, would seem harsh, but it was eminently practical. The doctor wrote: " If you want to be a fool, and give up opportunities for a promising career, you can go on the stage; but if you want to be sensible, and make use of your talents in a sensible calling, come home." Hannibal came home, but he always retained a love of the drama. In after life he made a practice of collecting and studying the standard plays he saw, and he had some lifelong friends among the noblest actors of his day. One was Edwin Forrest, whom he probably met before he entered public life, possibly when he himself wanted to go on the stage.

Coming home in the winter of 1827, Hannibal again set about to earn money to pay his way at college. An incident happened that was of practical benefit to him. An odd character named Ellis, who never seemed to be happy unless he was away from civilization, was engaged by Dr. Hamlin and others to survey a township of land they owned on Dead River. Ellis offered to take Hannibal on condition that he would cut wood and draw water for the cook. Hamlin saw an opportunity to learn surveying, and accepted Ellis's offer. A party of five or six was formed, and they fitted themselves out for a six weeks' expedition. They walked on snowshoes, and slept in their blankets on the snow, which was seven or eight feet deep. What impressed young Hamlin most strongly at first in his mid-forest life was the unerring precision with which Ellis and his assistants found their way from point to point back to camp. He saw that they had trained their powers of observation to a high degree, and learned by experience that the habit of noticing little landmarks became a second nature and a sure guide. He developed this practice to such a degree that he was never known to lose his way in the many times he tramped through forest, or in strange cities on either side of the Atlantic.

With the help of Ellis and his assistants Hannibal soon picked up enough practical knowledge about surveying to make a little money now and then after he returned home. He appreciated the kindness of his friends in teaching him how to survey, and returned it in a way they never forgot. The coming of Christmas found the surveyors still busy. The men were a little blue, thinking about the festivities at home, and were rather silent when they gathered in camp for the night meal. When they sat down around their rough board table, prepared to eat their customary supper of baked beans, coffee, and hard tack, Hamlin slipped out of the camp with the cook, and in a few minutes returned with an immense pan, while the cook was laden down with various pots and stewpans, all of which emitted appetizing odors. On the table was spread a feast for lords. During the few days preceding Christmas, young Hamlin, unbeknown to the surveyors, had tramped miles through the woods, shooting partridges, wild turkeys, and other game, and catching trout through the ice. He himself cooked a partridge-pie, which was the principal dish of the dinner. It was a red-letter night, and there was no merrier band of Christmas revelers in Maine that year than those who enjoyed Hannibal's dinner in the midst of its forests.

This dinner lived in the recollection of those who ate it, and an interesting result came from it nearly thirty years afterwards, when Hannibal Hamlin was running for governor in the most exciting and momentous campaign yet fought in Maine. He spoke one night in a little cross-road village, where the people gathered from miles around to hear him on the issue of slavery. There was something familiar about the face of the chairman, and looking at him again, Hamlin recognized his old friend Ellis, whom he had not seen since the dinner. Ellis had never forgotten his young friend, and had come out of his haunts in the wilderness to help a man whom he believed to be honest and disinterested.

After the surveying trip, Hamlin found that a teacher was wanted in his old school at Paris Hill, and he applied for the vacancy. Teaching a country school in rural Maine was not always a smooth and pleasant life. In the winter and early spring time it usually happened that many young men who had little to do on their farms came to the district school to repair the deficiencies of their early education. The Paris Hill school in the spring of 1828 had pupils who ranged from children in pinafores to young men and women. The master was called on to teach children their letters and fit boys for college. But there was another requirement that some failed to meet. Among the lusty farmer lads who attended this school was a rather unruly set, that looked on the teacher in the light of an enemy and their natural prey. When they heard Han Hamlin was to take the school, the story is, they talked him over and came to this decision, that if Han was "stuck up" in consequence of his appointment as school-teacher they would "chuck him out of the window," with the important proviso, if they could. Hamlin heard of the plot that was brewing, and knowing how some unfortunate college sophomores had been "chucked out of the window" on account of a little misunderstanding which could have been easily prevented, he took the initiative to let the boys know how he felt over his elevation in life. The day Hamlin entered upon his new duties, he began by calling the school to order. There was a look of mischief in the eyes of the big fellows sprawling on the back seats. Looking at them, Hamlin said in his sincere, quiet way: "Boys, out of school you will find that I will be as good a friend as ever, but here you will find that I will be the master." The boys exchanged approving glances, and passed around the word, "Han is n't stuck up." The new teacher was as good as his word. Out of doors he engaged in all the sports, and in school he lightened the hours by drawing on his knowledge of history and biography for the benefit and enjoyment of his pupils in connection with their routine work. He found his experience of value to him, and often advised young men to spend a winter or two in teaching, to learn how to impart their knowledge and also how to exercise power; in fact, he enforced these ideas on several of his sons at different times, twenty-five to forty years after his own experience.

In 1829 Hamlin was twenty years old, and had made up his mind to become a lawyer. He yet hoped to take a college course, but he determined to risk no chances. He had still to carry on his father's farm, and as he was fitted to enter college resolved to begin reading law by night, so that whatever happened he might prepare for the future. He had saved up a little money by teaching and surveying, and as Cyrus was now practicing with his brother-in-law, Dr. Job Holmes, in Calais, it looked to Hannibal as if he might be able, after earning a little more money, to enter college. In the winter of 1829, when he was released from his farm duties, young Hamlin secured a school at Columbia, where he lived for several months with his brother Elijah, working on his Blackstone at night. But in the spring, while Hannibal was enjoying his brother's delightful companionship, and pursuing his studies with advantage, news came from Paris Hill that a terrible blow had fallen on the happy home there. Dr. Hamlin was dead. He died of pneumonia after a few days' illness. His condition was not thought to be critical until a short time before he passed away, and the members of the family who were not at Paris Hill were not summoned in time to be with him when he died. The loss of a father who had been so devoted a parent and companion was a severe shock to Hannibal; but he voluntarily abandoned all hopes of obtaining a college education, and returned home, to become the prop of his mother and sisters.

CHAPTER IV

FARMER, PRINTER, AND LAW STUDENT

DURING the months that followed his father's death, Hamlin found distraction in the exciting presidential election of 1829. This was the first political campaign in which Hannibal Hamlin took part, and it is easy to see why he entered into it with heart and soul. Andrew Jackson was the Democratic candidate for President, and was the idol of his party. Hamlin saw Jackson in subsequent years, and often spoke of Old Hickory's wonderful personality. He was a born leader, picturesque-looking, very passionate, warm-hearted, and honesty itself. His eccentricities of temper and mistakes of judgment even served to make the masses of his party understand and love him all the better. If Jackson was not versed in the highest arts of statesmanship, and was narrow, he was nevertheless an iron-willed patriot, and rode fierce gales that threatened the safety of the young country. He checked the secession movement, which, with a weak man at the head of the government, might have succeeded; he crushed the United States Bank, and compelled the United States to do its own business and keep in the paths of Jefferson, — the simplest and easiest for the young nation to follow.

Jackson was the unique product of a unique period. When the little seaboard republic expanded into a continental empire, emigration to the great West followed. A new, strange, and fiercely exuberant civilization was developed there. New conditions were consequently created, and in this marvelous period of national growth, national faith in democracy as the cornerstone of the republic was enthusiastic. The spirit of democracy was rampant, as naturally befitted the crude state of affairs. Novel problems constantly arose, bringing with them unexpected dangers; in a word, the nation was in a formative period, the Republic was still an experiment. The country needed a strong man, who could be understood by the enthusiastic and headstrong masses. The colleges and schools were relatively few in number; the newspaper press a pygmy, and with the locomotive and steamboat in their infancy, and the telegraph not yet in existence, communication was slow. The difficulties of spreading information among the masses about the principles of self-government were a condition that does not exist to-day. Hence there is a philosophical consideration to be weighed in connection with Jackson's act in turning Federalists out of office by the wholesale, and replacing them by men of his own party who had never held office before, and who, according to the historians of the day, had at first but crude ideas of the principles of government. The absence of better means of instructing the masses of the people in the art of government, and informing them of what the government was doing, places Jackson's course in a new light. Necessity, the craving for intimate knowledge of governmental affairs among the masses, were a legitimate outcome of the times, and probably had as much to do with "raiding the offices," as desire to "get the spoils of war." Civil service reform came in due time, when the Marcy theory had degenerated into a source of danger and corrupt power ; but it was also the product of a new age, an enlightened period when communication was rapid through the press, the telegraph and mails, when the nation could learn of a governmental act the day it was executed and publish its reply the next. On the whole, it was fortunate the country had in this seething condition of affairs a man at the head of the government as human, honest, simple, patriotic, and inflexible as Andrew Jackson.

The campaign of 1829 was hotly contested, and was very exciting. Belief that Congress had cheated Jackson out of the presidency in 1825, by electing John Quincy Adams, stimulated the Democrats to great exertion. There was the glamour of 1812, too, about Jackson, and, on the other hand, President Adams, who was a candidate for reëlection, was believed to be cold and at heart a monarchist. This was unjust to Adams, as the country afterwards learned. But though Mr. Adams deserved reëlection on his merits, the conditions required Jackson. The new West created these conditions ; Jackson did not, though his recluse critics seem to believe it. The flood gates of democracy were opened, and Jackson was overwhelmingly elected.[1]

Although Hamlin was not yet old enough to vote, he spoke for Old Hickory, and shared in the exultation over his success. The campaign had an interesting effect on him. Plodding on the farm and reading law at night he found rather slow work, and he looked for an opportunity to forge ahead. One came in an amusing manner. Two years before this, Asa Barton, a bookseller of Paris Hill, had established a weekly newspaper under the title of the "Oxford Democrat." It was successful, but for some unknown reason Mr. Barton took offense at his surroundings, and one fine day the good people of Paris Hill woke up to find that Barton and his newspaper had disappeared. The night before, Barton had placed his entire establishment in an ox cart, and taken it over to the rival and neighboring town of Norway. Of course, Norway had a roar of laughter over the discomfiture of

[1] For the other view of Jackson, see his life by Professor William G. Sumner.

Paris Hill, and this incited the Jackson Democrats of the Hill to have a newspaper whose policy and movements also they could control. Accordingly, Judge Emery, Alanson Mellen, Moses Hammond, Thomas Webster, Alfred Andrews, Thomas Crocker, and Rufus K. Goodenow, who was afterwards a member of Congress, raised the money necessary, and started a weekly newspaper, under the title of the "Jeffersonian." Joseph G. Cole, a Harvard graduate and a law student in Judge Emery's office, was appointed editor at a salary of one dollar and a half a week, which, strange as it may seem, was satisfactory compensation, since it enabled the editor to live at the best boarding-house at Paris Hill.

Hamlin knew the Emerys well, and at this time was a frequent visitor at their house. He was attached to Judge Emery's daughter Sarah, and although no engagement as yet existed between them, it was understood that there was likely to be one when Hannibal's circumstances permitted him to declare himself. Judge Emery took a strong interest in the young man, and encouraged him to strike out into politics. Hamlin learned about this time that the "Jeffersonian" might be purchased. Without saying anything to outsiders, he had a quiet conversation with the owners, with the result that one day in May, 1830, he walked into the office of the "Jeffersonian," and finding there a young man of his own age, whose bright and frank face reflected a quick mind and honest character, said to him : —

"Horatio, Tom Witts and I have bought the 'Jeffersonian.' He is already sick of his bargain. Will you come into partnership with me ? "

This was Horatio King, who was at the beginning of his active career. He lived near Paris Hill, and saw a great deal of Hannibal Hamlin as boy and man. He was now the printer's devil, and pondering a career as a newspaper editor. In an amusing reminiscence, King told how it took him a long time to decide in what manner to submit an article to the "Jeffersonian." Finally he sent it to the editor-in-chief, Cole, as an anonymous communication, who, to King's great delight, published it. Then he announced himself to Cole's great amazement as the author.

King was taken by surprise at the sudden change in the ownership of the "Jeffersonian," but as it offered him an opportunity to promote his own fortunes he readily agreed. The young men did not have enough money to buy the paper outright; Hamlin had only two hundred and fifty dollars, which was his share of his father's estate. The owners of the "Jeffersonian," however, accepted notes for the balance of the debt, and on May 30, 1830, the paper appeared under the management of Hamlin and King. As Hamlin did not know how to set type, he consented to release Witts, the foreman, from his agreement to buy the "Jeffersonian," on condition that he would do two weeks' work in the office for nothing. Witts had to carry out his promise, and Hamlin learned enough from him to get started as a printer. King succeeded Witts as foreman and Cole remained the editor.

The office boy was Henry Carter, another lad with a future before him. He was distantly related to Hamlin, and ran away from his home in Portland to learn the newspaper business under his kinsman. The three lads had a busy time for the next six months, and Hamlin, who worked as writer, printer, farmer, and law student, used to refer jokingly to this experience as his college education. The "Jeffersonian" was printed on a Ramage press and required two pulls for each side of the paper. Cole wrote one dignified editorial, a week, Hamlin and King assisted and also turned in news. To save time Hamlin would often set his matter up "hot from the brain," without reducing it first to writing. When they worked the press, King handled the fly and Hamlin would ink the type. He used to say with a smile that a little ink would not hurt his complexion. His associates said that he was always jolly and full of fun, except at times when he seemed to be "wandering in dreams," possibly thinking of a career beyond that little office. King told a story to illustrate Hamlin's fun-loving disposition. A gaping boy applied for a position in the office, and when he asked how to learn the printing business, Hamlin told him that he must begin by eating printer's ink. Before any one could stop him, he scooped some of the stuff into his mouth. But the young partners squared things by teaching him how to set type.

In six months Hamlin found that the "Jeffersonian" was not making enough money for two proprietors, and he offered to sell out to King or buy him out. King decided to buy, and subsequently merged the "Jeffersonian" into a Portland newspaper, after which he entered the government postal service. Cole established a law office, and Hamlin and Carter read with him for a year or more. "All the leading traits in Hamlin's character," wrote Mr. Carter, "which distinguished him in public life were conspicuous in those days — only they grew with his growth and strengthened with his strength by coming in contact with the outer world. Never despising what he could learn from books and schools, he learned vastly more from his struggles and experience in actual life. In the village lyceum he was easily the best debater, although he had never studied elocution in the schools. He did not attempt any flight of oratory or rhetoric; he simply had ideas or points to present, and expressed himself in a natural, earnest, effective manner. He was always himself; always Han Hamlin; without any attempt at imitation or display. He was strongly democratic in all his ideas and manner. After the death of his father, the care of the Hamlin estate devolved on him, which brought him in contact with the plain people, and served to strengthen his natural tendency to turn from the artificial and cling to the real."

Other interesting glimpses of young Hamlin's personal character were afforded by his associate of those days. "We walked, rode, fished, hunted, and danced, and he always treated me as a companion, although four or five years older. I regarded him both as a companion and a mentor. Our most common amusement was hunting, and in our excursions over the country we were always accompanied by Hamlin's little dog Carlo. The two were inseparable. At home, in the office, or in the woods, there was Carlo by Hamlin's side. He was small, short-haired, swift of foot, nice head, and bright eyes, and always clean. He was very affectionate, and would show it by wagging his tail, barking, and looking up with his expressive eyes. Hamlin loved that little dog, and Carlo loved him, and it was exhilarating to see Carlo jump when Hamlin would take his gun. Carlo would dart ahead and sometimes in his zeal run out of sight. Occasionally we would play him a trick and switch off on another path. When he missed us we would hear his reproachful yells, and he would wag all over when he caught us again. I never saw a dog so clever in treeing partridges, nor one so affectionate. Years and years afterwards when Hamlin was collector of the port of Boston, I spent an evening with him, and Carlo was a prominent topic of conversation. And sixty years afterwards there is no picture of Han Hamlin so vivid in my mind as when he was walking across the green at Paris Hill, with Carlo by his side."

Hamlin's magnetism was recognized at that time, and a story was told that illustrated his power to soothe ruffled spirits. He planned a ride into the country one day with Carter and several young women, to spend the afternoon with the uncle of one of the women in the party. Hamlin forgot to inform those they intended to call on of their contemplated visit. They arrived at their destination about noon, and just as the young ladies were about to enter the house it occurred to Hamlin that he had made a blunder. The fact was, it was in the middle of the haying season, when their host was as busy as he could be in his field. Moreover, it was just dinner hour, and no preparations had been made to receive guests. What made it still worse was the fact that the enforced host was a retired sea captain, of a curt manner, developed from long life on shipboard. The girls, of course, knew nothing of the situation, and were chilled when the old captain, stern-looking, with a cue, and in his shirtsleeves, came into the room with a look that plainly asked, "What's your business?" "It was Hamlin's excursion," said Mr. Carter, "and I stood back to let him settle with the social function ; and how well he did it ! He explained and apologized with great skill and discernment, and gradually the captain's face lost its austere look. Then Hamlin with great tact drew out some of his best sea yarns, and in the end the old sea-dog was completely fascinated. He finally forgot his haying, and invited us to dinner, and actually compelled us to spend the evening with him."

Another incident foreshadowed the coming man. "In those days," wrote Mr. Carter, "Hamlin exhibited the same traits of loyalty to his friends for which he was noted in after years. One winter I was engaged to teach school near Paris Hill. There was a bitter sectarian war between the Baptists and the Universalists, and the teacher was usually the one who suffered. Hamlin invited me to a dance at Poland one night, and an immense fall of snow prevented me from returning to school the next morning. An illiterate busybody, who opposed the agent who appointed me, seized the opportunity to make war. He had a petition drawn up, asking the school board to dismiss me on the charges that I had 'neglected my duties as a teacher to indulge in worldly and sinful pleasures,' that I 'had used profane language,' and was 'inefficient.' Hamlin came forward and said that as he had got me into the scrape he would get me out. He had read some law, and had also studied the trial of cases in court. He had also investigated the school and knew that it was a success. He finally understood the animus of the charges and the character of the man who made them. He said to me, 'We will have some fun out of this,' and then planned to vindicate me. This he did in his own way, and without any help from his elders.

"The incident revived the old feud, and there was no little excitement when the hearing began in the schoolhouse. My enemy made a long speech, saying that his children had made little or no improvement in reading that he could ascertain, that I had been heard to swear, and was not competent. Hamlin at once put him on the stand and asked him to read and write on the spot. This staggered him ; he could do neither. Hamlin then called up my enemy's son, and asked him what profane words I had used. The boy replied that I had been heard to say that a certain man was a 'poor deaf old devil.' Hamlin asked him if he had heard anything stronger than that at home, and silence was the reply. Hamlin next placed a minister on the stand, and asked him if saying a man was a deaf old devil was swearing. The minister said no, and that it 'was not taking the name of the Lord in vain.' By this time the audience was in a roar of laughter, and yet Hamlin was not done. He was filled with righteous indignation, and made a speech that would have done him credit in later years, denouncing the spirit of warfare in the district as a disgrace to civilization, a detriment to education, and the petition as persecution. The committee at once dismissed the case, and publicly complimented me. The boys, who were all friendly to me, started to snowball my enemy, and it was all Hamlin, the agent, and I could do to stop them. But that was like Hannibal Hamlin. He could be as merciful to a fallen enemy as he was merciless in felling him."

This group of young men is of more than ordinary interest, and the subsequent lives of young Hamlin's companions were a source of pride to him. Cole became a successful lawyer, and was for many years a district judge in Maine. King rose in the government postal service to the top, and was postmaster-general in Buchanan's Cabinet during the latter part of his administration, when he called loyal men to his side. Carter returned to journalism and became editor of the "Portland Advertiser." He rendered valuable service when the Republican party was formed, and was one of the men who placed Hannibal Hamlin at the head of his party when he was elected governor. He was subsequently a member of the state Senate of Massachusetts, and for many years the municipal judge of Haverhill.

CHAPTER V

AFTER Hamlin sold out his interest in the "Jeffersonian," he tried to devote himself to the study of law in Cole's office. But he soon found that he could not give all his attention to the law without detriment to his mother's farm and live stock, and he had to adapt himself to circumstances as best he could. The farm hands noticed that when he was called to the field he generally brought a law book with him, and usually found a chance to make use of it. When he hoed potatoes they often saw him studying out a case while standing at the head of a row of potato hills. Presently he would put down the book, and con the case over in his mind while working down to the end of the row and back on the next. Then he would take up his book, read over another page or paragraph, and fix it in his mind while hoeing the next row in turn. But this was slow work, and Hamlin saw that to get ahead he must have a year's study in an office where he could get some practical experience with the mechanism of the law. To this end, he earned money by surveying land and copying legal papers for lawyers outside of his regular hours of work. By hard toil and careful saving, in two years' time he had got together more than enough money to pay his expenses for a year in Portland, where he had decided to go. At this time the leading law firm in Portland was Fessenden & Deblois. Young Hamlin called upon them, and asked to be accepted as a student in their office. They consented, and for the following year Hamlin had the opportunities he had sought.

In other respects, Hamlin's associations with Fessenden & Deblois were fortunate for him. They were not only able lawyers, but they were also fine men. The senior partner was General Samuel Fessenden, one of the most interesting and picturesque men identified with the legal profession and political history of Maine. He had a magnificent personality; his form was towering; he had a noble face, kindly, expressive eyes, and a calm, confident air. He was what he looked, a born leader and a man of heart and principle. He was descended from the pioneer Fessenden family of Massachusetts, and was educated at Dartmouth. He left his mark there as a scholar, and in after years the presidency of the college was offered to him.

Coming to Portland, he took and maintained a high position at the Cumberland bar, which numbers among its leaders men of national reputation, including Simon Greenleaf, William Pitt Fessenden, and Thomas B. Reed. General Fessenden disputed the leadership of the Cumberland bar with Greenleaf, until the latter attached himself to the Harvard Law School, but did not care for public life. William Pitt Fessenden was his son, but he was no abler man than his remarkable father. A difference was that one sought a political career, the other declined it. General Fessenden was best known in New England as a pioneer Abolitionist. Thomas A. Deblois, his partner, was a Massachusetts man. After graduating from Harvard he came to Portland, and for many years was associated with General Fessenden. He was a man of sterling qualities, of dignified presence, and was widely respected.

When Hamlin entered the office of Fessenden & Deblois, in 1832, the legal profession still enforced stringent rules upon students, and observed certain ideas of professional etiquette. Students, as a rule, were required to light office fires, sweep floors, run errands, and do other acts of a rather menial capacity. Lawyers usually wore the old-fashioned swallow-tailed coat, the buff waistcoat, and the stock. Fessenden & Deblois, however, had their own ideas about their duties and relations to their students. They believed in encouraging young men and in instilling high ideas of dignity and courtesy in them. They personally interested themselves in their student, and treated him almost as if he were of their own flesh and blood; in fact, they seemed to make little distinction between him and William Pitt Fessenden, who had just left Bowdoin to enter his father's office. General Fessenden was continually offering practical suggestions; Mr. Deblois gave earnest advice and explanation. They were very thoughtful about little things. Hamlin never forgot their kindness to him. Many years afterwards he used to tell a story that illustrated the consideration of his preceptors. One day a client, under indictment, called at the office to have a consultation. Hamlin was preparing to retire to the adjoining room when General Fessenden stopped him, saying, "Hold on, my son. You are a member of our legal family; we have no secrets from you. And I think you had better stay here, to see how the mechanism of the law works in such cases."

During this year the Abolition movement in the United States received great impetus from the election of a Parliament pledged to abolish slavery in the English colonies. Slavery became a subject of constant interest and discussion between General Fessenden and Hamlin. This noble man hated slavery and fiercely denounced it. He joined the New England Anti-Slavery Society when the only meeting place it could get in Boston was a barn loft behind the Marlborough Hotel, and he was also president of the society at one time. Hamlin had then fixed and positive ideas about slavery. In one of his conversations with Fessenden, he said: —

"General, I hate slavery, and I would fight it if ever I got a chance. I believe in Abolition, and hope it will come, but I do not believe in the Abolitionists with the exception of yourself."

In truth, the Abolitionists of this period, notwithstanding the humanity of their cause, with but few exceptions were as erratic, unpractical, and visionary as they were later when they proposed to dissolve the Union to prevent slavery from being extended into free soil. General Fessenden was a man too broad-gauged to overlook the practical side of the slavery question. He believed that the part the Abolitionists had to play was to agitate. He was too far-sighted, too patriotic, to sympathize with the disunionists among the Abolitionists. Fully a quarter of a century before the slaveholders' war of secession broke out, this far-seeing man created a scene in the old Portland court-house by predicting, in the presence of a number of pro-slavery men, that the slave power would bring on a war that would end in its own destruction. Fessenden liked Hamlin, it would appear, all the better for his frankness, and formed a favorable opinion of his ideas about slavery. In subsequent years, as will be seen later, he came to Hamlin's help when the slave power was trying to crush him. This was an outcome of their early associations. Mr. Deblois also proved himself a stanch friend in emergencies, to be related in other chapters. Another interesting friendship young Hamlin formed at this time was with Neal Dow, who was then entering his picturesque career.

The last thing General Fessenden did for Hamlin, with the approbation of Mr. Deblois, shows the nature of the two men. As Hamlin was about to leave Portland, he tendered his preceptors the usual fee exacted from law students. It amounted to several hundred dollars. General Fessenden handed the money back, saying, "I think you can make better use of the money than we can, my boy. Then again, if I know you right, and I think I do, you yourself will encourage deserving young men when you will be able to." This act of generosity was never forgotten.

This was an unexpected lift for Hamlin, and enabled him to strike out for himself at once. On returning to Paris Hill, in the spring of 1833, he was admitted to the bar, and complimented by the court on his examination. The same day on which he was admitted to the practice of his profession, he won his first case, with a pleasing result. The case was this. Just before Hamlin went to Portland, a man named Houghton came into Mr. Cole's office to engage him to try a case before the local justice. Cole was away, and Houghton insisted that Hamlin should take the case. A valuable cow of his, Houghton explained, had been kicked to death by a horse belonging to a neighbor, and he wanted damages. Hamlin argued the case and won, but an appeal was taken, and it came up for hearing before the court, just after Hamlin had passed his examination. Houghton asked Hamlin to appear for him, but when the young lawyer found that he was to be pitted against Judge Emery, for certain reasons he felt like declining. But Houghton urged him to retain the case, and, with some misgivings, he consented. Once started, he was on his mettle, and made an argument that not only won the case, but also drew praise from the court and Judge Emery. The pleasantest result of the incident was Judge Emery's graceful and good-natured prediction of success for his opponent, — a young man, he said, who was fortunate enough to begin his active career by winning his first case and a wife on the same day. This was the way the engagement between young Hamlin and Miss Emery was formally announced. Houghton, by the way, became a great admirer of Mr. Hamlin, and named a son after him, — Hannibal Hamlin Houghton.

After their marriage, which took place on December 10, 1833, the young lawyer and his wife went to the town of Lincoln, in Penobscot County, on the advice of General Samuel F. Hersey, a native of Oxford County, one of the leading lumbermen of Maine and one of Mr. Hamlin's lifelong friends. Hamlin opened an office and transacted enough business to say that he had practiced his profession in Lincoln, when he heard that there was a better opening for him in the town of Hampden. Charles Stetson, who had begun his career in Hampden, and who was afterwards one of the leading capitalists of Maine and a member of Congress, had acquired interests that demanded his removal to Bangor. Hamlin was the first lawyer to appear on the scene as Stetson's successor, and quickly ascertained that Hampden offered him an excellent field. Hampden at that time was a thriving country town of several thousand inhabitants, with large commercial interests. It is five miles below Bangor, on the banks of the Penobscot River, one of the finest streams of water in Maine. It is also one of the oldest towns in the State, and is historical as the scene of the battle of Hampden, where a brave but ineffectual stand by a small group of untrained militia was made against British regulars in the war of 1812, who came up the Penobscot, sacking the towns on their way as far as Bangor. Hampden was a shipbuilding and farming centre when Hamlin settled there, and he found plenty of business at the outset. He took possession of a little box-like office on the principal street, hung out his sign and went to work.

Hamlin's Law Office.

There were many hospitable people in Hampden, and they made the new squire, as they called him, feel at home. When Mr. and Mrs. Hamlin came to this place, they first boarded at the house of Asa Matthews, master of the village academy, and a rugged old-fashioned school-teacher. He was a graduate of Waterville College, and well informed. An account he gave of Mr. Hamlin is of interest. "Hannibal Hamlin's personality," said he, "at once drew attention to him when he was twenty-four, and settled in Hampden. The first time he came into my house and stood looking at me, I knew he was an uncommon kind of a man. He stood six feet, straight as an arrow. There was about him the natural air, simplicity, and nobility of an Indian sachem. There was a great power, too, in the steadfast look of his big black eyes. I thought he was one of the finest specimens of physical manhood I ever saw. There was iron in him, but it was tempered with a big heart. He was cordial, sympathetic, and magnetic. He was always a perfectly natural man. His career strengthened his rugged character, and developed his great mind, but his success did not affect his nature. When his old friends of Hampden called on him at Washington, when he was the war Vice-President, he was as simple and natural as when he came into my house for the first time, an unknown man, little dreaming of the honorable career before him."

At the outset of his life in Hampden, Mr. Hamlin told his clients that he had several rules and principles that he should always observe. One related to money, and it became known in this way. In this period there were few banks or money collecting agencies in the country towns of Maine, and this line of business was handled chiefly by the lawyers. Mr. Hamlin was soon called on to make writs ; in one year he made over three hundred. Thus he handled a good deal of money belonging to his clients, and it often happened that they did not call for it until some time after it had been collected. Mr. Hamlin, therefore, had at times considerable sums of money in his possession, and on one occasion he told a friend what disposition he made of such money and his reasons. He said : —

"When I collect money for a client, I inclose it in an addressed package, and lock the package up in my trunk until it is called for. I will not touch or use that money for my purposes under any circumstances, unless, of course, the owner should authorize it. The money belongs to the owner. I have no more right to use it, even if I could replace it in five minutes, than I would have to take money that he might happen to have in his pocketbook. A man should practice honesty in his heart and thoughts as much as in his deeds."

He not only followed this rule in all his business dealings throughout his life, but also endeavored to enforce it on others as the correct principle to be observed in matters involving trust and confidence. It was one of the first rules or maxims he enjoined on his law students and on all of his four sons, who lived to follow his profession.

Another thing the people of Hampden learned about the new squire, before he had been among them long, was that he would frankly discourage litigation, even if he was a pecuniary loser by so doing, when he honestly thought that a case could be settled out of court by a little common-sense advice on his part. Within a year after he had settled in Hampden, Mr. Hamlin was appointed town agent, and intrusted with all its public business. His own business rapidly increased, and in several years he laid plans to build himself a home. He and his wife now had two sons, George and Charles, and looked forward with pleasure to the time when they should own their house. The only set-back Mr. Hamlin received in the beginning of his active life occurred about this time. He went on the bond of a deputy sheriff named Grant for the sum of four thousand dollars. When he was signing his name, he said in a joking way : " My friend, if you should go wrong, it might cost me my home I am building." Unfortunately this jest came true. Grant became a defaulter for a large sum of money, and his creditors looked to his bondsmen. Mr. Hamlin acted promptly. He called a meeting of some of Grant's creditors in his office, and said to them :[1] —

" My friends, I have lived among you only a few years, but I think you know that I keep my word. I am poor, young, and struggling for an honest support for myself. This struggle will continue right among you, my neighbors. I am unable now to meet this just debt ; but if you will give me time, and God will give me strength, I will pay off every dollar I owe you, even if it takes me a lifetime to do it." As a matter of fact, it took him many years to settle this debt, for he had only his salary to live on while in public life, but he kept his promise to the last cent. " But," Mr. Hamlin added, in telling the story, "heavens! how long it kept my nose on the grindstone. Never willingly get into debt."

There was a great deal of social life in Hampden, for a village of its size, and although Mr. Hamlin worked hard he also believed in enjoying life himself. Out-of-door life was his passion. When he came to Hampden he had hardly been in the town a day before he was hunting around the country for its trout streams. Many an afternoon, when he could get away from his work, he would go off fishing for a couple of hours. At this time most of the States had compulsory militia laws, and there was, therefore, more interest in

[1] He related the story to S. F. Barr, representative to Congress from Pennsylvania in 1881–85.

military affairs in Maine then than now. In Hampden there were two companies, and Mr. Hamlin joined one, an independent organization called the Hampden Rifles. Incidentally, it may be said that this was the beginning of his political career. The company was composed of active, jovial young men, and when they found out the good-fellowship of their new companion they elected him captain of the company, and thereafter stuck to him throughout many a political fight. They had good times "training" in those days. A story is told of Captain Hamlin's physical agility. He and his men had attended a parade at Bangor, and returning to Hampden the men began to "skylark." When they were resting near a log fence, which reached up to an average man's chest, some one in the company shouted: "Hamlin, I'll stump you to jump over that fence without touching your hands." Dropping his sword, Hamlin was over the fence in a standing jump, without touching his hands, before another word was said. The company watched, and other men tried the same feat, but no one else could do it, and the fence was jocosely known as "Hamlin's stump."

Hamlin quickly made a reputation in Hampden as a speaker.[1] He had a simple, vigorous way of talking that he usually adopted, but he could be witty and sarcastic when the occasion demanded. He used to try his cases before the local justice of the peace, who was a more important functionary than now, and after a while the news that Squire Hamlin was going to argue a case always brought a crowd of farmers into the stuffy room to hear him. He also spoke frequently at the village lyceum, and on one occasion learned that he was becoming famous. A schoolmaster who heard him was strongly impressed. He met the Rev. George W. Field, then a young divinity student, and said to him: "They have a rising speaker in Hampden. His name is Hannibal Hamlin. He speaks so well that I am sure he will be elected to the legislature some day."

Hamlin's business rapidly developed, and he was often required to argue cases in Bangor. A story is told of one of the first arguments he made there, in a case that attracted considerable attention at the time on account of the prominence of one of the parties to the suit. He was a Federalist who lived in Hampden, and had undertaken to snub Hamlin because he was a Democrat, and depreciated his ability. The Federalist had a quarrel with his neighbor over the boundary line between their farms, and ultimately claimed that he was entitled to a slice of his neighbor's land. He retained a lawyer of established reputation to push his claim, while the defendant engaged Hamlin, who, after taking certain quiet steps, satisfied himself that the Federalist

[1] His first appearance as a public speaker was made in Hampden, on the Fourth of July, 1836.

had no right whatever to the land he was trying to get. The case was tried in Bangor. The old court-house was crowded. The Federalist's claim seemed to be established by positive testimony; but Hamlin threw a veritable bombshell into his camp by demonstrating, through an assistant he put on the stand, that he himself, a practical surveyor, had surveyed the land in dispute; that he had worked from the ancient landmark acknowledged by the Federalist, across the land, following the disputed line to the Penobscot River; that at the end of the line he had found on the ledge the original surveyor's mark, which proved beyond a doubt that the line was correct as it stood, and that the Federalist did not have a shadow of a claim to an inch of his neighbor's land. Then Hamlin turned on the exposed claimant, and arraigned him with great power and pitiless scorn as "a man who coveted his neighbor's lands." The Federalist left the court-house defeated and chagrined. In his hour of repentance he resolved to conciliate the fiery young Democrat upon whom he had hitherto affected to look down. When Hamlin returned home, he found at his house a number of choice young fruit-trees the Federalist had sent him as an olive branch of peace. Friendly relations afterward followed between the men.

Another story was told of Hamlin's shrewdness in dealing with a penurious client. The incident also illustrates his love of fun. One of the richest men of Penobscot County lived near Hampden. He was very parsimonious; in fact, his neighbors said he was "meaner than a skinflint." He sold some land one day, and being in Hampden called on Mr. Hamlin to get him to draw up the deed. He first inquired how much this transaction would cost him. Knowing the peculiarity of the old man, Mr. Hamlin thought he would see how far his meanness would carry him, and so he replied that the law allowed him seventy-five cents. Then he added: —

"Do you think that's too much?"

"Yes, yes, that's altogether too much," replied the old man, shaking his head, and contracting his thin lips.

"Well," continued Mr. Hamlin suavely, "do you think that two shillings (fifty cents) would be too much?"

"Yes," said the client, "that's too much."

"How about one shilling?" (twenty-five cents), Mr. Hamlin asked, with his blandest smile.

"Y-e-s," the old miser cautiously admitted, "one shillin' ain't too much."

Mr. Hamlin made out the deed, and when he received the shilling, he said in an apparently cordial, off-hand way: —

"Now seeing that it's you, I'll give you the deed for a shilling, and give you a treat besides. Come over to the tavern."

Mr. Hamlin ordered two glasses of the old man's favorite beverage, and paid for them with the shilling. As the client smacked his lips, his face lighted up with enthusiasm, and he broke out : —

"Squire, you air the most generoust man I ever knew. I'm going to give you my business, I'll be darned if I won't."

Now, this was not what Mr. Hamlin had been looking for, but it is an amusing fact that the old fellow became a valuable client, and afterward promptly paid Mr. Hamlin's charges without grumbling.

Another story was told at the expense of the Supreme Court of Maine, which added to the reputation of the young lawyer. The incident happened when Mr. Hamlin was a member of the town school committee. He had two colleagues, and in his absence from Hampden at one time they engaged a teacher named Jackson. Subsequently they became dissatisfied with Jackson, and dismissed him. He claimed that he had been engaged for a whole term, and sued the town for his salary for that period. The case was tried in the District Court, and went against Jackson, but he appealed for a new trial, claiming that it was not competent for two members of the committee to discharge him. Chief Justice Shepley of the Supreme Court, a man who was rarely caught tripping, upheld Jackson's contention, and ordered a new trial. When the case was tried the second time, Mr. Hamlin made the argument for the town. This is the way he made it : —

"Your honor," said he, addressing the court, "it is contended, is it not, that it was not competent for two members of the school committee to dismiss Mr. Jackson?"

"Yes, sir," replied the justice with great dignity. "The law court has so decided."

"Very well, your honor," Mr. Hamlin continued, "if it was not competent for two members of the committee to discharge Mr. Jackson, will you tell me if it was competent for the same two to employ him?" At the same time he exhibited Jackson's certificate, bearing the names of only two members of the committee.

Failure to perform military duties according to the law then was punishable by fines, and Mr. Hamlin's prominence in his company naturally brought him many cases to defend or prosecute. Eventually he was called all over the county of Penobscot to act in cases of this kind. One story is still told in a town near Bangor of his shrewdness in defending a suit against members of a company. He suspected that a family arrangement existed between four brothers to make what they could out of the compulsory military law. One brother was a justice of the peace, before whom the cases were tried against men charged with evading service. The writs were served by the second brother, who was a constable. The evidence against alleged delinquents was furnished by a third brother, who was clerk of the military company. The cases were prosecuted by the fourth brother, who was a lawyer. The first time Mr. Hamlin was called into the case he saw at a glance that the rolls were defective, because they had not been properly made up and certified to by the officers of the company as required by law. This was a fatal flaw, and the case was thrown out of court. Three months later, to his surprise, Mr. Hamlin was again summoned to defend the same clients against the same charge. Suspecting some trick, Mr. Hamlin asked to see the company rolls. He looked at the records very carefully for a moment, and then amazed the court and the spectators in the little room by suddenly stuffing the rolls in his pocket, buttoning up his coat, and planting his back against the court-room door. Before the startled justice could gather his wits, Mr. Hamlin was in command of the situation. Pointing his finger at the clerk of the company, he said : —

"I know you to be an honest man. Now, you shall tell me the truth, and I will not leave this room until you do. Have not these rolls been doctored since I was here on this case in September? At that time there were defects in the rolls; I remember that fact because the case was thrown out of court for that reason. Yet, the same charges against my clients are renewed, and the same rolls are now produced again, but dated back. Who has supplied the certificates that were missing in September? Answer me that question?"

Completely taken by surprise, the clerk stammered : "Well, Mr. Hamlin, er, the fact is, I er — I swore to the rolls which my brother (the lawyer) handed to me the other day."

This admission caused consternation among the rest of the family ; the lawyer raved, but Mr. Hamlin continued : —

"Your brother gave you the rolls, did he ? Then you signed the new certificates at his suggestion, did you not ? "

A reluctant "yes" came from the alarmed clerk. At this admission Mr. Hamlin took up his hat, and opened the door, firing this parting shot : —

"This case also," said he, "is thrown out of court, and to prevent it from being resurrected I shall carry the rolls home where you cannot get them."

He did so, and the militia of this town was not troubled again by these men.

Hampden's maritime interests were comparatively large at this time, and Mr. Hamlin was eventually drawn into admiralty law. When he had built up a large practice a suggestive incident occurred. He was called to Boston to take charge of an admiralty case, and there made the acquaintance of Sidney Bartlett, who was about his own age, and was already evincing those solid qualities of mind which

placed him at the head of the Boston bar for many years. Mr. Hamlin retained Mr. Bartlett as associate counsel, and subsequently Mr.
Bartlett engaged Mr. Hamlin to take charge of business for him in
Maine. In the course of a few years the two young lawyers developed a profitable line of business. But it was suddenly terminated by
Mr. Hamlin's election to Congress in 1843. Mr. Bartlett, it would
seem, had formed a favorable opinion of Mr. Hamlin's ability as a
lawyer and a liking for him as a man. When Mr. Hamlin started for
Washington, to take his seat in the House, he stopped at Boston, and
called on Mr. Bartlett. Now, Mr. Bartlett was perfectly devoted to
the law, and had a contempt for politics. He was rather reserved
and precise in his dealings with men as a rule, but when he saw his
former associate, he warmed up, and to Mr. Hamlin's quiet amusement, read him a vigorous lecture on entering politics. He seemed
to feel as if it were a personal grievance. In a tone of remonstrance
Bartlett began : —

"Hamlin, why do you go into politics ? There's nothing in political life, I tell you. You were doing well, and you should not have
got yourself elected to Congress. You may stay in politics and spoil
the making of a fine lawyer ! Hamlin, you will have a fine career as
a lawyer if you remain in your profession ; I know you will. Give up
politics. Stick to the 'larr,' my friend, stick to the 'larr.'"

In the following years Mr. Hamlin rarely made a visit to Boston
without calling on Mr. Bartlett for a few moments. Once when he
complimented the latter on his success at the bar, Bartlett replied : —

"Well, Senator, are you not sorry now you did not take my advice
and remain a lawyer ?"

"No," replied Mr. Hamlin, with a laugh, "but I will admit that
when I entered politics I spoiled the making of a good farmer."

Mr. Hamlin's early entrance into political life and its engrossing
duties soon withdrew him from his profession, and when he had been
fairly settled in the Senate he had to relinquish all thought of resum-
ing the practice of law. He did not, therefore, develop his legal possibilities, and in after life there naturally was no little speculation as
to the rank he would have attained at the bar. Sidney Bartlett's
opinion is suggestive. It was also recalled by a witty practitioner in
considering this, that Mr. Hamlin's success in winning cases during
his connection with the bar, which was regarded as remarkable, entitled him to a share in the story told of Rufus Choate by a farmer jury-
man : "He seemed to have the luck to be always on the right side."
But this brief phase is best summed up in the words of John A.
Peters, the distinguished Chief Justice of Maine, who knew him as a
lawyer, congressman, and friend : —

" There can be no doubt that Mr. Hamlin would have attained high
position as a lawyer, had not a strong natural taste for public life
allured him from the practice of his profession.   He naturally possessed a happy combination of the qualities that command success at
the bar, quickness and clearness of perception, conciseness of thought
and expression, discrimination, an intuitive insight into the motives
of others, industry and earnestness, and a personal magnetism which
made him acceptable to all classes of men.   And at the bottom, on
which this superstructure of character could most firmly rest, was a
strong, natural love of justice, a high order of integrity, and rare common sense.   We may well remember with pride that Hannibal Hamlin was a member of our bar." [1]

[1] Eulogy, Penobscot Bar Association, October 25, 1891.   See other remarks by
Albert W. Paine, S. F. Humphrey, Daniel F. Davis, and Eugene Hale.

CHAPTER VI

THE state and county musters were the great events of the year in Maine and other States, at this period. There was a good deal of rivalry between the various crack companies of Maine, and the approach of muster day stirred up more excitement among the men and boys than the coming of a circus to country towns does nowadays. The day before the muster towns were alive with moving troops on their way to the grounds. On the great day itself the muster place in the morning was a scene of arriving troops and soldiers marching and drilling. In the afternoon came the sham fight, with enough noise and dust for a real battle. Then the hungry soldiers charged on scores of booths that fringed the field, "stocked with enough food to feed an army, and enough liquids to float a navy," as the saying was. The absence of women was significant. Jamaica rum and punch were circulated in great quantities. The scene became hilarious. Barn doors were thrown down on the ground. Fiddlers scraped for men to dance. The double shuffle was a favorite step, the fore and aft a popular dance. Men jigged each other and the fiddlers down, and when the sun was sinking it lighted the way home for an hilarious crowd, marching and singing behind the heroes of the day.

The muster attracted the politicians, and they gathered to discuss candidates, and lay their wires. Two years after Hamlin came to Hampden, the rifle company, which he captained at the county muster, in 1835, proposed him as the Democratic candidate for the legislature, to represent Hampden and the associated towns of Newburgh, Orrington, and others. He was duly nominated at the regular caucus, and then entered upon his first campaign. This is of historical rather than personal interest, since it relates to the rise and formation of political parties in Maine. From 1820 to 1829 party lines in Maine were not strictly drawn in the state elections. In 1829 the ascendency of the Jackson Democracy was felt, and Jackson's followers there made a campaign on state issues. They were designated as the Democratic-Republican party, and their opponents as National Republicans. The Democrats were beaten by a small majority; but the next year they carried the State, and, with the exception of an occasional defeat, controlled its government until 1856. In 1833, the year in which Mr. Hamlin settled in Hampden and began to take an active interest in politics, the opponents of the Democratic-Republican party formally took the name of Whigs, and the Jackson party began to be known simply as Democrats.

At this time the Democratic party was most powerful in Maine. The year Mr. Hamlin was elected to the legislature, Robert P. Dunlap, the Democratic candidate for governor, received over 45,000 votes to only 18,000 for William King, the Whig candidate, the first governor of Maine, and a man of great personal popularity and ability. Party principle prevailed, and it is easy to see why the Democratic party was then supreme. First, it was truly the party of the people. This was because it was loyal to the principles of Jefferson and Jackson, and these were the safest for the young nation to follow in its formative period. They embodied a strict construction of the Constitution, and hence guaranteed the largest latitude of liberty to the individual citizen that was compatible with the welfare of society, while demanding thorough enforcement of the laws and maintenance of the government. The Democrats of this period looked on the Constitution as the Bible of their faith, because it gave the American people the best form of popular government yet given to mankind, and secured for the individual his personal liberty. The Democrats, therefore, opposed paternal legislation and centralization; they regarded the Whigs as the lineal descendants of the Federalists, whom they believed to have been monarchists at heart. They also believed in a low tariff for revenue only. Another thing to be credited to the party of Jefferson and Jackson was that it was the progressive and aggressive party of its day, the Whigs being the conservative element. While it did not have as many intellectual leaders as the Whigs did, it generally took the lead in cutting out the issues of the day. In several respects it embodied the life of the growing country in a striking manner. It was imbued with belief in the manifest destiny of the nation. To the Democratic party the country owes the acquisition of the Louisiana territory, under Jefferson, the opening up of the West under Jackson, the annexation of Texas, and the saving of Oregon from the British government. At this time it had the young blood of the day, and was the dominant party of the country.

Hamlin supported the principles of Jefferson and Jackson from conviction, and was in full accord with his party in its dominant ideas, although he believed in specific duties in connection with a tariff for revenue. New England was then a commercial centre, and many of her public men grew with her interests, and evolved naturally into protectionists when New England developed her great manufacturing possibilities. Hamlin was also attracted to the Democratic party partly on account of his democratic nature and aggressive disposition.

He thoroughly believed in the American people, and he was a born fighter for their rights. He enjoyed a contest, and entered on this campaign with zest. He was easily elected, and took his seat in the House of Representatives in the following winter.

The key to Hannibal Hamlin's political success is to be found in his legislative training and experience. He remained in the Maine legislature five successive years, and there he not only familiarized himself with legislation and parliamentary procedure, but also built up lifelong friendships that were as a rock for him to stand on in his long and arduous fight against the slave power, which is the most important service he rendered to his country and State. But at this time slavery was not an issue. The parties were divided on strictly party issues, and Mr. Hamlin's services in the legislature are interesting chiefly in showing his capacity for work and his grasp of public questions in the first stages of his political career. In point of ability, character, and individual success the legislature of 1835 was not equaled by any other body that met at Augusta in Mr. Hamlin's lifetime. The Democrats were in control. The Speaker was Jonathan Cilley, a promising man, classmate of Longfellow and Hawthorne at Bowdoin, who was killed in a duel while a member of Congress. Another leading member of the House was John Holmes, of Alfred, who had been a member of the United States Senate. Henry W. Paine, afterwards one of the leaders of the Boston bar, was then a Whig representative of Hallowell. Another lawyer who stood well up in his profession was Samuel Wells, a Democrat, who became governor and a member of the Supreme Court of Maine. The leader of the Whigs in the House was Elisha H. Allen, of Bangor, a graduate of Williams College, who afterwards was a member of Congress, chief justice of the Hawaiian government, and finally its minister to this country. Rufus McIntire, of Parsonsfield, Stephen C. Foster, of Pembroke, and Virgil D. Parris, then of Buckfield, were also subsequently members of Congress. Dr. Ezekiel Holmes, of Winthrop, achieved a national reputation as a naturalist and a writer on agricultural and educational subjects. There were also other men in the House who attained some prominence in the legislature, the governor's council, or the business affairs of the State. Among them was Moses Emery, of Saco, a sound lawyer and a clear observer of public affairs; Stephen P. Brown, a pioneer woolen manufacturer of Dover; William Conner, of Fairfield; Eliakim Scammon, of Pittston; William D. Sewall, of Bath; and Wales Hubbard, of Wiscasset. In the Senate, over which Josiah Pierce, of Gorham, presided, Luther Severance and Samuel P. Benson were future congressmen. Tobias Purrington was a powerful leader in the movement to abolish capital punishment. One who was long a picturesque figure in the politics of Maine was John C. Talbot, of East Machias.

There was a strong rivalry for the leadership on the floor of the House, and as this was a time of intense partisanship, many a rough and tumble fight took place in debate with exchanges of personalities. The Whigs prided themselves on the superior intellectual attainments of their leaders; the Democrats prided themselves on the democracy of theirs. Hamlin's associates of these days said that he at once stepped to the front, and became the recognized leader of his party on the floor of the House. Naturally his marked individuality, swarthy face, and vigorous way of speaking attracted attention to him. Finally, his ardent championship of Democracy involved him in several pitched battles. One story has been preserved that shows the personal nature of the times. Some of the old leaders were a little jealous of the newcomer's sudden ascendency, and of these John Holmes was one. He had been in the United States Senate for a dozen years, and was at one time famous as a speaker of great powers of sarcasm and humor, though of a rude quality. In the Senate John Tyler once sneeringly asked Holmes what had become of the famous political firm John Randolph had discovered: James Madison, Felix Grundy, John Holmes, and the Devil. Holmes withered Tyler by retorting: "The first is dead, the second is in retirement, the third now addresses the Senate, and the fourth has gone over to the Nullifiers, and is electioneering among the gentleman's constituents." Holmes was a free lance in this House, and tried to domineer over it. Hamlin disputed the leadership with him, and Holmes attempted to crush his young opponent by coarsely ridiculing his swarthy countenance. This was an unfortunate move for Holmes. Instantly Hamlin jumped to his feet, and pointing his finger at Holmes he retorted: "If the gentleman chooses to find fault with me on account of my complexion, what has he to say about himself? I take my complexion from nature; he gets his from the brandy bottle. Which is more honorable?" This fierce thrust at Holmes's unfortunate failing brought out a shout from the House. The fact was, the members of the House were glad to see so brave a young David fell the Goliath of the House at one blow. There were cries of "Go on!" Pointing his finger at Holmes, Hamlin continued: "I will also tell the member from Alfred that he is more conspicuous for trying to ride rough shod over young men than for trying to encourage them. He never extends a hand to them as they begin to toil up the rugged path of life; he has not even a kind word for them. But as long as they are true to themselves and to nature, and as long as the member of Alfred sticks to the brandy bottle, they need not fear him." The House cheered again, and Holmes, realizing that he had fairly brought down this fierce denunciation on his head, took the floor, retracted his words, and made a manly apology. Then there was peace.

"The young Carthaginian routed the old Roman," was one humorous comment on the incident, and then Hamlin was known and called the Carthaginian of Maine, a name that stuck to him throughout life.

But the encounter with John Holmes was one of the few exceptions to the general attitude Mr. Hamlin maintained towards his political opponents and party associates. Elisha H. Allen, the leader of the Whigs, became one of Mr. Hamlin's best personal friends through their intercourse in the legislature, and often in after years attributed much of Mr. Hamlin's success to courtesy, kindness, tact, and unwillingness to allow the incidents of party strife to interfere with his personal relations. Mr. Allen himself was a high-bred man, of social and scholarly inclinations. He had a polished address and a bright way of talking that made him a favorite speaker and visitor in political and social circles in Maine and at Washington, where he lived many years as the dean of the diplomatic corps at the national Capitol. One incident Mr. Allen related will illustrate his ideas of Mr. Hamlin's sense of courtesy and personal obligations to his friends and associates. At the request of a Portland editor Mr. Hamlin wrote some sketches of his fellow-members of the House. Feeling some delicacy about writing up Mr. Allen, who was his political rival on the floor of the House, Mr. Hamlin asked another member to do it, supposing that he had the right ideas of the courtesy to which Mr. Allen was justly entitled. The day the article appeared Mr. Hamlin did not see it until after he entered the House. To his utter amazement Mr. Allen cut him with a freezing look, and refused to return his greeting.

"Why, Allen," exclaimed Mr. Hamlin, "what is the matter? Why do you treat me like this? I demand to know the reason; it is my right to know it."

The newspaper that contained the sketch of Mr. Allen, written at Mr. Hamlin's request, was silently handed to him, and to his great chagrin and displeasure he found over the *nom de plume* he had used in writing, a virulent and utterly unpardonable attack on Mr. Allen as the leader of the Whigs.

"Good heavens, Allen!" Mr. Hamlin ejaculated, "I did not write this awful thing; you did not believe that I did, did you?"

"Knowing you, Hamlin," Allen replied with some emotion, "I could not believe you capable of such a thing; but the *nom de plume* misled me. Your word, however, is sufficient, and here is my hand. I am glad, very glad, that you acted so promptly, and prevented any further misunderstanding where another man might have allowed my pardonable error to have gone unexplained, owing to my natural resentment."

A hearty handshake followed. Then Mr. Hamlin insisted on explaining how the article happened to be written, taking upon himself the moral responsibility for it. In the mean time Whigs and Democrats in the House were reading and discussing the matter, with the result that the Whigs were incensed, while some of the bitter partisans among the Democrats were inclined to chuckle over the unmerciful lashing Mr. Allen had received. Mr. Hamlin at once went among the members of the House, and, without naming the author of the article, and accepting the blame attached, strongly condemned it as unmanly and totally unjustified. Both Whigs and Democrats were greatly pleased with Mr. Hamlin's action, and the affair ended there.

At the beginning of the session Speaker Cilley appointed Mr. Hamlin to several of the most important committees of the House. They dealt with questions that were looming up like dark clouds on the political horizon, and, therefore, absorbed a great deal of the legislature's attention. Several incidents occurred that revealed Mr. Hamlin's character while meeting new experiences. His colleagues of this day said that he soon earned the reputation of a worker, and never refused to face any problem. One question that was now constantly coming up in the legislatures, and frightening the time-serving politicians of that body, was slavery. The situation was interesting. There was a growing friction between the Abolitionists and the slave-holders that threatened to produce serious trouble. A favorite method the Abolitionists had of agitating was to flood Congress and Northern legislatures with petitions for the abolition of the peculiar institution. The slave party retaliated by passing the infamous gag-law in Congress, which prohibited the reception of anti-slavery petitions by that body, and also by sending remonstrances to Northern legislatures against abolition agitation. While the majority of people in Maine abhorred slavery, they nevertheless deplored the methods of the Abolitionists as likely to cause trouble without affording any remedy for the evil. There was also a small, but increasing faction in the Democratic party of Maine, composed chiefly of Federal office-holders, who frowned on any attack on slavery; in fact, in their eyes criticism of slavery was criticism of the Constitution itself. For did not the Constitution guarantee protection to the institution? Under the circumstances, the Abolitionists had but little encouragement in Maine, and found a rather chilly atmosphere at Augusta.

Mr. Hamlin was a member of the committee that received the petitions and remonstrances relating to slavery. There were some pretty stiff pro-slavery men in the House, and they insisted that the abolition memorials should be rejected, while time-serving members insinuated that it would be easy to smother them. One incident of interest in connection with this was Mr. Hamlin's action when both open and covert opposition was shown to the abolition petitions.

He insisted that it was the committee's duty to receive and report the petitions, and made a speech when the matter was brought before the House. He did not believe in the Abolitionists, but it incensed him to find that the gag-law had supporters in Maine. He spoke out his mind freely, and enunciated his anti-slavery principles and feelings about the Abolitionists, and adhered to these principles with perfect consistency to the end. The substance of the speech was well remembered by those who heard it, and was noted in newspapers of the day. It was on precisely the same lines as speeches Mr. Hamlin made subsequently on the stump and in Congress. He said : —

"I am opposed to slavery, and I will fight it if it becomes a menace to the liberty and welfare of our common country. I hope slavery will be abolished, but the Constitution could not be adopted without the recognition of slavery, and the free States are bound to maintain their sacred constitutional obligations. I believe slavery to be an evil entailed on us by the mother country, and we must do the best with it we can under the circumstances. In the words of Pinckney, 'Slavery blights all that it touches,' and as it is now a local trouble, we should try to confine it within as narrow a compass as possible to prevent it from spreading. It may die out, but God is sure in his own good way and time to put an end to it. It is a curse, a moral wrong, and hurts those who support it more than it benefits them. But the Abolitionists have a right to be heard. They are citizens of this country. They have the rights of free speech guaranteed them by the Constitution."

These declarations were practically the platform of the anti-slavery party until events set in motion by the slave power morally relieved the North from its constitutional obligations to tolerate slavery where it had originally existed. Yet in 1836 they were interpreted by the pro-slavery Democrats of Maine as an assault on the "Divine Institution." This speech irritated them, and they looked on the young Democrat of Hampden with disfavor. They were not numerous or well enough organized to make serious trouble at that time. But in their councils they denounced Hamlin, and began to oppose him. Thus the lines of cleavage were then faintly indicated in Maine which split the two parties asunder twenty years later, and with this incident begins the long and close struggle Mr. Hamlin had with the slave power, which is the most important service he rendered the country and State, and the most picturesque chapter in his life.

While this was an era of agitation, it was also an age of reforms. A movement that was creating widespread interest was to secure cheap postage and better government mail service. The postal service was in its infancy, and the cost of correspondence was excessive. It cost even twenty-five cents to send a letter of only one sheet over four hundred miles through the mail ; and with the increased service of the railroad and steamboat lines high rates of postage prevailed. Some relief was afforded in different parts of the country by express companies, which did a thriving business by carrying mail at lower rates than the government. In Maine, the mail service, necessarily of limited facilities, was accomplished chiefly by the old-fashioned stage-coach, and the people, therefore, were very desirous of a reform. This movement enlisted Mr. Hamlin's sympathies. He offered a resolution in the House that throws further light on the means for transporting mail within the State, and also the existing difficulties. It instructed the Committee on Railroads to inquire into the expediency of amending the general laws regulating the railroads so as to enable the Postmaster-General to compel a railroad to carry government mail whenever he required it to do so. The resolution was adopted, and from this time on Mr. Hamlin gave a great deal of attention to postal reform. Without anticipating, it may be added, he took his seat in the House at Washington the year the movement achieved practical success.

The legislature was a theatre that reflected the dark side of life as well as its political and business affairs. A touching and distressing circumstance, revealed to the legislature, was the condition of some old soldiers of the war of independence. Mr. Hamlin had found them living in poverty, although they were the victims of accident rather than of willful neglect. Maine had furnished more than her quota of soldiers in the war of the Revolution, and some who had suffered wounds had become dependent on the bounty of the State and their friends, through the government's inability to provide properly for them after the close of the war. They were independent old patriots, and greatly saddened to be regarded as objects of charity or pensioners. Their condition demanded relief, and Mr. Hamlin induced the legislature to increase their bounties to fifty dollars a year, which was the limit the State could then afford. This was not much, but it was an improvement, and a step in the right direction, and in the end it had a good result. The legislature, once becoming interested in the old soldiers, considered further measures proposed for their relief. At the next session, Mr. Hamlin offered a resolution increasing the land grants to the veterans from two to six hundred acres, and exempted them from taxation. The bill was adopted, and the veterans passed their last days in comparative comfort.

A fight then broke out between the Whigs and Democrats of Maine that is now historical, and which also served to push Mr. Hamlin more prominently before the people as a leader of his party. It happened to be a period of extraordinary expansion, and one consequence was that there was a strong land speculative craze in various parts of the country. Some States made a reckless use of public money in building railroads along routes where towns did not yet exist. Illinois was, perhaps, the worst sufferer of all in this respect. It was the Whig policy to favor internal improvements; and at this time it is an interesting fact that Abraham Lincoln, then a Whig member of the Illinois legislature, was supporting his party. Lincoln's honesty and candor, in accepting his share of the responsibility for the catastrophe that overtook his State, were characteristic of the man. Maine felt the trend of affairs, and the Whigs advocated the building of a railroad from Wiscasset and other seaport towns to Quebec, by the aid of state money, and their plan stirred up a great deal of excitement at the time.

The general policy of the Democratic party was to oppose the use of public money in aid of any enterprise that could be promoted through individual effort. The scheme savored of paternal legislation, and then, again, far-sighted business men saw that a reaction would follow the abnormal conditions of affairs described. Mr. Hamlin attacked the Wiscasset railroad plan in several speeches before the legislature. His reasons briefly stated were, that his party principles were opposed to the scheme; that Maine was a poor State and could not afford the money; that the promotion of such a plan might bring on a fever of land speculation, such as was raging in other States; that, finally, it was more or less of a Whig scheme, which, if realized, might become in their hands a dangerous piece of machinery that would enable them to get a firm grip on the state government. This provoked a fierce discussion, but in the end the Democrats triumphed and killed the bill. Not yet feeling quite secure against the temptations of speculation and paternal legislation, Mr. Hamlin, at a subsequent session of the legislature, led a movement that secured the adoption of an amendment to the Constitution of Maine prohibiting the State from increasing its debt over $300,000.

This prudent legislation saved Maine to the Democrats in the fall elections of 1837. This was a year of disastrous panics and depression in business. As a consequence, a reaction set in against the National Democratic party that reached high tide three years later in the election of Harrison to the presidency. In Maine, Governor Dunlap was reëlected, and the legislature was once more controlled by the Democrats. Mr. Hamlin's leadership, in the preceding House, made him his party's logical candidate for speaker, and he was elected, being at that time twenty-eight years old, the youngest man yet to fill the speaker's chair. Elisha H. Allen, still the Whig leader, was his competitor. Among the leading members of this House were Rufus K. Goodenow, a Whig, of Paris, and a member of Congress in 1849; the Rev. Ebenezer Knowlton, of Montville, who was one of Maine's first Republican congressmen; Alfred Reddington, of

Augusta, a lifelong friend of the Speaker, and adjutant-general of the
State in 1849; Atwood Levensaler, a powerful Democratic leader in
the shipbuilding district of Thomaston, and always Mr. Hamlin's
personal friend; Randolph A. L. Codman, a promising lawyer of
Portland; Ralph C. Johnson, of Belfast, and Joshua Lowell, of East
Machias. Over the Senate presided N. S. Littlefield, a Democrat of
Bridgton, who served in the Twenty-seventh and Thirty-first Con-
gresses. In the governor's council was another lifelong friend of Mr.
Hamlin's, General Samuel Veazie, a leading banker of Maine, and
one of that patriotic group of financiers who, at the outbreak of the
civil war, came forward and offered the government large loans to
meet its immediate needs in confronting the crisis.

One of Speaker Hamlin's first acts was to give a hearing to a number of students at Waterville College, who had started a movement
to abolish capital punishment in Maine, and wanted an opportunity to
present their arguments to the legislature. The times and conditions
were hardly favorable for such a movement, but the young men were
very earnest, and determined to make a beginning at least. The
death penalty was then the law of every State in the Union and of
every nation. In the United States it was generally upheld as a
necessity, and supported by a conservative religious elements in the
belief that it was sanctioned by the Bible. One of the students was
J. Young Scammon, then of Bath, who, as a young man, was giving
promise of great talents. In subsequent years he ranked among the
first men at the Chicago bar, and was a Republican leader of note in
Illinois. Scammon at once impressed himself on Mr. Hamlin as a
sincere and able young man, and he obtained for the student a hearing before the Judiciary Committee. He gave close attention to their
arguments; it was the first time the subject of the death penalty had
ever been pressed on him for his consideration and action. His inclinations were against it, and now that he gave his thoughts to it, he
saw it in the light of a reproach to civilization. To the great pleasure
of the college boys he warmly indorsed their views, and when the
Judiciary Committee agreed to report favorably, Mr. Hamlin promised
that he would present the bill to the House and make a speech. He
told Scammon that "he had enlisted in this war to win."[1] He made
a speech that stirred up a vigorous discussion throughout the State.
He never lost interest in the matter. He wanted to see the death
penalty abolished by civilized nations, and in his family and among

[1] It is an interesting coincidence that, practically, Mr. Hamlin's first act as the
official representative of his party, and his last appearance before the legislature
of Maine, just half a century afterwards, were in opposition to capital punishment.
The law was repealed in 1887 for the last time, after a short revival, as a result of
his plea. Thus he literally fulfilled his promise to J. Young Scammon.

his friends spoke with a good deal of feeling against the law of capital punishment. He adhered to the same views he presented before the legislature in 1837. His general argument was as follows : [1] —

"I am opposed to capital punishment on general humane principles, and also because it does not serve as a deterrent; finally, because it is not in accordance with the great and fundamental truths of the Sacred Book. The world has become more merciful and kinder since the coming of Christ. It is learning to prefer his teachings, 'Love thy neighbor as thyself' and 'Return good for evil,' to the law of Moses, 'An eye for an eye, a tooth for a tooth.' The world, also, better understands the frailties of mankind and the laws of heredity. Capital punishment is now inflicted chiefly for two offenses against God and man, — murder and treason. But death was once the penalty for several scores of offenses in England, including even petty larceny. It is on record that a woman was once hanged in London for stealing bread for her starving children.

"That was truly said to be an age of barbarism, and we would not sanction these barbarous acts. Capital punishment belongs to that age ; it is, indeed, a relic of barbarism, and a blot on our progressive civilization. It ought to be wiped out. It is not a deterrent because it does not deter. The lessons of history teach us that executions draw crowds of morbid curiosity-seekers, and act as an incentive to the unfortunates who are naturally depraved to commit crime. It is the duty of society to protect itself, not to take revenge. Men who have taken lives should be immured and kept apart from society. With only their thoughts for company, their punishment is more terrible than death. The prospect of solitary confinement, without hope of pardon, might act as a stronger deterrent on habitual criminals, who see in their execution a chance to glory in their brutal notoriety. But the history of criminal jurisprudence also teaches us that criminals do not always consider the penalty for their acts. An unfortunate man may lead a criminal life on account of bad associations in his youth. Society ought to consider these things, and give him the benefit of corrective influences.

"The argument that capital punishment is sanctioned by the Bible is inconsistent with the spirit of that holy book and the teachings of Christ. The thing about the Bible that impresses me most is that it teems with love for humanity. Christ is the one great and divine figure in that Book, and do we not take our teachings from him? He is the one we believe in all things, for he is the Son of God. Moses was not, and why should we follow his commands in this matter? Moses said God commanded him to kill a man for working on Sun-

[1] This was reproduced from memory, but is believed to be literally correct. — C. H.

day. Does mankind believe that? The Old Testament also says: 'When a man has taken a wife, and it comes to pass that she finds no favor in his eyes, then let him give her a bill of divorcement, and give it into her hands and send her out of his house.' What would become of our modern society if we lived up to that? Suppose we lived verbatim up to the command, 'an eye for an eye, a tooth for a tooth'? All that take life, whether in self-defense or in the heat of passion, would come under that penalty. Moses did not discriminate, but society does discriminate, for it draws the line between murder and manslaughter. Thus it rejects the exact letter of Moses' teachings, although there are those who insist that in inflicting capital punishment society literally interprets the Scriptures. They have as little authority for claiming this as they have for justifying capital punishment on the saying, 'Whosoever shall shed man's blood, by man shall his blood be shed.' That saying is doubted by some of the greatest students of the Bible. The original can be translated a dozen different ways. But, to my way of thinking, the whole question, from a Biblical point of view, is that it is more Christian to follow the merciful Christ than the revengeful Moses. Christ never justified the taking of life.

"The most terrible thing society can do is to hang an innocent man. But it has done that awful thing more than once. Let us remember what that good and great soldier and statesman, Lafayette, said: 'Not until you can prove the infallibility of human tribunals, will I approve the justice of capital punishment.'"

The result of the agitation of capital punishment in 1837 was, that a moral victory was won by the passing of a law that dated the execution of a criminal convicted of murder one year after his sentence had been pronounced on him, and also requiring the governor to issue the death warrant. There was a steady growth of sentiment after this in favor of repealing the statute, and the law was subsequently abolished, to be revived by a small majority vote in the legislature in 1883, and finally revoked four years afterwards.

For several years there had been trouble brewing over the boundary line between Maine and New Brunswick, and this year it threatened to bring on serious consequences. In the preceding legislature, Mr. Hamlin served on the committee that had this question in charge for Maine, and by familiarizing himself with the facts of the case at that time he was now able to act and speak with authority. There was a growing friction between the inhabitants of Maine and New Brunswick, along the disputed territory, and far-seeing men in Maine believed that, unless the government took steps to settle the dispute, there might be danger of national complications. One of the first things Mr. Hamlin did, after taking the speaker's chair, was to appoint a committee to investigate the situation in coöperation with a committee from the Senate. The two parties in Maine were entirely in accord on the Northeastern boundary question, and passed a resolution authorizing Governor Dunlap to call on President Van Buren to have the boundary line explored and surveyed, and monuments erected in accordance with the provisions of the treaty of 1783. But the national administration failed to see the necessity of acting. In putting the matter off, the government allowed Maine's interests to become entangled with other affairs, which were bunched together, so to speak, and settled at a cost to the State, under the Ashburton treaty of 1842, of 1,200,000 acres of land.

But, not to anticipate further, although the government was slothful, not understanding the watchfulness of the British diplomat, the legislature of Maine was on the alert. Plans were discussed and pushed for constructing military roads through the County of Aroostook to the scene of contention, and for providing the State with adequate coast defense. Mr. Hamlin enlisted in this work with a great deal of interest. He came to the conclusion that the country needed a thorough system of coast defense, and when he entered the United States Senate strongly urged the government to protect the country in this way. But nothing came from the military preparations the government made this year, and the legislature adjourned without leaving anything else to be recorded of public or personal interest.

The tide was still running against the Democracy on account of the panics of 1837, and this year the Whigs elected their candidate for governor, Edward Kent, of Bangor, over Gorham Parks, a former Democratic congressman from the same city, by a plurality of less than five hundred votes. The Whigs also carried the House in Maine by a substantial majority. This campaign became historic, and Governor Kent attained a national prominence. He was an able, scholarly man, a graduate of Harvard, very popular personally, and well qualified to sit in the Senate. He did not desire a national career, however, and declined a post in President Taylor's Cabinet in 1848, although he did accept the consulship at Rio Janeiro, and later in life was a member of the Supreme Court of Maine. Governor Kent, on taking the executive chair, at once applied himself with zeal to the Northeastern boundary question, to bring about a settlement if possible. To quote Israel Washburn, Jr., Maine's war governor: "Governor Kent knew more about this question than anybody else in the country."

The Whigs organized the House, and elected Elisha H. Allen speaker over Mr. Hamlin, who returned to the floor as the leader of his party. In this legislature, Mr. Hamlin made some strong friends.

In the House was John Searle Tenney, then a Whig, of Norridge-wock, who subsequently became chief justice of Maine. Abner Coburn, of Skowhegan, was later governor of the State, and is remembered also for his substantial and practical philanthropy. Ebenezer Webster, of Orono, was one of the leading lumbermen of Penobscot County, and always a close friend of Mr. Hamlin's. George F. Patten was a large shipbuilder of Bath. John West, of Franklin, was one of the first men President Lincoln appointed to office under the revenue law. At Mr. Hamlin's request, Mr. Lincoln made Mr. West collector of internal revenue, in spite of the fact that the entire Maine congressional delegation had united in support of another man. Richard H. Vose was a prominent lawyer of Augusta. Noah Barker, of Exeter, was afterward state land agent. N. S. Little-field still presided over the Senate, which the Democrats controlled. Among Mr. Hamlin's friends in that body were Daniel Emery, of Hampden, and Job Prince, of Turner. Timothy Boutelle, Thomas Robinson, and Benjamin Randall, leading lawyers of that period, were other prominent members of the Senate.

The depression in business following the panic caused a great deal of suffering among the poor people in the country, and in Maine a peculiar condition of affairs existed that would not be tolerated to-day. The poor-debtor law had some technical features that enabled shys-ters and Shylocks to take unfair advantages of men in debt at a cost of unnecessary suffering and expenditure of money. There were some hard-hearted men, who made a practice of issuing a writ, arresting a debtor and clapping him in jail before he could take advantage of the law that was framed for the poor debtor's benefit. It happened that some deserving men, who would have paid off their debts in time, were thrown into prison by shysters in order that the latter might get business. A great deal of complaint was heard, and when some distressing cases came to Mr. Hamlin's personal knowledge, he went to work to prevent this gross misuse of the law. He incorpo-rated his ideas in a bill, and presented them in a speech, sternly denouncing the causes of the misery. Legislatures are conservative bodies, and while Mr. Hamlin made a good beginning in this House, he did not wholly accomplish the reform he desired until the next legislature met. He succeeded then to his satisfaction, and chapters 366 and 412, Statutes of 1839, and chapter 58 of the Statutes of 1840, embody the results of his work.

As the state campaign of 1838 approached, the Democratic party resolved to make a supreme effort to win. Mr. Hamlin appears to have come into the councils of his party soon after he was elected to the legislature. One of the men talked of as the Democratic can-didate for governor was John Fairfield, of Saco. Mr. Hamlin knew

Mr. Fairfield well, and not only advocated his nomination, but organized the eastern part of Maine in his interests. Mr. Fairfield had been reporter of decisions of the Supreme Court of Maine, and was now serving his second term in Congress. He was able, far-seeing, upright, and a decided power in his party. Mr. Hamlin believed that Mr. Fairfield had a future before him, and might have a national career.[1] Mr. Fairfield was nominated by the Democracy, and in an exciting campaign was elected over Governor Kent by about three thousand plurality. The Democrats also carried the legislature, and reëlected Mr. Hamlin speaker over his friend Mr. Allen. In this legislature there were also men who attained some distinction in Maine. Joseph G. Cole, Mr. Hamlin's former law preceptor, was a leading member of the House. A man of promise was Charles Andrews, of Turner. He read law with Mr. Hamlin, who encouraged him to enter politics. He became speaker of the House in 1843, was elected to Congress in 1850, but died during his term. Ezra B. French, of Nobleboro, was a member of the Thirty-sixth Congress, and afterwards second auditor of the United States Treasury Department. Shepherd Cary, of Houlton, served one term in Congress. W. B. S. Moor, of Waterville, was elected attorney-general of Maine in 1843, and was a member of the United States Senate by appointment for a session. Other members, well known in Maine at the time, and among Mr. Hamlin's friends, were Samuel Dyer, of Sebago, and Lyman Rawson, of Rumford. In the Senate were Isaac Reed, of Waldoboro, Hiram Belcher, of Farmington, and Hezekiah Williams, of Castine, all of whom were subsequently members of Congress. Job Prince, president of the Senate, and Charles Holden, an able journalist of Portland, were among Mr. Hamlin's closest friends, and with him joined the Republican party in 1856.

Party lines now became more strongly defined in Maine. Governor Fairfield led off at the opening of the session with a message in opposition to internal improvements as a national measure, and taking no less strong grounds upon the boundary question than did Governor Kent. He said in part : —

" The general government must soon feel it to be its unavoidable duty to insist upon a termination of this question — peaceably, if possible, but at all events and at all hazards to see it terminated. If, however, the general government, under no circumstances, should be disposed to take the lead in measures less pacific than those hitherto pursued, yet, I trust, we are not remediless. If Maine should take possession of her territory up to

[1] During the few years Mr. Fairfield was in the Senate, he impressed his party as a strong man. He received a large vote for Vice-President in the Democratic National Convention of 1844. His sudden death in 1848 cut short a promising career.

the line of the treaty of 1783, resolved to maintain it with all the force she is capable of exerting, any attempt on the part of the British government to wrest that possession from her must bring the general government to her aid and defense, if the solemn obligations of the Constitution of the United States are to be regarded as of any validity. This step, however, is only to be taken after matured deliberation. Once taken it should never be abandoned."

Governor Fairfield was warranted in taking this strong tone in his message. In a short time after the governor had defined the position of Maine towards the disputed territory, the State was electrified at the news that a large body of Canadians were robbing the disputed land of its timber. The governor promptly ordered Sheriff Hastings Strickland, of Penobscot County, to organize a posse of men and drive out the intruders. Great excitement prevailed, and an unmistakable war fever arose. With two hundred men the sheriff rapidly proceeded to the scene of action in what is now Aroostook County. The Canadians heard of the sheriff's movements, and possessing themselves of arms in the province arsenal in Woodstock, they prepared, three hundred strong, to stand their ground. But when the Canadians heard that the Americans had a cannon they fled, and, as luck would have it, Land Agent McIntire went after them. He and his men captured twenty poachers, but the same night a body of Canadians dropped down on Mr. McIntire, and carried him and his men off to Woodstock. Maine and New Brunswick began to arm themselves. The legislature appropriated $800,000, and the governor ordered a draft of 10,000 men to protect our claims. Congress appropriated $10,000,000, and authorized the President to call for 50,000 volunteers to help Maine. General Scott came to Augusta to take charge of the military operations. He opened up diplomatic negotiations between Governor Fairfield and Governor John Harvey, of New Brunswick, with the result that each promised to withdraw his forces from the disputed territory, and leave it in charge of a peace posse until a settlement should be arrived at by diplomatic methods.

Thus ended the famous Aroostook war. It was a bloodless affair, and yet it was a narrow escape from a collision between the two governments. Both sides were prepared to fight, and the loss of a single life might have prevented a peaceful settlement. The wonder is that no harm came out of all that excitement and manœuvring. As a major on Governor Fairfield's staff, Mr. Hamlin was ready to take the field. With Lincoln he could have said in after years that he, too, had a military record, and told a humorous story of the war that was never fought.

Mr. Hamlin was reëlected to the House in the fall of 1839, and chosen speaker for the third time. In this House were some new members who were among Mr. Hamlin's closest friends and political associates. Among them were General John J. Perry, of Oxford, a lawyer and afterwards member of the Thirty-sixth Congress; William C. Hammatt, of Howland, a man of uncommon political sagacity for his circumstances; Philip A. Eastman, of Strong, and a judge of probate of Franklin County; Joseph W. Eaton, of Plymouth; Dennis L. Milliken, of Burnham; Aaron P. Emerson, of Orland; S. R. Lyman, of Portland, and William Delesdernier, long a unique character in the politics of Washington County. Samuel Trafton, of Cornish, and Joseph Dane, of Hollis, Mr. Hamlin always remembered as faithful friends and legislators. Ebenezer Everett, a Whig, of Brunswick, was a sound lawyer and a member of the State's commission to revise its statutes. He was the father of the Rev. Dr. Charles Carroll Everett, for many years dean of the Unitarian Theological School of Harvard University. Edward O'Brien, one of Maine's largest shipbuilders, was a member of this House. A newcomer, who was destined to have a national career and enduring fame, was William Pitt Fessenden, then a young Whig, of Portland. Over the Senate presided Stephen C. Foster, who, with two of his colleagues, Isaac Reed, of Waldoboro, and David Hammons, of Oxford County, was to sit in Congress with the Speaker of the House. Samuel H. Blake, of Bangor, was a future attorney-general of the State. Levi Bradley, of the same city, was a leading lumberman of the State. Franklin Smith, of Anson, was a prominent landowner. A coming governor and rival of Mr. Hamlin's for senatorial honors was John W. Dana, who was then beginning his legislative career in the House. Another future associate in the House, at Washington, was Elbridge Gerry, of Waterford, who was clerk of this House.

During this session of the legislature an effort was renewed in the United States Senate to repeal the fisheries bounty of $250,000. This was a movement that was aimed directly at one of Maine's chief interests. Mr. Hamlin gave his earnest attention to the subject. With other leading members of the legislature, Mr. Hamlin met this movement with a prompt remonstrance. This was accomplished by the appointment of a select committee chosen from both Houses at Mr. Hamlin's suggestion. He interested himself in the committee's work, and its report was his argument in favor of retaining the bounty. Briefly, Mr. Hamlin demonstrated that the fisheries bounty act should be maintained because the fisheries produced brave sailors for the navy in the wars of 1776 and 1812, and because the act also fostered the shipbuilding business. Hence, the fisheries bounty was national, not entirely sectional in its workings, and hence the considerations of national interests and safety demanded its maintenance. This was still another subject with which Mr. Hamlin became prominently identified in his national career.

Another question of national and state interest that obtained Mr. Hamlin's active support in this legislature, and throughout his whole term of public service, was the settlement of the French spoliation claims. By the treaty of 1831, France agreed to pay the United States the sum of $5,000,000 for despoiling our navy in the last Napoleonic war. The payment was delayed for several years, and when the money was received it was used for government purposes. John Quincy Adams ascertained the fact of the government's delinquency, and called it severely to account. Senator Ether Shepley, afterwards chief justice of Maine, declared in the United States Senate, speaking of the claims: "Our government pocketed the consideration and repudiated the debt." Maine had suffered severely from the depredation France and England had made on her ships, and even four years after Senator Shepley had urged the government to satisfy these just claims, the restitution had not been made. On March 13, 1840, Mr. Hamlin procured the passage of a resolution through the legislature admonishing the government that it was "bound upon every principle of equity to make provision for an indemnity to those who suffered by French spoliation upon American commerce prior to September, 1840; that, having compromised all claims upon the French government for such spoliation, and received an ample indemnity therefor, a longer delay on the part of the general government in making provision for those individuals whose property has been appropriated for the common benefit would be neither expedient nor just." The sequel to this was the hard and conscientious work Mr. Hamlin accomplished at Washington on many private claims which the government had ignored.

This was, on the whole, a good working legislature, but unfortunately its reputation suffered from a senseless joke some one played on it in the winter. The incident was the most trying Mr. Hamlin experienced while speaker. There was great rejoicing among Governor Fairfield's friends over his large plurality. One of his admirers was Mrs. Longley, the wife of an extensive farmer of Greene. Remembering how an admirer of President Jackson had presented him with a mammoth cheese, she bestowed on Governor Fairfield a similar token of her esteem. It weighed fully four hundred pounds, and Governor Fairfield presented a large portion of it to the legislature for luncheon on a certain day. The Whig members of the legislature contributed cider and brown bread to the feast. A recess of half an hour was taken, and the legislature adjourned to the room where the cheese, cider, and brown bread had been set forth. The cider was in a large keg. Some of the representatives drank freely, and it was noticed that they became voluble and animated. When the Speaker called the House to order, these members, at least twenty in number, jumped to their feet and demanded recognition. He recognized a member, and a yell of protest from the others arose. The Speaker saw that something had gone wrong, and received a motion to adjourn the House. But the motion was voted down in a storm of "Noes!" A second met with a similar fate, and when a third motion was introduced, the excited members rushed to the Speaker's desk, shouting and waving their arms. Bedlam reigned. Speaker Hamlin grasped the situation, and amidst frantic demonstrations and efforts to secure his recognition, declared the House adjourned. When they found themselves standing on the floor before an empty speaker's chair, the sudden change of situation brought the noisy representatives to a realizing sense of their conduct. One by one the representatives slunk out of the House into the luncheon room. The cider keg was still there. Some one, who had not drunk any of its contents, made a quiet investigation. Lo! brandy, in large quantities, had been mixed with the cider. The affair created a great scandal, but it was never found out who had perpetrated the trick, although some ardent Democrats called it a Whig joke. It is hardly necessary to add that Speaker Hamlin's ruling was eventually upheld.

This session closed Mr. Hamlin's terms of consecutive service in the legislature. He often referred to this period as the happiest in his public career. Undoubtedly, the experience he thus gained gave him the key to his success in national fields.

CHAPTER VII

THE presidential election of 1840 was preceded by the most picturesque campaign in the history of the country. The Democrats renominated President Van Buren, and the Whigs presented General William Henry Harrison as their candidate. In the summer of this year Mr. Hamlin entered national politics, and sought his party's nomination for Congress, in what was called the Penobscot district. He was supported by the same elements that elected him to the legislature and the speakership of the House; and he was opposed by the party leaders of Bangor, because they thought him too young, and also because they had a candidate of their own, A. G. Jewett, an able lawyer and a leading politician of Bangor. The convention was held at Levant, on the fourth of July. Mr. Hamlin received ninety-six votes, and Mr. Jewett seventy-six. This was a great surprise to Mr. Hamlin's opponents. Two of the Bangor leaders were John S. Chadwick and Jefferson Chamberlain, sheriff and register of deeds of Penobscot County. When the result of the ballot was announced, Chadwick and Chamberlain held a short consultation. Then approaching the successful nominee, one of them said: " Mr. Hamlin, we did not know you, but we do now. Hereafter we propose to train in your company." The nomination was made unanimous, and the convention bestowed an additional compliment on Mr. Hamlin by electing him a delegate to the Democratic National Convention, which was held at Baltimore. After Mr. Van Buren's renomination, which Mr. Hamlin favored, he returned to Maine and took part in the closest election ever held in the State during his lifetime.

For a year or more there had been signs of a political revolution. Times were hard; the people were in a state of unrest. A low tariff had done its work. Mr. Van Buren had given the country a good administration, but he was doomed to go down before a whirlwind of popular wrath that followed the panic of 1837. He became the target for abuse such as few presidential candidates have had heaped on them. He was represented as an unscrupulous schemer and a thoroughly insincere man. This was unjust to Mr. Van Buren. He was the first perfectly polished machine politician to reach the presidency, and was more of a politician than a statesman; but he had statesmanlike qualities, and having been governor of New York, United States senator, secretary of state, vice-president, and president, he was better equipped by experience for his high position than General Harrison was. If Mr. Van Buren was too suave in address and manner to be thought sincere, he nevertheless could rise above popular clamor and partisanship. He stood firm for the adoption of his sub-treasury plan, although his position on this question was one of the causes of his unpopularity. Although a pro-slavery man, Mr. Van Buren believed in maintaining the status of affairs as established by the Constitution. Hence, he was not a willing instrument of the slave power. His opposition to the annexation of Texas proved that. But the people demanded a change. The Whigs were quick to see their opportunity. An incautious sneer at General Harrison's early life in a log-cabin gave them their cue. They started a movement to elect Harrison, the like of which has never been seen since in the United States. The log-cabin was the Whig emblem. Thousands were erected throughout the country, and miniature representations were carried in processions. The Whig meetings were without precedent in size, enthusiasm, numbers, attendance, and procedure. Tom Corwin, the brilliant Whig orator, addressed audiences in Ohio, some of which fully numbered 20,000 people. Hard cider was liberally dispensed. People came miles on horseback, or even on foot. Huge balls, with campaign mottoes painted on them, were rolled at the head of processions. Some balls were started even in Maine, and rolled through other States. Campaign songs, another new feature, swept over the country, glorifying " Tippecanoe and Tyler, too."

In Maine the two parties contested every inch of the ground.[1] The Democrats renominated Governor Fairfield, and the Whigs Mr. Kent. By an interesting coincidence, Mr. Hamlin's opponent was his competitor for legislative honors and his personal friend, — Elisha H. Allen. Governor Fairfield had proved himself to be a strong man. He would have achieved a conspicuous national career had not death suddenly cut him down a few years after he had entered the United States Senate. Mr. Kent had the prestige of having once defeated a Democrat for governor. Mr. Hamlin and Mr. Allen "stumped" their district together, discussing in debate the political questions of the day. This was an innovation in the political customs of Maine, and the two candidates spoke to large audiences from the same platform nearly every night for the greater part of two months. Often Mr. Hamlin and Mr. Allen had to room together, for the hotel ac-

---

[1] W. W. Story, the sculptor-artist, who was then a law student in Boston, and an ardent Jackson Democrat, stumped Mr. Hamlin's district for him, having made his acquaintance on his professional visits to Boston.

commodations in the country districts were primitive. The times were rather boisterous, and the two candidates had some trying experiences, but they remained good friends, and in subsequent years had many a laugh over their experiences in this campaign. One incident caused some merriment at Mr. Allen's expense. He had been in the habit of opening the debate. The last night of the campaign the candidates were to speak in the old city hall, in Bangor. Mr. Hamlin said: "Allen, you have had the advantage of speaking first. Now let me fire the first gun to-night." Mr. Allen assented. He had been in the habit of beginning the debate with a set speech, in which he told some capital stories, to illustrate his position. To Mr. Allen's utter amazement, he heard Hamlin reel off his stories with original applications that brought out peals of laughter. His discomfiture was complete when Hamlin closed and whispered to him in the suavest manner imaginable: "Allen, old fellow, your stories are so good that I thought they ought to be told twice."

But Mr. Allen had the last laugh. In the election he had 200 votes more than his opponent, in a total poll of 15,000. Mr. Hamlin had the satisfaction of running ahead of his party's ticket, which was beaten in the State. Out of 91,000 votes, Mr. Kent defeated Governor Fairfield by a bare plurality of sixty-seven. As Maine was a pillar of the Democratic party, Kent's election electrified the Whigs, and in wild enthusiasm they expressed their joy in the following famous doggerel verse: —

> " Have you heard the glorious news from Maine?
> Maine, she 's gone hell-bent for Governor Kent,
> And Tippecanoe and Tyler, too."

In the opinion of their opponents, the Whigs in Maine exulted a little too much over their victory. They had a log-cabin and a big gun at Hallowell. Whenever they received favorable news they set the gun booming. When the great news came in October that Ohio had fallen in line, the Whigs of Hallowell paraded their gun all over town; but when they returned to fire salutes, lo! their powder had disappeared. Some Democrats had pitched it into the Kennebec. Thus the cider trick was offset, and the laugh was turned on the Whigs. But in the following month pandemonium reigned wherever there were Whigs. They had carried the country by an immense majority, and elected Harrison and Tyler President and Vice-President.

For the next three years, Mr. Hamlin remained at home, practicing his profession, though he maintained a prominent part in his party's affairs. The Whigs' jubilation was turned into grief, by the death of President Harrison within a month after his inauguration, and their sorrow into bitterness over their betrayal by Mr. Tyler. Out of their great victory in 1840 the Whigs reaped only disappointment. Tyler vetoed a bill to restore the United States Bank, and was hostile to Whig tariff ideas and other legislation proposed. An immediate result of Tyler's recreancy was the recuperation of the Democratic party in Maine, in 1841. Mr. Fairfield this time defeated Governor Kent by 10,000 plurality, and the next year was reëlected for a fourth term by more than 14,000 plurality. To accommodate the new apportionment under the census, the congressional election was postponed from 1842 to 1843. Mr. Hamlin was renominated for Congress in the Penobscot district, and this time was elected by a majority of 1,000 votes over Mr. Allen.

Traveling facilities were decidedly limited when Mr. Hamlin made his first journey from Hampden to Washington. He had to pass over a circuitous route, in a number of different conveyances. From Hampden to Portland, he proceeded in a stage-coach, and thence by boat to Boston. From that city he traveled by railroad to Norwich, whence he crossed the Sound to Greenport. There he took the Long Island railroad to New York, and thence to Philadelphia. He made his way to Baltimore by boat and stage, finishing his journey by rail. Washington was not an inspiring spectacle to one who had made this long journey. It was a small, straggling, overgrown, and ill-kept city of twenty thousand inhabitants. The streets were full of grass and dirt. Cows were even pastured in some of the principal streets. The houses were cheerless-looking. Pennsylvania Avenue was paved with dust or mud, according to the weather that prevailed. On a windy day immense clouds of dust swept over the street, sometimes making it hard for pedestrians to see their way. On a rainy day the avenue was a bank of thick, black mud. One of the few picturesque sights was the old Capitol. The Washington of that period was a disgrace. Few congressmen brought their families to live with them, and it was the custom for them to club together, hire a house, and contract with the landlord or a caterer to provide the table. These clubs were called "messes," and they were more important and exclusive than the name would seem to imply. Many famous measures were planned at "messes," and their champions appointed. It was the invariable rule that no member of a "mess" should invite an outsider to dinner without having obtained the permission of his associates. Strange to say refusal rarely gave offense.

Congress was a more demonstrative and talkative body than the one which now assembles at Washington. Many members wore the old-fashioned swallow-tailed coat, and others the buff waistcoat. Mr. Hamlin adopted the former garment, and wore it all the rest of his life. Although there was not that brilliant social atmosphere of to-day, yet in their polite intercourse the members of Congress were very ceremonious. The speeches were ornate, full of high-sounding periods, and, as a rule, very long. It was the closing period of a picturesque era — one full of extravagant talk and demonstration that preluded an approach of a time of violent action. There were still orators in Congress who regularly announced in their speeches their willingness to shed their blood on their country's altar, simply to gratify a weak fondness for playing on their own emotions. Personal habits were not as good as now. There was much drinking and card-playing. Public altercations were not infrequent. Personal allusions in debate were frequent. Dueling was still practiced. Party feeling, too, was intense, and party discipline was rigid. There could not be much intercourse between the people of the various parts of the country, on account of the scant and expensive facilities of travel. Hence, provincialism and partisanship of a narrow kind were to a considerable extent the outcome of the order of things.

When Mr. Hamlin took his seat in Congress, slavery was looming up as a political issue, and events were soon set in motion that formed a momentous epoch in the history of the Republic. It was not generally perceived at this time that the North and the South were each fostering a civilization of its own, and that the two people each looked at the Union from a totally different point of view. The North had developed its civilization through free institutions, and was a democracy; the South had developed its civilization through slavery, and was controlled by a slaveholding aristocracy. Through the encouragement of free labor the North had been able to master its own resources, and had become a community that was self-supporting and the embodiment of progress. Through its blind attachment to slave labor, the South had narrowed down into an agricultural, free-trade section, whose productive capacity was practically limited to that of the slave, and was dependent on the world for the staples of life in exchange for its cotton, tobacco, rice, and indigo. The two sections had been bound together by the possession of a common glorious heritage, and their desire to remain in union with each other had been cemented by various acts of legislation, such as the recognition of slavery by the Constitution and the Missouri Compromise. But slavery had proved to be the evil genius of the South; it had blinded a generous and chivalrous people to its moral evils and its blighting effect. It had become so thoroughly the basis of Southern business, social, and political life, that it could be thrown out of the body politic only by a gigantic convulsion. But this was not realized until years later.

Mr. Hamlin entered Congress when the slave power, not content with controlling the entire South, was beginning to extend the institution in the hope that it might control the entire country. But this was developed year by year, and the part he played in frustrating this conspiracy is the rôle of his life. It is interesting to observe his point of view at this juncture. One of the anti-slavery men in this Congress, with whom he was associated, was Henry Williams, of Taunton, Mass. Mr. Hamlin told Mr. Williams that, before leaving his home, he had made up his mind that he would not interfere with slavery in the Southern States, and would give the South all its constitutional rights; but if the Democratic party went farther than this and made the extension of slavery over free territory its policy, he would abandon the party. In other words, this was the position taken by Northern men, such as Lincoln and Hamlin, at this stage. They regarded slavery as an evil entailed on the United States by the mother country, and they also believed that the Constitution could not have been formed and the Union established without the recognition of the peculiar institution. But they also held that the Constitution was to be fairly interpreted when it gave the States that right to regulate their own affairs. The Northern States had expelled slavery, while the South had retained it. Under the Constitution, neither had a right to interfere with the other in the matter of local affairs, and slavery was a local institution, and could be regulated by the individual States precisely as the lottery was.

But John C. Calhoun and his school of statesmen, who saw the North outstripping the South, hoped to maintain the political prestige of the South by making slavery national. These protagonists of the drama of 1860 are now to be regarded as products of slavery, — as examples of its warping and narrowing influence. They were sincere and personally pure men, and in censuring them for their acts, their birth, circumstances, and environments are to be considered. They are to be judged as singularly blind to the debasing effects of slavery, and as reckless in deluding their people into a course that they might not have followed if they could have clearly understood the progress the North made under free institutions. Yet, in the case of Calhoun, it is to be remembered that he was not in advance of his environments. The idea that the government was a compact, and that each State could withdraw when it desired, was evolved to give slavery protection, a last refuge to insure its existence. This was the natural fruit of the institution itself. But Calhoun cannot escape the responsibility of doing more than any other man of his day to implant the doctrine of state sovereignty in the minds of his generation as the shibboleth of the South, and to initiate the gigantic conspiracy to fasten slavery on Northern soil. When Mr. Hamlin now entered public life this baneful doctrine had thoroughly impregnated the Southern mind. The Southern statesmen of this era were probably abler dialecticians and orators than their Northern colleagues; but in reasoning from false premises they reached false conclusions. Hence, believing in slavery and thinking that they still lived under the old confederacy, they held the Abolitionists, protective tariffs, and fishery bounties to be the cause of friction between the two sections. The North was also guilty of temporizing with its conscience, and made compromises in the delusive hope of maintaining peace. This, then, was the situation when Mr. Hamlin became a member of the House, and a glance at the personnel of this Congress is interesting.

While the Twenty-eighth Congress did not rank intellectually with its immediate predecessors and successors, it was one of the most important and interesting assemblages that ever legislated on issues affecting the vital welfare of this nation. Webster, Clay, and Calhoun were missed in the Senate, and the House was filled with young men who had yet to make themselves felt in public affairs; still, there were strong men in either branch, and future leaders were to play leading rôles in the greatest drama of the American people. Thomas H. Benton, of Missouri, was the Roman of the Senate. He was a massive defender of the Constitution, and the Democracy's ablest expounder of the pure Jeffersonian doctrine of government. He was honest and a born leader. Hence, he was often a rock in the way of the slave power. In contrast to Benton was his colleague, David R. Atchison, who was high in the inner councils of the slave hierarchy, as was proved by his leadership in the nefarious effort to force slavery into Kansas. He is also remembered as the "one-day President," for he claimed to have acted as President the Sunday on which General Taylor refused to take the oath of office. Personally, Mr. Atchison was well liked. The divided state of sentiment at the North was represented in Levi Woodbury and Charles G. Atherton, the one a strong type of the Jackson school, the other a Northern man of Southern principles, who figures in history in connection with the so-called "Atherton gag," an infamous rule of Congress which forbade the introduction of any petition relating to slavery. Another commanding figure of the Jackson school was the able and upright Silas Wright, of New York. One of Pennsylvania's senators was the unfortunate Buchanan. Prominent among the Whigs was Rufus Choate, the greatest of all American advocates, a wizard of oratory, a patriotic but unsuccessful statesman. Willie P. Mangum, of North Carolina, and John M. Berrien, of Georgia, were among the ablest statesmen of the Whig party, and worthy representatives of the national idea of government formulated by the South's greatest men, which was now being undermined by the insidious state-rights doctrine of Calhoun. George McDuffie was the typical South Carolina state-rights man. Robert J. Walker, of Mississippi, was another Northern man of Southern ideas, for he was Mr. Calhoun's most active agent in popularizing the Texas scheme among the Northern States, though in all justice to Mr. Walker it must be added that he was sincere, and in 1861, after hostilities had begun, won the respect of Mr. Lincoln's administration for his valuable services to the government in upholding our credit in Europe. William R. King, who was Vice-President under Mr. Pierce, was the other senator from Alabama, an amiable man, — a gentleman of the old school of deportment. From Ohio came William Allen, a plain, blunt-spoken man of the people. William C. Rives, of Virginia, may be regarded as one of many Southern men who honestly regretted the secession movement, and yet allowed their course to be shaped by their respective States. R. H. Bayard represented the powerful Bayard following of Delaware. William L. Dayton, who was the first candidate of the Republican party for Vice-President, and Benjamin Tappan, of Ohio, were among the scant number of anti-slavery leaders this Senate was to produce.

John Quincy Adams, sixth President of the United States, was the most commanding figure of the House of Representatives. He was now in his final battles for the rights of free speech and petition. Fortunate it was for the republic that he was not reëlected to the presidency, for he sought a vindication by entering the House. There he achieved that career which is one of the inspiring pages in the annals of the nation. In this Congress he was blazing the way for the coming of the Republican party, and some of its future pioneers were already assembling by his side. The most active representative of the Calhoun doctrine in the House was Henry A. Wise, of Virginia. The most conspicuous opponent of slavery on the floor was the towering Abolitionist of Ohio, Joshua R. Giddings. George C. Dromgoole, of Virginia, a clever parliamentarian, was the leader of the Southern Democrats. Samuel F. Vinton, of Ohio, a man of pronounced ability and high character, was prominent among the Whig members. Another leading Whig was Robert C. Winthrop, of Massachusetts, a man of fine scholarship, who afterwards became speaker of the House, though he did not retain his prominence, owing to his conservative tendencies on the slavery issue. Still another coming speaker was Linn Boyd, of Kentucky. R. Barnwell Rhett, of South Carolina, Howell Cobb and Alexander H. Stephens, of Georgia, Jacob Thompson, of Mississippi, John Slidell, of Louisiana, Thomas L. Clingman, of North Carolina, with Wise, of Virginia, formed a group of imperishable memory, both in the inception of the plot to break up the Union and its attempted execution. In contrast was a group of anti-slavery Democrats and Whigs. Chief among them was John P. Hale, one of the few avowed Abolitionists of that period, — a man whose witty and caustic tongue the slavery men feared, while they could not help liking the frankness, honesty, and geniality of the man. Robert Dale Owen, of Indiana, was another vigorous and fearlessly outspoken advocate of abolition. A distinguished member of the New York delegation was Preston King, short and stocky in body, weighty in argument, and, to use Mr. Hamlin's estimate of King, "as true as steel to his convictions." George Rathbun, of New York, Robert C. Schenck and Jacob Brinkerhoff, of Ohio, Solomon Foot and Jacob Collamer, of Vermont, and Daniel Putnam King, of Massachusetts, were also members of this group with which Mr. Hamlin acted on questions relating to slavery. There were also among Mr. Hamlin's colleagues several men who were to attain greater distinction. Andrew Johnson was a coming President. Stephen A. Douglas was already a rising leader of his party, and ambitious for its greatest honors. Hamilton Fish was destined to leave an enviable record as secretary of state in President Grant's Cabinet. Caleb B. Smith, of Indiana, was to be Mr. Lincoln's secretary of the interior. Washington Hunt was a future governor of New York. Alexander Ramsay, then of Pennsylvania, was to represent Minnesota in the Senate, and to be secretary of war in Mr. Hayes's Cabinet. Cave Johnson, of Tennessee, was to leave this House to become postmaster-general under Mr. Polk's administration. In marked contrast to each other were Kenneth Raynor, of North Carolina, who was a loyal Union man during the civil war, and Thomas H. Seymour, of Connecticut, who was a leader of the so-called copperhead element.

The House was not wanting in quaint personal characteristics. It had probably the largest man and the smallest man that ever were members of the House. The first was Dixon H. Lewis, of Alabama, who was a mountain of flesh, and had to have a chair made for him. But he was a giant in intellect as well. The other was Alexander H. Stephens, who was so small and frail in appearance that he seemed a youth in the last stages of consumption. But he, too, belied his appearance. An exceedingly eccentric character, the court jester of the House, was Felix Grundy McConnell, of Alabama. He was a man of brilliant mental qualities, but his habits were responsible for his grotesque performances. At a fashionable concert given by Ole Bull, the Norwegian violinist, who was then the reigning musical favorite, McConnell interrupted the violinist in the midst of a delicate passage by shouting out : " None of your highfalutin' fiddling ; give us 'Hail Columbia,' and bear hard on the treble." A sensation followed. The audience called for the police, and the officers had to use their clubs to eject the unruly congressman from the hall.

The new members of Congress rapidly formed their associations. In the words of another writer : " Naturally enough, in what was then the small and contracted political and social circle of Washington, a

REPRESENTATIVE HAMLIN. AET. 36.

man of Mr. Hamlin's striking appearance and many attainments was not long in making his mark. Tall and graceful in figure, with black and piercing eyes, a skin almost olive-colored, hair smooth, thick, and jetty, a manner always courteous and affable, the new member soon found his way into the best society of the capital. His advancement to a commanding position in the political world was quite as rapid." [1] Mr. Hamlin was soon associated with Preston King, Jacob Brinkerhoff, George Rathbun, and other members of his party who eventually constituted a notable group of anti-slavery Democrats in the House. In their councils they both formulated practical and important measures and appointed their champions. Mr. Hamlin made many pleasant acquaintances outside of his political circle. A Unitarian church had been founded at Washington, and as the new faith it upheld was not popular, it had to struggle for its existence. Mr. Hamlin naturally inclined towards an independent religious belief. Among the small congregation were a few congressmen. One was Daniel Putnam King, a man of high character and fine fibre, a graduate of Harvard. Mr. Hamlin and Mr. King worked together to build up this little church. They became greatly interested in the church through its pastor, Edward Everett Hale, who had come from Boston to begin his ministerial duties at Washington. Mr. Hale was already manifesting those noble qualities of character and mind that have made him one of the most widely beloved citizens of his country and the foremost Unitarian of the land in his day. A strong personal affection grew up between the young congressman and his pastor, which developed into a firm and lasting friendship. In a personal letter to the author under the date of February 27, 1896, Dr. Hale wrote : "I supplied the pulpit at Washington for one winter. My memory of him (Mr. Hamlin) is as one of the pillars on whom the little church relied with absolute confidence. The support of members of Congress meant more than it does now to such a church. The whole attendance at the Unitarian church, of all the worshipers, seldom amounted to two hundred persons, and we knew very well that the presence among them of eleven or twelve congressmen was a matter of great importance in the prestige of the church. Of these eleven or twelve Mr. Hamlin and Mr. King were two — absolutely reliable. There were, alas! gentlemen who were sound Unitarians in New England, who were never in our little church. But we were sure of the two I have named. I am not speaking simply of the winter when I lived in Washington, but of many years after, when I maintained my interest in the church and its affairs. As you know, I renewed my personal acquaintance with your father in Spain, where I owed much to his constant kindness and to that of Mrs. Hamlin.

[1] Carroll's *Twelve Americans*.

I trust that you will understand how high was the esteem in which they were held there, and how important he made his place by the cordiality of his intercourse with all travelers and with the diplomatic circle. I was disappointed when I found no memoranda from his own pen which would show his interest in the affairs of our Washington church. But you know how active he could be without saying anything of what he was doing."

CHAPTER VIII

WORK OF THE TWENTY-EIGHTH CONGRESS

WHEN the House was being organized a parliamentary snarl ensued that is of both personal and political interest. The preceding Congress had enacted a law directing the States, that elected representatives to Congress on a general ticket, to follow the more popular method of electing by districts. This was regarded as a Whig law, and several Democratic States, in the election of 1843, flatly disregarded the act on the ground that it was unconstitutional, because it interfered with the rights of the States. The Whig members of this House were determined to enforce the law if possible, and accordingly drew up a protest against the seating of Democratic representatives from New Hampshire, Georgia, Mississippi, and Missouri, which were the States in question, in order to prevent these representatives from voting in the election of a speaker. When the clerk called the House to order, that it might proceed to effect a permanent organization, John Campbell, a Democrat, of South Carolina, questioned the right of the members of New Hampshire to take their seats until the House had inquired into the mode of their election, and he submitted a resolution to take proceedings accordingly. But the clerk, believing that he was clothed only with authority to act in the capacity of an initiatory officer, refused to accept Mr. Campbell's resolution. The House was in a predicament, and David D. Barnard, a tenacious Whig, of New York, tried to read the Whigs' protest. In the unorganized condition of the House, the majority members refused to hear him, and proceeded to elect John W. Jones, a Democrat, of Virginia, speaker by a vote of 128 to 59 for John White, of Kentucky, the Whig candidate.

The members whose seats were disputed took part in the election of speaker, but this did not close the affair. The next day the Whigs were greatly exercised to find that the clerk had not incorporated their protest in the journal of the House, in spite of the fact that it had not been read. A violent wrangle followed, lasting two days. The Whigs tried to have the journal amended so as to have their protest appear in the records of the first day. The issue was on the duties of the clerk, and yet the debate, after eddying around this point, drifted off on to the constitutional rights of the minority and majority members of the House, and discussions of abstract principles that were supposed to be involved. The Whigs did succeed in having their protest entered in the journal on the second day in the form of a resolution, but this did not satisfy them. The House became confused on the question as to what constituted a House. Finally, on the third day, Mr. Hamlin offered a resolution directing the clerk not to print the protest. Robert C. Winthrop vehemently protested, and asked if there was a single precedent in the whole history of Congress directing the clerk as to the discharge of his duties. As he understood, the clerk was sworn by a solemn oath to God to discharge his duties to the House, and was responsible for the journal.

Mr. Hamlin quietly pointed out the forgotten fact that the protest had not yet been read in the House, and that there was no legislative evidence that the document at issue was the same one which was offered on the opening day of the session, although members would be willing to take Mr. Barnard's personal word for it.[1] This put a new aspect on the debate, and in the end the House upheld Mr. Hamlin's position by striking the protest in the form of a resolution out of the record.

Mr. Hamlin was appointed a member of the Committee on Elections,[2] and was thus immediately thrown in contact with the extreme Southern members of the House. Among his associates on the Committee on Elections were Stephen A. Douglas, Robert C. Schenck, and Garrett Davis. Speaker Jones's seat was contested by John Minor Botts, who won distinction by his loyalty to the Union, when Virginia was the seat of war. The contest between Mr. Jones and Mr. Botts was admittedly close, and the session of the Committee on Elections aroused great excitement in Congress and interest throughout the country. Garrett Davis, the leading Whig member of the committee, was of that peculiar hot-headed, argumentative type of Southern politicians who seem to rely on the act of speech to enable them to come to a decision, and as Davis rarely knew his own mind, Mr. Hamlin's patience was more than once exhausted over Davis's waste of time. Finally, Davis and some of his sympathizers thought they could intimidate Mr. Hamlin and Mr. Douglas. The result was not satisfactory to Davis, and some fire-eaters indulged in wild threats about shooting Douglas and that "black Penobscot Indian," as Davis stigmatized Mr. Hamlin. The details of this affair were not then fully revealed, but the fact is apparent that Mr. Hamlin and Mr. Douglas believed that they had good reason to remember the old proverb that "to be forewarned is to be forearmed." As dueling was still in vogue, Southern fire-eaters carried pistols, and

[1] *Congressional Globe*, December 11, 1843, p. 240.
[2] *Ibid.*, December 14, 1843, p. 36.

drunken brawls among quick-tempered congressmen were not infrequent. For the first and only time in his life, Mr. Hamlin armed himself. Mr. Douglas also put a pistol in his pocket, and a signal was agreed upon in case Davis or his friends should attempt to shoot Mr. Hamlin or Mr. Douglas.

At the next session of the committee, Davis once more endeavored to intimidate Mr. Hamlin, thinking that his threats might have had an effect. But he met with an emphatic resistance that completely threw him off his balance.

"You shan't speak so, sir; you shan't!" Davis fairly screamed in his rage.

"Well, no matter how I may speak, I will think as I please," replied Mr. Hamlin.

"No, sir; no, sir; dam'me if you will. I'll be damned if you will think as you please. You have no right to think at all, sir," Davis howled.

The shout of laughter that came from Mr. Hamlin and the other committeemen covered Davis with mortification at his absurd blunder; but when he cooled off the session ended without further efforts to override Mr. Hamlin.

General Schenck, who was an amused spectator of Davis's performance, subsequently encountered the same fiery element in a dramatic scene on the floor, in which Davis also figured, strange to say, as a friend of the sturdy Ohioan. Joshua R. Giddings had been accused by Southern slaveholders of stealing slaves and secretly sending them out of the District of Columbia, and he had been violently abused on the floor of the House in connection with this charge. Mr. Giddings determined to make a personal explanation, but when he rose to speak there came cries from all over the House: "Don't hear him. Don't hear him. We object. We object." Great confusion prevailed, but finally General Schenck got the floor and insisted that, in the interests of justice, Mr. Giddings should be heard. He closed his argument by saying: "I repeat, Mr. Speaker, that under the circumstances, no gentleman would object," with emphasis on the word "gentleman." Mr. Giddings was then allowed to have the floor. But this was not the end of the matter. Jacob Thompson told Mr. Schenck that the impression was that he had reference to Slidell, of Louisiana, when he insisted that "no gentleman would object." Schenck denied that he had Slidell in mind when making this statement, but Thompson, who was curious to know who the man was whom Schenck indirectly reproved, managed to badger him into making a public disavowal the next day that Slidell was the one. But Slidell was not satisfied with this, and proceeded to ask Schenck so many annoying questions that Mr. Schenck lost his patience. In spite of the efforts of his friend, Governor Vance, of Ohio, to restrain him, Mr. Schenck took the floor and said : —

"It is evident that what the member from Louisiana desires to know is to whom I referred yesterday, when I said that no gentleman would object to the explanation of my colleague. Lest there should be any further doubt upon this subject, I will say here and now that I meant and referred to the drunken member from Alabama, Felix G. McConnell."

A wild uproar immediately arose. McConnell rushed down the aisle to Schenck's seat, shaking his fist, and threatening dire revenge on the blunt member from Ohio. But an encounter was averted, and order finally restored. After the House had adjourned, Garrett Davis approached General Schenck, and asked him if he carried a pistol. Learning that he did not, Davis said : —

"You had better carry one to-day ; McConnell is swearing that he will shoot you on sight."

"Still, I have n't one," replied Schenck, "and I don't know where to get one."

"Take mine — take mine," said Davis, pushing his weapon into Schenck's hand.

For three days General Schenck kept Davis's pistol, but when he met McConnell face to face, the fiery Alabamian made no demonstration, and Mr. Davis received his pistol unused.[1]

Another incident that characterized the temper of the House was a personal encounter between George Rathbun and John White.[2] Rathbun was a high-spirited Democrat and one of the Northern representatives who heartily despised the so-called "dough-faces" and "fire-eaters." White was a talented man, but of a passionate disposition, and had an unruly tongue. As speaker of the preceding House he had offended many Democrats by his alleged partisan conduct. In the latter part of this session, when the House had one day resolved itself into the committee of the whole, some discussion arose as to the language that Henry Clay used in regard to the Missouri Compromise, which is immaterial. White contradicted a member who alluded to Mr. Clay's alleged words, and Mr. Rathbun spoke up, and said that the truth of Clay's statement was known throughout the House. White leaned over towards Rathbun, and in a low tone of voice cursed him, and applied an opprobrious epithet. According to Mr. Rathbun, White at the same time raised his hand to strike. Rathbun was too quick, and dealt White a blow. Bystanders, however, grasped the two men, and the general struggle threw the House into an uproar. At this moment an outsider named William S. Moor,

---

[1] Carroll's *Twelve Americans*.

[2] *Congressional Globe*, April 23, 1844, p. 578.

who evidently wanted to take a hand in the fray, rushed into the House, and installed himself behind the railing in front of the Speaker's desk. The sergeant-at-arms ejected Moor, but in Moor's efforts to escape he drew a pistol and shot an officer in the leg. This brought the House to its senses. Messrs. Rathbun and White apologized and shook hands. Nevertheless an investigation was ordered, and when the report was made, Mr. White took exceptions because, forsooth, the report neglected to state that he had sworn at Mr. Rathbun in a low tone of voice. John P. Hale saw the Pickwickian trend of the affair, and with some sarcasm observed that if Mr. White did whisper his insult to Mr. Rathbun, it magnified the offense, because White must have been calm and cool at that moment. The usual motion to expel was made with the usual result, — the report was tabled. White left Congress at the end of the term, and the next year died by his own hand.

A true index of the attitude of public men of the day towards slavery is to be found in the records of this House on the question of retaining or abolishing the twenty-first rule, which is better known as the "infamous gag-law." From the beginning of the government, Congress had received petitions in opposition to slavery, and in 1836 the slave power passed a rule in Congress to table without discussion any petition relating to slavery. The immediate result was that anti-slavery sentiment at the North was increased, and feeling between the two sections of the country became more embittered. It was even charged by John Minor Botts that the slave power conceived the gag-law with this very object in view, in order to help bring about a separation. But whether this claim was correct or not, the adoption of the obnoxious measure had that effect. The debates that the gag-law gave rise to in Congress were widely circulated throughout the country, and the Southern leaders of the slave party eventually systematically deceived the Southern people as to the sentiments, intentions, and character of the Northern people. But in the end the gag-law became a mighty engine in the hands of John Quincy Adams for the destruction of its own creator. As a natural champion of free speech and the right of petition, this measure aroused his sense of justice and his pugnacious nature. Certainly no more despotic rule was ever passed by a body of men calling themselves the representatives of a self-governing people than this gag-law. Under its provisions a complaisant speaker would refuse to allow a petition to be presented that seemed to him to reflect on slavery, no matter what its language might be. The House of Representatives then did have a "czar."

Mr. Adams had been waging unremitting warfare on the twenty-first rule since its adoption, and now victory seemed nearly within his grasp. It was in the preceding House that the effort was made to censure him. In this House Mr. Adams knew there were new members on whom he could count, and he was desirous of getting them into action against the tyrannical rule. Mr. Adams was now seventy-seven years of age, and yet his mind was as clear, his will as inflexible, and his heart as stout as ever. He was both hated and feared by the slave representatives, and still they were forced to acknowledge his superior ability even to their cost. The old Puritan undoubtedly enjoyed a savage delight in fighting the slave party in the House single-handed. One day, when Adams was laying round him with terrific effect, and opponent after opponent had gone down under his deadly fire of facts and withering sarcasm, a despairing Southern member turned to Mr. Hamlin, and said : " It is useless to debate with Adams. He knows so much that, one way or another, and despite the devil, he can, when he will, make the greatest wrong appear the greatest right." The respect in which Mr. Adams's ability was held was shown in the fact that although Speaker Jones knew that the veteran intended to reopen his batteries on the twenty-first rule, he nevertheless appointed Mr. Adams chairman of the Committee on Rules, the very body that would first act upon the question of retaining or abolishing his *bête noire* — the gag-law.

A few weeks after the House had been organized, the committee was ready to make its report, when a story was circulated that Mr. Adams had induced the latter to omit the twenty-first rule. Members poured out of the cloak rooms on to the floor, and great excitement prevailed. Mr. Dromgoole, the skillful Democratic leader and a member of the Committee on Rules, practically confirmed the story by saying that his colleagues had made material changes in the rules, and that he would like to have the report recommitted, because their important sessions had not been fully attended. By admitting in the next breath that he had absented himself from the meetings of the committee, Mr. Dromgoole unwittingly revealed the fact that there had been perfect confidence that the old rules would not be changed, and that he and the other slavery representatives had been beaten through inattention to their duties.

But the incautious E. J. Black, of Georgia, at once put the anti-slavery men on their guard by boldly charging that the committee had dropped the twenty-first rule, and he announced with vehemence his intention of defying any committee, or House, that would allow his constituents to be assailed by " incendiaries and Abolitionists " by abolishing the twenty-first rule. " Talk to me," he exclaimed, "about Whigs and Democrats when abolition is the question before the House ! " Motion after motion followed Black's outbreak in rapid succession, and another parliamentary snarl threatened to ensue. Mr.

Hamlin made up his mind that it would be best to declare his convictions on the gag-law, and try to bring matters to a crisis. He took the floor, and in a few words pointed out that the question before the House was on the motion to recommit the rules with instructions to the committee. He said he was opposed to both recommitting and instructing, because the real question involved, which was the retention or the rejection of the twenty-first rule, must be decided in the House, and there was no use in a recommitment. Mr. Hamlin next proceeded to enter an impersonal and yet emphatic protest on behalf of the anti-slavery men in the House against the intimidating tactics of Black, in these words : —

"The time has gone by, if it ever existed, when the galvanic starts of any member can produce an impression on this House. I for one shall vote on every question according to the dictates of my judgment. I shall vote against the motion to recommit and instruct, . . . because this question can be determined in the ordinary way of doing business. If the rules should be reported again without the twenty-first rule, it will involve the decision of the question of restoring it; if they should be reported with it, this would involve the decision of the question of abolishing it. . . . A word as to the position in which I am placed. I do not wish to have my views on this important subject mistaken, nor my votes misconstrued by giving them on mere collateral issues. I shall vote against this twenty-first rule, because I believe the right of petition to be a constitutional one, and not dependent on the judgment of any member of the House, or any other body. When this House declares in advance that it will not receive petitions of a certain class, it prejudges the matter and comes in conflict with a constitutional right. I know that any action on these petitions must proceed from the votes of a majority; and, therefore, it is inferred that a majority must decide against them in advance. But if a constitutional right can be taken away in the judgment of a majority on this question, the same thing may be done on any other question. I am in favor of rejecting the twenty-first rule, and in favor of receiving all petitions that may be offered; and I am for referring them to committees in favor of the objects embraced. Let this committee report to us what are the duties we owe — not to the South, but to the Union, the whole Union, and nothing but the Union. Then it will be seen if we do not come up to the mark; and we will stand by the Union and those institutions reared by the wisdom of our forefathers and cemented by their blood. We will stand by the Union at the expense of our lives and the desolation of our firesides. All we ask, then, is that our friends of the South will not mistake us; that they will not subject us to misconstruction on mere collateral issues. Give us but an opportunity to spread on your journal the obligations we owe to our fathers and ourselves, to perpetuate the blessings conferred by the glorious Constitution they have bequeathed us. Then it shall be seen how we shall perform our duty, not to the South, but to the whole Union."[1]

[1] *Congressional Globe*, January 5, 1844, p. 110. Stenographic reporting had not

John Quincy Adams paid Mr. Hamlin marked attention during his speech, and when the latter had closed his remarks, Mr. Adams rose in his seat, and with a pleased smile on his face walked across the floor towards him, holding out his hand. With unusual cordiality of manner Mr. Adams grasped Mr. Hamlin's hand, and said: " Light dawneth in the East, sir; light dawneth in the East." Mr. Hamlin's attack on the gag-law won for him Mr. Adams's interest, and he always held Mr. Adams in reverence as the father of the Republican party.

The battle against the twenty-first rule was continued in the House, and ultimately Mr. Hamlin and his friends were defeated by a small vote. But they had won a victory even in defeat; Northern Democrats, like Mr. Hamlin, Preston King, John P. Hale, Jacob Brinkerhoff, Robert Dale Owen, George Rathbun, and John Wentworth rose above party affiliations when the slavery issue arose, and associated themselves with Whigs like Mr. Adams, Robert C. Schenck, Daniel Putnam King, Solomon Foot, Jacob Collamer, Caleb B. Smith, and others, many of whom are now remembered as among the founders of the party that abolished slavery. The next Congress saw Mr. Adams victorious. But it must be understood that the majority of these men were not Abolitionists in the sense the word was then used. They hoped slavery would cease to exist; they saw that the unawakened public conscience would not yet sanction direct warfare on the institution itself. They realized, therefore, that it was their duty to resist the encroachments of the slave power. Mr. Adams expressed the feelings of this group of men towards the Abolitionists when he said in a speech that, although they were a noble-minded people, they were not practical. The Abolitionists were required to agitate and educate the conscience of the masses, and practical men like Mr. Adams and his followers were needed in congressmen who were wise in the ways of a work-a-day world, who could detect a plot of the slave power when in its incipient stages in the committee room, check it resolutely on the floor of the House, — men, in short, who could successfully cope with a foe that could be as "bold as a roaring lion or as wise as a serpent."

been introduced in Congress, as this imperfect record of Mr. Hamlin's speech demonstrates.

ANTI-SLAVERY LEADERS IN CONGRESS OF 1845.

CHAPTER IX

MR. HAMLIN AS A REFORMER

THE debate on the "gag-law" brought Mr. Hamlin conspicuously before the House as a determined opponent of slavery, and yet events followed that tended to win for him the respect of his Southern colleagues, even though they did not like his views of slavery. It must be borne in mind that while slavery was as yet an intermittent issue, and did not wholly dominate legislation at Washington, it was nevertheless a sacrilege in the eyes of the slave party to denounce the institution. Hence, if a congressman publicly attacked slavery, as Mr. Hamlin did in one of his first speeches in the House, he prejudiced the Southern members against him, unless, of course, he had strong qualities that would compel respect. In this Congress the Southern men were an abler body than their Northern associates. They were the élite of the South, and trained to politics as a profession. The presence of Northern men in Congress of inferior ability and character was due to the fact that the best minds of the North were required at home to develop the professions, the educational institutions, the material resources of the nation, to foster invention, further manufacturing and the building of railroads, which would unite the country, and for the launching of other large enterprises. This inferior type of men who misrepresented Northern character represented indeed a sycophantic pro-slavery element which fawned before the slave power, and intrenched itself in power with the patronage it obtained. Men of this kind did much to blind the eyes of the South to the real character of the Northern people. They themselves were stigmatized as "dough-faces" by that picturesque individual known as "the Southern fire-eater." The epithet was not elegant, but it was truthful, it was appropriate and merited. It may be needless to add that the honesty, sincerity, independence, and ability of the group of anti-slavery men with whom Mr. Hamlin was identified placed them as individuals in the right light before the best of their Southern colleagues.

The breeze that John Quincy Adams's opening attack on the gag-law raised soon subsided, and the House returned to its regular routine. There were other important things for the House to consider ; the business of the nation had to be transacted. Mr. Hamlin's business capacity had been developed by his experience in the legislature of Maine. He devoted himself to his duties, and was soon regarded as an absolutely reliable, conscientious, and practical worker. In debate he was recognized as an effective speaker ; indeed, he was often selected to champion measures. He had the inherent editorial faculty of speaking to the point, and presenting his case briefly in his opening remarks. He never spoke for rhetorical effect, he rarely prepared a speech, and never revised one for publication. He was modest and indifferent. But his most conspicuous characteristic was brought out when the House was forming its estimate of the new members. An incident occurred that Mr. Hamlin's friends related to illustrate his conception of the duties a public man owed his country and constituents, and also his idea of honor.

One McNulty was clerk of the House. He was charged with improper practices, and had the effrontery to call the yeas and nays on a resolution ordering his dismissal. He was discharged, and Mr. Hamlin was instrumental in securing the election of Major Ben B. French, at one time a famous politician, as McNulty's successor. For this service Major French was ever afterward most grateful. One day, full of feeling, he came to Mr. Hamlin in the House and said : —

"At last, Mr. Hamlin, I have an opportunity of repaying you for your kindness to me. Three squares of the District of Columbia are to be sold, — the one for seven mills a foot, the second for five, and the third for three. We can secure this property quietly, and I know of public improvements, shortly to take place near it, which will so increase its value as to make our fortunes."

"That's all very well," said Hamlin, "but if the property were to be sold for one mill I have no money to buy it."

"In that case," replied French, after consideration, "I'll tell you what I will do. I will raise the money, and buy a portion of the property in your name. When the improvements I know of are made, and the great increase in value comes, — as it must come, — you can sell a small portion of the land and pay me what I have advanced."

"You are very kind," said Mr. Hamlin, fully grateful for the offer, "but the fact is, while there is no actual wrong in your proposition, I do not think that it would be right for me to use information which I secure as a public servant to advance my private fortune." So the matter was dropped. The principles implied in Mr. Hamlin's answer to French he lived up to all his life. The property which he might have bought for five mills a foot, as described, is now in the heart of Washington, just back of the Interior and Post-office departments, and readily sells for three dollars a foot.[1]

One of the first reform movements which engaged the attention of

[1] Carroll's *Twelve Americans.*

this House was one that strongly interested Mr. Hamlin, because it touched the honor of the nation. This was a movement to keep the franchise pure, and was an outcome of the presidential election of 1840. An anomalous condition of affairs prevailed which rendered corruption easy in the elections. The election for President was not held on the same day throughout the Union. In some States the ballot-box was kept open for several days, to accommodate voters who were unable to be present on election day. In many country districts people went to bed even without locking their doors. Mr. Hamlin, for one, rarely fastened up his house in Hampden, before retiring. But the ballot-box stuffer, the burglar and tramp, were to work a change. There were signs of danger threatening the franchise, and practical statesmen were agreed that the elective methods in vogue were in need of reform. The real difficulty presented was how to handle the question without stirring up party feeling. Alexander Duncan, a Democrat, of Ohio, had the right idea of how to remedy the evils, but he did not go about it in the right way. He offered a bill in the House, making it compulsory on all the States to choose their presidential electors on the same day; but he made a violent attack on the Whigs, and charged them with carrying Ohio in 1840 by importing Kentuckians across the borders, after they had given their own State to Harrison. This angered the Whigs in the House, and tended to alienate strict state-rights Democrats, who were naturally opposed to measures strengthening the power of the general government, and would thus regard the bill in the light of a bludgeon to be used on the heads of the Whigs for mere party effect.

With the spirit of partisanship inflamed, and the fears of the strict interpreters of the Constitution aroused, the Duncan bill had poor prospects of success. Several times the bill was brought up in the House and failed to reach a vote. The debate on the measure dragged on for weeks. Mr. Hamlin was earnestly in favor of the bill, and it appears from the records that he was ultimately appointed its champion on the floor of the House. After the discussion had developed into an unusually acrimonious wrangle one day, the bill was brought up, and a great effort was made to secure a vote. Mr. Hamlin took the floor and made a speech that illustrates his clear and concise style of argument. A little tact was needed to soothe the ruffled feelings of the disputing members. In his opening remarks, Mr. Hamlin quietly referred to the unfortunate partisan discussion which attended the introduction of the bill, and said that while he had once desired to make a reply to charges against his party, he had changed his mind and would confine himself exclusively to the bill and its merits.

"This bill," said Mr. Hamlin, "is intended to prevent — and I believe it will, if it has favorable action — frauds that have hitherto been perpetrated

in our elections. I have no accusations to bring against any political parties; I have no criminations or recriminations to make; I have simply to
say that I believe the bill will prevent frauds and preserve, as far as is
possible, the great and fundamental principles of the elective franchise in
their purity. If there is a principle that addresses itself with greater force
than any other to American statesmen, it is the principle involved in this
question. If we can by any legislative action preserve and protect the
rights of electors, it is our duty to take such action. The question, then,
arises, Can we adopt a measure regulating the time for holding elections?
Have we the constitutional right? By reference to the fourth clause of the
first section of the second article of the Constitution, it will be found that
the States gave Congress the clear and undoubted right to determine the
time when the elections shall be held. I will read the clause : —

" ' The Congress may determine the time of choosing the electors and
the day on which they shall give their votes, which day shall be the same
throughout the United States.'

" There is a variety of causes and circumstances that might induce a
State to be in favor of holding the presidential election at the same time
as the state elections ; and other periods might be selected by other States
for good and sufficient reasons ; but by the law now in existence all the
States are compelled to hold their elections for presidential electors within
a period of thirty days from the first Monday of December. Now, by
changing the period of the elections for President, it would not affect the
State elections. We do not ask the States to alter the manner and place
of holding their elections, but only to fix on a particular day. Another
objection has been offered; that it would compel, in certain cases, two
elections, inasmuch as some of the States elect their presidential electors
and state officers on the same day. Having taken some pains to inform
myself on this matter, I have ascertained that there are only two States in
which two elections are held on one day. I am opposed to the amendment of the gentleman from New Jersey (Mr. Elmer), because it is unnecessary. The bill reported by the Committee on Elections is sufficient
without the aid of any additional regulation. The Constitution gives Congress the power to prescribe the day for holding the presidential election,
and no other power on that subject. Congress can fix on the time, but
not on the place and manner. It has been suggested that the passage of
this act would require a convention of the legislatures of several of the
States to carry it into effect. This I do not believe to be the case ; but
even if it were so, I should vote for the bill." [1]

This speech brought the House to a vote. The bill was passed by
a large majority, and sent to the Senate; but the Whigs were still in
control of that body, and although approving the purposes of the
measure, they laid it on the table by a strict party vote, because
they did not desire their opponents to obtain the credit that would
come from the passage of a bill which would in its enactment work

[1] *Congressional Globe*, May 15, 1844, p. 634.

salutary reforms, and create capital for its Democratic sponsors. Nevertheless, the friends of the bill were not discouraged, and prepared themselves to renew the fight for a pure ballot at the next session of Congress, when they were successful.

When Mr. Hamlin came to Washington he heard loud complaints from old soldiers of the war of 1812, and also from heirs of veterans, over the difficulties they had in obtaining bounty lands from the government to which they were entitled. Mr. Hamlin's experience while a member of the legislature of Maine with this subject determined him to probe it, and try to remove the obstacles of which the veterans complained. In Mr. Hamlin's opinion the government was pursuing a mistaken policy in withholding from the public the names of those who deserved the lands. The explanation furnished by the government authorities for this course was that the Pension Department was infested with unscrupulous claim agents who made a business of hunting up claimants and cheating them, often getting fully one half of the land involved in payment for their alleged services. But to a broad-minded man it was evident that while the government might save some claimants from dishonest agents in the end, it would prevent by this course many heirs from learning that they were entitled to government land. Thus, between the government's over-caution, departmental red tape, the cunning of the claim agents, and the ignorance or feebleness of claimants or their heirs, many found themselves unable to obtain bounty land which they were morally certain belonged to them.

One of the first things Mr. Hamlin did after taking his seat in the House was to strike at the root of this evil by offering a resolution calling upon the Secretary of War to furnish the House with a list of the names of those who were entitled to bounty lands, of those who had not received warrants, and also those who had obtained patents but had not procured warrants. This resolution aroused the conservative spirit of the House. Cave Johnson, of Tennessee, was a good example of the honest but narrow class of congressmen who instinctively clung to precedent and feared departure from beaten tracks. Mr. Johnson opposed Mr. Hamlin's resolution on the grounds that the publication of names of those deserving bounty lands would not benefit the widows and orphans, but speculators and agents. William P. Thomasson,[1] of Kentucky, supported Mr. Johnson, and told the House that he himself had called at the War Department to obtain information about a claim, and that it was refused, though he gave the name of the claimant; that Mr. Johnson had informed him that this was the practice of the department, because making public

[1] Thomasson was one of the few Southern anti-slavery members of Congress. He became a Republican, and was one of Mr. Hamlin's personal friends.

information about the claims would help the agents and speculators, who were constantly on watch for their chance to prey on applicants for bounties. For these reasons Mr. Thomasson said he was unwilling to depart from the government's custom.

Mr. Hamlin replied by showing that the fact that Mr. Thomasson, a member of the House, could not obtain information at the War Department about a just claim for bounty lands, that he could not learn from the government's books the names of the people he knew to be interested in land claims, was a convincing reason in itself why the House should adopt the resolution he, Mr. Hamlin, had offered. Addressing himself to Mr. Johnson, Mr. Hamlin asked, if the government expressed a willingness through its laws to reward those who had imperiled their lives for it, was it proper to withhold evidence that would show to whom reward was due? "Would the gentleman from Tennessee," Mr. Hamlin continued, "stand like a miser over his gold, and refuse the relief offered? . . . But is it to be the policy of this government to say to meritorious citizens, 'We will give you this bounty land,' and the same moment turn and say in the same breath, 'We will withhold from you the very information which will enable you to enjoy the benefits we offer'? Is this not 'to keep the word of promise to the ear and break it to our hope'"? [1]

John P. Hale supported Mr. Hamlin's resolution, and asserted that the publication of the information desired would tend to defeat the speculators. Mr. Hopkins, of Virginia, strengthened the argument in favor of the resolution by pointing out that concealment alone would aid unscrupulous agents in their designs on worthy land claimants. In fact, under the present system they had managed to bribe clerks to give them data that placed claimants in their hands. The House came to the opinion that Mr. Hamlin was right, and that it was better to transact public business in the open light. The resolution was passed by a vote of two to one, and Mr. Hamlin soon enjoyed the satisfaction of seeing many a veteran of 1812 rewarded for his services. It may be added, without anticipating, that this was the beginning of a long service to the country's old soldiers which earned Mr. Hamlin the lasting gratitude of many a home.

While Mr. Hamlin was endeavoring to work a reform in the pension office, he was also lending his aid to the movement to obtain cheaper postage. During the first few days of his membership in the House, he introduced a petition praying for lower postal rates, and then joined with prominent members of the House in an effort to pass a bill to accomplish the desired reform. This was one of the many topics which Mr. Hamlin and his "mess" associates considered, and one outcome of their deliberations was a bill that was offered

---

[1] *Congressional Globe*, December 27, 1843, p. 76.

by Preston King making uniform reduction in the cost of transporting mail. The public was strongly in favor of the reform. In a speech by Charles H. Carroll, of New York, a circumstance was brought out that in these days seems amazing. Mr. Carroll said that it cost one cent and three quarters more to transport a letter from Geneva, N. Y., to New York city, than it did to transport a barrel of flour between the same places. The timidity and conservatism of the government were the real obstacles to the success of this reform movement. It was feared that a reduction in postage rates would make the Post-office Department a burden to the government. A general understanding was arrived at in the House, that action should be deferred until the petition in circulation throughout the country had been laid before the House.

In the mean time the desire for postal reform increased among the progressive people of the country, and when Congress reconvened a determined effort was made to reduce the postal rates from an excessive average of fifteen and one half cents to a uniform rate of five cents a letter; at the same time it was planned to make an attempt to abolish the franking privilege, which had become a great abuse. Opposition to the reform was strong, and was chiefly based on the plea that a sweeping reduction of postage rates would decrease the revenues of the Post-office Department to so low a figure that the service would become a burden on the national treasury. A reading of the debates on this question discloses the different points of view the Northern and Southern congressmen held on economic questions. In this instance, the Southern members were influenced to a considerable extent by their ideas of state rights, which seemed sometimes to act on them with the force of a religion, and to be the conscious or unconscious motive of their acts. Sectional considerations also operated among them. Mr. Hamlin favored the bill, and he made several speeches in which he embodied the Northern argument in favor of it.[1] The main idea was that as cheap postage had increased the business of the Post-office Department in England, and tended to spread intelligence throughout the masses, the same measures ought to bring about the same results in the United States. As a simpler illustration he showed that the reduction of postal rates, like the reduction of railroad and steamboat fares, would also increase the business and revenue of the Post-office Department.

These views, however, were not accepted by the Southern members as a rule. Howell Cobb feared that the contemplated reduction was too radical, and, moreover, would lodge too much power in the Post-office Department. William L. Yancey supported Mr. Cobb's argument, and claimed that only the large cities favored the reform. It

[1] Principal speech, February 24, 1845, *Congressional Globe*, p. 339.

was his belief that this would be taxing the many for the benefit of the few. Mr. Hopkins, of Virginia, asserted that the government could never compete with the private expresses that now transacted a large amount of the postal business. But the *reductio ad absurdum* was a speech by William W. Payne. In reply to Mr. Hamlin he said that the postal bill was a New York and New England measure, and that the letter writers who paid the cost of postage were merchants, business men, love-sick swains, and city belles. They should be made to pay it.

But without going into the subject further, it may be added that although the five-cent bill passed the Senate, it did not triumph in the House. An amendment was added establishing five cents as the rate for letters under 300 miles, and ten cents over that distance. The progressive and unprogressive elements in the House divided on this bill almost identically as they did on the slavery question. Eighty-five members, including Mr. Hamlin, John P. Hale, Preston King, Jacob Collamer, Daniel Putnam King, Hamilton Fish, Caleb B. Smith, Robert C. Schenck, Joshua R. Giddings, George Rathbun, Freeman H. Morse, Alexander Ramsay, and others who generally affiliated on progressive matters voted against this amendment; but 110 voted for it, and the Senate concurred on the principle that "half a loaf was better than no bread." The franking privilege remained unchanged. The beginning of postal reform has thus been briefly described in order to show Mr. Hamlin's interest in it. He accomplished more work in the committee room than in debate. He retained his interest in this reform movement when he entered the Senate, and when more important results were attained. From the first he opposed the franking privilege. But this is anticipating, and the narrative returns to the chronological order of events — beginning with the annexation of Texas.

CHAPTER X

MR. HAMLIN accepted an invitation to join President Tyler and a party in a trip down the Potomac River, on the man-of-war Princeton, of the United States Navy, on February 28, 1844, when a new gun that had been added to the Princeton's armament was to be tested. As he was about to proceed to the ship, Mr. Hamlin unexpectedly found that his presence was required in the House, and to his regret he was compelled to forego what he had expected would be a very pleasant outing. But it proved to be a day of tragic and portentous significance for the entire nation. The gun exploded, killed Mr. Upshur, the Secretary of State, Mr. Gilmer, the Secretary of the Navy, and nine others, and also wounded nine sailors. It happened that President Tyler had stepped into the cabin just before the gun was fired, and so escaped injury. The death of Mr. Upshur had a momentous effect on this administration. Mr. Tyler had schemed to annex Texas in order to give lustre to his administration, and also in the hope that he would be enabled to force the Democratic party to nominate him for President. To this end Mr. Tyler had negotiated a treaty with Texas, looking to the annexation of the young republic with the Union, when Mr. Upshur's tragic death interrupted the proceedings. The Democratic party took the practical view of the situation, and favored the annexation of Texas; the Whigs opposed the project on the ground that it might involve the United States in a war with Mexico. Like an inspiration, the thought came to Henry A. Wise that the master-hand of John C. Calhoun could guide the Democratic party to success in the emergency now presented, and he induced Mr. Tyler, against his personal preference, to make Mr. Calhoun the successor to Mr. Upshur. Here was a young nation on our borders asking to be taken into our Union as a sister State, and increase our domain and power. The fact was that Texas was able to separate itself from Mexico, and maintain itself as an independent community by its own efforts. Now, if the United States did not accept its offer, there was manifest danger that Texas might remain an isolated power, and become a prey for adventurous European governments, a danger that was well exemplified only twenty years afterwards, when Louis Napoleon attempted to seat Maximilian in Mexico on a throne propped up by bayonets.

Mr. Calhoun emerged from the retirement into which Jackson had driven him, and became the Secretary of State. He favored the annexation of Texas, and, moreover, his comprehensive mind grasped the great possibilities of party success in a joint Northern and Southern movement to acquire more land for the Union. The Texas question also suggested the advisability of adjusting the boundary line of Oregon with Great Britain. Thus, before the National Democratic Convention met at Baltimore, in May, Mr. Calhoun had already provided it with winning issues. The proposal to increase the nation's territory fired the Democratic party with zeal and enthusiasm; but it must be added that Mr. Calhoun had an ulterior motive in raising these issues besides seeking party success. Mr. Van Buren and Mr. Clay had both written letters opposing the annexation of Texas. Mr. Calhoun, believing that Mr. Van Buren had robbed him of the presidency by poisoning Jackson's mind against him, was naturally desirous of avenging himself upon him. Mr. Calhoun seized on Mr. Van Buren's opposition to the annexation of Texas as a means of defeating his aspirations for renomination. Mr. Calhoun welded the slave States into a compact body against Mr. Van Buren, and accomplished his defeat in the convention by enforcing the two thirds rule. When a deadlock seemed imminent, James K. Polk was brought forward as a compromise candidate, and nominated amidst enthusiasm. Silas Wright was named for Vice-President, but declined, and in five minutes sent a dispatch to Baltimore to that effect.[1] He was Mr. Van Buren's confidential friend. George M. Dallas, of Pennsylvania, was substituted. The Whigs having nominated Mr. Clay and Theodore Frelinghuysen as their leaders, this session of Congress closed amidst preparations for one of the most important and exciting presidential elections in the history of the country.

Mr. Hamlin returned to Maine after the adjournment of Congress, and was renominated for another term. Although he preferred Mr. Van Buren, he accepted Polk's nomination, and supported him loyally. Mr. Hamlin was a strong party man, and believed that the right would prevail in the end. No man had yet arrived who possessed the power of prophecy or divination; the truth was but half suspected, — that Mr. Polk had been secretly selected by the slave power weeks before the convention nominated him. Mr. Polk was a man of irreproachable private character, and his candidacy was received by his party with great favor, except among Mr. Van Buren's intimate friends, although Mr. Wright, for the sake of the party, waived his own feelings, and became the Democratic candidate

[1] The telegraph had just been established, and the convention did not know whether to believe Wright's dispatch of declination. A committee was sent to Washington to ascertain the truth.

for governor of New York. It was his influence that decided the result of the campaign, for New York elected Mr. Polk. Mr. Clay soon perceived that the Democratic party was making great progress with the slogan, "Annex Texas; 54° 40' or fight." The South would naturally look with favor on a plan to increase its slave territory, and as the feeling against Great Britain, on account of the war of 1812, had not yet died out, the cry, "54° 40' or fight," roused a spirit of enthusiasm that nearly threatened to bring on another war with that nation. To his great mortification, Mr. Clay found himself for the first time on the defensive in a political campaign. To stem the turning of the tide, Mr. Clay wrote a letter denying that he was opposed to the annexation of Texas, and adding that he would be glad to have Texas brought into the Union under honorable conditions. This so-called Alabama letter was Mr. Clay's death warrant. It drove a sufficient number of anti-slavery Whigs of New York into the ranks of the Abolition party to give that State to Mr. Polk. It weakened Mr. Clay even in Kentucky. In the gubernatorial election in Kentucky that occurred in the month of August, William O. Butler, the Democratic candidate, cut down the Whig majority from 28,000 votes to less than 5000. This reduction of strength in Mr. Clay's own home created consternation among his friends and proportionate jubilation among the Democrats. Before this, Mr. Hamlin was but little known outside of Maine as a campaign speaker. After the Kentucky election, Mr. Hamlin made a speech that attracted considerable attention to him beyond the borders of his own State. In characterizing Mr. Clay's attitude towards Texas, which was called "facing two ways," Mr. Hamlin said that Clay, after the Kentucky election, reminded him of the old woman who went to sleep on the highway, to wake up and find that her petticoats had been cut off about her knees. She lamented : —

> " ' If this be I as I hope it be,
> I have a little dog at home and he knows me.
> If it be I he will wag his little tail;
> If it be not I he will loudly bark and loudly wail.'
> Forth went the little woman all in the dark,
> Up jumped the little dog and began to bark.
> Up jumped the little woman and began to cry,
> ' Lawk a mercy on us, this is none of I.' "

"Kentucky, my friends," observed Mr. Hamlin, "does not know her old woman." Campaign oratory, it need not be added, was then noted for vigor, sarcasm, and its personal nature. This rude shaft proved exceedingly effective and was widely used as an apt, if homely, illustration of Mr. Clay's unfortunate predicament.[1]

[1] Mr. Hamlin made his first speech in New York city in this campaign. He addressed a large audience at Castle Garden.

In the Maine election, the total poll was over 90,000 votes, a gain of more than 30,000 over the previous year, which indicated the great interest the campaign commanded in the Pine Tree State. The Democrats reëlected Governor Anderson, a popular and able man, by 10,000 majority. Mr. Hamlin was reëlected by a large majority over Abraham Sanborn, a Whig of ability as a campaign orator and a leading lawyer of Bangor. For several weeks after the presidential election in November the result was not generally known, owing to the delay of getting the returns from New York, and the lack of facilities for spreading the news. Democrats and Whigs alike passed through agonies of uncertainties. Mr. Hamlin awaited the result at his home in Hampden. One day a group of Democrats gathered before the little village post-office to wait for the news, when a horseman was seen in the dim distance on the old Boston highway, galloping towards Hampden like mad. In his hand he held a long shining thing, and there was curious speculation as to what it was and what the man was doing. When he came a little nearer he lifted the shining object to his mouth ; it was a speaking-trumpet, and the impatient Democrats were transported with almost uncontainable joy when they heard these words : "Polk elected ; New York goes for him by 5000 majority." In a cloud of dust the jubilant and smiling messenger dashed on to carry the glad tidings of Polk's election to Bangor. In this way the news of Polk's victory was spread throughout Maine. Polk had a popular majority of about a quarter of a million of votes and an emphatic majority in the electoral college. The significance of the election was that the people favored the annexation of Texas and the reoccupation of Oregon.

An incident that followed the election of Polk indicates Mr. Hamlin's position as a leader in the House. Shortly before the adjournment of Congress some members of the House asked him to be a candidate for speaker at the next session, when a new House would come into existence. He said nothing about this, however, at the time to his colleagues from Maine. But after the presidential election he received a letter from Major French, clerk of the House, who wrote that, judging from what the incoming members of the next House were saying, Mr. Hamlin stood as good a chance as anybody to succeed to the speaker's chair. Mr. Hamlin, however, made no effort, so far as is known, to become speaker. He never mentioned the affair to his family. All he did that is a matter of record was to lay the facts in a letter before Robert P. Dunlap, who had been governor of Maine, and was then in the House and a personal friend. In this letter he expressed no desire for the speaker's chair, but asked Mr. Dunlap's opinion. Oldtime politicians of Maine remembered that Mr. Hamlin's name was freely used in connection with the speakership, which appears to have been the beginning and the end of the affair. His name was not presented. The tone of his letter to Governor Dunlap indicated that he had doubts whether it would be worth while to make a contest. He knew that the slave party was in control, and would probably choose a man of its own. This was the case. But the incident was a compliment worth noting.

Congress reconvened in another month, and the Democratic members returned to Washington rejoicing over the brilliant victory their party had achieved. But when the Texas affair began rapidly to develop its real aspect, the happiness of the anti-slavery Democrats changed to apprehension. The fact was the North had only dimly realized the danger to free institutions involved in the admission of Texas into the Union. The North had, indeed, good reasons for believing that a part, if not half, of Texas would be free. Up to this time it had been a part of the unwritten Constitution of the United States to preserve the balance between the free and slave States of the Union by admitting new States in pairs, — one free, the other slave. Texas had enough land for five States, and if the anti-slavery voters of the North had grasped the purpose of the slave power to seize that immense territory for slavery, Mr. Polk would never have been elected President. In the presidential campaign there were developments that disturbed far-seeing men ; a frenzy seemed to possess the slave party in several Southern States. The cry of "Texas with or without the Union" was often heard. Declarations of this kind were regarded by the great masses of loyal people in all parts of the country as utterances of superheated, irresponsible fire-eaters. This belief had some truth for its foundation, and yet the excited condition of the South over the issue of annexation was the result of a systematic agitation which was begun in order to create a demand in the South for the admission of Texas into the Union as a slave State.

When Mr. Calhoun became secretary of state he perceived that the plans of the slave power could not succeed without the aid of Southern Whigs. Personally, Mr. Calhoun was a pure and honorable man, but his failure to reach the presidency had embittered him probably more than he realized. He believed in slavery as a patriarchal institution ; he defended it with the intensity of a fanatic, and saw its opponents with a distorted vision. Just prior to Mr. Calhoun's entrance into President Tyler's Cabinet, some Abolitionists conceived a plan to purchase the slaves of Texas and set them free. They visited London in the hope of inducing the English government to help them raise the money needed, — $10,000,000. It had been England's policy to encourage emancipation, since she had freed

the last of her slaves ten years before this; but in this instance Great
Britain could not" act without incurring the danger of bringing on a
war with the United States and Texas too.   Assistance was refused
the Abolitionists, and the British government, through Lord Aber-
deen, informed Secretary Upshur, ten days before the latter's tragic
death, that while it was England's policy to encourage emancipation
throughout the world, it would neither secretly nor openly resort to
any measure that would tend to disturb the domestic tranquillity of
the slaveholding States.   This was an explicit and honorable declaration, and yet Mr. Calhoun and his coöperators saw in it only a revelation of a Machiavelian policy, — an intention on England's part to
thwart the annexation of Texas.   When Mr. Calhoun became secretary of state he made effective use of the Abolition incident to elect
Mr. Polk and to intensify Southern sentiment in favor of annexation,
by charging England with hostility to the slaveholding policy of the
country.   Thus Mr. Calhoun stirred Southern hatred of the abolitionist, and national dislike for the English government.   In a letter
of instructions to William R. King, the American minister to France,
Mr. Calhoun said that England regarded the defeat of annexation
"as indispensable to the abolition of slavery in Texas," that "England was too sagacious not to see what a fatal blow abolition in Texas
would give to slavery in the United States," and finally, that the
effect of the abolition of slavery "to this continent would be calami-
tous beyond description."

Mr. Calhoun and his faction continued to harp on these themes
even after the election of Mr. Polk, and their object is easy to understand.   When Congress resumed its session, and the purpose of the
slave power to grab all of Texas was revealed, there were signs of a
defection of the anti-slavery Democrats from their party.   Mr. Hamlin and his associates were justly indignant, and vehemently in private
and in public denounced their Southern party colleagues for their
practical breach of faith and abandonment of custom.   The anger of
the Northern anti-slavery men in Congress was after all only an episode
in the eyes of the crafty slave power.   The next thing to do was to
win over the men needed, and to do that the Calhoun party kept
Southern excitement up to the fever pitch as long as they could, in
hopes the requisite number of Southern Whigs would yield under the
pressure of public sentiment, and deliver Texas over to slavery.   The
final step Mr. Calhoun arranged was to rush Texas into the Union by
forcing through Congress joint resolutions framed by his adroit brain.
Senator Robert J. Walker, of Mississippi, was chosen to manage the
resolutions.   On December 12, Charles J. Ingersoll, of Pennsylvania,
chairman of the Committee on Foreign Relations and a Northern
man with Southern principles, introduced the resolutions into the

House, and the battle was begun that closed two decades afterwards.

The measure presented by Mr. Ingersoll only "cleared the deck for action." In general terms it provided for the admission of Texas into the Union, the appointment of a commission to investigate questions that needed settlement, and other details which do not require recapitulation. But not one word was said about slavery; no intimation was given of the slave power's intention to make five States out of Texas in order that they could send ten senators and at least twice as many representatives to Congress in the interests of the slave oligarchy. The debate that opened a few days later was not an oratorical contest of note, but an exposition of the diametrically opposite views the North and the South held on slavery, and another proof that there could no longer be any compromise on that issue, because it had become a political factor which was to be settled only in the last court, — the field of war. But prophets had not yet arrived who were to be believed in their day, and the battle over Texas was regarded as a great political contest, although the nation's degradation was keenly felt at the North, and fears for the country's future aroused over the display of the slave party's power and arrogance.

In another respect the debate was interesting and important as an exposition of the Southern belief in slavery as a useful and beneficent institution, and also that the North made war on the South through tariffs, laws, and bounties. As the slave party controlled the situation far more surely than its opponents knew, the leaders did not favor the making of speeches that would tend to inflame the Northern congressmen; but they could not hold some of their own number in check, and there were a few outbursts of more than ordinary interest in the course of the debate. William L. Yancey, of Alabama, was one of the most eloquent and extreme representatives in the House of the selfish, sectional spirit of the slave party. He was a man of great ability, though of a vindictive nature. He hated the anti-slavery men, and was not unwilling to stoop to the tactics of the demagogue to "fire the Southern heart" against them. Mr. Yancey was one of the first to lead off in the debate on Texas, and his speech is one of peculiar interest, because he made a base attack on New England, to which Mr. Hamlin replied, and an onslaught on Thomas L. Clingman, a Whig, of North Carolina, who was opposed to annexation, which brought on a duel. With extreme Southern men like Mr. Yancey it was a favorite practice to slur New England as a centre of disunion on account of the Hartford convention and the ideas of the Abolitionists, for both of which New England could not be held responsible. Two brief extracts from Yancey's speech will suffice to illustrate. "Looking at New England," said he, "I see her plains made fertile and her villages springing up by the bounties wrung from the South." "Men are now there," he continued, "who, forgetful of their fathers, are seeking to weaken the bonds of the Union, and are content to live on the bounty wrung from the sweat of Southern brows." But of more importance was Mr. Yancey's declaration, bold and unqualified, that "the slaveholding States were losing their relative strength in the representative branch of the government," that "they had compromised away all possibility of retaining an equality in the Senate by the fatal Missouri Compromise," and finally, that "the highest considerations of individual, sectional, and national interests urged the South on to annexation."

Several other speeches were made following the lead of Mr. Yancey's remarks, although not so severe in their reflections on New England. Isaac E. Holmes, of South Carolina, a man of generous disposition and honorable nature, but who was naturally imbued with the Southern idea of New England, claimed that that section opposed annexation for purely commercial reasons, and in further allusion to the anti-slavery movement said that a tremendous whirlwind was gathering in blackness and fury to drink up all that was estimable in Southern institutions. "Men," he continued, "have talked of dividing this country in two parts, from one of which slavery is to be excluded. A Southerner who would agree to this — a Southerner who would manacle and fetter the energies of his children — must be either a knave or a fool. Admit Texas and give us but two slave States, what will our condition be? With our exhausted soil, a dense population which without a field for industry and enterprise must grow idle, let gentlemen figure the consequences for themselves."

It is not necessary to pursue this line of Southern argument further. Anti-slavery men met and refuted it when it was advanced. The development of the manufacturing interests of the South subsequent to 1865 completely upset this theory. But at this time something else claimed the attention of the anti-slavery men in Congress, and that was the avowal of the extreme pro-slavery leaders that they would not restrict their ambitions for extending slavery with the annexation of Texas. Another thing was becoming clearer, and that was the fact that the slave party was growing more confident with the progress of the debate of its ability to force the joint resolutions through the House. There were reports that the slave leaders had been promising the patronage of the incoming administration to unscrupulous and dough-face Northern Democrats, which were unhappily verified. Realizing the tremendous efforts the slave party was making to push the joint resolutions through Congress, and that the chances of success were favorable, and having a clear idea of the practical difficulties before the anti-slavery men, Mr. Hamlin resolved to present a dispassionate view of the annexation issue in the hope, faint though it was, that the South might yet be brought to see that a compromise ought to be effected which would satisfy the North. On January 23, 1845, he made a speech on Texas that was conciliatory in tone, though firm in its denunciation of slavery. Mr. Hamlin was then thirty-four years old. This speech was inadequately reported in the "Congressional Record," the eulogy on New England was even omitted entirely. His poetic tribute to New England was saved by the newspaper correspondents, who sent it out over the country. The speech was in part as follows : —

" We have a country stretching from the frozen regions of the North to the tropical climate of the South. We have a seacoast extending from the rocky shores of New England, washed by the Atlantic, to our western boundary, bathed by the peaceful waters of the Pacific, vast in extent, and embracing in its circuit almost every climate and almost every industrial pursuit known to the world. It must occur to every thinking mind that a government stretching its powers over such a vast domain must be one of compromise. On compromise our Republican form of government was based. Viewing the question of the annexation of Texas in such a light, let us come to the consideration of it with feelings and purposes equal to its importance. Gentlemen who have preceded me in this debate have so ably discussed the constitutional question involved that I shall not enter upon it. I shall content myself with simply saying on this point . . . that I will give my sanction to the annexation of Texas upon conditions and restrictions which will make it what I claim it to be, a national question. Moreover, I am for immediate annexation, although I had indulged the hope that the consummation of this measure would have been left to the coming administration, which will have, as I trust and believe it will, the confidence of the people. The present administration possesses the respect and confidence of no party and no man. . . .

" I first propose to show that this question has not been presented to the House in a national aspect, and I shall then proceed to show in what manner it ought to be presented. . . .

" I regret that this great and important national question has been dragged down, down, down from its proper sphere to a wretched, contemptible, and groveling position. Let us trace the development of this question from its first appearance in this hall to its present aspect. I know that the acquisition of Texas has been the desideratum of several administrations for national purposes, purposes which I approve. But what is the origin of the measure of the annexation of a foreign power to this Union? A mere rumor reported in a letter . . . that the British government designed to abolish slavery in the republic of Texas. . . . This was the basis on which the authorities of Texas were invited to open negotiations with this country. Yes, an idle rumor had force enough to engage the attention of our government.

" This is an attempt to strengthen the slave power. Let us examine the correspondence of the Tyler administration on this subject, which shows that the object of annexing Texas is to uphold and extend slavery, and the alleged design of the British government to abolish slavery in Texas has been brought to bear upon the annexation issue. I quote from Mr. Calhoun's elaborate argument defending slavery and urging the annexation of Texas as a means of maintaining the institution. . . .

"What! is it true that the slave institution in this country is the great upholder of the power in this Republic? Is it the means of spreading civilization over the world? . . . If we should return home and tell our constituents that we voted for annexation on such principles and with such a name, we should be pronounced recreant to our duty, traitors to our country. I deny Mr. Calhoun's reasonings and conclusions. If the government should extend its domain for such as he sets forth, it would give national power, importance, and dignity to a purely local affair.

"The general government has no right to interfere with slavery. But if the government can extend the institution for an alleged beneficial purpose, it can restrict it. . . . This is an attempt to make a national question of a purely state issue, and those who are endeavoring to give it a national character would be swift indeed to prevent Congress from taking a restrictive action. The question of annexation is fully and clearly national, not one where the government should act for a cause over which it has no right to interfere. . . . I myself am in favor of the abstract proposition of annexation, and I am willing to leave the details for the future if they could be fairly settled. . . . That the people decided in favor of annexation in the last election, I believe ; that they prescribed and settled the details, I do not believe. . . . In my State we took the ground that recourse must be had to compromise, but we concluded that it would be the means of admitting more free States than slave States. I refer you also to the resolutions adopted by the legislature of New Hampshire — I also refer you to the bill introduced into the Senate by Mr. Hayward, the senator from North Carolina, a bill which speaks much for his heart, but more for his head.

"Of slavery I do not intend to speak. The eloquent Pinckney spoke for me when he declared that slavery's footsteps were marked with blight wherever it had touched the earth ; but again I say, I am willing to enter into compromise, because I believe that annexation is of national importance. It will promote Northern commerce, agriculture, and industrial pursuits ; it will also benefit the South in giving the monopoly of the cotton-growing industry for the supply of foreign markets. . . . I am desirous that a portion of this territory should be left free for the industry of Northern people. When they shall have established themselves, leveled the forests, cultivated the earth, built up their industries, I would leave it to them whether they would admit slavery. There would be no fear of that.

"I recall the jeers and taunts that have been thrown out in the progress of this debate, and when I heard them, my heart impelled me to hurl them back. Reflection, however, has softened my indignation. It does not become public men in discussing great national questions to descend to taunts and to provoke sectional feelings and prejudices. If there are any here who can find consolation in this kind of debate, they are welcome to it. I protest against the reproaches that have been heaped upon the North. If the North has acted wickedly, I offer for her no apologies — that wickedness was not the crime of her people; it belonged to her politicians alone. . . . The hardy sons of the ice-bound regions of New England have poured out their blood without stint to protect the shores of the South, and to avenge her wrongs. Their bones are even now bleaching beneath the sun on many a Southern hill; and the monuments of their brave devotion may still be traced wherever their country's flag has floated on the battlefield or in the breeze, upon the lakes, the ocean, and the land.

> " ' New England's dead ! New England's dead !
>   On every field they lie,
>   On every field of strife made red
>   With bloody victory.
>   Their bones are on our Northern hills,
>   And on the Southern plain ;
>   By brooks and river, mount and rills,
>   And in the sounding main.'

" I glory in New England and New England's institutions. There she stands with her free schools and her free labor, her fearless enterprise, her indomitable energy! With her rocky hills, her torrent streams, her green valleys, her heavenward-pointed spires, there she stands a moral monument around which the gratitude of her country binds the wreath of fame, while protected freedom shall repose forever at its base.

" While I thus glory in New England, however, I meet not my Southern brethren with any brand of discord, but with the olive branch of peace. I meet them in the spirit of harmony ; still, I desire above other considerations to meet them on even ground, — a ground alike respectful to the North and the South, — and I invoke them to perform this great national act, — the annexation of Texas — that Southern and Northern hearts may rejoice to behold the stars and stripes floating together over the rich and fertile Texan plains. I ask, will not the gentlemen of the South meet us here ? Will they not rescue this measure alike from danger and reproach and put it in a form which will gratify us all ? I entreat them to look at the question in all the lights of cool reflection before they finally reject the compromise which, while it secures them an inestimable benefit, does equal justice to all sections and all interests of the Union."

The resolutions to annex Texas were now to be read for the last time before a vote was taken, when Stephen A. Douglas, whose presidential ambition had not then eaten away his sagacity, offered an amendment providing that the States to be formed out of Texas be admitted to the Union with or without slavery as their people should desire. This was rejected by a majority of only eleven votes. Mr. Hamlin promptly presented another amendment providing that the terms on which the new States should be admitted to the Union should be determined by Congress at the time of admission and in accordance with the Constitution. But this was rejected, and so were other amendments presented or framed to secure some recognition of the anti-slavery sentiment of the North. The result of all these efforts was to secure the adoption of an amendment offered by Stephen A. Douglas providing that there should be no slavery in any territory of the States to be formed out of Texas that laid north of the Missouri Compromise line. This was practically a reaffirmation of the Missouri Compromise. The only honorable course left for all members of the House who favored annexation, but who were opposed to it as a means of extending slavery, was to vote against the joint resolutions. The resolutions were passed by a vote of 120 to 98. An analysis of the vote shows that nearly thirty Northern Democrats braved the slave power on this occasion and that some eight Southern Whigs yielded to it. A few changes of votes would obviously have defeated the joint resolutions and thus compelled the framing of a fairer measure. Among the Democrats who put their country before their party in this struggle were : Preston King, George Rathbun, J. E. Cary, Joseph H. Anderson, Charles S. Benton, Amasa Dana, Richard D. Davis, Byram Green, Horace Wheaton, Orville Robinson, David L. Seymour, Lemuel B. Stetson, and S. M. Purdy, all of New York ; Edward S. Hamlin and Jacob Brinkerhoff, of Ohio; John P. Hale and John R. Reding, of New Hampshire; George S. Catlin and John Stewart, of Connecticut ; Joshua Herrick, Robert P. Dunlap, and Hannibal Hamlin, of Maine; Henry Williams, of Massachusetts ; Paul Dillingham, Jr., of Vermont, and James B. Hunt and Robert McClelland, of Michigan. Prominent among the Whigs who were actuated by high moral reasons rather than political were John Quincy Adams, Daniel Putnam King, Joshua R. Giddings, Robert C. Schenck, Samuel F. Vinton, Washington Hunt, Hamilton Fish, Caleb B. Smith, Freeman H. Morse and Luther Severance, of Maine, Solomon Foot, and Jacob Collamer. The old proverb, " Politics makes strange bedfellows," is illustrated in finding Thomas L. Clingman in company with these Whigs, — a man whose principles and friendship for Clay held him against the annexation of Texas, but whose attachment to his State led him to favor disunion in 1860. In this portentous division on the slave issue, it is significant to find Alexander H. Stephens as the leader of the small handful of Whigs who deserted their party to serve the interests of the slave power. John B. Ashe, Milton Brown, James H. Payton and William T. Senter, of Tennessee, A. H. Chappell, of Georgia, and James Dellet, of Alabama, were the other Whigs who followed the lead of the coming Vice-President of the Confederacy in this issue. They worked hand in hand with Democrats who became conspicuous disunionists, — Howell Cobb, Jacob Thompson, John Slidell, William L.

Yancey, Thomas L. Seymour, and R. Barnwell Rhett. The strength of the slave party is better appreciated when the fact is recorded that others who supported this measure were John W. Davis, of Indiana, who was speaker of the next House; Charles J. Ingersoll, of Pennsylvania, an influential member of Northern birth and Southern principles; Aaron V. Brown, Mr. Polk's law partner and postmaster-general under Buchanan; Cave Johnson, who held the same office under Polk; Stephen A. Douglas, whose presidential aspirations split the Democratic party in 1860, and Andrew Johnson, who was then a consistent defender of slavery.

The last chapter in the story of the joint resolutions of annexation is of personal interest. In the Senate there was a small group of Democrats who opposed the House resolutions for fear that the annexation of Texas, accomplished by their adoption, would bring on a war with Mexico. Thomas H. Benton was the leader of these men, and he succeeded in inducing the Senate to pass an amendment to the House bill providing for the annexation of Texas by negotiation with Mexico. President-elect Polk, who was now in Washington in conference with President Tyler in regard to the annexation of Texas, gave his assurance to several senators, that if Colonel Benton's amendment was passed by Congress, he would act within its lines and appoint a commission, composed of men of the highest character, to acquire Texas on terms honorable to the United States and satisfactory to Mexico. The Senate then rejected the House joint resolutions and passed Colonel Benton's amendment. This measure was next introduced into the House, and Mr. Hamlin and all the anti-slavery Democrats except three or four, trusting in Mr. Polk's assurances, voted for the Senate amendment, which was carried by a majority of more than fifty. The parliamentary phase of these proceedings confused some good Free-Soilers of Maine, and they thought that men who supported the Senate amendment had withdrawn their opposition to the Texas grab scheme. There were also others who misunderstood the votes of anti-slavery members of the House in this latter incident. The following extract from a private letter which Mr. Hamlin wrote to a friend in Maine makes his position clear : —

" The resolutions were offered in the House for annexing Texas. They passed the House and went to the Senate. I voted against those resolutions in the House. They passed the Senate with an amendment prepared by Colonel Benton. The amendment left the manner and terms to be fixed by negotiation. By that course (I mean Colonel Benton's) we believed, if annexation took place, we could prevent a war and secure at least half of the territory as free. Well, the amendment of Colonel Benton's was carried in the Senate, and the resolutions so passed the Senate. The amendment only was sent to the

House, and I voted for it, as making the resolutions better. Bear in mind that the original resolutions were never sent back to the House. Nothing but the amendment came back there. That is the way of proceedings here. It is different in our state legislature. Hence, I did not vote for the original resolutions at any time."

But the country was to be deprived of the fruits of the patriotism and wisdom of the honorable members of Congress. Zealous to snatch the credit of annexing Texas for his administration, President Tyler's last-important official act was to sign the Texas bill, and send a messenger off to Texas post haste with the legislative clause without the Senate's peace-bearing amendment, to announce to the impatient republic that it had been incorporated into the Union. It was the most perfidious act of a perfidious administration. Mr. Tyler usurped the rights of the incoming President, who in a few days was to take the oath of office. Senator Benton vehemently denounced this conduct of Tyler and Calhoun, and asserted that at least five Senators would have voted against the resolutions, had they known Mr. Tyler contemplated this act. Their votes would have blocked the annexation scheme of the slave power at that juncture, and possibly averted what John Tyler was justly responsible for, — the precipitation of a cruel and unjust war with Mexico. In the words of Senator Benton: " The flight of the winged messenger from this capital on the Sunday night before the 3d of March, dispatched by the then Secretary of State, in the expiring moment of his power, and bearing his fatal choice to the capital of Texas, was the direct cause of the war with Mexico. It broke up all the plans of peaceable men, slammed the door upon negotiations, put an end to all chance for accommodations, broke up the camp on the Sabine, sent the troops to Mexico, and lit up the war."

The danger of misunderstandings that every honest public man must meet was exemplified in Mr. Hamlin's experience in the Texas issue. His speech so incensed the slavery members of the House that they seriously considered the advisability of passing a vote of censure. At the same time there were anti-slavery Whigs in Maine who, not understanding the purport of the Benton amendment, failed to understand Mr. Hamlin's votes. Some historians, moreover, have failed to grasp the significance of the Benton amendment. Anti-slavery Democrats like Mr. Hamlin opposed the joint resolutions for fear that Texas would be annexed as a slave State, and also for fear that these resolutions would precipitate a war with Mexico. The adoption of the resolutions of annexation created a dangerous situation. The duty was devolved on the anti-slavery men of modifying the situation. They tried to do this by voting for the Benton amendment, which sought to accomplish annexation by negotiation, now that annexation had been decreed by an arbitrary slave power.

CHAPTER XI

NATIONAL feeling against the practice of dueling had been greatly intensified by the death of Jonathan Cilley in a meeting with William J. Graves, of Kentucky, on February 24, 1838, to which brief allusion has already been made. This was one of the least justifiable "affairs of honor"—if the word justifiable may be used—which ever occurred in this country. Mr. Cilley was a man of great courage and spirit. On entering Congress he encountered the fire-eating element, and when he heard their braggadocio and sneers at Yankees, he unfortunately allowed his temper to show itself. He returned Southern sneers at Northern men, and asserted that he would fight if challenged. From the day Mr. Cilley gave way to his anger he was a marked man. In a short time he made a speech in which he criticised an article that appeared in a newspaper, edited and published by General James Watson Webb, in the city of New York. General Webb was a duelist; he had fought the year before with Thomas F. Marshall, of Kentucky. Thinking that Mr. Cilley's remarks were intended as a reflection on him, General Webb sent Mr. Cilley a challenge through Mr. Graves. Mr. Cilley, however, disclaimed any intention of reflecting on General Webb, and declined to meet him. There the affair should have ended, but it did not; it was even currently reported that Graves consulted Henry Clay, Henry A. Wise, and other Southern duelists, who urged him to challenge Mr. Cilley. Mr. Hamlin, who knew much about the affair, openly charged Clay with being morally responsible for Jonathan Cilley's death. Graves made Webb's alleged grievances a personal affair, and Cilley, finding his courage questioned, and although unfamiliar with firearms, and near-sighted, designated hair-trigger rifles as the weapons.

The duel took place at Bladensburg, Md. Henry A. Wise was second for Graves, and George W. Jones, then a representative from Wisconsin, and afterwards a senator from Iowa, acted for Mr. Cilley. One shot was exchanged without effect, and then, according to the "code" as practiced by Southern experts, the affair should have stopped. Mr. Jones took that ground, but Cilley's murder was intended. Wise asserted that Graves's honor was not yet vindicated. A second shot was fired also without effect, and once more Mr. Jones insisted that honor was satisfied and that the duel should end. Not so with Wise; he demanded that the unequal contest should go on. A third shot was fired, and Cilley fell, mortally wounded. This foul murder created a tremendous feeling against dueling at the North and in some parts of the South. Graves and Wise fell under the ban of public censure; the former was peremptorily retired from Congress by his constituents, and died from remorse. It was the fate of Wise to receive one of the most awful excoriations ever heaped in public on the head of a wrong-doer. A few years afterwards, when Thomas F. Marshall, of Kentucky, Wise, and their fellow conspirators had John Quincy Adams at bay, and were trying to prevent him from exercising the rights of a freeman in presenting a petition to the House, the grand old Puritan roused himself like a lion. Pointing his trembling finger at Wise, he uttered these words in his shrill voice with all the power he could command: "Four years ago there came into this House a man with his hands and face dripping with the blood of murder, and the blotches of which are yet hanging upon him." Before leaving the incident it should be added that Mr. Adams's denunciation of Wise caused him to be feared more than ever by the fire-eaters of the House, and yet respected by the best of Southern representatives. When another attempt was set on foot to expel Joshua R. Giddings for his anti-slavery sentiments, Tom Marshall was asked to lead. Marshall had some splendid qualities. "No," said he, with a look of disgust; "when I had the old lion, John Quincy Adams, at bay, and he turned on me, you people deserted me. Now, damn you, skin your own skunks."

The duel between Yancey and General Clingman was fought right after Yancey's speech. It was one of those curious meetings which were termed complimentary affairs, — that is to say, the participants would fire one shot without intending to hit each other, after which their seconds would go through the farce of declaring honor satisfied. Emotion having been relieved, reconciliation followed, and the great men basked in the sunshine of each other's praise of his courage and willingness to vindicate his honor. But there was some mystery about the duel between Yancey and General Clingman, and garbled reports were soon flying around Washington. Probably to clear the matter up, the "National Intelligencer," a Washington newspaper, was authorized to state that a duel had taken place, and that after one shot had been fired friends intervened, and a reconciliation effected. This duel revived in Mr. Hamlin's mind the circumstances of Mr. Cilley's death, and he saw that a fitting opportunity had come for him to try to induce the House to adopt more stringent measures against dueling. Mr. Hamlin never lacked the moral courage to do what he believed to be his duty. One of his first declarations of principle

was this: " I believe that nothing is ended until it is ended rightly."
With this feeling he approached the Yancey-Clingman duel. For
General Clingman, Mr. Hamlin always entertained a high personal
regard; for Yancey he had no regard whatever; but the duel was in
his mind a moral wrong, and he did not hesitate to pursue the course
his conscience dictated, no matter what personal danger he might
encounter.

Mr. Hamlin took action in the midst of the Texas debate when
attacks on slavery had inflamed the extreme Southern members to a
high degree against their Northern colleagues. The morning the
" Intelligencer " published the news of the duel, January 16, 1845,
Mr. Hamlin prepared a resolution, and asked Preston King to offer
it. The reading of the resolution fell on the apologists of dueling
like a clap of thunder from a clear sky. It called for the appointment
of a committee to investigate the story in the " Intelligencer," with
power to recommend the expulsion of Yancey and Clingman should
it prove to be true. Now to reveal their real sentiments on the subject of dueling would place the upholders of the " code " under the
ban of public opinion; but if they should permit the passage of the
resolutions they would accomplish the expulsion of two of their number: and Southern members who opposed dueling, and voted for the
resolutions, would expose themselves to the danger of angering their
colleagues, neighbors, and constituents. A serious dilemma was presented, but a way out of it was quickly perceived; in fact, the first
incidents of the debate proved that the leaders of the " code party "
proposed to defeat the passage of the resolutions on a convenient pretext. Hence, the first thing to do was to find the pretext. After
Mr. King had read the resolutions, William W. Payne, an excitable
member from Alabama, sprung to his feet and objected to their reception. But that looked too much like intolerance, and the crafty
Slidell tried to table them in the usual way. The House, however,
believed that the resolutions should receive at least a semblance of
fair play, and refused to accept Mr. Slidell's motion. An interesting
debate then opened which shows how disingenuous fire-eaters could
be even when professing high-sounding ideas of honor and chivalry.

Kenneth Rayner, of North Carolina, made one of the chief arguments against Mr. Hamlin's measure. He was thoroughly impregnated with the purely Southern view of slavery and dueling; but he
grew, and when the crisis came in 1861, the true Rayner revealed
himself a man of great courage, high sense of duty, and pure patriotism. He attacked the anti-dueling resolutions largely for sentimental
reasons, and although professing himself an opponent of dueling,
yet took the apparently inconsistent ground that dueling was not
an act of immorality which rendered a member an unfit associate

for the other members of the House. His view of this duel and the resolutions was that there might be extenuating circumstances, and in expelling those who took part in it the House might inflict a grievous wrong. "But," Mr. Rayner unhappily added, "I know how fruitless it is to appeal to the sensibilities and justice of the men who sit here with the halter of fanaticism about their heads. I, however, appeal to no feelings of humanity, but to the everlasting principles of justice." [1]

The attitude of the typical fire-eater towards the resolutions was well illustrated in a speech by William W. Payne, the man who objected to the reception of the resolutions. His speech was long, rambling, coarse, and humorous in its inconsistency and naïveté. He asserted, for example, that the resolutions would accomplish nothing but a useless waste of time, and himself made the longest speech of the occasion. He declared that legislation on dueling could not check the evil, and then proposed a law. He betrayed a ludicrous ignorance of the rules of the House, by claiming that it had no right to act in the case brought before it, and insisted that there was no evidence before the House that a duel had been fought, ignoring the fact that the resolutions were introduced primarily to find out whether there had been a meeting between two of its members. The character of Mr. Payne's speech may be better judged from the following verbatim passages : "I have had a good deal of experience in the world for my age," said he, "and I tell you that every law passed for the suppression of dueling has only augmented the evil. If you really desire to apply the axe to the evil, you should pass a law disqualifying every one who fights a duel, if the distance at which he fights exceeds six feet. Pass such a law," Mr. Payne went on triumphantly, "and assume it to be dishonorable to fight at a greater distance, I can assure the House that there would be none, or very few duels — there would be none but which involved a man's reputation if he did not vindicate his honor." Dropping the rôle of the prophet, Mr. Payne proceeded to his peroration, and wound up in a blaze of pyrotechnic wrath. "What are we asked to do ?" he demanded. "Why, suppose we should carry out the investigation and expel a member of this House for dueling, do you suppose that there is a single district in this Union which would not send back such an expelled member by an overwhelming majority. If I were one of the gentlemen rumor said were engaged in a duel, and if the House should expel me, I would scorn and spit upon your act, and come back with increased majority." As a final word, Mr. Payne expressed the hope that the resolution would not pass.

The most sarcastic effort came from Isaac E. Morse, of Louisiana,

[1] *Congressional Globe*, January 16, 1845, pp. 144, 145.

whose masterpiece was the following resolution, which he offered as an amendment to the original measure : —

" *Resolved*, That the said committee be authorized to inquire whether any of the members of this House have violated any of the laws of the decalogue, or of the Ten Commandments, within the District of Columbia, or any of the States ; and that they be authorized to send for persons and papers ; and if they shall find any of the members here guilty of a violation of any of these laws or Commandments, or having left this District with an intention of so violating them, that they be required to bring in a resolution to expel all such members."

When Mr. Hamlin arose to participate in the debate, there was great curiosity to hear what he would say, because he was known to be the sponsor of the resolutions, and also because he had proved himself to be one of the very best shots in Congress. A short time after Mr. Hamlin came to Washington, he accepted an invitation to join a party of congressmen in target shooting, which was a favorite pastime of the day. Long experience in hunting and target shooting at the musters in Maine had made Mr. Hamlin a crack marksman with the rifle. On this occasion he made the best record by hitting the bull's-eye three times in succession, at a distance of one hundred yards. This gave Mr. Hamlin a reputation as a great shot, which secured him against the danger of encountering the fate that befell his friend, Jonathan Cilley. There were several interruptions from members when Mr. Hamlin began his remarks, in answer to his arguments, but after he reached his proper theme the House paid him the unusual compliment of maintaining a perfect silence until he had completed his speech.

" Gentlemen have asked," said Mr. Hamlin, " what is the object of this resolution. Its object and design are manifest, and I hope that it will receive the favorable action of this body. . . . I am in favor of the proposition. The gentleman from North Carolina (Mr. Rayner) asks by what authority we undertake to interfere in this affair, the duel. I answer upon the authority of the highest and most sacred law of the land — the Constitution of the nation. . . . The gentleman also asks by what authority we propose to proceed. Again I tell him that we plant ourselves on the Constitution as the platform and basis of our action. The Constitution says, ' Each house may determine the rules of its proceedings, punish its members for disorderly behavior, and with the concurrence of two thirds, expel a member.' . . . The common law incident to the power we exercise under this clause of the Constitution overrides all mere rules. Are we to be told that should a member rise in his place and commit a cool, deliberate murder of an associate, we have no law to meet the exigency ? "

Mr. Payne : " That would be a violation of the privileges of the House."

Mr. Hamlin : " Yes ; that would be a violation of the privileges of the

House, and more too. The decalogue mentioned in the amendment of the gentleman from Louisiana tells us that idolatry may be committed in the heart as plainly as in the overt act. Now, if I understand the provisions of the Constitution, we have the clear and undoubted right to exercise whatever powers might be in accordance with the rights of individual members, and which should comport with that breach of privilege which had been committed.

"Again, the gentleman from North Carolina remarked that before any member should be expelled from this House, he should be found guilty of some immoral act. Let me tell the gentleman from North Carolina, that there are men . . . in this Union who solemnly believe that when any man deliberately attempts to take the life of another there is immorality in his act."

Mr. Rayner: "I am as much opposed to dueling as the gentleman from Maine; but I said that dueling was not an act of immorality which would constitute a member an unfit associate for his brother representatives on this floor."

Mr. Hamlin: "I accept the gentleman's explanation. I had not heard the latter part of his remarks; but now that I understand him, I confess that it would take a nicer casuist than I to make a distinction between the language I attributed to the gentleman and the language which he now avows. I asked if there was no immorality in the act of dueling, and the gentleman himself admits the fact. I then asked if it was not an act of immorality which justified, nay, demanded the expulsion of any member who should deliberately commit it; but the gentleman, while admitting that dueling was immoral, remarked again that it was not of that degree of turpitude that would justify the expulsion of a member who should have been engaged in it. I hardly know what is the gentleman's notion of a moral course of conduct. He speaks of men here who, he says, stimulated by fanatics at home, might ask an investigation into this alleged duel. To whom does the gentleman refer? . . . I stand up for the North, and I say that this charge cannot be laid at our door.

"But, gentlemen, I speak with feeling on this subject. I remember, alas, too well when a favored son of the State I have the honor to represent, in part, was sent to his 'long and narrow home;' I remember that a wife and an infant child that had never gazed on its living father's face were left to mourn sadly over the fate of the man who should have been a husband and a father to them through weal and woe. I remember the excitement that pervaded my State, and I recall we were told that a man could not stand up here under the fire of reproaches unless he defied the laws of God and man and poured out the blood of humanity. It is the time, it is the hour, it is the day, for this republic to speak out against this inhuman practice in tones that shall thunder across its vast domain. It is time to set here an example of moral courage and rectitude. . . . Let us act as becomes us; let us act as it becomes the great institutions bequeathed us. Let us find out if there are moral influences here, and show that we are not representatives of fanatics."[1]

[1] *Congressional Globe,* January 16, 1845, p. 146.

It was not to be expected that a House of Representatives under Southern influence would expel two Southern representatives for engaging in a practice sanctioned by Southern sentiment. Political considerations also influenced Northern members who were closely allied with their colleagues on the slavery issue. Obviously, it was impossible for this House to take an heroic course, whatever it pretended its sentiments were. The wonder is that the resolutions obtained as large a vote as they did. The record was 102 against 86. The individual record is not given in the official report of the debate, which is inadequate in all respects, often leaving the reader in doubt as to the meaning of the speakers. Mr. Hamlin won a moral victory in obtaining so large a vote for his resolutions ; but it was useless for him to continue agitation on the subject, and with the announcement of the vote the Yancey-Clingman duel was dropped. But Mr. Hamlin's speech, although not intended as an oratorical effort, but as a manly protest against a barbarous practice, attracted a great deal of attention at the time throughout the country, and was one of the many things that established him firmly in the esteem of people who value public men for their strength of character, purity of principles, and genuine humanity, rather than for brilliancy of intellect and accomplishments of partisan leadership. Among Mr. Hamlin's associates who held the same views he did of moral questions, this arraignment of dueling strengthened him, and he was accepted as a coming leader of great measures.

Before dismissing this episode in Mr. Hamlin's life, it is interesting to recall the fact that when legislation failed to suppress dueling among congressmen, ridicule became an effective weapon against it and supplemented the moral argument. This was the natural course of events, for ridicule follows denunciation as a factor in a movement against an evil. About this time an incident occurred that was one of several which turned the laugh of the nation on "knights of chivalry," whose ideas of honor and courage were as absurd as their practices were unfair and dangerous. Joshua R. Giddings was challenged to fight a duel, and in accepting named raw cowhides as the weapons, and as conditions stipulated that he and his challenger should tie their left thumbs together and lash each other until one should die under the whip. Now, considering the fact that Mr. Giddings was not a practiced shot, while his challenger was an experienced marksman, Giddings's proposition was on the whole the fairer. For a duelist to ask a man unaccustomed to the use of a rifle or pistol to fight him was tantamount to asking him to stand up and be shot in order that the former might satisfy his ideas of honor and vindicate his courage. Giddings had the advantage of weight and height, but it does not follow that he would have had the greater advantage in the end in a duel with cowhides, because his challenger was a slaveholder.

More incidents happened that placed Southern duelists in the position of would-be tragedians in burlesque. One affair of this sort nearly extinguished Roger A. Pryor in a gale of laughter which swept over the North. He "called out" John Fox Potter, a native of Maine and a representative from Wisconsin. Potter accepted the challenge, and with pretended savageness chose bowie knives as the weapons. This was the *reductio ad absurdum* of the code; but affairs had not progressed to that stage in 1845 when Mr. Hamlin attacked dueling, and his speech remains a part of the suasive movement to kill the barbaric custom.

CHAPTER XII

THERE was a strange crossing of political interests and a singular reversal of fortunes when James K. Polk became President of the United States on March 4, 1845. Martin Van Buren made Mr. Polk speaker of the House in 1835, and John C. Calhoun, the bitter personal enemy of Jackson and Van Buren, made him President. Yet, Mr. Polk was also a protégé of Old Hickory; and as Clay was his opponent, Jackson roused himself in his last days to secure a final triumph over his rival. Jackson's friendship for Polk made him a "Young Hickory" in the eyes of his party, and the feeling for him that this created was no doubt a factor in electing him President. Mr. Polk's good fortune did not stop with the success of his campaign, for coming to the presidency in a period of great activity and development, he is remembered now as the Executive of one of the most important administrations in the history of the government. Mr. Polk was a pleasant man to meet; he was exceedingly courteous, of a rather grave demeanor and striking appearance, with his silver hair falling to his shoulders. One of the most industrious of presidents, Mr. Polk was nevertheless always accessible to members of Congress, and very patient. His private character was irreproachable, and his well-known piety won him the confidence of the conservative people of the country. He was not a great man; but while he was thoroughly subservient to the slave power, he was sincere in believing that slavery was a blessing, and honestly deprecated agitation of the subject. He was much the superior of Pierce or Buchanan, although he marred his administration by his complicity in the conspiracy to bring on the Mexican war.

The Twenty-ninth Congress was a more intellectual body than its predecessor. In the Senate the Whigs were strengthened by the return of Webster in full possession of his great powers; of John M. Clayton, an able and upright statesman of Delaware; of John Davis, one of the purest men Massachusetts ever sent to the Senate; and by the acquisition of Thomas Corwin, of Ohio, the most brilliant platform orator of his time; Reverdy Johnson, the distinguished jurist of Maryland. The Democrats, on the other hand, were reinforced by the return of John C. Calhoun in the zenith of his power and fame;

by the appearance of General Lewis Cass, who was to be the Democratic candidate for President four years later; by Simon Cameron, the shrewdest political manager of his day; and of Daniel S. Dickinson, an able pro-slavery man of New York, and John A. Dix.

The anti-slavery group in the House was increased by the appearance of several Northern men who achieved distinction, or made creditable records. One was David Wilmot, of Pennsylvania, whose name is perpetuated in the famous anti-slavery proviso. He was of splendid physique, had sound common sense, coolness, and persistence. He quickly associated himself with Mr. Hamlin, Judge Brinkerhoff, Preston King, and their friends, and was a popular member of their circle. A prominent figure was Edward D. Baker, of Illinois, "The eloquent Baker," as he was affectionately called by his admirers. He was, indeed, one of the most brilliant champions of freedom the North produced in *ante-bellum* days, and fell at the head of his troops at Ball's Bluff. It is an interesting circumstance that Baker had obtained his nomination for Congress in a contest with Abraham Lincoln. A cool, well-balanced, and popular anti-slavery man who took his seat in this House was George Ashmun, of Massachusetts, who presided over the Republican National Convention of 1860. A newcomer from Vermont, who attained international distinction as a linguist, writer, and diplomat, was George P. Marsh. Another Vermont man of honorable record was Paul Dillingham, Jr., who served the Green Mountain State as its war governor, with credit to his State and himself. The new representatives from Maine were Cullen Sawtelle, J. F. Scammon, and Hezekiah Williams, friends of Mr. Hamlin, especially Mr. Sawtelle, who was long active among Mr. Hamlin's most trusted associates in his political career. Of historic interest was the entrance in this House of Allen G. Thurman, "The Old Roman of Ohio," with whom Mr. Hamlin formed a lifelong friendship, and with whom he retired from public life thirty-five years later.

The picturesque group of coming Confederate leaders, which was partially formed in the preceding House, was completed by the appearance of Jefferson Davis, Robert Toombs, and James A. Seddon. The future president of the Confederacy was tall, of commanding appearance, and of the manner of one born to lead. Able, forceful, scholarly, and courteous, Davis soon made himself felt, and was recognized as a coming aspirant for the robes of John C. Calhoun. In marked contrast to Mr. Davis was Alexander H. Stephens, the future vice-president of the Confederacy, small, emaciated, sprung from the people, self-educated, but able, resourceful, and adroit. "Bob" Toombs embodied the arrogant, truculent, and aggressive spirit of extreme Southern sentiment. His black hair stood up all over his head, and his eyes flashed when he was stirred. He was very effective in debate, and a daring leader ; yet his best qualities are forgotten, and although he denied the story, Toombs goes down in history as the man who made the foolish boast that he would call the roll of his slaves at the foot of Bunker Hill Monument. Mr. Hamlin affirmed the truth of the incident, but said that Toombs did not use the exact words attributed to him. Howell Cobb, who was forging to the front as a candidate for speaker in the next House, was, on the other hand, the personification of the *bonhommie*, generosity, and true courage of the South. There were few men who could not like Howell Cobb ; of all Southern men Mr. Hamlin knew in the House, he liked Howell Cobb best. Henry W. Hilliard, a new member from Alabama, who achieved some distinction under the Confederacy, and afterwards served the national government with credit as its minister to Brazil, was another Southern leader with whom Mr. Hamlin entertained pleasant relations.

The House was organized by the election of John W. Davis, of Indiana, as speaker. Mr. Hamlin's status among his party associates may be judged by the fact that he was appointed chairman of the Committee on Elections and a member of the Committee on Rules. After the House had perfected its organization, it plunged into the Oregon question, which would admit of no further delay. This marked the beginning of an open conflict between the champions of freedom and slavery, and American and British diplomacy, which now reads like a romance. If inheritance, discovery, exploration, and survey constitute a better claim to territory, rather than pretension based on false evidence and occupation under permission, then all of the land on the Pacific slope which was then called Oregon belonged to this nation. This embraced what is now included in the States of Oregon and Washington, and British Columbia, and Great Britain claimed it all except the lower part of the present State of Oregon, without the shadow of a legal title to it. The energy and patriotism of the Northern Democracy saved Washington and half of Oregon to this country ; the slave power betrayed the territory that is now British Columbia into the hands of the English government, and would have fastened its "peculiar institution" on Oregon had it not been defeated by the same men who rescued this territory from the other danger. Mr. Hamlin was on Oregon's side in her long struggle for her rights and liberty, and thus the story can be repeated because it has a personal interest in these pages.

The history of England's pretensions to Oregon brings out more clearly the duplicity of the slave power, because it indirectly and secretly supported claims that were at best but a tissue of ingenious versions of the exploits of English adventurers and explorers, and thus morally proves that the slave power opposed the reoccupation of

Oregon, because it was unwilling to risk a controversy with Great Britain which might prevent it from engaging the United States in a land-grabbing war with Mexico. Here are the facts.[1] Oregon was discovered and occupied by the Spanish. In consequence of a collision at Nootka Sound between Spanish and English sailors, Spain allowed Great Britain the rights of trade in Oregon, but yielded no rights of sovereignty in the territory. Charles James Fox, in a satirical speech in Parliament, demonstrated the substantial worth of the Nootka treaty when he asked what had England actually gained from the convention that she did not possess before. In 1819 the United States came into amicable possession of the Spanish lands in this country and also their titles. The year before, the United States and Great Britain had agreed on the forty-ninth parallel as their boundary line from the Lake of the Woods to the Rocky Mountains. As Spain then claimed some sovereignty in Oregon, our government and England agreed to leave the Oregon boundary line unfixed, and to occupy the territory jointly for ten years. The reservation was that the joint occupancy should not enter into the final settlement of the boundary line, and that it should be terminated only when one of the contracting parties gave twelve months' notice.

For this reason the question did not come up again until 1827–28. Now, for many years Great Britain had been carrying out her well-known land-seizing policy in Oregon, through the instrumentality of the Hudson Bay Fur Company. This company had pushed its way down through Oregon to the Columbia River, erecting forts and settlements which bore the British flag. When the boundary question arose in 1827–28, Great Britain, feeling secure in her position, since there were few American citizens in Oregon, and the attention of our government was given to more serious matters than the adjustment of a boundary line on an extreme western frontier, claimed territory in Oregon as far south as the Columbia River. The utter worthlessness of Great Britain's pretensions are easily recognized. One claim was based on the assertion that Vancouver discovered the Columbia River. The fact was, Vancouver himself, in an honorable statement, gave the credit of the discovery to Captain John Gray, of Boston, the first man to carry the American flag around the world. Another equally false pretension was that McKenzie had explored Oregon. The fact was, he did not cross the Rocky Mountains, whereas Lewis and Clarke surveyed Oregon under the direction of President Jefferson. A more preposterous claim to British sovereignty was that the Nootka convention gave the British govern-

---

[1] The chief authorities consulted are the speeches by John Quincy Adams and others in the House and the *History of Oregon and California* by Robert Greenhow (1845).

ment full right to Oregon. The fact was, a war occurred between England and Spain in 1796, shortly after the adoption of the Nootka convention, which circumstance, according to English precedents, destroyed the treaty. A final incident may be cited to show how weak England's title to what is now the State of Washington, and more than half of Oregon, was in her own eyes. In 1827 the life of the nation was still east of the Alleghany Mountains, and the government, not appreciating the value of Oregon, offered to compromise with Great Britain on the forty-ninth parallel; but the British government, realizing the value of delay, refused to accept this offer, in hope that it might ultimately acquire all the land north of the Columbia River. Yet, twenty years later, Great Britain yielded these claims, and accepted the forty-ninth parallel as the boundary line.

In 1835 the tide of emigration rolled into Oregon, and American citizens found themselves living in an American country under the jurisdiction of a foreign power. They began to petition Congress to fix a boundary line, and extend United States laws over them. The Democratic party responded to their petitions, and on this issue won the sympathies of the North. With the return of the Twenty-eighth Congress to Washington, after the triumphant election of Mr. Polk, the Northern leaders of the Democracy prepared to redeem the Democracy's pledges to Oregon, and planned to pass a resolution giving Great Britain the twelve months' notice to terminate the treaty of joint occupation of Oregon. Mr. Hamlin made an incisive speech, urging Congress to take immediate action, and there was an interesting debate that, however, is now important only as a prelude to a great contest which followed in the next Congress. No one can doubt the sincerity of the leaders of the Northern Democracy in insisting that their party should fulfill its pledges. Their anger, chagrin, and dismay may easily be imagined, therefore, when they detected signs that the Southern leaders of the Democracy intended to betray the party if they could. The fact transpired that the day the Democratic National Convention affirmed that our claim to all of Oregon up to 54° 40' was clear and unquestionable, Mr. Calhoun, as secretary of state, was secretly negotiating with Great Britain to compromise on the forty-ninth parallel. Taking their cue from Calhoun, the leaders of the slave power began to change base on the Oregon question. The resolutions to give Great Britain the treaty notice was not passed, and the Twenty-eighth Congress expired under these conditions.

This breach of faith aroused great indignation among the Northern Democrats, and the war feeling against Great Britain which arose grew out of their anger over their betrayal; and was an intimation to the slave power that the Northern Democrats were fiercely in earnest over the Oregon question. The Twenty-ninth Congress convened under these circumstances, with a considerable war party in it led by General Cass. President Polk opened the question in his annual message, in which he reaffirmed our rights to Oregon in plain but dignified, courageous terms. The next crucial move was made by General Cass, who introduced in the Senate a resolution instructing the military and naval committees to investigate their departments and ascertain their condition. This was a significant expression of the war feeling of the hour. The debate that followed breathed war, and the Democratic press teemed with declarations of hostility to Great Britain. The natural consequence was that there was an outburst of ill-feeling in England. Lord Palmerston, the leader of the opposition, characterized the President's message as bluster, and Sir Robert Peel and other leaders in Parliament avowed Great Britain's determination to maintain her claims in Oregon. Thus a war scare arose, and the leaders of the slave party were quick to take advantage of the opportunity to array the conservative element of the country against a controversy with England, by emphasizing the horrors of war, although they had deliberately pursued a course towards Mexico that was destined to plunge the country into war with that nation. The Whigs embodied the conservative spirit of the country, and thus the slave party had respectable and powerful allies. But there was a large and strong party in Congress led by no less a man than John Quincy Adams, who favored giving the treaty notice to Great Britain, and did not believe that England would go to war over the Oregon question. Mr. Hamlin stood with Mr. Adams.

Mr. Adams's position is the best authority the history of the times affords of the legality of our title to all of Oregon. Both as secretary of state and President, he had dealt with the Oregon boundary-line question, and urged our title up to 54° 40'. He was the best representative of his day of the educated conscience of the nation. He knew we were right in the Oregon controversy; his vast experience in diplomacy taught him the value of British bluster. Nominally a Whig, Mr. Adams broke away from his party on this occasion, and in a unique speech proved that the American title to 54° 40' was "clear and unquestionable." Mr. Adams's position is strengthened by the fact that it cost him an election to the United States Senate. The incident is, therefore, another measure of his devotion to principle and truth. His speech was most embarrassing to the slave party; but, having made up their minds to retreat from the declaration of the Baltimore convention, the leaders continued their tactics of opposition. A speech by R. Barnwell Rhett, of South Carolina, illustrated these tactics. Rhett was an adept in raising hair-splitting questions.

His speech was an ingenious tissue of quibbles, evasions, and insinuations. Evidently it was Rhett's purpose to embroil the Northern and Southern wings of the Democracy in a controversy in the hopes of weakening the former. But by an unlucky chance he indirectly insinuated that John Quincy Adams served only the interests of New England by charging him with opposing the war of 1812, and voting against the granting of supplies to our troops. The old Puritan completely exposed Rhett's malice, and floored him at one blow, by simply stating the fact that he was out of the country at the time as the United States minister to Russia.

When the debate was resumed, Rhett regained his courage, and renewed the charge against Mr. Adams. But the old lion was ready this time for the whole slave party. Mr. Adams was always at his best in debate when his temper was at white heat. Then he forged thunderbolts.[1] Rhett's attack induced Mr. Adams to explain his position in the war of 1812, and as he reached the climax, he declared impressively that he did not believe there would be war between Great Britain and the United States, even if our government should send troops to Oregon the day after the treaty notice was served on England. He followed up this assertion with a vehement and positive charge that he apprehended other circumstances would prevent a war, "the ultimate backing out of the present administration and its supporters from the ground they have taken." This was the first time the slave party in the House had been squarely told to its face what its opponents suspected of its purposes in the Oregon matter, and pandemonium reigned for a few moments.

Speeches that were made by other members of the slave party were more adroit than Rhett's, though aimed at the same object, and following the same lines, emphasizing the horrors of an armed conflict, as if one was certain to be provoked should the United States reoccupy Oregon. Yancey, of Alabama, spoke eloquently on the subject of war, and, in denying that the nation's honor demanded that it should insist on its rights in Oregon, alluded to honor as that "blood-stained god at whose red altar sit war and homicide," regardless of the fact that he himself had recently worshiped at that altar in an affair of honor. Toombs, of Georgia, made a speech in opposition to giving the treaty notice to England, basing his reasons on his alleged belief that the United States did not hold title to the limit the government claimed, in spite of the fact that all the best authorities in the country supported the claim, whether or not they were prepared to enforce it. Toombs followed up this line of argument with a crafty and plausible indorsement of a suggestion of Henry W. Hilliard, of Alabama, which had the merit of sincerity, that power be delegated to the

---

[1] Mr. Hamlin's description.

President to settle the controversy with England by negotiation, a plan that would obviously suit the slave party's desire for delay. These tactics moved Mr. Hamlin to speak out his mind, and obtaining the floor after Toombs, he made a speech that was a calm survey of the situation in the House and the country and a patriotic appeal to the House to perform its duty.   As an oratorical effort it was the best of Mr. Hamlin's early service in Congress, and discloses ideas of form and symmetry which are absent from the practical and plain style of address he finally chose in speaking before the people.   Mr. Hamlin began his remarks by making a respectful recognition of John Quincy Adams's speech, and by corroborating the veteran's charge that the war-cry was raised to defeat the treaty notice resolutions. Mr. Hamlin said : —

"I come to the consideration of the question before us, I trust, with a full understanding of its momentous importance, and of the magnitude of the interests that are committed to our hands to be affected for weal or for woe by the right or wrong decision we make.   The eyes of twenty millions of people are watching our action here, and the hearts of twenty millions of freemen are beating with anxiety as to the action we shall finally take.   It has been well said by the venerable gentleman from Massachusetts (John Quincy Adams) that, for the years that are to come, there would not be a question submitted to the American Congress equal in its importance, equal in its moment.

"But proceeding directly to the subject, I design to refer, and in a few remarks to reply, to . . . gentlemen who have preceded me in this debate. . . . . 'War,' 'war,' has been shouted within these walls and echoed over our vast country to react on this body. . . . I care not whether these shouts of war were manufactured here or elsewhere ; I shall not be diverted from my path of duty by that stale and senseless cry.   I have heard it before, and upon this subject a year ago at the other end of the Capitol. When it was there, it was the same master spirit that raised this cry of 'war,' 'war,' to defeat this measure.   Why is it gentlemen assume this position, a position which the facts do not justify?   Rome had her Punic war ; it is reserved for us to have our panic war.

"Let us examine the position of the question before us.   In 1818 a certain convention was entered into between the respective governments of the United States and Great Britain, relative to the territory upon our northwest coast known as the Oregon Territory.   That treaty was by its own limitations to remain in force but ten years.   In 1827 it was renewed by a treaty which was to be terminated whenever either of the two high contracting parties should give twelve months' notice of its desire to terminate it.

"And now, forsooth, because we come here in the way marked out by the treaty, to exercise the power thus especially provided for in the treaty, we are to be met as the war party.   I repel the imputation, and I hurl it back again.   It is that very cry in and of itself that tends more to produce a war than any other course. Which course can be taken here? We on this side of the House are the peace party. Timid counsels tend to war; 'fear admitted to our councils betrays like treason.'

"I cannot sympathize, then, with gentlemen who use this argument, although they may use it honestly; nor will I permit it to divert this discussion, so far as I am concerned, from its true and legitimate track; we ask nothing on this side of the House but the exercise of our constitutional rights; rights that are pointed out and defined by this very treaty under which we are acting. And is it true that the exercise of these rights, as we propose it, is any cause of war, — No, sir. 'Old men see visions, and young men dream dreams,' the gentleman from Virginia (Mr. Hunter) tells us, and, my word for it, it was but the dream of the gentleman's waking hours when he made the anti-war speech, — or calculated to be a war measure? While with gentlemen in all parts of the House I most cheerfully concur that peace is to be desired above everything else save the preservation of our national rights and our national honor, I do not hold war to be an evil from which we should shrink, when the preservation of our national rights and our national honor demand it. . . .

"There is another remark to which I must allude. Too often within these walls, in the discussion of various measures, I have heard taunts and reproaches, either directly or by implication, cast upon various sections of this Union; and when they have been directed to that section where it is my pleasure and pride to reside, I have felt a thrill along my nerves like an electric shock, and the impulses of my heart have been on my lips, to hurl them back again. But time and reflection have chastened my feelings, and I passed them by in sorrow that they should come from the lips of any individual on this floor; and while it is my glory and my pride to be an inhabitant of that section whose motives have been so often questioned here, I have a single word to say in behalf of that people. I have no objections to interpose here in defense of what may have been errors or the wickedness of her politicians; but in behalf of her citizens I have a word to say. I believe them to be as patriotic as any other class of citizens in our Union. They have exhibited their patriotism and their valor on many a well-fought field. Their bones have bleached on many a Northern hill, and the barren sands of the South have drunk their best blood.

"Sir, I point you with pride to the North, and invite you there to witness a system which has grown up with us, and which is our ornament. I point you to our system of free labor. I point you to our common schools, to our churches with their spires pointing toward heaven, and I glory in them. They are the monuments that belong to a people who have the true spirit of citizens of a free government. But I stop not there; I ask you to go with me throughout this broad nation. I point you to her — I point you to the whole Union — as a monument of political grandeur towering towards the heavens — upon which the friend of freedom, wherever upon our globe he may be, may gaze; around whose higher summit the sunlight of glory forever shines, and at whose base a free people repose, and I trust forever will repose. So much for New England, my home. So much for the Union, my country. . . .

"If there is a single duty which arises over, above, and beyond all others, it is that of the American republic to afford protection to every American citizen wherever he may be found on American soil. It is one of the highest duties incident to the charge committed to their hands; wherever our nation's flag floats upon the breeze, it should be a certain index of ample protection to the American citizen in all his rights of person and property. Why is it true that in the nineteenth century, which we believe to be the best the world has ever seen, the cry, 'I am an American citizen,' shall not be as sure a safeguard and a pledge of protection as the cry, 'I am a Roman citizen,' was in the palmy days of Rome?

"It was said by an ancient philosopher that the government which feels most sensibly, and which redresses most promptly, every injury visited by a foreign power upon its most humble citizen has but only discharged the duties incumbent upon it. And is it not so? What in a greater degree than the strict discharge of its duty to its citizens will call forth their affections and their loyalty, and will draw them forth to protect the institutions and defend the standard of their common country in the hour of their common perils? . . .

"How then is our government to extend that protection and that aid which are required from it to its citizens — to those wanderers to the distant portion of its territory westward of the Rocky Mountains? Sir, those citizens have been wrested from American soil to be tried for alleged offenses by foreign law. They have been dragged from their peaceful homes — from their own domestic firesides — and have been tried and held amenable to the laws of the British provinces, and here in the nineteenth century, from this stale clamor of war ringing in our ears, are we to stop and fold our arms about us, and say, We will pause awhile before we give this notice — we may rouse the lion from his lair — England, with her chain of military posts around the world, may be aroused — and we do not precisely foresee what will be the consequences?

"No, the notice should be given now, and protection to American citizens should be extended wherever they are found on American soil. And then that flag that has been borne aloft in triumph in the battle and in the breeze, upon the ocean and upon the lakes, the emblem of protection to each and every one of our citizens, will float forever over the homes of a free and happy people. That flag which now

"'So proudly drinks the morning light,
        O'er ocean wave, in foreign clime,
        A symbol of our might.'

"This faithful discharge of governmental duties will be one of the strongest arguments in favor of the advancement of the principles of our own free government. The feeling of every citizen, that protection in person and property is secured to him by the laws and by the flag of his country, will serve more surely than aught else to extend and widen our broad domain. Let it be done, and our government will pursue its onward course by its moral power, until it shall extend from the Isthmus of Darien to the frozen regions of the North — from the rough, rock-bound coast of the Atlantic, back to the gentle murmurs of the Pacific. Then, in the inimitable language of our own distinguished poet, —

> " 'Wide shall our own free race increase,
> And wide extend the elastic chain
> That binds in everlasting peace
> State after State — a mighty train.'

" Oregon is ours, it belongs to us, and the question of title I have no disposition here to examine. It has been thoroughly and ably examined by those who are in authority, and the result has been presented to the American republic. I have no disposition to go into that examination. I should be well satisfied to rest myself on him who may well be considered the Achilles in this question in the position that our title was better than that of England. It was more, it was a perfect title. This being our territory, then by the laws and rules established by Great Britain herself, let us examine into its importance in a commercial point of view.

" We have been told, on another occasion, within these walls, that it was necessary to extend our public domain in the southwest, for the purpose of securing to our country a monopoly of the cotton-growing interest ; and the argument was as broad as the Union ; it came home to the feelings, to the interests, and to the principles of action of the representatives from every section of our country. Let us weigh by the same rules — the rules established on that occasion — the commercial considerations involved in this question. The Northern and Middle States are essentially manufacturing States, — the Northern States particularly ; they are situated in a high latitude, under a forbidding climate, and yet they have the industry of their citizens, the water-power and the facilities given them by nature, to render them a manufacturing people. The South, the sunny South, may grow the staple product of the country, and the West may be the granary not only of our own country, but — give it an outlet — the granary of the world. Then I say, — in a commercial point of view, — this matter comes home to the feelings and interests of every citizen of every section of our widely extended country. The North must necessarily be the manufacturing section of the Union. Let them have an outlet ; let there be an easy mode of transportation and communication to the far West, and we would become the manufacturers almost of the world. The Northern and Middle States must be that portion of the Union which will supply not only India, but China, and all the Eastern portions of the world, with their manufactured articles. But I do not stop here. The matter comes home equally to the interests of the South, because for the supply of those manufactured articles, the South would be called upon for their staple, for increased production of their staple, which in its manufactured form is thus destined to find its way to the markets of the East. It is a question in which the West has no right to assume a particular interest. It is a question that comes home equally to the North, South, East, and West. It is a great national question, co-extensive with our Union. Why! we are already opening our markets in the East. We have already established our treaty stipulations with China. We have already sent our cotton and manufactured goods into the Eastern empire. Last year more than six millions of dollars of American manufactured goods were sent to the Eastern continent, and of that amount four million dollars is believed to have been of cotton goods. We have opened the Chinese market; and in opening that market, with the advance which commerce will give in that distant portion of the globe to civilization, to refinement, and to Christianity, we have opened a market which will call for untold millions of the manufactured articles of the Northern and Middle States — manufactured from the staple of the South.

"Besides, the commerce of the North is deeply interested in the whaling ships. The ocean is now covered with nearly seven hundred ships and half a hundred smaller vessels, manned by more than 20,000 of our citizens, who are sending home as the fruits of their labor more than 3,000,000 gallons of oil annually. The trade between the United States and the East Indies is already very important. But it will be vastly increased when we shall find a route for that trade overland to the Pacific and across that ocean to India. Wherever the people of the East have become enlightened by commercial intercourse with us, she will consume a vast quantity of our products, while they will supply us liberally with theirs. Who can tell what uncounted millions of manufactured goods from the United States will be marketed in the East Indies? Commerce is therefore greatly interested in preserving the integrity of our domain. I would gladly pursue this subject farther, if time were allowed, and show that this question is one which concerns the commerce of the whole country, and that the whole people of the United States are interested in it. But I am limited in time, and cannot pursue the subject in all its details.

"I am in favor of giving this notice, as I have already declared. I am still in favor of giving it. For this course I will give reasons. First, I trusted that by giving the notice, the danger of delay and of obstruction in our councils would be obviated. The gentleman who immediately preceded me in the debate (Mr. Toombs) preferred the amendment of the gentleman from Alabama (Mr. Hilliard), which leaves it discretionary with the President to give notice at such time as he may see fit.

"This will lead to serious difficulties. I will say that this proposition came with no good design, so far as I can judge of it, though I have no doubt of the honorable motives of the gentleman who offered it. It will change the issue that ought to be made. Instead of inquiring whether we would act now, we would, by this course, give a discretionary power to the Executive to act or not, and either now or at a later period. Some would think that the President had acted too soon, if he acted now; others would think he had acted too late, if he postponed it. It would give an opportunity to many to shelter themselves from responsibility, and to reproach the President with having acted out of time.

"The true question is, whether we should give the notice now. Shall we assume the responsibility of action or throw it on the President? That is an important question. Why should not we take upon ourselves the responsibility of action in the matter?

"Many gentlemen wished to shift the responsibility from themselves; and then, if the President should act promptly they would say that he had let slip the golden moment. Why, if the subject had been referred to us, and if the power belonged to us, should we not exercise the power and give the notice at once? If there was any advantage in giving the notice at all, it was proper to give it at the earliest moment, without loss of time. If we do not give it now, in what position shall we be left? The whole subject would be suffered to take its chance without an effort on our part to maintain our rights. I know that it has been recommended to us to adopt 'a wise and masterly inactivity' — that was to do nothing. I should rather call it masterly duplicity, or masterly dishonesty, to take measures in an indirect way, to get possession of the country without suffering our object to be known. How long do gentlemen wish to carry on this masterly duplicity? Some of them have fixed a limit to it of twenty years. Sir, I have a single idea on that point. We have told our people that they might occupy that country. Are they to be thus encouraged to go there and settle, and yet not be entitled to our protection? If you do not take them under your wing can you expect to retain their affection? No. They would be faithless to themselves if they gave you any confidence or affection after such treatment. As well might a mother expect the love of her children whom she repelled from her bosom, and cast out into the world without protection. It would be a most unnatural mother that would cast off her children, as we would do, were we not to give this notice. Should we acquire a colony by this course of masterly dishonesty, it would make us the reproach of all nations. There is one thing in the British government which I admire, much as I despise all the vanity about her power, and greatness, and glory. I admire it for one special quality — its care of its subjects. It gives protection to its subjects all over the world. Wherever the subject of England might be, he is covered with the protection of British laws and British power. This, in my opinion, is an example worthy of imitation.

"I will go a step farther than the notice, and extend the protection of our laws over our citizens in Oregon. If we do not we shall fall short of our duty. After doing this, I would go still farther, and create those bands of iron which will bind indissolubly together in our Union the people of the Atlantic and the people of the Pacific. I would go for a railroad across the Rocky Mountains — for annihilating time and space between us and the inhabitants of the Pacific coast. From a military point of view, this railroad would be necessary. We would be obliged, for the protection and defense of the country, to establish this mode of communication. While it would afford military protection for the defense of the country, it would be the means of creating a vast trade between the Eastern and Western portions of the continent. The immediate consequence of such a trade will be to open a traffic in our manufactures with the people of the East Indies; next, we shall be able to drive out all competition on the part of the British fabrics in that lucrative and important trade.

"We would by means of this overland communication soon be able to create immense commercial depots on the coast of the Pacific. We could make voyages to the East Indies in half the time that Great Britain could. Our manufactures would thus compete in that important and increasing market with those of Great Britain, and, indeed, drive out all competition, and thus they would become established on a firm foundation, without the aid of a black tariff to maintain them.

"I have always opposed internal improvements by the general government, but I would adopt this improvement as a military work — one necessary for the public defense, though it would be used for civil and commercial purposes. Should the United States delay to do their duty to their citizens in Oregon, the British government would avail itself of the delay to take measures for securing the territory to its subjects. Great Britain has already, by force and fraud, covered the world with more than a hundred colonies. She has done this by blood and carnage, and in violation of the rights of all nations with which she has been connected as an ally, or opposed to as a foe.

"The history of India will tell the whole story. In the year 1600, during the reign of Queen Elizabeth, a charter for commercial purposes was granted to some private trading adventures. This company have spread death and desolation over the East. Under Warren Hastings every crime, every species of perfidy and cruelty and rapine, was perpetrated for the acquisition of territory and of wealth by the company. So fearful and prodigious was his rapacity and cruelty that he became the theme of universal execration by orators and poets. It has been remarked in one of the invectives against him that when some wretch, laden with horrid crimes without a name, should stalk through earth, and we want curses for him —

> "'We'd torture thought to curse the wretch,
> And then to damm him most supreme
> We'd call him Hastings.'

"It would be easy to run a parallel between the East India Company and the Hudson Bay Company. It would show us the necessity of taking hold of this matter in due time, and of giving this notice now.

"Government after government has submitted to British power in the East, — some being reduced by fraud and treachery, and others by force, — until now the population brought under sway amounts to more than a hundred millions. I would be glad to trace the progress of this government in the East Indies; but not having time I would say, from beginning to end it is stamped with infamy. I call the attention of the committee to these facts, in order to show that, unless we give the notice, the Hudson Bay Company, which is formed upon principles akin to that in the East, will, by gradual encroachments, become possessed of all the strong positions in Oregon, and be more difficult to dislodge. We might find a parallel in their progress to the corporation that has so long oppressed and devastated the East. By what waters were the Hudson Bay Company originally bounded? By those waters that emptied into Hudson's Bay. But still that company had by virtue of a connection with the Northwestern Company stretched across to the Pacific. It is the policy of Great Britain to plant and maintain colonies ; and one of the modes of doing it is to operate through chartered companies. This policy she is now applying to the Territory of Oregon ; and it will succeed there, as well as it has elsewhere, unless we interfere in behalf of our settlers to protect them, and give the notice of the termination of the joint convention.

" No longer ago than the year 1790, the British government claimed the right to make settlements on the Pacific coast, north of the Spanish settlements. Delay has taken place on the other side, and encroachments of Great Britain have not been observed. At length Great Britain has not only made settlements above the oldest Spanish settlements, but also far below them, and has now come down to the Columbia River. Originally her territorial pretensions were only to points beyond the oldest Spanish settlements, but soon she will come down to forty-seven. [A member here said, ' She is really there now.']

" Yes, sir ; she will soon be there, even if she is not there now. What, then, can be gained by delaying the notice, which is the only means by which we can arrest her progress ? While men talk of war, — which still only exists in the visions of old men, and the dreams of young ones, — while this bugbear is held up, we are losing the opportunity to secure for ourselves and our children an important and valuable country. What will arise is only an inference on the part of these gentlemen. They have not shown how it will arise. They have not shown us the *modus operandi*. But we well know that the British pretensions will be strengthened by eternal delay. The longer we delay the notice, the more arrogant will the British pretensions become. One point more. ' Our old men,' the gentleman from Virginia says, ' see visions, our young men dream dreams.' I am not old, and I can see visions ; and the dreams I leave to the gentleman from Virginia. Let those who dream, imagine that a war will arise from our assertion of our rights ; I do not believe it. But the vision I see is that of a populous and enterprising State on the Pacific slope, with manufactures, and commerce, and navigation. The waters rushing down to the Pacific will turn thousands of wheels and spindles.

" Our people will move to that region, and carry with them all their arts and skill, in all the various branches of manufactures which they have established in this region. In due time they will supply a large portion of America, as well as Asia, with their fabrics. It will not be long before our settlement will extend down to the Mexican boundary. I appeal to the gentlemen from the South to come to our rescue, and avail themselves of this fair opportunity to obtain Oregon. I ask your attention to the position we occupy before the American people and the world, in regard to this subject ; and assure you that for us there is no retreat from the responsibility of this act, without incurring the just reproach of the people of the United States, and, indeed, of the whole world. The Executive has presented his views to Congress, and has recommended to us the passage of the measure now before us. He has asked for our early action upon it.

The stale cry of war ought not to prevent us from discharging this duty, and if we should falter in performing it, we should be branded as unfaithful to our trust.

"The Executive has laid before us a statement of our just claims, showing that they have a solid and stable basis. The whole world will be convinced of their truth and justice ; and can an American Congress be found slow to defend and assert them ?

"I would appeal again to the South, and to the spirit of their fathers, of Sumter, Marion, and Pinckney, and call upon them to come up to this duty of defending our soil. Should fear of consequences prevent us from vindicating our rights from foreign aggression ? Should the horrors of war deter us from pursuing our line of duty? Will they not come up to the struggle, if need be, and like ' reapers descend to the harvest of death' ?

"True, the South has peculiar interests that would be hazarded in a war; but has not the whole Atlantic border a deep stake in the countenance of peace ? We, sir, in the Northeast have an extensive commerce. Our ships are found in every sea, and we have cities on the seaboard exposed to the assaults of an enemy. But, sir, we are willing to hazard everything in the defense of our country, and to lay all our wealth as an offering on the altar of the public safety. But who can believe, sir, that England will go to war because we do an act that we are entitled to do by treaty stipulations? This is too absurd an idea to be for a moment entertained by any one.

"But there is another view of the subject. I do not pretend to be a wizard, nor to foretell future events, but coming events sometimes cast their shadows before them. Judging of the future by the past, I would say the moral force of our institutions would spread them over every portion of this continent. Their progress is as certain as destiny. I cannot be mistaken in the idea that our flag is destined to shed its lustre over every hill and plain on the Pacific slope, and on every stream that mingles with the Pacific. What would monarchical institutions do ? what would tyrants do — in this age of improvement — this age of steam and electricity?

"The still small voice in our legislative halls and seminaries of learning would soon be reëchoed in distant lands. Shall we fold our hands and refuse, under all these circumstances, to discharge our duty? No, let us march steadily up to this duty, and discharge it like men, —

> "'And the gun of our nation's natal day
> At the rise and set of the sun
> Shall boom from the far Northeast away
> To the vales of Oregon.
> And ships on the seashore luff and tack,
> And send the peal of triumph back.'"[1]

Our rights to Oregon were set forth so clearly before the House that even Whigs, who had opposed the issue in the Polk campaign as a catch-vote device, came to the support of the treaty notice resolu-

[1] *Congressional Globe*, January 12, 1845–46, pp. 186–188.

tions, influenced, no doubt, by Mr. Adams's powerful and authoritative speech. The slave party practically abandoned the fight in the House, and yet Messrs. Yancey and Rhett, who had indorsed the Oregon declarations of the Democratic National Convention, continued to act in concert with Mr. Calhoun to the end, knowing that defeat awaited the resolutions in the Senate. But there were Southern Democrats who resented the attempt to betray their party. One was Jefferson Davis and another was Howell Cobb, who were conspicuous for their high sense of honor. Events had not yet come to pass that wrenched many a man from his anchorage. The support that Davis, Cobb, and their friends gave to the resolutions tends to heighten the duplicity of the slave party as exemplified in the course of Yancey and Rhett.

But if the weighty accusation made by Mr. Adams and supported by Mr. Hamlin and the action of members of the House in falsifying their positions are not conclusive evidence of the duplicity of the Calhoun party, its action in the Senate is final proof. Edward A. Hannegan, of Indiana, in a sharp retort to a Southern Democratic senator, told the truth about the slave party in these words: "If," said he, "Oregon were good enough for the production of sugar and cotton, it would not have encountered this opposition. Its possession would have been secured at once." The Senate defeated the blunt House resolutions by a vote of 32 to 22. An analysis of the vote shows that Mr. Calhoun drew away from the party, which had declared in its national convention that our claim in Oregon to 54° 40' was "clear and unquestionable," six Southern senators, who, with the Whigs, as the conservative element, accomplished the defeat of the measure. The reason given by these senators was the danger of war, and they were supported by Mr. Webster, although in his speech he neither denied nor affirmed the legality of our claim. If these defecting senators had stood by their party, the House resolutions would have passed the Senate, and all of Oregon would have been saved to the United States.

The refusal of the Senate to concur in the House resolutions provoked a storm of wrath in the Democratic party. A newspaper at Washington pointedly charged that secret caucuses were held by the Democratic and Whig senators, at the house of the British minister, for the purpose of arranging a compromise. The Senate appointed an investigating committee, which insisted that the editor should withdraw his charges under penalty of exclusion from the correspondents' galleries in both Houses of Congress. He refused, and submitted to the penalty rather than withdraw a charge that he believed to be true. But Mr. Calhoun and his supporters had won their point; they were soon able to wind up the Oregon affair and stop the administration in its straightforward course. Resolutions couched in diplomatic language and conciliatory in tone, authorizing the President, "at his discretion," to give Great Britain notice, were adopted as a substitute, and passed by the House through the mediation of a conference committee. This was a defeat for the House, for it was an intimation to Great Britain that the Senate would not support the House in its desire to take Oregon without further negotiation. Still, it had the saving grace of "the glue of compromise" that the American people then loved so well. Trusting in the President's sincerity, most Northern Democrats in the House, Mr. Hamlin among them, accepted the substitute, as did John Quincy Adams also. The substitute was passed by a large majority, and Mr. Buchanan, who was secretary of state, negotiated a treaty with England, fixing the boundary line on the forty-ninth parallel.

The recession of the House was called a disgraceful surrender by the satirical Whigs. But what else could be done with the conservative Whigs and Calhoun Democrats in control of the Senate? This incident in our history has been generally treated from the Whig point of view, and the course pursued by the slave party only faintly indicated. Mr. Blaine may be quoted in illustration, on page 55 of his "Twenty Years of Congress:" "It is not improbable that if the Oregon question had been allowed to rest for the time under the provisions of the treaty of 1827, the whole country would ultimately have fallen into our hands and the American flag might be waving to-day over British Columbia." But how is that theory tenable when Great Britain began steadily to work her way down in Oregon towards the Columbia after the adoption of that treaty? In 1844, the Hudson Bay Fur Company had erected as many as thirty settlements or outposts across Oregon, which were practically garrisons, and claimed territory below the Columbia River or nearly to the northern line of California. Gold was discovered in California only four years after England had claimed the Oregon territory, and if the boundary line had not been settled in 1846, the cupidity of the English government would never have allowed it to give up without a contest a foot of land in Oregon, a country that might yield it a rich harvest in the precious metal. Thus, in view of the discovery of gold in California, it was fortunate, indeed, that the Democratic party had the heart to listen to the prayers of the American citizen in Oregon in 1844, since a postponement of the question would more certainly have brought on a war with England in 1849 than reoccupation of Oregon in 1845, when nothing was known about the existence of gold on the Pacific slope. The Northern Democracy saved Washington and Oregon to the nation, opened up commerce with the East, encouraged the building of the Pacific Railroad, and perhaps averted greater trouble than the country incurred in 1844–45.

CHAPTER XIII

THE MEXICAN WAR

THE war with Mexico broke out on April 14, 1846, the day our government backed down and withdrew its claim to all of Oregon. It was as if fate wished to emphasize the apparent victory of the slave power and the humiliation of the anti-slavery Democrats. As the annexation of Texas was the cause of the war, the events that followed the reception of Texas into the Union seemed to be a natural consequence. It is useless to speculate on the course pursued by the Polk administration. This may have been designed to precipitate the outbreak of hostilities, and it may have been shaped according to the necessities of the times. The progress of events, however, appeared to give the administration a plausible pretext for adopting vigorous measures that led to the conflict. Mexico had never acknowledged the independence of Texas, although several foreign powers and the United States had recognized the Lone Star State as an independent power. When the United States took Texas into the Union, it therefore assumed all of Texas' grievances against Mexico. One was a long standing quarrel over the boundary line between the two countries. Texas asserted that it was the Rio Grande, while Mexico maintained that it was the River Nueces. There were frequent collisions in the disputed territory, and when Texas became a member of the Union her government naturally called on the administration to maintain her position. President Polk sent some troops under the command of General Zachary Taylor into the country of the Rio Grande, and their presence there infuriated the Mexicans. General Ampudia ordered General Taylor out of the country, and an encounter occurred in which several American officers and soldiers were killed. The news created great excitement throughout the United States. The cry was raised, "American blood has been shed on American soil." President Polk sent a message to Congress, declaring the existence of a state of war, and urging prompt action. Congress passed a bill empowering the President to call for 50,000 volunteers, and appropriated $10,000,000 to carry on the war.

The Mexican war threw an ominous light on the slave power, and also gave thinking men a clearer insight into the rôle, doctrines, and character of its leader, — John C. Calhoun. He was now at the zenith of his power and fame. Few men have had a stronger moulding influence on this country than Calhoun. He had a great mind, an iron will, wonderful prescience, and a unique personality. His grim features, surmounted by stiff, bristling, gray hair, seemed to have been stamped by an iron process. His powers of logic and the purity of his private life were conceded by his opponents. But the one fact above all else in Calhoun's career that stands out clearly now is that he was the genius of the slave power. It is logical to conclude, therefore, that if the master mind of that party conceived plans, and intrusted them for execution to the organization itself, he was fully aware of the responsibility he assumed. When Mr. Calhoun stood up in the Senate, and proclaimed his opposition to having a war with Mexico, it was his intention to clear his skirts of a war and a land-grabbing conspiracy for which he more than any other man was responsible. He was simply stating the abstract proposition that he did not like war. No doubt Mr. Calhoun would have preferred to have Mexico of her own accord contribute a large slice of her domain to this country for the mere asking. No doubt it would have been more agreeable to confine the war within Texan territory; but it was not, because it was a land-grabbing conspiracy to perpetuate the organization Mr. Calhoun adroitly directed. Moreover, if he had desired to avoid a war with Mexico, and had wished to annex Texas by peaceful means, he would never have allowed President Tyler in the last hour of his administration to send the articles of annexation to Texas without the Senate's peace-bearing clause. It is absurd to suppose for a moment that when Mr. Calhoun started the events in progress that led to the Mexican war, his wonderful prescience could not foresee the result. He was not in the Cabinet when the actual fighting began, and could apparently disclaim responsibility for it.

Calhoun's complicity in the plot to betray Oregon was a natural and necessary sequence to the part he played in planning the Mexican war. In colloquial parlance, Mr. Calhoun "buncoed" the North in sacrificing its interests. He was the master of the Democratic convention that nominated Polk on the Texas and Oregon platform. He kept secret his negotiations for a compromise with England until Polk was elected on the Oregon issue. While Mr. Calhoun pleaded the dangers of a conflict with England in the Oregon controversy as a pretext for withdrawing our claims, he pursued the opposite tactics in the case of Texas, and urged annexation on the ground that England might take Texas. He artfully stimulated the war scare to which Mr. Hamlin made allusion in his speech on Texas, by publishing his correspondence with Mr. King, our minister to France. Senator Hannegan was right when he charged in the Senate that if Oregon had been essential to the interests of the slave power, our claims to the entire territory would have been enforced.

But that for which history will most severely censure Calhoun is his authorship of the doctrine of state sovereignty, and the terrible results that sprung from it. To quote from an able and dispassionate critic of Calhoun, who, writing of his doctrine of nullification, said:[1] "It is not to be doubted that it sowed the seeds which in another generation produced the opinions that made the right of secession from the Union a firm political faith, which multitudes of men have sealed with their blood on the battlefields of a civil war."

The Mexican war also throws more light on Mr. Hamlin's Americanism and political principles. When the crisis came Mr. Hamlin deeply deplored the situation; in fact, he never ceased to regret the necessity of meeting Mexico on the battlefield, and said so in a speech he made half a century afterwards before a Grand Army reunion in Portland, Maine. Favoring the abstract proposition of the annexation of Texas, because he honestly believed that Texas had never belonged to Mexico, he opposed annexation under the terms and conditions arranged by the slave power, because they were not honorable, and were likely to lead to war with Mexico. But the beginning of actual hostilities changed the situation; an emergency was presented that required prompt action. Bitterly as he regretted the necessity of fighting Mexico, Mr. Hamlin felt with Decatur, when he said: "My country, right or wrong, always my country." He held that with the angered Mexicans preparing to shoot down American citizens, destroy property, and resist American laws in American territory, a congressman could no more properly refuse aid to the government than a physician could decline assistance to a man who had brought sickness on himself by some act of his own folly or wickedness. He voted for the war bill, and firmly supported the government. Only fourteen members of the House, the so-called fourteen immortals, and a few members of the Senate opposed the war. The Whigs, as a rule, sustained the government, because the nation's welfare demanded it. It was a trying position for Mr. Hamlin and congressmen who felt as he did, but they believed that they had a duty to perform, and however repugnant it was they discharged it.

While Mr. Hamlin upheld the administration in its general plan of war, he nevertheless had his ideas about the campaigns in Mexico and our military establishment, which he did not hesitate to urge on the government. An incident of this kind that is of importance to this record in its personal and political significance occurred in the winter of 1846–47. An anomalous condition of affairs existed. With a successful war going on the regular army fell off in numbers to

[1] George Ticknor Curtis in the *Life of Webster*, vol. i. p. 449.

10,000 men, and the administration could not recruit enough men to fill up the quota allowed by law, — 17,000 men. The reason was it was more popular to enlist in the volunteer branch of the service, which was winning the glory of the war. The government had more offers than it needed for the volunteer service, but more men were wanted in Mexico on account of the depletion of the regular army. Desiring to keep the standing army up to its complement, the administration determined to try once more to obtain the necessary enlistments. The Military Committee of the House prepared a bill to meet the wishes of the administration. This authorized the President to raise ten additional regiments, and as an inducement to enlist, men were to be allowed to choose their term of service — for five years or for the war — and were to have bounties. A feature of this measure that commended it to many congressmen who were looking for patronage to distribute among their constituents was a provision that the President should have the authority to name the commissioned officers to be appointed, — some four hundred in number.

This bill seemed assured of success. It had the support of the administration, it had been favorably reported by the Military Committee, and was drawn on the same lines as a bill which had passed the House at the preceding session. But Mr. Hamlin found the measure very objectionable, and decided to defeat it if he could. It contravened what he believed to be the correct principles of government, and also appeared to him to be unjust to the volunteer soldier. When the army bill came before the House on January 4, 1847, Mr. Hamlin led an attack on it which placed the measure in its right light before Congress as an un-American, un-Democratic bill, a usurpation of state rights. Hence, the situation presented to the interested House was a Jeffersonian Democrat arraigning a Calhoun administration for abusing a principle which it professed to uphold as its cardinal doctrine. Taking up the bill item by item, Mr. Hamlin clearly established all his points.

He argued first that the bill should be radically changed to enlist ten regiments in the volunteer service instead of in the regular army. One reason he gave was that the administration itself had informed Congress at its last session that an independent or volunteer corps was preferable to a regular army, and it was on that principle that Congress authorized the President to call for 50,000 volunteers. Another reason was that the volunteers had acquitted themselves with great credit, and no one had yet complained they had not realized all expectations. Still another reason was that there were grave doubts whether ten regiments could be raised for the regular army, since the Secretary of War reported that only 2500 men had enlisted since Congress had passed the other bill for that purpose.

Coming now to general principles, Mr. Hamlin discussed the abstract idea of maintaining a large standing army. A descendant of revolutionary stock and a sincere Jeffersonian Democrat, he was opposed to this. He favored a standing army only when an absolute necessity, as a nucleus for recruiting and drilling raw troops in an emergency. He believed that large standing armies were a menace to peace, an unnecessary source of expense, of intrigue and class distinction, and the natural props of monarchies. The essence of his views was that the citizens of a true republic will always volunteer to defend its welfare and honor. To increase the standing army with more volunteers ready to enter the service than were needed would be absolutely unnecessary.

In view of the development of the Calhoun doctrine of state sovereignty into the doctrine of nullification, and the method employed by both the North and the South in forming their armies during the civil war, Mr. Hamlin's ideas of how troops should be raised in the Mexican war are interesting. They illustrate in their turn his creed of government, that the United States was a government founded by the people, and derived its existence from their support; that it was not a compact or league of States, but that each State, while preserving the rights of autonomy, owed its allegiance to the general government; that the people were bound to come to the support of the government in times of war through their States, which should exercise their acknowledged functions in raising and equipping the troops. On this score, Mr. Hamlin severely criticised the war bill, because it infringed state rights by giving the President the appointment of the officers of the regiments called for. Mr. Hamlin's language makes his points clearer. He said : —

"I am now and always shall be in favor of restricting the executive patronage whenever it can be well done, and when there is no necessity for extending it. This I believe is the doctrine of the old Jeffersonians. It seems to me that there is no necessity for placing the appointments of four hundred officers in the hands of the Executive to be wielded for good or evil, as the case might be, though it be exercised with all the prudence the best man on earth could employ. . . . Who has complained of the officers of the brave volunteers? . . . They have always led their forces. . . . There are other considerations I would like to dwell on. One is that under this bill men raised in one State would be officered by men from another. Would it not be expedient for these corps to officer themselves? . . .

"The House may not recollect a bill introduced last session (by James A. Black, of South Carolina); but I do, for I had reason to confer with the gentleman who offered it. What was one of the grand features of that bill? It is one too often derided, too often laughed at. It is the great and glorious doctrine of state rights, state pride, and state duty; and these doctrines are not to be forgotten in this connection. The gentleman proposed to organize the several corps of militia in the Union into corps to be denominated legions, each State to have its own legion and its own colors. Well, there was something in that suggestion. When called into active service, if there are substantial honors to be gained, laurels to be reaped, the pride of each State would be roused to gather its share. This would tend to preserve the principle of state rights. But it is a serious objection to the pending bill — and a serious one with myself — that by building up this large standing army there would be a constant and tremendous tendency to centralization. How different it would be with the independent corps — each impelled and directed to a common purpose, and yet meeting in different places of rendezvous, respecting their individual rights, and contending each for the glory of its own State.

"But how would it be with a standing army? Why, all individuality would be swallowed up, and all state lines obliterated. Now that fact alone is sufficient to lead me to prefer a modification or change of this bill so that it shall be made one by which men can be enlisted as volunteers. . . . Let us then avoid unnecessary extension of executive patronage; let us raise a volunteer corps; let us permit the corps to be officered by men of their own choice, and let the officers and the men be dismissed simultaneously. With these provisions attached, the bill will receive my hearty coöperation and support."

Mr. Hamlin planned his attack on the army bill with the assistance of his friend, George Rathbun, who introduced a substitute for the original measure embracing Mr. Hamlin's ideas. This the House accepted, by a vote of 98 to 96, in preference to the bill offered by the Military Committee. The Senate concurring, the new troops were raised as volunteers, and commanded by officers commissioned by the States. The government has not since departed from these principles. It is an interesting fact, too, that the Union armies raised during the civil war were formed in about the same way Mr. Hamlin advocated in his speech on the army bill in 1846.

An incident happened during the Mexican war that Mr. Hamlin related with keen pleasure as an illustration of the kind of volunteer soldiers Maine produced. Major C. N. Bodfish, of Bath, a personal friend of Mr. Hamlin's, was one of the leading lumbermen of the State, and was noted for his practical ways in overcoming obstacles. The division he was attached to in the Mexican war came one day to a wide river, flowing between lofty and precipitous banks. The corps of trained civil engineers belonging to the division gave it as their opinion that they could not transport the army across the river in less than a week. When Major Bodfish heard this decision, he was disgusted, and, after making an examination of the river's banks, he asserted that he could transport the army inside of forty-eight hours.

Knowing Major Bodfish's reputation, the commanding officers ordered him to go to work on the problem upon which the engineers were figuring. He detailed a large body of men, working in relays, to dig a path, in a diagonal direction, down the bank on which the army was camped, to the river, which he bridged over with pontoons; and while the army was defiling down the first path and over the bridge, other men cut a diagonal path up the second bank. The army was transported within the time Major Bodfish stipulated, and the incident became famous. After the war had closed, Mr. Hamlin related the story to the President, who, at his request, appointed Bodfish collector of customs at Bath.

Mr. Hamlin continued to follow closely the details of the Mexican war. On one occasion he was brought in opposition to the dominant forces in the House, when he did not succeed in carrying his point. The incident evidences the petty and arrogant spirit of the slave party in small things. Daniel Putnam King was one of the fourteen Whigs who voted against the war bill in the House. For this reason the slave party in the House did not treat him at times with the courtesy his high character deserved. At this session of Congress, Mr. King presented a memorial from the Society of Friends of New England praying that measures might be adopted to put an end to the war. Mr. King moved that the memorial be referred to the proper committee and printed. A curious objection sprung up to this motion. One Southern member protested against the printing of the memorial because it was presented by Quakers, who were always in favor of peace; another, because it was a private affair, and would involve the spending of public money.

These and other petty subterfuges disgusted Mr. Hamlin, and he made a few remarks which expressed his ideas of toleration and courtesy towards an honorable opponent. He argued as Mr. King did, that the memorial should be printed, because it came from a respectable body of nine or ten thousand people living in New England. The paper was short and respectful, and by printing it the House neither indorsed nor contradicted its sentiments. "This memorial," Mr. Hamlin continued, "may deny the justice of the war, and yet I, who am one of the firmest and most decided supporters of the war, am disposed to print it. To refuse might look like shrinking from the freest investigation of the subject, and the fullest expression of public sentiment in regard to it. I am in no wise disposed to do either." But the House was in a particularly intolerant mood, and rejected Mr. King's resolution by a vote of 77 to 65.[1]

Although the Mexican war, in its political aspect, is a discreditable page in the history of our government, yet, as a feat of arms, it

[1] *Congressional Globe*, December 29, 1846.

reflected credit on the military prowess of the young nation, and won it more respect among the nations of the Old World. The victories our arms gained at Vera Cruz, Buena Vista, Chapultepec, Churubusco, and other Mexican strongholds now read like romances. The Mexicans were brave, and greatly outnumbered our men; but they were inadequately equipped, badly officered, and divided by internal political dissensions. On the other hand, it is doubtful if there ever was a more efficient army for its numbers than the one that won the Mexican war. The men were mostly volunteers — the flower of American citizenship. They were young, unusually intelligent, brave unto rashness, and fired with ambition. They were commanded by Scott and Taylor, two of the best generals of their times, who had among their subordinates Grant, Sherman, Hancock, Hooker, Kearny, McClellan, Lee, Jackson, Johnston, Longstreet, and others whose names are now among the military geniuses of the age. In another respect, the Mexican war is of personal interest to these pages, since it gave Mr. Hamlin experience that enabled him to render practical aid to the Committee on the Conduct of the War when he was the war Vice-President.

CHAPTER XIV

MR. HAMLIN's antagonism to slavery during his first three years' service in the House had a far-reaching effect in Maine, and the narrative now turns to the political situation in the Pine Tree State. When the slave power betrayed its plan to nationalize slavery by annexing Texas, the people of Maine, like those of other free States, were aroused from their passive attitude towards the peculiar institution. At first the slavery question was not a burning issue, but served in the beginning as an opening wedge in splitting the old parties asunder. The line of cleavage in the Democracy of Maine was indicated first by the development of two wings, one called the Free-Soilers, the other the Wild-Cats. As events progressed, the Free-Soilers were filled with foreboding over the increasing demands of the slave power and the attempts it made to suppress free speech, the persecution of anti-slavery people, the killing of Jonathan Cilley, and the red-handed murder of the Rev. Elijah P. Lovejoy, also a son of Maine. All these things, and others, revealed the temper of the slave power in its sinister light to the liberty-loving people of that State. Mr. Hamlin's continued fight against the slave party on the floor of the House, his denunciation of slavery, in Pinckney's words, as "an evil that blighted all it touched," his attacks on dueling, his resistance to the annexation of Texas as a slave State and to the betrayal of Oregon, — all these acts warmed the anti-slavery Democrats of Maine towards Mr. Hamlin, and although he was only thirty-six years old, they rallied around him in greater numbers than ever, and in the fall of 1845 brought him forward as their candidate for the United States Senate. Then followed one of the most exciting and interesting elections in the history of the State. It is of peculiar importance to this record, since it throws a strong light on Mr. Hamlin in one of the most trying struggles of his life, and also because it marks the beginning of the efforts of the slave power to dominate the Democratic party in Maine. Mr. Hamlin's success in his fight with the slave power at home was perhaps his best political work. His defeat in 1846 was a preparation for this long struggle. The contest he waged with the slave power this time lasted six weeks. The result hung on the turn of a single vote.[1] If Mr. Hamlin had agreed to modify his opposition to slavery, he might have been elected. He refused.

But to understand this contest in all its phases, it is necessary first fully to understand the political status of the slavery question in Maine. When slavery began to force its way into politics as an issue, men began to array themselves on either side according to their convictions, interests, and natures. Although the senatorial election of 1846 was in the main a square fight between the anti-slavery and the pro-slavery factions of the Democracy of the Pine Tree State, yet it would not be right or just to rank all of Mr. Hamlin's opponents as pro-slavery men, as the term is now understood. There were many good men in the country at this time who, while personally abhorring slavery, nevertheless felt that it had a constitutional status which could not be assailed without assailing the Constitution itself. It is necessary to emphasize this fact, that the positions of many may be justly understood, who subsequently saw their error, and fought the upholders of slavery on the field of battle. George F. Shepley, for many years a distinguished judge of the United States Circuit Court, was one of the most conspicuous Democrats of this class who first fought Mr. Hamlin because they thought he was too radical on the slavery question, but afterwards joined hands with him in the real crisis. There were other conservative Democratic leaders in Maine at this time, such as Hugh J. Anderson, who was governor of the State, and as a strong party man accepted the policy of his party and opposed Mr. Hamlin. He was also ambitious to go to the Senate himself. Then there was a non-political element which instinctively arrayed itself against Mr. Hamlin because he was of a radical nature. The members of this feared a change, and they saw in Mr. Hamlin's aggressive leadership dangers that they thought the country could avoid by pinning its faith to the Constitution. Strange as it may seem, at this time slavery had supporters among the colleges and churches in Maine. Among these men were Rev. Dr. Leonard Woods, president of Bowdoin College from 1833 to 1866, and the Rev. John O. Fiske, of Bath.

But there was also an aggressive pro-slavery party in the Maine Democracy at this period, and it strengthened itself by drawing on the national administration for support. As the administration had

---

[1] Mr. Hamlin wrote Leander Valentine, of Westbrook, on March 2, 1848: " I was nominated some half a dozen times in the House, receiving about two thirds or three fourths of the whole party, perhaps the largest majority ever given in the popular branch in the legislature. Three times I came within one vote of a nomination in the Senate, once receiving just one half. But two or three Mormons (pro-slavery men) prevented me from getting that one vote necessary."

developed a distinctively pro-slavery policy under Secretary Calhoun, it is hardly necessary to add that it filled the offices with its friends. Of this party Nathan Clifford, afterwards United States attorney-general and associate justice of the Supreme Court of the United States, was the most prominent leader. Mr. Clifford was a man of great industry and unbounded ambition. He had already served in the national House of Representatives, was a personal friend of President Polk, and desirous of promoting his fortunes. His ambition was soon gratified, and he was taken into Mr. Polk's Cabinet, where he exercised a considerable control over the federal patronage in Maine. There were other leaders in this faction, who, while they were of less repute than Judge Clifford, were none the less men of decided political ability. One was Wyman B. S. Moor, who was several times attorney-general of Maine, a member of the United States Senate for a short time, and afterwards United States consul-general to the British-American Provinces. Another was Bion Bradbury, of Eastport, a man of talent and address, who for many years was one of the most skillful managers of the Democratic party of Maine. A third was Shepard Cary, of Houlton, who served a term in the House and exerted considerable influence in his party. A fourth was Benjamin Wiggin, of Bangor, a smooth wire-puller; and a fifth was Leonard Jones, proprietor of the " Bangor Democrat," the leading party newspaper in Mr. Hamlin's congressional district.

In the beginning of the canvass Mr. Hamlin and his supporters had easily the best of it. They carried the majority of the caucuses in the summer of 1845, at which the Democratic candidates for the legislature were chosen, and nominated men who pledged themselves to vote for Mr. Hamlin when his name came before the legislature. The Democrats carried the State at the September election, and Mr. Hamlin's friends confidently counted on his elevation to the Senate. He probably would have been chosen had the legislature met shortly after the state election, but it did not convene until the spring of 1846, and in the interim the opposition relaxed no effort to turn every little advantage to account. Mr. Hamlin, on the other hand, was at this time in the thick of the fight at Washington against the plot to betray Oregon. He knew, of course, that in the beginning of his candidacy for the Senate his anti-slavery course would be used as an argument against him. Indeed, he was told by his enemies that they would defeat him if they could, because he was an anti-slavery man ; he was also urged by well-meaning friends to modify his course. His most substantial reply to his enemies and timid counselors was his speech on the Oregon matter, and it is therefore to be considered in one sense as a measured expression of his anti-slavery convictions.

In spite of the fact that the party machine led by the governor was against Mr. Hamlin, his friends were confident of his success, because the people of the State were for him, in preference to a pro-slavery man. As the time for the convening of the legislature drew near, Mr. Hamlin's opponents, both the avowed pro-slavery men and the conservative element, concentrated their forces in a movement to nominate Governor Anderson as the most available man they could present against Mr. Hamlin. Mr. Anderson was a popular man personally and a shrewd politician, but the fact that he was supported by men who believed in slavery, and were opposed to the principles of the Wilmot Proviso, was sufficient to defeat him. He was out of the race at the start, but certain unscrupulous pro-slavery members of the legislature, who did not propose to respect the will of the majority of their party, made use of Governor Anderson's name. When the legislature assembled in May, 1846, it was generally believed that Mr. Hamlin would be nominated by his party. He had a large majority assured him in the House, and while there were some doubts about the Senate, there was no question that he was the choice of the majority members of the legislature, and his party could be defeated only by unfair tactics.

There was only one way in which this could be done, and that was by bringing about a deadlock. Circumstances conspired to favor this plot. It was the custom then for each House to make its own nomination for senator in a separate caucus, instead of meeting in a joint assembly as they do now. Thus if the two Houses did not agree, a deadlock was sure to follow, when a small minority could dictate terms to the majority. If any man had predicted on the opening of the legislature that a plot of this kind had been planned, and that it would be carried out, he would have been laughed to scorn; nevertheless, a small number of bitter pro-slavery men who had been elected to the Senate were working desperately, when the legislature came together, to bring about a deadlock, and thus block Mr. Hamlin's election. They found that they could succeed only by breaking pledges made to their constituents to support Mr. Hamlin, and by resorting to questionable tactics. They were equal to this sort of work, and were therefore responsible for the success of the slave party in the Maine Senate election of 1846.

While the machine was working against Mr. Hamlin, he nevertheless had strong friends in the state government and the legislature, who had served their political novitiate, and who under ordinary conditions could have carried the day for him. Prominent among these men were Ezra B. French, secretary of state, and Alfred Reddington, adjutant-general. In the Senate were General John J. Perry, Alpheus S. Holden, Elisha M. Thurston, Asa Smith, Joseph S. Monroe, John H. Pillsbury, Charles G. Bellamy, Benjamin F. Mason, Randall Skillin, Rufus Porter, Joseph Berry, Henry Barnes; in the House were Hugh D. McClellan, Atwood Levensaler, Sylvanus T. Hinks, Horatio G. Russ, Hiram Ruggles, Thomas H. Norcross, Lyndon Oak, Benjamin B. Thomas, John Gardner, and the Rev. Ebenezer Knowlton, the Speaker. The testimony of Mr. Hamlin's friends in this contest is interesting, and no one is better qualified to speak than General Perry, an Oxford County man, a lifelong friend of Mr. Hamlin's, and whose personal character and services to the State as a legislator and congressman render him a reliable witness. General Perry read an address before the Maine Historical Society, at Portland, in which he said: "The defeat of Mr. Hamlin, by the legislature of 1846, was the result of one of the most corrupt bargains that ever disgraced any legislature." At another time, General Perry gave the details.[1] One point, however, must be explained before quoting him. The custom had not yet been established of holding a joint caucus in the legislature to make nominations for senator, but each house made its own nomination and balloted independently of the other. This circumstance gave Mr. Hamlin's enemies their first opportunity to make a stand against him in the Senate. Had the nomination been made by a joint caucus, Mr. Hamlin would have been chosen by a large majority. To quote General Perry: —

"A canvass of the Democratic members of the House soon settled the fact that Mr. Hamlin would be the nominee of that body, and his friends had the best of reasons for believing that he would be nominated in the Senate caucus also. But subsequently there appeared to be some uncertainty about the Senate; it was developed that Mr. Hamlin had some bitter personal enemies in that branch of the legislature who would not hesitate to use any means within their power to defeat him. We found that they had been working day and night to accomplish this, and not meeting with the encouragement they had expected were at one time ready to abandon the fight. But they received reinforcements from a body of 'Wild-Cats' who came over to the Capitol, and it was announced that Mr. Hamlin would be defeated in the Senate caucus. The House had its caucus on May 28, and Mr. Hamlin was nominated by a handsome majority, receiving 44 votes to 29 for Governor Anderson and a few for other candidates. The result was announced to the Senate before it voted, but even in spite of this demonstration of Mr. Hamlin's popularity with his party, in spite of the fact that a majority of the Senate had been nominated under the supposition that they were Mr. Hamlin's friends, the Senate, after twelve ballots, nominated Governor Anderson, the pro-slavery candidate. He received 14 votes and Mr. Hamlin 11. On the last ballot, the supporters of the minor candidates combined on Mr. Anderson; it was 'anything to beat Hamlin.'"

The next day the situation remained unchanged; each house stuck

[1] Letter to the author.

to its candidate. A week was passed without an election, and then the news of the deadlock spread over the State. When it became evident that a plot had been formed by pro-slavery men in the Senate to defeat Mr. Hamlin on account of his anti-slavery record, the greatest indignation prevailed among the Free-Soil Democrats. They brought great pressure to bear upon several recalcitrant senators, but without avail. Charges of broken pledges and plain warnings that the delinquent would be punished by peremptory retirement from the Senate by their constituents had no effect. The slave power was in an ugly mood, and proposed to punish Mr. Hamlin for defying it. Compromising stories about corruption were next heard in explanation of the course several senators were pursuing, regardless of their instructions and the wishes of the people who had elected them, but nothing could be proved, and the long fight went on week after week, Mr. Hamlin's friends clinging to him with a pertinacity worthy of the cause, and the slave party in the Senate sticking to its candidate with a zeal worthy of a better cause. Again and again the slave party presented a new candidate, but at every House caucus Mr. Hamlin was put forward as the candidate of the Free-Soil Democrats of Maine. Mr. Hamlin's timid friends tried once more to urge him to listen to suggestions of compromise, but he firmly and emphatically refused to modify his opposition to slavery, or to entertain any offer of compromise from his enemies in the Senate. He continued his course in Congress, apparently undisturbed by the unexpected happenings at Augusta. When a change of one vote would have elected him at one time, if he had given assurance that he would be less pronounced in his attitude towards slavery, he remained as grimly opposed to the slave power as ever before.

The contest dragged on for six weeks without an election. Mr. Hamlin's friends were morally sure that corrupt means had been employed to block his election, and they hated to yield; but Mr. Hamlin, a few days before the time for adjournment arrived, decided not to prolong the contest further, because he did not wish the State to go unrepresented. He therefore wrote a letter to his friends advising them to withdraw his name in favor of James W. Bradbury, of Augusta, who professed to be friendly to Mr. Hamlin. They did it with great reluctance, and the legislature finally elected Mr. Bradbury, who held conservative views on the slavery question, and whose selection was therefore regarded as a drawn battle between the two wings of the Democratic party.

Immediately after the election of Mr. Bradbury had been declared, an episode occurred that General Perry relates as follows: "About a week before the legislature adjourned, Stephen H. Chase, of Fryeburg, who was president of the Senate, resigned the presidency, and

David Dunn, of Poland, was elected to fill the vacancy. Chase was bitterly opposed to Mr. Hamlin, and voted against him, although he came from Oxford County, Mr. Hamlin's old home, where three fourths of the Democrats wanted Mr. Hamlin elected. Dunn was supposed to be Mr. Hamlin's friend, until the final test came. This incident has never been explained, and is recited without comment. There were other senators also who betrayed the wishes of their constituents. Some of the senators who betrayed their constituency by opposing Mr. Hamlin were not met on their return home with 'shouts of applause and bands of music,' but were invited to political graves which know no resurrection. Chase,[1] for example, was retired from the Senate the next year before a withering fire of denunciation, while I, who was one of the other senators from Oxford County and Mr. Hamlin's friend, was unanimously renominated and reëlected by an increased majority, — two convincing circumstances which show what the Democrats of Oxford County thought about the defeat of Mr. Hamlin. But I should add that the people of Maine took Mr. Hamlin into their own hands, and thereafter sent him to the United States Senate as long as he was willing to remain there."

If either Chase or Dunn had kept his pledges or respected the wishes of his party, obviously Mr. Hamlin would have been elected. This and other circumstances escaped the chroniclers of the times. The newspaper press was but an infant in those days. Years afterwards, when this defeat had lost its sting, and men who had opposed Mr. Hamlin had acknowledged their mistake and joined hands with him in fighting the enemy, an amusing circumstance came out in connection with the contest of 1846 that tended to place it in a somewhat humorous light. One vote in the Senate was diverted from Mr. Hamlin, not on account of his opposition to slavery, but on account of a personal grievance which one member held against him, but which, however serious to the senator, is an amusing illustration of how little things may control the course of events. " Misfortunes do not come singly." Mr. Hamlin happened to have an enemy in the Senate, whose hostility he had innocently incurred in an accident, the story of which, as related by him on the occasion of a legislative reunion at Augusta, nearly forty years afterwards, may be instructive to young politicians. As has been said, Mr. Hamlin in his early life was something of a "practical joker." He enjoyed a little harmless fun even at his own expense, but he did not dream one day, when an amusing idea popped into his head, that the execution of it would cost him an election to the United States Senate. While he was serving as speaker of the House some eight or ten years previous to this time, there was a

[1] Chase afterwards sought the Democratic nomination for Congress in his district. He was defeated by the anti-slavery men, and left the State.

member who prided himself on his faultless personal appearance. He was growing bald and was very sensitive about it. To conceal this approaching calamity, he was in the habit of using bandoline and other preparations to keep each hair in its proper place. One day, while sitting in the speaker's chair, Mr. Hamlin, who was in a particularly happy mood, happened to cast his eye on this man's carefully dressed hair, and not knowing his peculiarity — for he would not purposely have offended the old gentleman for the world — Mr. Hamlin beckoned to him, shaking with repressed laughter at the same time. Full of importance at being summoned by the Speaker to his chair in the presence of the House, this member marched pompously up to Mr. Hamlin, who smilingly whispered : —

"Old fellow, I just wanted to tell you that you had got one of your hairs crossed over the other."

Had the Speaker suddenly slapped the representative in the face, he could not have angered the sensitive man more than he did by playing this little joke on him. His face turned red with fury, and he spluttered: "You insult me, sir; you insult me!" He marched to his desk in a state of great indignation. Mr. Hamlin was profuse in his apologies, but the irate man cherished the fancied insult for nearly ten years in the hopes of avenging himself. In 1846 the opportunity came. He was elected to the state Senate, where he joined the proslavery men, and with great satisfaction wiped out the insult to his hair. What aggravated the offense was the fact that he was elected to the Senate, pledged to vote for Mr. Hamlin. When the York County Democrats held their convention to nominate a candidate for the state Senate in the fall of 1845, the subject of Mr. Hamlin's innocent joke sought the honor. Learning of his candidacy and knowing that he still nursed some feelings of resentment towards Mr. Hamlin, the latter's friends suspected that he might prove an unsafe man to send to the state Senate. They were in control of the convention, and to guard against any misunderstanding as to his position, they called on him to state in the convention who was his choice for United States senator. He took the floor and declared that if Mr. Hamlin should be a candidate before the legislature, he would vote for him in accordance with the wishes of the convention. Rome was once saved from capture by the hiss of a goose. That was a narrow escape. In political annals it could be paralleled only by the escape of the slave power of Maine from defeat in 1846 by a hair. But this contest only nerved the Free-Soil Democrats of Maine to greater effort two years later, when their battle was renewed, and that time there was no slip between cup and lip.

CHAPTER XV

ONE of the most important measures connected with the cause of freedom in ante-bellum days was the Wilmot Proviso. In one respect this proviso operated like the gag-law; although framed for a different purpose, it compelled the parties and public men of the day to divide in opposition to, or in support of, the slave power. Again, like the gag-law, the Wilmot Proviso became a tremendous weapon in the hands of the anti-slavery men in fighting their foe. Although they lost the preliminary battle, they won a greater victory in the end: the Wilmot Proviso aroused the free States and caused them, slowly at first, it is true, to join hands against the slave power. The Wilmot Proviso may be called the first plank of the young Republican party, which was gradually evolving from the free-soil elements that united in support of this measure. The Wilmot Proviso is of both historic and personal interest to these records, and the complete story of how this famous measure happened to be devised and presented is now related in its entirety for the first time, in order that all the chief actors in the drama may have their just share of credit. Although the proviso goes down in history bearing the name of its presenter, David Wilmot, of Pennsylvania, yet, without desiring to detract from Mr. Wilmot's well earned reputation, it must be stated that the facts show that Jacob Brinkerhoff, of Ohio, is entitled to the credit for originally drafting the proviso, and that Hannibal Hamlin is also entitled to the distinction of bringing the measure to a final issue against the slave party in Congress.

The proviso was a moral result of the Mexican war. When it became evident that the Mexicans were willing to listen to negotiations for peace, President Polk asked Congress for an appropriation of $2,000,000, to bring the war to an end, the understanding being that the United States should indemnify Mexico for land that the government should take. As the Mexican troops were occupying California and New Mexico, it was certain that this territory would be acquired, and the anti-slavery men were considering among themselves ways and means for preventing the slave power from using this territory for its purposes, when the so-called Two Million Dollar Bill was introduced in the House. The idea of excluding slavery from the territory to be conquered and purchased from Mexico had occurred to many anti-slavery members of Congress. Mr. Hamlin, Judge Brinkerhoff, Mr. Wilmot, Preston King, George Rathbun, Martin Grover, of New York, Paul Dillingham, Jr., of Vermont, and others of the anti-slavery Democrats, had already discussed at their "messes," and in their conferences in the House, the possibilities of such a move by the slave power as was made in the presentation of the Two Million Dollar Bill, but no definite line of action was decided upon. When the bill was read, on August 8, 1846, the House was in committee. Brinkerhoff was quick to see that the time for action had come, and so were his friends, too. In the incident that then occurred, there were several men who took part, each of whom might have said afterwards that he had a narrow escape from lasting fame.

The Two Million Dollar Bill had been referred to a committee, and while it was considering the measure, Judge Brinkerhoff sat down at his desk, and, to use his own words in a letter to Henry Wilson, April 4, 1868, he "drew up the proviso in the exact language in which it now appears on page 1283 of the (congressional) 'Journal.'" The proviso embodied the language of the Ordinance of 1787, prohibiting slavery in the territory northwest of the Ohio, and followed it as exactly as Judge Brinkerhoff could recall it. Looking over the House, he saw Samuel F. Vinton, the leader of the Whigs, and an anti-slavery man. He showed the draft of the proviso to Vinton, who read it, and asked if the members on the Democratic side of the House would support it. Judge Brinkerhoff answered that some would. Mr. Vinton advised him to be on the alert, to get the floor and offer the proviso. Judge Brinkerhoff replied : " No, I am suspected, and the floor will probably not be awarded to me. Wilmot is the favorite of the Southern members, and he can get the floor when I cannot ; and he is all right I know, for I have talked with him ; he is the man."

Vinton promised Brinkerhoff that he would rally the Northern Whigs to the support of the proviso, and the latter turned in search of his Democratic friends. Just at this time Mr. Hamlin, John P. Hale, Preston King, George Rathbun, Martin Grover, Timothy Jenkins, Paul Dillingham, Jr., and others had formed a group, and were holding an excited conversation. As Mr. Brinkerhoff approached several members of the group, Mr. Hamlin, Mr. King, Mr. Grover, among them, passed him amendments to the bill similar in character to the proviso he had written, which shows that all these men had acted under the same impulses. He immediately read his proviso, and Mr. Hamlin said at once, " That 's the best yet, because it 's the shortest," and there were assents of " Yes, that 's so." When Mr. Brinkerhoff added that he had asked Mr. Wilmot to introduce the bill, since he was popular with the Southern members on account of his free-trade ideas, there was a chorus of approval. Further action was taken before the group dissolved, which shows the annoying difficulties the anti-slavery members of Congress had to cope with. Obviously to accomplish anything in the way of legislation, it was necessary for a member of the House to get the floor. ·As the House was controlled by the slave power, it was not easy for an anti-slavery member to obtain the Speaker's recognition, in a great emergency that involved the interest of the slave party. To meet any contingency of this kind that might arise from the presentation of the Two Million Dollar Bill, Mr. Hamlin and his friends agreed among themselves that they would all, ten or twelve in number, try to get the floor as soon as the bill was reported, with the understanding that if one other than Wilmot should succeed, he should yield to Wilmot. The wisdom in choosing Wilmot to present the proviso was vindicated. Out of the ten or a dozen anti-slavery men who sought the floor when the Two Million Dollar Bill was reported, Wilmot was recognized by the presiding officer of the House.

In well chosen words, Mr. Wilmot offered the proviso, which briefly declared it to be " an express and fundamental condition to the acquisition of any territory from Mexico, that neither slavery or involuntary servitude should ever exist therein." The proviso was presented when the House was still sitting in the committee of the whole, and as the slave party was completely taken by surprise, it was passed by a vote of 83 to 64. Unfortunately, there is no individual record of the vote. When the proviso a few minutes later was brought before the House, after the committee of the whole had risen, once more the anti-slavery men triumphed, but by the close vote of 85 to 79. The slave party had made a desperate but unsuccessful rally. Some votes were changed, but each side rallied recruits and increased its vote. It was an ominous division ; it was practically a solid free North, against a solid slave South. Only two Southern men voted for the proviso : Henry Grider and William P. Thomasson, of Kentucky, both of whom remained consistent opponents of slavery until the contest was ended by its downfall. Of the few Northern members who opposed the proviso, the strangest case was that of Samuel F. Vinton. He had pledged his support to Judge Brinkerhoff, and the records give no reason for his change of position. Yet it is only just to Mr. Vinton to add that he subsequently voted for the proviso when it was presented by Mr. Hamlin. The circumstance is alluded to only to give a clearer idea of the discouraging difficulties the anti-slavery men met, even in the ranks of their friends. Stephen A. Douglas, who was now currying the favor of the South, and his two henchmen, John A. McClernand, and Orlando B. Ficklin, also voted with their

Southern colleagues. The Two Million Dollar Bill, with the Wilmot Proviso attached, next went to the Senate, where John Davis, of Massachusetts, prevented action by holding the floor, by speaking against time, until the session expired. Mr. Davis's motives were misunderstood at the time. He felt certain that the Senate would defeat the proviso if it came to a vote, and he thought that if he prevented a vote the country would discuss the proviso during the interim, and create a sentiment in its favor Congress would not dare to resist.

Congress adjourned under these circumstances, and during the summer and fall of 1846 the Wilmot Proviso became the most widely discussed topic of the time. When Congress reconvened in December, the friends and supporters of the proviso had to shape their action according to the course pursued by the administration. Soon a bill was framed appropriating $3,000,000 to end the war, and it was arranged to close all debate on this bill at the hour of noon on February 15, 1847. Wilmot was again selected to present the proviso, and on the day for action both sides prepared for a desperate struggle. The slave party, having had one unpleasant experience with the proviso, laid plans to defeat it that were worthy of Indian warfare. When the Three Million Dollar Bill was reported by the committee that had it in charge, the House was again sitting in the committee of the whole, and the slave party managed to keep the bill back until fifteen minutes of twelve o'clock with the intention of rushing it through the House while in committee, so that no opportunity could be given to present the proviso. Furthermore, steps were secretly taken to prevent Mr. Wilmot from being present in the House before noon.

It was a cunningly contrived plot, and the details and unfolding of the conspiracy demonstrate how desperate the slave party was. The anti-slavery men of the House, on the other hand, were as determined to win as their opponents, and had planned to meet certain contingencies, although they had not expected to encounter downright dishonorable tactics. At Mr. Hamlin's suggestion, they had substituted another proviso for the one drawn up by Judge Brinkerhoff, which read as follows: "There shall be neither slavery, nor involuntary servitude in any territory on the continent of America which shall hereafter be acquired by or annexed to the United States by virtue of this appropriation (the $3,000,000), or in any other manner whatever, except for crime whereof the party shall have been duly convicted," etc. This substitute was thought more fully to embody the principles for which the anti-slavery men were contending than the original proviso which Judge Brinkerhoff had drawn up in a hurry. All the leaders among the supporters of the proviso took copies and prepared in other respects for the coming contest.

The moment the committee reported the Three Million Dollar Bill, Mr. Hamlin, Judge Brinkerhoff, and the other anti-slavery Democrats in the secret looked round for Wilmot. To their surprise he was nowhere to be seen. Another writer describes the scene : —

" ' Now is the time ! Where is Wilmot ? Where is Wilmot ? ' was anxiously whispered by one and another of the anti-slavery men. But to the question, ' Where is Wilmot ? ' no man could give a response. The supreme moment had come, and the chief actor in what had long been anticipated as a great scene was not at his post.

" ' Run into the cloak-rooms ! ' cried Preston King. ' Search for him in the lobbies,' said Rathbun.

" But none of these suggestions resulted as was hoped — Wilmot was nowhere to be found. The anti-slavery men were in the direst confusion, Hannibal Hamlin alone being entirely calm and collected." [1]

In the mean time the pro-slavery men, perceiving the confusion of their opponents, resorted to parliamentary tactics to prevent the offering of the Wilmot Proviso by any one. Dromgoole, the leader of the slavery forces, claimed that the time for debate had expired, and that the time for action had arrived. When the chair overruled him, he talked about raising the question of order on the Wilmot Proviso, and insisted that if overruled he should attempt to show that the proviso contemplated the exercise of a power not granted by the Constitution. " The Wilmot Proviso," said Mr. Dromgoole, " is an arrogant assumption of power ; it represents a pernicious tendency, and is calculated to produce confusion and discord in the Democratic party."

Preston King tried to offer the proviso, but a heated discussion arose which produced an uproar. The chairman had to suspend all proceedings several times until order could be restored. Mr. Hamlin and his friends in the mean time held a hurried conference, and the proviso was intrusted to Mr. Hamlin's hands. Watching his opportunity, Mr. Hamlin, when there was a sudden subsidence of the confusion, quickly took the floor and moved the adoption of the proviso as an amendment to the Three Million Dollar Bill. Immediately Dromgoole raised a point of order, but Mr. Hamlin met that difficulty by promptly revising his motion on the lines Dromgoole claimed that it should be framed. John A. McClernand, who had continued his opposition to the proviso, came to Mr. Dromgoole's aid with a flank movement. He insisted, possibly to gain time for the slave party, that he had been entitled to the floor, and when he was overruled, he took an appeal from the decision of the chair, which caused another uproar. When this subsided, Mr. Hamlin grimly insisted again that

[1] Carroll's *Twelve Americans*.

the Wilmot Proviso should be accepted, and McClernand reluctantly yielded the floor to him. Mr. Hamlin read the measure as he had redrafted it. The fertile Dromgoole rose to a point of order, and claimed that Mr. Hamlin's amendment was out of order on the ground of irrelevancy, and when he was overruled once more, the pro-slavery men appealed from the decision, to be beaten. Until this time, Stephen A. Douglas had remained quiet, but now he emerged, and, true to his calculating nature and ideas of expediency, presented a compromise amendment which would bring the territory to be ac-quired into the Union under the conditions of the Missouri act of 1820. But the anti-slavery men were not deluded this time, and they voted the Douglas amendment down, and also another framed on about the same lines. And now Mr. Hamlin's amendment came to a vote. The tellers rapidly polled the House, and the anti-slavery men cheered with joy when the result was announced. The proviso was adopted by a vote of 110 to 89.

The next thing in order was for the committee to rise, and the House to reorganize itself to act upon the bill. Thus, the proviso was again voted upon, and was adopted by a vote of 115 to 106.

The following scene is described by another writer : —
"While the roll call was in progress, David Wilmot — stout and unwieldy of form, out of breath, and perspiring at every pore — rushed into the chamber.

"'There he is, there he is, the —— traitor !' cried half a dozen of those who had been his warm friends. To them Mr. Hamlin said quietly : 'Don't be in a hurry, gentlemen ; don't condemn him with-out a hearing. Let us see how he votes.'

"At that moment the clerk called, 'Mr. Wilmot !' For an instant there was a hush in the House ; and then in a strong, firm voice, Wilmot voted 'aye !' Immediately afterwards a score of his old associates, Mr. Hamlin among the number, crowded about Mr. Wil-mot in the cloak-room, and, with more or less excitement, demanded to know why he had not been in the House to present the proviso.

"'Give me a moment to get my breath, gentlemen, — give me a moment to get my breath,' Mr. Wilmot replied, and then went on : —

"'Just as I was coming to the House I received a note from Presi-dent Polk, asking me to come to the White House immediately. On one pretext or another he kept me in conversation for a long time. I had no watch with me, and did not know how rapidly the moments flew. When I left the White House, however, I found to my con-sternation that I might not be in time to offer our measure ; then with all the rapidity I could, I hastened to the Capitol. The rest you know. This, my friends, I declare to you, upon my honor as a man, is the whole truth.' Saying which Mr. Wilmot paused, and then added: 'But, by Heaven! I shall believe to my dying day that the President purposely detained me, with the expectation of defeating the proviso.'

"It is almost needless to say that Mr. Hamlin had never doubted Wilmot's integrity or his fidelity to the anti-slavery cause. He, together with Preston King, Rathbun, and the rest of their circle, offered Mr. Wilmot their warmest sympathy for the circumstances that prevented him from presenting the measure which bears his name, and so the matter ended." [1]

To this may be added that Mr. Hamlin and Mr. Wilmot remained close friends and associates. Mr. Wilmot was also one of the founders of the Republican party; he was temporary chairman of the convention that nominated Mr. Hamlin for Vice-President and for several years a member of the United States Senate when Mr. Hamlin presided over that body.

The proviso was rejected by the Senate. Public sentiment of the North was in favor of the measure; Daniel Webster lent it his powerful aid; but the administration had determined on the defeat of the proviso, and that most powerful engine of corruption — patronage — was the means employed. The Three Million Dollar Bill was passed in the Senate by almost a strict party vote, and sent back to the House for its concurrence. Here again evil forces triumphed, or else men were guilty of unpardonable inconsistency. On the last day of the session the courageous Wilmot and his determined allies made another stand in the last ditch, as it were, for the cause of freedom. Mr. Wilmot offered his proviso once more, and this time the House rejected it by the narrow vote of 107 to 97. Of the men who stood by the Wilmot Proviso it need only be said that they were the same upright friends of freedom who have been mentioned many times in these pages, and those who opposed had many among them who afterwards risked their all to disrupt the Union to perpetuate slavery. Honorable mention should be made of Alexander Ramsey and Samuel F. Vinton, who first opposed the proviso when it was presented in the House in August, 1846, but supported it when public sentiment was aroused. The change of a few votes accomplished the final defeat of the proviso in the House, and those votes, alas! came from the Northern men, — Joseph E. Edsall, of New Jersey; Henry D. Foster, William S. Garvin, and James Thompson, of Pennsylvania; Joseph Russell and Thomas M. Woodruff, of New York, and Thomas J. Henley, of Indiana. Thus, the Three Million Dollar Bill was passed by Congress without any restrictions whatever on the slave power. Thus, once again a slowly awakening people heard

---

[1] Carroll's *Twelve Americans*, pp. 132–134.

in their slumbers a dim echo of the firebells that were warning those fully roused to the dangers which threatened the republic. The slave power was now conscious of its strength, and was beginning to boast of its future conquests. It was no child's play to battle with such a foe; not orators, not speeches, were needed to grapple with the enemy, but practical men, who could rise to any emergency at a moment's notice, combat carefully laid plans, watch the enemy in his ambuscade or meet him boldly in the open, fight treason in their own ranks, and keep up the courage of their friends. The future looked dark, but the pioneer anti-slavery men who rallied around the Wilmot Proviso had the stuff of the men of '76.

CHAPTER XVI

THE plot to betray Oregon to the British government was no sooner executed in part, as before stated, than another plan was set on foot, to establish slavery in Oregon. This developed when the settlement of the boundary controversy rendered it necessary to organize a territorial government. The leaders of the slave power exercised more caution and self-restraint in the first stages of this affair than in the latter; nevertheless, they took a bolder stand in enunciating and defending the doctrines of slavery extension than ever before. Their chief contentions were that the slave was " property," and that a slaveowner could, therefore, take his " property " or " chattel " wherever he liked; and also that Congress had no right to interfere with the institution of slavery. These claims had been heard before in connection with Texas and Missouri; but now they had a different sound when applied to Northern territory. There was an ominous meaning in these theories, and yet while the Northern anti-slavery leaders fully caught the significance of the slave party's attitude, the North was slow to believe. The general talk at the North was that this was more " Southern bluster." But it proved to be the beginning of a gigantic movement to force the peculiar institution into free soil, to make slavery national. The crisis of 1860 was the ultimate outcome of the train of events thus set in motion. The anti-slavery men in Congress were on their guard at the outset. Mr. Hamlin was one of their leaders in exposing and fighting this new move by the enemy.

The bill to organize Oregon as a free territory was introduced into the House on December 23, 1846, by Stephen A. Douglas. This bill reaffirmed the Ordinance of 1787, which excluded slavery from the Northwest, and the slavery leaders pretended to oppose the Douglas measure on the alleged ground that the ordinance was not constitutional. Their apparent object in pursuing this course was to lead the House into the labyrinth of a debate on the constitutional aspect of the Oregon case, in which they might be able to effect a compromise to their advantage over the territory to be acquired from Mexico. Stephen Adams, of Mississippi, gave a hint of this programme by introducing on January 12, 1847, an amendment that read, " Nothing in relation to slavery in this act shall be construed as an intention to interfere with the provisions or spirit of the Missouri Compromise; but the same is hereby recognized as extending to all territory which may hereafter be acquired by the United States." The House was then in the committee of the whole, with Mr. Hamlin in the chair, but he took the floor to reply to Adams. Mr. Hopkins, who succeeded to the chair, ruled that so much of Mr. Adams's amendment was out of order as referred to territory other than that of Oregon. Mr. Hamlin's short, vigorous speech was a notable warning, in view of subsequent events, to the slave power and a challenge to his enemies at home.

" I shall vote," said he, "under the belief that the Missouri Compromise has no more to do with the territory of Oregon than it has with the East Indies. Gentlemen ask me why put this restriction into the bill? I will tell them. If the restrictive clause were not inserted, slavery would creep into Oregon as surely as Satan crept into the Garden of Eden. . . . The Missouri Compromise did not apply to any territory in the Union at the time it was effected. . . . That compromise was effected by drawing a line along the latitude of 36° 30', separating so much of the territory of Louisiana as should be open to slavery from that part from which it was to be forever excluded. Now, it is obvious on every principle of justice that when other territory is to be taken into the Union, the compromise line must be run on a different parallel to suit the changed state of circumstances. I desired to have this principle of compromise introduced into Texas and made a condition of her annexation. But I was told by gentlemen who opposed me that this course would be unnecessary because a part of Texas must be free by the laws of Heaven, it not being adapted to a slave population; and finally, the compromise was refused, and slavery is now lawful in every part of Texas. But it is now time that it should be fully understood that the resolution has been taken, and will prevail in all the free States, that there shall be no more slave territory admitted to the Union. This doctrine will prevail, and woe! woe! unto the man coming here from any Northern State who shall not govern himself accordingly. Such a man may escape destruction for a short time; but as sure as he has an existence so surely will the resistless tide of public sentiment of the North roll over and overwhelm him forever." [1]

Mr. Adams withdrew his amendment. The slave party returned to the attack with different tactics. Armistead Burt, of South Carolina, offered an amendment to the Douglas bill to extend the Missouri line of compromise to the Pacific slope, and he made a speech, prophesying disunion unless compromise was agreed to in the case of Oregon and the new territory to be taken from Mexico. R. Barnwell Rhett, of South Carolina, enunciated the extreme theory held by men of his class, that the ownership of Oregon resided in the sovereignty of the

[1] *Congressional Globe*, January 12, 1847, p. 169. See correction, p. 177.

States, and that neither Congress, nor the entire federal government, had a right to legislate on the question of slavery touching Oregon.

The anti-slavery Democrats undoubtedly had a private understanding when the time arrived for action. Preston King introduced a bill that was more popular with them than that which Douglas had offered, since it was a reaffirmation of the Wilmot Proviso, and dealt with other subjects. It is evident, also, that Mr. Hamlin was chosen to champion King's bill, and to make reply to Rhett and his friends; but the Douglas bill had the floor the last day of the debate, and as it was a good measure the anti-slavery men supported it. Mr. Hamlin made the principal speech of the debate. This was delivered on January 16, 1847, and was one of the most elaborate efforts he ever made in Congress. It is an exposition of his constitutional knowledge and his views as a Jeffersonian Democrat and Free-Soiler of the powers of the government and the individual States in the matter of slavery. One sentiment that Mr. Hamlin uttered was heard throughout the country: " To any proposition for taking territory now free and sending there the shackles and manacles of slavery, I will never consent; never ! " A necessarily compressed report of the speech is presented.

Mr. Hamlin began his speech by charging the pro-slavery party with misrepresenting the attitude of the anti-slavery party. If a stranger had listened to the discussion, he might have supposed that the anti-slavery members of the House were engaged in a crusade against the rights of the States. But they did not propose to disturb one solitary right; on the other hand, they pledged themselves to stand in a common brotherhood engaged in a common cause with the States.

" As members of this great confederacy, however, we do ask and demand that in all things submitted to our deliberation we shall have the right to speak, and speak with manly frankness and boldness, to maintain and defend the rights of constituents. We will ask no more, we will take no less. What is it, then, that we would propose to do? We propose to say . . . that we will stand by the clearly defined rights of each individual State in reference to the institution of slavery; but to territory now free it shall never be extended with our votes and consent, nor shall its limits in any way or manner be enlarged. . . . What provisions of the Constitution do we violate? What right of a single State do we disregard? . . . Now the question submitted to us, and it is not a question to be winked out of sight, is: Are we to acquire other and foreign territory . . . that it may be converted into slave territory? Never, sir; never, to the end of time, with my aid and my assistance, shall that acquisition take place. . . . We here understand perfectly if nothing be said, if nothing be done, that slavery will surely advance and invade the territories which we may hereafter acquire."

Mr. Hamlin reviewed the acquisition of Louisiana and Florida, and the annexation of Texas, to show the purpose of the people was to enlarge the Union, not to extend slavery. He referred to the Missouri Compromise, and while he was willing to agree to a fair compromise in the division of Texas at the time, now he would discard at once and forever any talk about compromises on any parallel of latitude named by man.

"To any proposition of taking territory now free, and sending there the shackles and manacles of slavery, I will never consent, never. . . . On that rock I build, sir, and the waves, the strength, the power, of that institution of slavery shall never prevail against it. Why should we say it now? Because if we do not say it now, it will be too late hereafter. Now is the golden moment. . . . I hope we may be able to pass a declaratory act forever prohibiting slavery in any territory we may hereafter acquire, and that, when admitted, the compact will be made to exclude slavery after it shall have become a State of this Union. I know that gentlemen may tell me that such an act may not have force or validity; that Congress has not the power to restrict slavery in any State. I have no fear on that subject. . . . Sir, the Supreme Court of the United States has affirmed this doctrine with reference to the Ordinance of 1787, that slavery was absolutely prohibited northwest of the Ohio River by that ordinance; and the Supreme Court has also decided that no State formed out of that territory has the right to establish slavery within its limits."

Mr. Hamlin affirmed the power of Congress to pass the declaratory act he advocated, and asserted that the people of the North desired it, although here and there there was

"a shackled press muttering its dissent" and "here and there a dough-face with feelers on his lips, uttering his faint protest against it. But it is the doctrine of the North, it is the doctrine she will march up to; she will live up to it in all coming time. . . . But the gentleman from South Carolina (Barnwell Rhett) denies to us the power of passing this declaratory act. If I understood the gentleman's argument — and I believe I did, although it is somewhat fine-spun and bordering too much on the transcendental — . . . the gentleman holds clearly and distinctly that we may acquire foreign territory, . . . but can do nothing with it. The answers to these propositions are full and to the point. They need only to be stated : —

"1st. If the general government have the power or sovereignty sufficient to acquire, they have the sovereignty to take care of, these territories.

"2d. If there is no sovereignty in the general government, and if it is with the people, we as representatives of that sovereignty can acquire territory by legislative enactment. We have done so. . . .

"3d. The gentleman holds that . . . the Constitution which authorizes us to pass all needful rules applies only to property. . . . Well, does he not hold that slaves are property?

"4th. California and other territory are now free. By the law of nations the moment a slave treads their soil he becomes free. Slavery, then, must exist there in violation of that law."

Mr. Hamlin reviewed constitutional and congressional authorities to support his contention of the right to pass the declaratory act. He found authority in article four, section three, of the Constitution, which said : —

"Congress shall have the power to dispose of and make all needful rules and regulations respecting the territory or other property belonging to the United States. . . . But it is too late even to raise this question when the whole and uniform action of the government has been one way. . . . Why, there has not been a time since the adoption of the Constitution, when Congress at each session has not exercised that power, — the power of legislating over territories. One thing more. I wish to see no cordon of free States thrown around the slave States. . . . I would leave a transit open through which they may pass into Mexico, where they may find a government in which they may participate. But I would leave this for those who are interested to do this without force or coercion. . . . God in his own good time will put an end to that institution, as He will as certain as time will roll on. . . . A few words more and I am done, and in reference to the stale, worn-out cry of the dissolution of this Union. . . . The Union cannot be dissolved. The mutual interests and benefits enjoyed by the different sections would not permit it. The great West is bound to the South by its commerce, and cannot be separated while its mighty waters roll on to the Gulf of Mexico. The North and the South, too, are equally bound by their commerce and exchange of products. These are all ligaments that cannot be rent or dissolved.

"The talk of it is folly, as well as madness. A dissolution of this great and mighty republic, erected by the wisdom of our fathers, and cemented by their blood. And for what ! Spread it out that the public eye may gaze upon it ; proclaim it that the public ears may hear it ; utter it from the groaning press and thunder it from the pulpit. A dissolution of the Union because we will not extend the institution of negro slavery ! The man who would utter that sentiment should blush when it falls from his lips. Dissolve this great and mighty republic for this miserable pretext ! That is not the doctrine of the great and patriotic South ; — she has rallied, except the time when she was about to go to the death for sugar, — she has rallied for this Union. She will stand by it when others desert it, — stand by it in all coming time, and will regret that her sons proclaimed it to the world, in this nineteenth century, in this freest country on earth, that we are to dissolve this fair fabric for the miserable reason that we will not extend the institution which is a curse to all States in which it exists.

"Whatever may be the action and course of Northern representatives here, the great mass of the Northern people have but one single impulse in their bosoms — to stand by this Union through good and evil report — to rally round the blessed stars and stripes of our glorious confederacy wherever they float — to peril their lives and pour out their blood and treasure, if need be, in its defense ; but to the institution of slavery they say, ' Thus far hast thou gone — no farther shalt thou go.' "

A clearer insight into the plans of the slave power regarding Oregon may be glained from what John C. Calhoun said in the United States Senate, on February 19, 1847, a little more than a month after Mr. Hamlin's speech had defined the feelings and intentions of the anti-slavery party towards Oregon : —

" Sir, the day that balance between the two sections of the country, the slaveholding States and the non-slaveholding States, is destroyed is a day that will not be far removed from political revolution, anarchy, civil war, and widespread disaster. The balance of this system is in the slaveholding States. They are the conservative portion, — always have been the conservative portion — always will be the conservative portion, and with a due balance on their part may for generations to come uphold this glorious Union of ours. But if this scheme should be carried out, if we are to be reduced to a handful, if we are to become a mere ball to play the presidential game, — to count something in the Baltimore caucus, — if this is to be the result, woe, woe, I say, to this Union."

As the slave party saw that it was beaten in the House, it made no effort to defeat the Douglas bill, in the hope that the pro-slavery Senate would check the passage of the measure. This was the case. The Oregon bill was delayed in the committee until it was too late for the Senate to take action. Mr. Hamlin was, personally, greatly disappointed, for his efforts to guard Oregon against slavery were among the last services he rendered in the House. He left Washington at the expiration of his term, little dreaming that he would be sent to the Senate in a short year, in time to help Oregon secure her liberty.

The record of Mr. Hamlin's second term in the House may be closed with a brief reference to other acts of his that are of lesser interest and importance, which should not be entirely omitted. He voted for the Walker tariff bill, but in a speech on July 7, 1846, said that it did not fully meet his approval. On July 8, 1846, he spoke at length on the sale of public lands, defending the right of the government to sell to those who would settle on them and "transform a wilderness into cultivated fields and happy homesteads." This right was denied by some theorists. Mr. Hamlin laid special stress in his remarks on the necessity of the government taking pains to prevent the land to be sold from falling into the hands of speculators. He was also active at this time in pushing the independent treasury bill, though he had little to say about the measure in debate. It is noticeable that Mr. Hamlin several times, when postal bills were under discussion, advocated the repeal of the franking privilege. On different occasions he offered amendments to this effect, but without avail, —

April 24, 1846, February 24, 1847, and at other times. He opposed franking on principle, and to the end of his career in Congress urged its abolishment. One more incident may be referred to since it shows Mr. Hamlin's ideas about suffrage. A bill was before the House on May 21, 1846, to extend the right of suffrage to citizens living in the District of Columbia. Mr. Hamlin, in the discussion of suffrage, on this and other occasions, favored the measure and declared himself opposed to property qualifications. One argument he made was that if some people had no money they had rights that were infinitely above money. A unique incident was his introduction of a bill to close the " refectories in the basement of the Capitol, unless the keepers should suspend the sale of intoxicating liquors." This was offered on December 29, 1846. A motion to table was lost by a vote of 120 to 18.

A movement was started to elect Mr. Hamlin to the House for a third term. He wrote his friend, A. M. Robinson, who should have been his successor, and who was for many years a leading Democrat in Piscataquis County, that this was originated without his knowledge or desire. He did not allow his friends to proceed farther, and it appears that he supposed that he would not return to public life.

CHAPTER XVII

ELECTED TO THE SENATE

WHEN Mr. Hamlin came home from Washington in the summer of 1847, in describing his life in Congress to his friends, he said that he felt "cooped up" at the national capital, and he now proposed to "get back to nature." Out-of-door life was always his passion ; farming and fishing his pastime. When he settled in Hampden he began planning to have a farm of his own, but it was not until he left Congress this summer that he was able to gratify his wishes. He bought a farm in Hampden then known as the Haskins place, on the eastern or river side of which is the site of fortifications that Captain Charles Morris, of the United States frigate John Adams, threw up in the war of 1812, when the British fleet came up the Penobscot River. Captain Morris was prepared to rake the fleet, but a fog arose, and in the end he had to burn the Adams and spike her guns to prevent the British from capturing a great prize. For many years subsequent the charred remains of the Adams were seen near the foot of the bluffs of the old Hamlin farm when the tide was low.

The land extended easterly from the village highway to the bluffs overlooking the Penobscot. It commanded a beautiful view of the river stretching to the right and left, and was refreshed by the breezes wafted up from the waters below. The farm comprised about fifteen acres of worn-out land ; but the regeneration of land was one thing in which Mr. Hamlin especially delighted, and he set about his work with enjoyment. He had a little garden near his house, and he planned to make his farm and garden supply his table and live stock, and also leave a surplus for him to sell.[1] He worked on his land every day he could spare, and also insisted that his sons, and, later, his grandsons, should do likewise. He never said much about his reasons for this, but it was easy to see that he believed in the dignity of manual labor, and that it purified men to get back to nature. "God made the country, and man made the town," was one of his silent, guiding maxims of life. In a few summers' time he renovated the Haskins place, and thereafter it yielded him all the produce necessary.

---

[1] Mr. Hamlin kept a farm in Bangor and worked on it nearly every year from 1861 to 1890. He rarely failed to make it produce all he needed for his table and live stock, with a surplus that he sold.

A pretty reminiscence of Mr. Hamlin's life on the Hampden farm is associated with the bobolinks that nested in a large plot in the centre of a field. He had been too busy to pay attention to them until mowing in their neighborhood. He then noticed that the bobolinks flew up out of the tall grass in large numbers, uttering cries as they circled off, as if trying to draw him away. This Mr. Hamlin recognized as a sign that the birds had nests in the grass. He could not think of disturbing the pretty little songsters, and although they laid claim to a large plot of land, he mowed around the spot, leaving the bobolinks in undisturbed possession of their home. Before long Mr. Hamlin became very much attached to his bobolinks, and often in the early morning, when they sang their symphony, he would go to his farm and listen. "This is music," he would say. In haying time, whenever the farm hands approached the birds' homing place, they would see Mr. Hamlin turn around now and then and look at the plot in the centre of the field. So the bobolinks continue to nest and sing on the little farm in Hampden to this day, as they did more than half a century ago.

When Mr. Hamlin returned to Hampden from Washington he had little idea of reëntering active political life immediately, but circumstances conspired to bring him out of retirement before he had hardly entered it. A political tangle occurred in the Hampden legislative district. There were three tickets in the field and three successive failures to elect. Mr. Hamlin's friends urged him to take the Democratic nomination to prevent further factional troubles in his party. He did not desire to return to the legislature, and would have declined could he have seen his way out of the difficulty. But a final argument was brought to bear upon him, and that was, if he resumed his seat in the House, he could effectively fight the pro-slavery wing of his party, and perhaps materially improve his chances of going to the Senate. This prevailed, and Mr. Hamlin accepted the nomination. His election was by no means an assured success, nor was it a purely local affair. There were hard-headed pro-slavery Democrats in Hampden who honestly believed that the Constitution morally forbade criticism of slavery and with whom it was a toilsome task to labor. They liked Mr. Hamlin personally, but they felt it a solemn duty to offer him up as a sacrifice, and they were encouraged by the leaders of the pro-slavery Democracy.

But Mr. Hamlin was elected in spite of this opposition, and, as it afterwards turned out, his return to the legislature was an exceedingly fortunate thing for him. The anti-slavery men all over the State had bestirred themselves, and sent men to the legislature who could be depended upon. Among them was a group of men who were as true supporters as any anti-slavery leader in this country ever had. Mr.

Hamlin made their acquaintance, and for the rest of his fight against the slave power in Maine they stood by as his old guard. The ablest was William P. Haines, of Biddeford, who possibly might have sat in the Senate with Mr. Hamlin had he desired, as will appear in a subsequent chapter. Hugh D. McClellan, of Gorham, the Speaker of the House, was another leader. Leander Valentine, of Westbrook, was one of Mr. Hamlin's lifelong friends. Others were Ira T. Drew, of Waterboro, one of the leading lawyers of the State; Nathan White, of Bucksport; Horatio G. Russ, of Paris; Campbell Batchelder, of Corinna; Andrew D. Bean, of Brooks; David S. Flanders, of Monroe; Ozias Blanchard, of Blanchard; Samuel Mayall, of Gray; Benjamin B. Thomas, of Newburgh; and William R. Flint, of Somerset County. General John J. Perry, of Oxford County, and Charles Holden, of Portland, who had served before in the legislature, were members of this group of Mr. Hamlin's friends. Mr. Hamlin's brother, Elijah, was prominent among the anti-slavery Whigs of the House.

Mr. Hamlin's record of services in this legislature shows that he was closely attentive to his duties. While his record need not be detailed, several of his acts cannot be omitted. The most important was an attack he made on the doctrine of slavery extension. The Mexican war had not yet closed, and the question of the extension or restriction of slavery was slowly but surely bringing about a revolution in public sentiment at the North against slavery. Maine had not yet given an official expression of the feelings of her people on this question, although their general sentiment was strongly against the extension of the peculiar institution. Mr. Hamlin still felt that it was the duty of the North to maintain its constitutional obligations and confine slavery to the territory where it had previously been agreed by the founders of the government that it should exist. This was the opinion held by the coolest heads of the day, and it was vindicated in the end. In attempting to extend slavery, the South violated the implied moral obligations placed on it by the Constitution, and therefore was responsible for bringing on the crisis of 1860. But men were not prophets in 1847. The leaders of the anti-slavery party saw the necessity of maintaining their lines of defense intact. They knew how slow great movements were in crystallizing, and how important it was to move slowly until events began to operate. "The feeling in the air" was that this line of action would place upon the slave party the responsibility of any dire results that might follow its aggressive conduct.

Mr. Hamlin offered some resolutions in the legislature that clearly illustrate his feelings at this time. The first declared that, "Maine, by the action of her state government and representatives in Congress, should abide honestly and cheerfully by the letter and spirit and concessions of the Constitution of the United States, *at the same time resisting firmly all demands for their enlargement or extension.*" The second said that, " The sentiment of this State is profound, sincere, and almost universal that the influence of slavery upon productive energy is like the blight of mildew ; that it is a moral and social evil ; that it does violence to the rights of man as a thinking, reasoning, and responsible being. Influenced by such considerations, this State will oppose the introduction of slavery into any territory which may be acquired as an indemnity for claims upon Mexico." The third asserted that, " In the acquisition of any free territory, whether by purchase or otherwise, we deem it to be the duty of the general government to extend over the same the Ordinance of 1787, with all its rights, privileges, conditions, and immunities."

When the committee having these resolutions in charge reported them, a member of the House who had a constitutional habit of disagreeing with everybody offered some substitutes, and in the course of his remarks criticised Mr. Hamlin's resolutions on the grounds that they were the same thing as the Wilmot Proviso, which he said was "nothing but an abstraction."

Mr. Hamlin replied to this astonishing doctrine with some sarcasm. He pointed out that the Wilmot Proviso embodied the principle of the Ordinance of 1787, which prohibited slavery in all territory northwest of the Ohio River, and was a fundamental law passed by Congress, and, therefore, not an abstract doctrine. Taking up the Wilmot Proviso he said : —

" Upon this question I chose my ground on the side of freedom — against the extension of the accursed system of slavery into territory now free. There I plant my feet with deliberation and with a fixed determination to abide. There I shall rest while reason controls the helm. The gentleman has said that the discussion in Congress upon the Wilmot Proviso was nothing but talk about abstractions. Indeed! it was proposed to pass a fundamental law prohibiting forever the introduction of slavery into territory now free, and which might be hereafter acquired, — to enact the principles of Jefferson, who originated the idea of the Ordinance of 1787, as applicable to the new States that might be embraced within the folds of this republic. And this to the gentleman's apprehension was an abstraction. Well, I would like to have him define what is not an abstraction. . . . Deprecating the system of slavery the friends of the Wilmot Proviso would provide against the extension of that system into free territory. In this the gentleman sees nothing but abstractions, but in his own propositions that condemn slavery as a moral and political evil, the further extension of which should be resisted by every just and honorable means, he avoided recommending any course of action. . . . But is it not a little singular that one who has said so much about the wrongs of slavery should be so easily satisfied that he should fold his arms in a listless way, and say to our brethren of the South, 'Your institution is a vile one, its extension ought to be resisted, but we have no disposition to interfere to prevent its extension.' Oh, no ! any effort of that kind would be an abstraction. For myself I care very little for that enthusiasm which wastes itself in words. I shall never be found pluming myself on my hatred of any particular form of error, and putting forth no hand to prevent its spread — hurling anathemas against the moral and political evils of slavery, yet not daring to maintain the right, but shrinking back before the menaces and frowns of the friends of the peculiar institution. I will not stultify myself by asserting a moral and political evil, and yet refuse to say that I will not prevent an extension. Withholding action is declaring that one will not say the truth about this thing of slavery, and we should act. . . . The first resolution is in accordance with the old Democratic doctrine of a strict construction of the Constitution. . . . The second resolution declares that Maine will resist the extension of slavery in free soil. The third makes out distinctly the manner in which it shall be accomplished. . . . We not only say that we will resist the extension of slavery into free territory, but we say precisely how we will do it. The substitute is vague and uncertain, and it might be explained away at the time of action. Upon questions like this there should be candor and frankness. We owe that to ourselves, to the State, and to the Union. . . . The only slave territories that have been joined to the original Union were received with their slaves, and the guarantees accorded to the old States were extended to them and kept in good faith. May we not require them in even-handed justice that free territories shall be added to the Union without change? And who and what kind of men at the North will demand anything else? I should, indeed, consider myself regardless of a becoming state pride, recreant to the impulses of humanity and to all the obligations resting upon me as a man, if I should falter on this question. I will not speak of the motives and actions of others; but occupying the stand I do, if I should fail to maintain the principles of the resolutions I should be entitled to the opprobrium of an outraged constituency, and to the scorn of every man worthy to breathe the free air of our native hills, or to drink the pure water of their crystal springs."

In another part of his speech Mr. Hamlin urged the adoption of his resolutions on the ground that it would also shape any further legislation Maine might make on this issue. But he particularly favored this act because he believed that it would have a moral effect. Years afterwards Mr. Hamlin was questioned about this, and he broke his habit of taciturnity about himself to say that he regarded the offering of these resolutions as one of the most important acts of his life. He did not make any explanation of this, but the events that follow seem to offer the explanation. The legislature passed the resolutions with only six dissenting votes out of one hundred and thirty in the House. Standing at the head of the column of States,

Maine's official and political acts have always carried weight. Mr. Hamlin's resolutions were looked on as the Pine Tree State's formulated views on the extension of slavery, and nine years later were practically the principles adopted by the young Republican party at its first presidential campaign.

The legislature adjourned in July to welcome President Polk, the first chief magistrate to visit Maine since Andrew Jackson. Mr. Polk was received at Augusta with many honors. William P. Haines made the speech of welcome, and he and Mr. Hamlin were the President's honorary escort in his departure from the city. Mr. Polk made a very favorable impression on the people of Maine. He was a speaker of no mean ability, and was an undoubtedly sincere Union man. Born and brought up at the South, he regarded slavery as a patriarchal institution, and earnestly desired that agitation against slavery should cease. His sentiments are to be found in his speech at Augusta on this occasion. His ideas of disunion, and the evils that would follow, may now be read with a clearer understanding of the man who uttered them than he received in his lifetime. Mr. Polk said in part : [1] —

" Sir, in other countries the monarch rules — he is the sovereign — but in this country, thank God, we know no monarch, no sovereign — save the people. . . . Sir, under our republican system we are all equals. It is the noblest structure of human government ever devised by the wisdom of man. This government, founded by our ancestors, is intrusted to our keeping, and we owe it to ourselves, to posterity, and to mankind to cherish and preserve it. . . . And permit me to add, that he who would upturn and destroy this fairest fabric of human wisdom would inflict an irreparable evil upon mankind.

" Sir, the government under which we live is one of compromise. Embracing interests so opposite, and comprehending within its limits so many degrees of latitude, with production so varied and pursuits so dissimilar, it could not well have been established upon any other basis than that of mutual concession. That band of statesmen, the noblest the sun ever shone upon, whose wisdom gave birth to our glorious Constitution, declared it to have been founded in compromise. The spirit of Washington presided in their counsels, and concession characterized their deliberations. They gave us their present institutions, and what do we witness as a result of their influence and operations ? . . . a territory inhabited by a thriving, an industrious, a contented, happy, and free people. Who, then, I repeat, will have the boldness to strike a blow at this fair framework ? . . . It is, therefore, to a Union of the States, sir, that we must look as the pole-star to guide us onward in the career of prosperity and greatness. . . . Sir, let that Union be dissolved, and these States pass into petty prin-

[1] Reported in the *Augusta Tri-Weekly*, July, 1847.

cipalities, with jarring interests, and incessantly at war with each other, and the last hope in the capacity of man for self-government is fled forever. Our example is now spread abroad to the world — the result of our experiment is watched with intense interest. . . . Sir, how shall the local jealousies which disturb us compare with the great object of binding and continuing this free and happy people? . . . Why, then, should the thought be entertained that this Union should be dissolved into its original elements? Let us rally round the Union as our safeguard. At that altar, thank God, we may all worship, and in pleading for the preservation of our institutions, pray for the advancement of the good of mankind." . . .

In December, 1847, news came from Washington that Senator Fairfield had unexpectedly succumbed to a surgical operation. The tidings of his sudden death caused great sorrow in Maine, for it was generally believed that he was a man of national possibilities. The immediate result of Fairfield's untimely end was the reopening of the old fight between the anti-slavery and pro-slavery wings of the Maine Democracy to nominate a man to fill out Fairfield's unexpired term of three years. Mr. Hamlin's defeat in 1846 served to strengthen him with the anti-slavery wing of his party, and they brought him forward again as their candidate. The pro-slavery men again opposed him for the same reasons as in 1846, and even more vehemently on account of his course in the preceding legislature. For the following six months a warmly contested canvass was carried on among the members elect of the legislature, and the bitter cry was heard again: "Anything to beat Hamlin." [1]

For a second time Mr. Hamlin had to fight the party machine, and the opposition to him was more formidable than in his first campaign, although it was not as cunningly managed. There were four candidates against him this time, and it was thought by his opponents that this would draw strength away from him. The candidates represented different shades of opinions and convictions on the slavery question — from the hard-headed Hunker Democrat to the artful dodger who sheltered himself behind the Constitution, while trying to ascertain which way the wind was blowing. The best known was Nathan Clifford, who, as a member of the Cabinet, had the moral if not the practical support of the administration. Mr. Polk's courtesy and sense of propriety precluded him from interfering in behalf of his friend, Mr. Clifford, nevertheless the government office-holders in Maine were in sympathy with the administration, and constituted a strong Clifford machine. Ex-Governor Anderson was also a candidate, and still retained a large personal following. The

[1] Mr. Hamlin wrote Leander Valentine, on March 2, 1848: "I am to be hunted down with the ferocity of bloodhounds."

third was Samuel Wells, a man of force, who became governor of the State a few years afterwards. A fourth candidate was John D. McCrate, a member of Congress, who was friendly to Mr. Hamlin.

John W. Dana was governor, and he had been elected as an anti-slavery man. In his message to the legislature of 1847, Mr. Dana took strong grounds against the doctrine of slavery extension, and for this he was commended by Mr. Hamlin in his speech on the Wilmot Proviso, which is partially reproduced in preceding pages. But while Mr. Dana was naturally inclined against the institution of slavery, he was a type of the well-meaning men of his day who allowed themselves to be guided in their difficulties by the fetich of party fealty. Men of this kind preached party duty first, and that a Democrat should "vote for the devil, if the regular party nominee." The emancipation of the American voter from this fetich is a story by itself. It will suffice now to say that the events that led to the crisis of 1860 found Mr. Dana a convert to slavery, because it was supported by a majority of his party. His change of position was indicated at this time by his appointment of Wyman B. S. Moor to fill Fairfield's seat until the legislature acted. This was a distinct triumph for the avowed pro-slavery element of the Democratic party. Moor was a leader of that faction, and had publicly announced his opposition to the Wilmot Proviso.

With the pro-slavery element in control of the party machinery, and two of its men in the United States Senate, the outlook was not encouraging for Mr. Hamlin at first. But appearances were deceitful; the appointment of Moor caused an awakening of anti-slavery sentiment throughout Maine. It forced a direct issue between principles rather than men, and caused the defeat of the pro-slavery men. They contested every inch of the ground from the beginning of the fight. An idea of the extreme lengths to which they went in their efforts to defeat Mr. Hamlin may be gathered from the position Senator Bradbury took. When he was elected to the Senate in 1846, he took a conservative attitude towards the slavery question, and his election was regarded as a draw between the two factions. Mr. Hamlin threw his strength to Mr. Bradbury in the belief that it would be better to send him to the Senate than an avowed pro-slavery man. Mr. Bradbury acknowledged his obligations to Mr. Hamlin, and professed his intention of standing by him in the future. But he was a man of a gentle nature and conservative disposition; the internal wranglings of his party disturbed him.

But Mr. Hamlin had active and reliable friends. Ezra B. French was still secretary of state; Alfred Reddington, adjutant-general, and Samuel Cony, who was afterwards governor of Maine, was then the land agent. Mr. Hamlin's friends in the Senate were Thomas Dyer,

3d, Ira T. Drew, Samuel W. Fox, Samuel Mayhall, Charles Holden, Hiram Chapman, Adams Treat, Benjamin B. Thomas, Henry Richardson, Gilman M. Burleigh, William R. Flint, Jacob Hale, and William Tripp. In the House were Hugh D. McClellan, the Speaker, George M. Freeman, Leander Valentine, Nathan White, Ziba Thayer, John Thissell, Stephen D. Jennings, James Patten, Jr., John Tobin, George P. Sewall, William Merriam, Ebenezer Knowlton, Willard P. Harriman, and others who were prominent in the political affairs of their day. They were not only good anti-slavery men, but they were also practical, and experienced in the ways of politicians. They profited by the lesson of the previous senatorial election, and won their victory when perhaps one false move might have defeated them.

When the legislature convened, the pro-slavery men were confident that they had Mr. Hamlin beaten. Their plan was to enter their four candidates in the Senate caucus, and ultimately concentrate their strength on the one who should develop the largest following and pit him against Mr. Hamlin, in hopes of forcing a deadlock, as they had done in 1846. Mr. Hamlin's friends prudently refrained from disclosing their strength for the reason that a knowledge of their numbers might lead the corrupt element that seduced David Dunn in 1846 to attempt a renewal of dishonorable tactics. They said nothing, but quietly accepted the professions of the pro-slavery men at their face value, and suggested that an agreement be made that both sides support the party nominee, whoever he might be. Confident that they could beat the Hamlin forces in the Senate, the pro-slavery men bound themselves to this agreement. Among themselves they argued with no little merriment that if they could nominate their man in the Senate, and if the House should select Mr. Hamlin, there would be no party nominee, and in that contingency they would be free to carry out their original programme.

Each house held its caucus on the same day — May 29. The House nominated Mr. Hamlin by a handsome majority, as was generally believed it would. Interest was focused on the Senate. On the first ballot Mr. Hamlin lacked a few votes necessary to nominate him. He had a plurality over each of the four candidates against him, but not a majority over all. The balance of power was held by a few men who had been waiting to see which way the tide was going to turn before taking sides. They naturally favored the nomination of an anti-slavery man, but they did not like the idea of going counter to the dictates of the machine. Mr. Hamlin's friends, for this reason, did not throw their full strength on the first ballot. On the second ballot they increased Mr. Hamlin's vote by one; on the third by two, and on the fourth the wavering senators joined the Hamlin forces and gave him fourteen votes, a majority of one over Clifford, Wells,

Senator Hamlin. Aet. 39.

Anderson, and McCrate. The pro-slavery men were dumfounded at the result, but when they recovered from their surprise, they found their pledges to support the nominee staring them in the face. They could do nothing but redeem their promise, and they acquiesced in Mr. Hamlin's nomination, comforting themselves by reminding each other that his term was only three years, and that in the mean time they could prepare themselves for the fight against him in 1851. These pledges they kept, as will appear later. Mr. Hamlin was duly declared the nominee, and elected United States senator. Elijah L. Hamlin was a member of the House, and as a Whig voted for George Evans, the nominee of his party. A few weeks later Elijah L. Hamlin was nominated by the Whigs as their candidate for governor, and Senator Hamlin had to take the stump against his brother, who was defeated.

The same month in which Mr. Hamlin was elected to the Senate, the National Democratic Convention assembled at Baltimore to nominate a candidate for President. The events of the Polk administration proved that the slavery leaders were the power behind the throne of the Democracy, and there were signs of a bitter struggle for the mastery of this convention. The factional differences between the New York Democracy had precluded the renomination of Mr. Polk. Mr. Van Buren still desired a vindication, and his friends cherished a desire for revenge on the Southern Democracy for setting him aside in 1844. The sudden death of Silas Wright reopened old wounds, and his followers in New York were opposed to Mr. Polk's renomination on account of his course in rejecting advice he had sought from Governor Wright in appointing his secretary of the treasury. Thus the anomalous spectacle was presented of anti-slavery and pro-slavery Democrats joining hands to punish the slave power of their party. This faction, led by Mr. Van Buren, was known as the Barnburners; the other, led by William L. Marcy, the Secretary of State, was called the Hunkers. Each sent a delegation to the convention, and refused reasonable offers of compromise. The Barnburners withdrew and announced their intention of making war on the ticket, should it displease them.

This action on the part of the Barnburners not only rendered Mr. Polk's renomination inadvisable, but also peremptorily forbade the selection of Mr. Marcy, who was, perhaps, the ablest leader of the pro-slavery faction, next to Mr. Calhoun. The convention was therefore restricted to making its choice from General Lewis Cass, James Buchanan, and Levi Woodbury, who were the chief candidates considered. Of these three Mr. Hamlin preferred Woodbury. He knew Woodbury personally; he believed him to be safe on the slavery question, and to be amply qualified by ability, character, and experience to fill the presidency. He had also been one of Andrew Jackson's lieutenants, having been secretary of the treasury during Jackson's second term. He had been senator, and was now associate justice of the Supreme Court. In short, Woodbury was a wheel-horse of the Democracy, and would have been a good President. General Cass was a man of high personal character and pronounced ability, but he took the politician's view of slavery and did not seem to see the moral side of it. Mr. Buchanan appeared to Mr. Hamlin to be too pliant and weak to be President. The convention was dominated by the Southern wing, and its leaders, not daring to put forward one of their own men, dictated the nomination of General Cass in the belief that he was a "Northern man with Southern principles." It is perfectly proper to add that when events, in 1860–61, opened General Cass's eyes to the dangers of slavery, he proved his loyalty to the Union by withdrawing from Buchanan's Cabinet.

The nomination of General Cass was displeasing to Mr. Van Buren and his friends. They charged that General Cass, by allowing the use of his name in the convention of 1840, contributed to the defeat of Mr. Van Buren. They decided to bolt Cass, and called a convention of their own at Buffalo. Mr. Van Buren professed his concessions to the principles of Free-Soil, and in this move the more optimistic of the anti-slavery men thought they saw the dawn of a better day. The result was that a sympathetic movement was begun among the Free-Soilers of both parties to coöperate in forming a new party at this convention. Good and true anti-slavery men favored this movement and came to Buffalo. There were Democrats present, such as Salmon P. Chase, Preston King, James S. Wadsworth, John A. Dix, David Dudley Field, and Benjamin F. Butler, of New York. Among the Whigs was Charles Francis Adams, and among the Abolitionists was Joshua R. Giddings. Mr. Van Buren was nominated for President, and Mr. Adams for Vice-President. The Whigs completely begged the issue of slavery extension by nominating General Zachary Taylor on his military record as their platform. All that the public knew about General Taylor at the time was that he was a good soldier who was highly respected by his associates, and was also a large slaveholder. The situation did not seem promising to anti-slavery Democrats. General Cass apparently pledged himself to oppose the principles of the Wilmot Proviso by writing what was called the Nicholson letter. Senator Hamlin was a strong party man, and it was his custom to stand by his party. He believed that great results in national affairs could be best obtained through party coöperation, but he also held that parties erred like men and were to be judged as men were. He was disappointed at the defeat of Woodbury, and he was disturbed over General Cass's apparent repudiation of the Wilmot Proviso. But he was not in the habit of judging men before he tried them, or leaping before he looked. He saw General Cass, and from him obtained a definite statement, that if he should be elected President he would not veto a bill prohibiting the extension of slavery into territory then free.[1] In the political game between the Northern and Southern leaders of the Democracy, General Cass appeared to believe that it was the North's time to take its turn. But if Senator Hamlin found General Cass's position inconsistent with his own ideas of truth and candor, he also found equal insincerity in the professions of Mr. Van Buren. He well knew the lengths to which a political feud would carry men, and he also understood that the Buffalo convention was manipulated by the friends of Mr. Van Buren.[2] He concluded that they were animated by a desire of revenge rather than by a sincere wish to promote the principles of Free-Soil. There was a final consideration that decided Mr. Hamlin to stand by his party. He had been elected to the Senate as an anti-slavery leader, and it was a part of his duty to keep his party in Maine from falling into the hands of the slave power. If he left his party he would lose his hold on it, and there was now a pro-slavery Democrat from Maine in the Senate, Mr. Bradbury. Mr. Hamlin was engaged in the difficult task of "leading his constituents out of the woods," and by remaining with them he exerted an influence he never could wield outside of his party. His reasoning was vindicated within one year by events. Cass was defeated, and Van Buren enjoyed the exquisite satisfaction of polling more votes in New York than Cass did. All Van Buren wanted was revenge, for after beating Cass, Mr. Van Buren threw his Free-Soil professions to the winds and returned to full alliance with his party as a pro-slavery man. In the words of Henry Wilson, then a Free-Soil Whig, "Who then could have imagined that within one brief year the very men who made this gallant fight . . . should return to the ranks they had so effectually broken, . . . aid by voice and vote in again placing in power the men who were found ready to indorse the wicked compromise of 1850 ? "[3]

[1] When a candidate for reëlection to the Senate in 1851, Senator Hamlin wrote to George F. Emery, of Portland, as follows: "I had such information as led me honestly to believe that Cass would never veto a bill prohibiting slavery. I believed so; and was I not in a position to aid all who with me went for Free-Soil? Could I not stand up in the Senate, demand a restriction of slavery, and demand it on the ground that I went for Cass's election with that expectation? I believed then, as I do now, that I could truly aid the cause of freedom by my course. What the Free-Soil men will do, I cannot tell. I only know that I will battle faithfully for Free-Soil, whether defeated or successful."

[2] Lincoln satirized the elastic plank of the Buffalo convention by saying that it reminded him of what the Yankee peddler said of a pair of trousers he had for sale, "large enough for a man and small enough for a boy."

[3] Wilson's *Rise and Fall of the Slave Power*, vol. ii. p. 158.

THE golden age of American oratory was still in its glory when Mr. Hamlin entered the Senate. Webster was at the height of his powers and authority. Calhoun, although on the decline, was still the master mind of his party. The return of Clay reunited this Titanic trio for the last time in the Senate. Another great figure was Benton, the Roman of his party. The most brilliant campaign orator of this period was Thomas Corwin, and he was one of the senators from Ohio. Willie P. Mangum and George E. Badger, of North Carolina, John McPherson Berrien, of Georgia, John M. Clayton, of Delaware, John J. Crittenden, of Kentucky, and Reverdy Johnson, of Maryland, were a notable group of high-minded, cultivated, able statesmen, and pro-slavery Union Whigs, who represented a conservative element that was soon to be supplanted by the aggressive Southern wing of the Democratic party. Jefferson Davis was now recognized in the Senate as a coming leader of that faction, and an aspiring heir to Calhoun's mantle. With him David R. Atchison, of Missouri, David L. Yulee, of Florida, James M. Mason, of Virginia, author of the Fugitive Slave Law, formed a group of historic interest. John Davis, of Massachusetts, and William L. Dayton, of New Jersey, represented the element of the Whig party that was merged into the Republican party eight years later and nominated Mr. Dayton for Vice-President. Stephen A. Douglas was forging to the front as the leader of that wing of the Northern Democracy that regarded slavery as a political rather than a moral issue, and was considered as a presidential candidate. General Sam Houston, of Texas, brave, able, and picturesque, was a Southern man of the Jackson type, and believed by many to be a coming President. Still another presidential possibility was John Bell, of Tennessee, able and statesmanlike, and now an opponent to the slave power. Charles G. Atherton, of New Hampshire, author of the Atherton gag, and Jesse D. Bright, of Indiana, who was subsequently expelled from the Senate for treason, were conspicuous as Northern men with Southern principles. Roger S. Baldwin and John M. Niles were worthy representatives of Connecticut. R. M. T. Hunter, of Virginia, was a Southern leader of distinction who was highly esteemed by his opponents for his per-

EARLY ASSOCIATES IN THE SENATE.

sonal qualities. Andrew Pickens Butler, of South Carolina, was impulsive and generous by nature, and his impassioned utterances rarely left a sting. Henry S. Foote, of Mississippi, brilliant but erratic, was the disturbing factor in the Senate, and often as much a thorn to the disunionists as to the anti-slavery party. Daniel S. Dickinson, a self-made man of ability and character, and the soldierly John A. Dix maintained a conservative attitude towards slavery, the policy the New York Democracy generally followed. In John P. Hale, brilliant and whole-souled, the anti-slavery party had a devoted champion who had stood virtually alone until Mr. Hamlin entered the Senate. Another indication of the great changes working among the masses at the North was the fact that Salmon P. Chase had already been chosen the successor to William Allen, of Ohio. Simon Cameron, the shrewdest political manager this country has yet produced, was beginning his long career as a senator from Pennsylvania. In truth, the Senate of 1848 was an assembly of great and interesting men, nearly all of whom consciously or unconsciously helped cast the shadows of the drama of 1860. The place this Senate holds in history is told in Mr. Blaine's well-chosen words : " At no time before or since in the history of the Senate has its membership been so illustrious, its weight of character and ability so great."

The senate chamber was the room now occupied by the Supreme Court of the United States. Modeled after the Grecian theatre, it was noted for its fine acoustic properties. The proceedings were conducted with great dignity and decorum, although an occasional bitter personal encounter took place. Senatorial courtesy had not yet reached that stage of development which transformed the Senate into an offensive and defensive alliance. Vice-President Dallas was the presiding officer, and he was truly the embodiment of senatorial dignity and diplomatic courtesy. The two senators from Arkansas differed as to pronunciation of the name of their State. Mr. Dallas rose above the difficulty by recognizing one as the "senator from Arkansas," and the other as "the senator from Arkansaw." Ideas of dress as well as of etiquette prevailed that are now absent from the Senate. There was a recognized senatorial toga, and this was the claw-hammer coat. Certain deferential customs were maintained in the public intercourse among the senators, to accentuate the importance of the senatorial function. For example, when a punctilious orator had to refer to a remark of a colleague, he would usually say, "It fell from the senator," as if he had shed words of wisdom.

Behind the scenes the senators relaxed themselves. They were like lawyers who, after having launched their thunder at each other in court, found recreation in enjoying each other's society. The god-like Webster would sometimes signalize his release from duties by wrapping his powerful arms around Mason and Douglas, and give them a bear-like hug. Calhoun ceased to be a Spartan, and became one of the most delightful of men. Henry Clay's imperious manner vanished, and he was soon the centre of a story-telling group. Benton was no longer the Roman, but a cordial, warm-hearted man, who seemed to have no other object than to entertain his friends. Andrew Pickens Butler, after one of his attacks on John P. Hale, would seek what was known as the "cave in the wall," and having cooled down, would engage in repartee and anecdote with his anti-slavery antagonist with the enjoyment of a generous nature. Jefferson Davis, high-bred and courteous, was active in the social life of the Senate. Mr. Hamlin enjoyed pleasant personal relations with Webster, Clay, and the Great Nullifier, although he did not believe in their principles. From the first he was drawn to Benton as the representative Jackson Democrat of his day, and the relations he sustained with the latter are a chapter for another place in these pages. He early formed a close social and party intimacy with Jefferson Davis, the story of which is to be told elsewhere.

When Mr. Hamlin entered the Senate, Congress was once more embroiled in the Oregon controversy, which had been renewed since he left the House. This time the question of Oregon's rights arose for final settlement, and thus it happened that Mr. Hamlin took his seat in the Senate in season to help Oregon save herself from slavery. While this was a famous struggle in its day and severely agitated the country, it was overshadowed by the greater events that ensued. It is of historical importance and personal interest to this narrative. In the latter stage of the Oregon controversy may be found the genesis of the plan to bring the Supreme Court of the United States to the aid of the slave power. The debate also led Mr. Hamlin to make his first anti-slavery speech in the Senate. This speech, by the way, resulted in interesting Abraham Lincoln, who was then a member of the House, in Mr. Hamlin. He heard it and gave it his warm approval.

When Mr. Hamlin was in the House, it will be recalled, the bill was passed granting Oregon territorial government, and prohibiting slavery within her borders. Although the people of Oregon demanded a free government, the pro-slavery Senate was bold enough to repudiate the first principles of self-government by refusing to pass the bill in the face of a strong demand. But action could be delayed no longer now. Lawless men were flocking to Oregon, and the citizens of the territory were compelled to take the law into their own hands. President Polk referred to this in a message to Congress. Further delay by Congress to give Oregon the simple means of self-defense from marauders was certain to create a national scandal.

What Oregon asked was what had been granted to other territories, — Iowa, for instance, — the machinery of law and the right to
regulate her own internal affairs. Why was Oregon singled out as
an exception to the general rule? It was plain now to the leaders
of the slave party that they must show their colors and make their
intentions known. What they wanted was to force slavery into all
territory out of which States were likely to be formed in the near
future. This territory then included Oregon, Upper and Lower California, and New Mexico.

This scheme was generally understood throughout the North; but
it must not be forgotten that the slave party had not yet directly
acknowledged its purpose, and was not a unit in working to this end
until the Oregon controversy came up for final settlement. Undoubtedly the leaders of the slave party intended to make as fierce a
fight as possible for the possession of Oregon as well as California
and New Mexico; but, failing in the case of the former territory,
they planned to make use of the controversy over Oregon as a basis of
compromise in dealing with the other territories. They were determined not to lose the hard-earned results of the Mexican war, — California and New Mexico. The thought that they might infuriated
them. Events were therefore ripe for a fight to a finish, so to speak,
when Stephen A. Douglas, at the beginning of this session of Congress, introduced a bill organizing a government in Oregon similar
to that which Congress had granted to Iowa, and which forbade the
introduction of slavery. John P. Hale offered an amendment embracing the principles of the Ordinance of 1787. These measures
together were too much for the slavery leaders. Their pent-up anger
escaped; they threw prudence to the winds, and in their wrath they
let out their desires. Mr. Calhoun had the audacity of his wishes.
He boldly proclaimed his doctrine, that "the national flag carries
slavery wherever it floats." He laid down some dogmas in support
of this doctrine, that "Congress had no right to prevent a citizen
of a slave State from emigrating with his slave property to any territory, and holding his slaves there in servitude;" that "the people
of such territory have no right to legislate adversely thereto," and
that "Congress has no right to vest such authority in a territorial
government."

The significance of these declarations was that the slave controversy had entered on a new stage. The terms " Whigs" and " Democrats" had little meaning now among the Southern members of
Congress. They rallied around the standard of Calhoun, and accepted
his declaration that "the national flag carries slavery wherever it
floats" as their shibboleth. Conservative Whigs, such as Berrien, of
Georgia, and Clayton, of Delaware, worked with Jefferson Davis, the

leader of the young, aggressive Southern Democracy. Mr. Davis made an extreme speech, in which he defined the slave as a chattel, and claimed that for that reason the owner could take his property wherever he liked. According to this the doctrine of state rights was inoperative in a free State if a slaveholder chose to appear in it with his "property." But the debate popularized this theory with the slave party, and it was adopted as a cardinal principle, whereas before it had been tentatively presented. Although Mr. Davis's speech was extreme, it sounded the note of compromise. He was a spokesman of the slave party, and its leaders were now evidently looking beyond Oregon and at California and New Mexico.

But there was nothing to compromise, and so much the better for the slave power. If it could hoodwink the Northern congressmen into believing that a compromise was the only way out of the difficulty, it was sure to gain a point. Mr. Clayton, of Delaware, moved that the Douglas bill be referred to a select committee of eight, — four from the North and four from the South. This motion appealed equally to the senators who supported slavery, and those who believed in "the glue of compromise," and those who worshiped the function of committee deliverance. Only fourteen senators opposed it, and among them were Messrs. Hamlin, Hale, Dix, Niles, Baldwin, and John Davis. Two of the Northern men appointed were Jesse D. Bright, of Indiana, who was expelled from the Senate for treason in 1862, and Daniel S. Dickinson, of New York, an honorable man, but one who never saw the slave power in its true light until the war. Mr. Dickinson said that he beheld "a gleam of sunshine" in Mr. Clayton's motion. That is why he was placed on the committee. There was but one anti-slavery man on this committee, — S. S. Phelps, of Vermont. It was a packed court.

The deliverance of this committee was called the Clayton compromise. It was an extraordinary affair. Instead of dealing with Oregon exclusively, or with each territory separately, the committee lumped the three territories together in a log-rolling scheme. Instead of taking action on the slavery question, it dodged and recommended that the matter be referred to the Supreme Court of the United States. This was a crafty plan, and it failed by a miracle. The court was a strong pro-slavery body, and although its members were pure and high-minded men, they were biased, and so strongly tinctured with slavery ideas that, had they sat on this question, Oregon, California, and New Mexico would have been doomed to slavery, or the final struggle might have been precipitated then. It is not necessary to add that the anti-slavery senators fought this bill resolutely, and the main discussion was on the abstract and concrete questions that slavery involved. Mr. Hamlin's speech differed somewhat from the general order of remarks heard in the Senate. While he denounced the institution of slavery with characteristic bluntness and force, his speech is more interesting as an exposition of the character of the bill. In this respect it is one of the best to be found in the " Congressional Record." He condemned the bill as a fraud, a snare, and a delusion. The speech was widely circulated in pamphlet among the anti-slavery documents of the time.

This was the year of '48, " the year of revolutions," when a democratic movement swept over Europe and seemed to presage the springing up of republican institutions all over the Old World. Mr. Hamlin, in opening his remarks, pictured in a few terse sentences the contrast afforded.

" It is indeed startling," said he, " that in the middle of the nineteenth century, — in this model republic, with the sun of liberty shining upon us, and while the governments of Europe are tottering to their base from the lights reflected from our own, and while they are striking down the shackles of tyranny over the minds of men, — we have been gravely discussing the proposition whether we will not create by law the institution of human slavery in territories now free. Such is the question in direct terms before us ; such, in fact, is the issue now. Sophistry cannot evade it; metaphysics cannot escape it. . . . The crisis is now upon us. . . . We are about to shape and mould the character of these territories, which in time will become a mighty empire. Whether that country shall present all the elements of a free government, in which man is elevated as an intellectual and moral being, or whether the despotism of slavery shall imprint its soil, are matters depending entirely on us. We must act. . . . The issue cannot be avoided. . . .

" The bill like the proposition discussed by the Senate does not profess to establish slavery by law. It leaves slavery to extend itself by the 'silent operation' of the law, without restriction. It does not guaranty slavery; but will it not permit slavery ? And after it has found an existence, will it not demand a guaranty ? Thus, without inhibition will it not become certain and fixed by the process of time ? . . . I solemnly believe that this bill will allow of the extension of slavery as certainly as if it created slavery in express words. The bill, as I understand it, concedes practically all the ultra-doctrinaires of the South demand. Let us then erect a barrier to this tide of moral evil. . . . It will thrill the country like an electric shock when it is known that the acquisition of territory from a foreign power necessarily subjects it to the institution of slavery, that the flag of this Union carries slavery wherever it floats. This is a new principle in the doctrines of slavery propagandism. It is not the doctrine of the founders of the republic. Democracy has been called progressive, but my word for it, she goes along in the old-fashioned stage-coach style, while this doctrine of slavery propagandism has mounted the railroad cars. . . . I repeat, it will startle the North when it is known that it is gravely announced here that the Constitution of the United States . . . carries with it and extends the institution of slavery; that it, in fact, abrogates the laws of the free and gives instead the powers of servitude. . . . These doctrines are not to be deduced from the Constitution, but are in derogation of its letter and spirit; that instrument is, in all its terms and in all its scope, an anti-slavery instrument. It was conceived, it was enacted, it was approved by the States of this Union, not in the spirit of extension or creation of slavery, but in a spirit which looked to the future emancipation of the slave in this country."[1]

With this introduction, Mr. Hamlin discussed the Calhoun dogma, that the Constitution contained within its provisions a power to establish and extend slavery over free territory. This amounted to the notion that as the territories belonged to all the people, and as the Constitution recognized slavery, it therefore authorized the institution in the territories. Mr. Hamlin quoted from articles one and four of the Constitution, and showed that it simply recognized slavery as existing; it did not provide for the creation, or extension of the institution. In one instance, the Constitution spoke of slaves as a basis of taxation and representation, and in the other with regard to the laws requiring the free States to return fugitive slaves. That was all. The falsity of the interpretation that the supporters of slavery placed on the Constitution was exposed by Mr. Hamlin in these words : —

"The argument that slavery is recognized by the Constitution is used as an equivalent to establishing it. The laws of the State support and maintain it," Mr. Hamlin continued, "not the Constitution. It is a state institution resting on the local law of the State, without the aid, without the support, without the maintenance, of the Constitution in any way whatever. . . . If the institution of slavery is one which has its foundation in the Constitution, and not one resting upon the laws of the State, where is the limit to its extension? What is the next step in the application of the argument? After you have overrun your territories, what power can prevent the slaveholder from coming into the free States with his slaves? If his right is a constitutional one, if he rests his claim there, and is correct, a state law could not affect him, because it would be in conflict with the Constitution. . . . The Constitution gives no right, it creates no right; it merely recognizes a right which is created by the laws of the State. That slavery is a local institution there can be no doubt. The courts of nearly all the States have so decided. . . . The moment a slave goes beyond the limits of a State where slavery exists, he becomes free. Slavery, therefore, must look alone to local laws for its support.

"I hold that the Constitution in and of itself, and by its express language, authorizes Congress to inhibit this institution in our territories. . . . What is the language of this clause of the Constitution? 'Congress shall have power to dispose of and make all needful rules and regulations respecting the territory or other property belonging to the United States.' "

Mr. Hamlin traced the history of this clause. No such power

[1] For example, the slave trade was abolished.

existed in the articles of confederation, and when the Constitution was formed this power was granted to Congress. It was exercised by numerous presidents, and declared valid by the Supreme Court.

"Again," said Mr. Hamlin, "the power is contained in the bill upon which we are acting. It continues the laws of Oregon in force for three months after the meeting of the legislature. It provides in the territories of California and New Mexico that the legislative power shall not pass any laws on the subject of religion or slavery. . . . If the Constitution was silent, as it is not, yet under that power which can acquire we can most certainly govern. It matters little where you can find the power to acquire ; if you do acquire you must have the power to govern. The first is the major, the second is the minor proposition. It would not be good sense to contend that we have a power to acquire public domain, and yet could not pass needful rules and regulations for its government. . . . Casuists have been known to deny their own existence and satisfactorily to prove it to their own minds. That may be a plausible and practical doctrine when contrasted with the one that we have no power to govern our own territories. . . .

"Having the power to act, what is the responsible duty which I feel imposed on me ? It is that I should exert all the power which the Constitution gives to exclude the institution of slavery from our territories now free, because it is a social, moral, and political evil. That such is its character needs no argument to prove. They are conceded facts — supported by the declarations and admonitions of the best and wisest men of the South,

"'In thoughts that breathe and words that burn.'

"I would resist the introduction of that institution in justice to a superior race of men, — men who are capable of a higher state of social and political refinement. I would institute such governments as are best calculated to advance the true interests of our own Caucasian race, and not degrade the dignity of labor by fastening upon it the incubus of slavery. I would resist it because I would not invoke or use the name of Democracy to strike down as with the iron mace of a despot the principles of social equality and freedom. I would not profane the sacred name of Freedom while using it to impose a tyranny upon the minds or persons of men. Jefferson has said that 'God has no attribute which can take sides with us in such a cause.' The eloquent Pinckney has declared that 'the earth itself, which teems with profusion under the cultivating hand of the freeborn laborer, shrinks into barrenness from the contaminating sweat of the slave.' Sir, my course is a plain one, and clear from all doubt. Our position is unquestionable. We stand in defense of free soil and resist aggressive slavery, and we demand enactments for the protection of free soil against this aggression. We will not disturb that institution, but we will stand in defense of the freedom of our soil as right in principle and beneficial to free white labor in all parts of our common country."

Mr. Hamlin next discussed compromise, and in connection with that subject he revealed again the fraudulent nature of the bill and the crooked record of the slave party in dealing with Oregon. He briefly related the history of Oregon's efforts to secure a free government, and charged the pro-slavery Senate with killing every bill the House passed for Oregon's relief. The Douglas bill had a provision inhibiting slavery, but it was recommitted to the committee of eight, and reported back "chained" to other territorial bills, with the anti-slavery provision so modified that it secured freedom for Oregon for three months only after the first territorial legislature should meet.

"This bill," said Mr. Hamlin, "is called by some a compromise; all that I can see which entitles it to that name is that it does provide that the laws in Oregon which exclude slavery shall remain in force for three months. A compromise, indeed! . . . Why was the law regarding the exclusion of slavery not permitted to remain in force until the territorial legislature should see fit to change it? Why abrogate and then compel them to change their laws? Sir, it is not worth the name of compromise. This is the fundamental objection: It repeals all the laws of the territory after three months, and the seventeenth section provides that 'All laws passed by the legislative assembly shall be submitted to the Congress of the United States, and if disapproved, shall be null and of no effect,' thus making the legislative acts of Oregon depend upon our approval or disapproval. Is it not, then, literally true that this bill concedes the free principle to Oregon for only three months, after which it must depend on our action here?"

Mr. Hamlin next exposed two grossly inconsistent features of the bill, and the causes of their adoption. One gave Oregon a territorial government with the right to elect a legislature; the other denied California and New Mexico a territorial government and legislature, but vested all authority in the governors, secretaries, and judges, to be appointed by the President, and forbade them passing any laws respecting religion and slavery. Mr. Hamlin stigmatized the provision relating to California and New Mexico as creating an "odious oligarchy." He asked:—

"Why adopt one system for Oregon and another for California? Is it said that the people of California are not yet suited to participate in a free government or in the enactment of laws? If such were the fact, why wholly exclude them from all rights? But senators know that even at this day there are some five or six thousand American citizens there, and they are ruthlessly excluded. Is their capacity for free government to be mistrusted? Is it not rather from the fact that they would set up a free government that they are deprived of all power? I know there is a mixed population in California; and so there is in Oregon; but the same limitations and restrictions which apply in one case can be applied in the other. The right of voting has been confined in Oregon to the 'free white inhabitants.' The same limitations may apply to California. No sound distinction can be drawn in these cases; yet a republican government is established in one case and an oligarchy in the other. . . . Is it not better to authorize our own people to participate in this government and allow the free Castilian race the same power? Is it not sound policy as well as correct in principle? Will it not fraternize them with our people and our government? On the other hand, without power in the local laws by which they are governed, will they not be alien to our Union and un-fraternal to our people? It must not be forgotten that all laws which would be passed in California, as in Oregon, would be subject to the approval or disapproval of Congress. This system is wholly repugnant to our form of government. It is in violation of the fundamental principle which recognizes the 'consent of the governed' as the basis of government."

Mr. Hamlin's most convincing exposition of the artful character and insincere purpose of the bill was made when he took up the claim that the measure was framed to settle the question of slavery in the territories by referring the matter to the Supreme Court of the United States from the Supreme Court of the territory. It actually prevented such a reference. He read a clause in the bill which provided that appeals from the Supreme Court of the territory should " be taken to the Supreme Court of the United States in the same manner, and under the same regulations, as from the Circuit Court of the United States." But it happened, as Mr. Hamlin demonstrated, that the right of appeal from the Circuit Court to the Supreme Court of the United States was granted " where the matter in dispute exceeds the sum of two thousand dollars." Thus, slaves that were worth less than this sum were barred out from taking an appeal. On this and other points Mr. Hamlin said : —

" The settlement of the question of slavery by this bill, it is said, is to be determined by the Supreme Court. . . . This is the first instance in the history of legislation where a question purely of a historical character has been transferred to the judiciary. It is avoiding what necessarily belongs to us to determine. Is this the part of wisdom, or manly dignity and firmness, to avoid settlement of a question which is political and which belongs to us? I think not. . . . Suppose slavery steals into the territories, as it will (under the bill), how can the slave avail himself of this right of appeal? Who is to aid him in the first instance to obtain his writ of habeas corpus on which to try his right to freedom? And if he should get that process and take his first step, how could he appeal? Who would be his surety? And at the distance of three thousand miles from Washington, by what means could he reach the court? This right of appeal, if it existed by law, could have no practical effect whatever. It leaves all unsettled, in fact, while two lines in a law we may pass, by simply inhibiting the institution, will settle all. . . . If it could apply to one case it would be powerless in thousands. It is all delusive. It does not allow an appeal at all.

"How, then, stands the case? You establish a government in California; a governor and secretary are appointed by the President, and three judges who are not removable. To them you submit the legislative power of the territory; you deny them the power to legislate at all upon the subjects of religion and slavery, even if every person in the territory should desire to exclude the latter. You deprive the people of the right to act at all, — you refuse to act here, nearly one half of the Senate denying the power to act. Is this not virtually building up a wall around that territory which will and which must serve as a protection to that institution? What is the origin of slavery? It is never created by law; it steals into territory and then claims a law to recognize it. . . . It exists by brute force, in violation of the rights of everything human or divine. . . .

"Looking to the lights of other days — the patriots of other times — the eloquent warnings which we have from our Washington, Madison, our Jefferson, our Mason, aye, and from our Pinckney, too, and all that long list of patriotic men of the South who have adorned this Union, who have pointed out the evils that would come upon us by perpetuating and extending this institution, I owe it to the constituents whom I represent, to our posterity, to all the toiling millions who are seeking an asylum in our land, to embrace this opportunity of opposing, with unshaken firmness, any attempt to introduce or permit this institution to flow into any territory now free. Let these vast and fertile regions be preserved for the cultivation of free labor and free men, so well calculated to advance the arts of civilization. Do this, and the busy millions of future ages shall bless our acts with grateful hearts."

The story of Oregon's struggle for free soil should be followed to the end in order to get a complete idea of the tenacity of the slave power in its desire to make Oregon a slave State. The debate continued for several days, and on the morning of July 22, at eight o'clock, after a continuous session of twenty-one hours, the compromise bill was passed by eleven majority. Among those who voted against this surrender to the slave power were Messrs. Hamlin, Hale, John Davis, William Allen, Bradbury, Dayton, Dix, Niles, Corwin. Badger, of North Carolina, Bell, of Tennessee, and Metcalfe, of Kentucky, were the only Southern senators who were still obedient to their implied duty.

But Oregon was still to be saved. When the bill was sent to the House, Alexander H. Stephens moved that the measure be tabled, and his motion prevailed. The bill had a chance of success in the House, where the arguments for compromise were potent also. Whether Mr. Stephens threw away this opportunity by reason of timidity or an attack of mental blindness was a matter of speculation. While he did not always serve the slave power blindly, the fact is obvious that the cause of freedom in this instance received opportune aid from one who was generally allied with the slave party.

Still the struggle continued. Caleb B. Smith, in February, had introduced into the House a bill to organize a territorial government in Oregon, and it was passed in March by a large majority, in spite of the leaders of the slave party, who objected to its free clause. In August, Mr. Douglas introduced this bill into the Senate, with an amendment applying the Ordinance of 1787 to Oregon, with the reason, "Inasmuch as said territory is north of the parallel of 36° 30' north latitude, usually known as the line of the Missouri Compromise." Once more a bitter debate ensued on the question of slavery — the alleged rights and wrongs of the North and the South. Mr. Douglas told the Senate that the Ordinance of 1787 had been incorporated in his bill by the Committee on Territories, in which it was formed, because "it desired that no senator should commit himself on the great question." But this artful plea induced only two senators to vote for the amendment, — Mr. Douglas himself and Bright. Yet the everlasting merits, virtues, and necessities of compromise were again officially brought before the Senate, and that weary body agreed by eleven majority to Mr. Douglas's next proposition, to extend the Missouri Compromise line to the Pacific Ocean. Mr. Hamlin voted against this compromise, and it is an instructive and interesting circumstance that among his companions in this vote were John C. Calhoun and Daniel Webster, the latter having spoken strongly against the attempt to rob Oregon of her rights.

But all this manœuvring in the Senate went for naught. The House, with only three dissenting votes, rejected the compromise amendment when it came from the Senate, and the bill was returned. The genius, courage, and force of Benton came to the rescue. He moved that the Senate recede from the amendment. Perhaps it was the indiscreet utterance of John C. Calhoun, that "the great strife between the North and South is ended, the separation of the North and South is complete," that was the final cause which decided the fate of the bill to give Oregon her freedom. At all events, John Bell and Sam Houston disavowed Calhoun's sentiments as representative of the South, and General Houston was among those who changed their votes. The debate continued day and night, until the exhausted Senate was driven to close it on August 13, at nine o'clock in the morning, after an all-night session. At midnight, before the vote was taken, the incorrigible Foote announced his ability and intention of speaking continuously for two days and nights. The senators expressed their willingness to have him try it. He was actually speaking at nine o'clock the next morning, when debate was shut off. Mr. Douglas, General Houston, and a few other senators followed the lead of Benton in changing their votes, and by a majority of four votes the unprecedented struggle between the anti-slavery and pro-slavery parties, that had lasted for many months, was closed, and Oregon was a free territory forever.

Soon after Mr. Hamlin took his seat in the Senate, he heard of Abraham Lincoln, who was serving his first and only term in the House of Representatives. Mr. Lincoln did not make much of a mark as a legislator or debater; he was in the House too short a time to make his peculiar personality felt to a great extent in shaping legislation. Mr. Hamlin first heard Mr. Lincoln spoken of as a "rattling stump orator," the "champion story-teller of the House," and the "most striking-looking man in Congress." The general impression about Lincoln, as Mr. Hamlin related in subsequent years, was that he was the personification of geniality and democracy, a faithful worker, and always ready for a good story. He was often seen in the cloak-room of the House tilted back in a chair, with his legs crossed, and a crowd around him listening to the fund of interesting and amusing stories that rolled out of him.

The day Mr. Hamlin made his speech on the compromise bill, he observed among his auditors a man who towered up above the outsiders who crowded the outer aisles of the Senate floor, like an oak in a forest of saplings. His appearance was so unusual — of immense size, loosely hung frame, homely, but expressive face — that Mr. Hamlin could not fail to note him. Mr. Hamlin knew that it must be Lincoln, and he observed that Lincoln followed his speech with apparent interest, nodding his head from time to time, as a sign of approval, when Mr. Hamlin made a good point against slavery.

A few days after this Mr. Hamlin was called into the House, where he found Lincoln in the middle of a speech. Part of the speech was of the rough-and-tumble order he made in his early days, when he was struggling to get a hearing with the masses in Illinois; but the most was pure good-nature. While Lincoln's face was homely, and his movements seemed awkward, when his face was lighted up with a smile, his countenance took on an appearance of irresistible good-humor and frankness, and men felt drawn to him. When he reached the heart of his subject, he was bubbling over with fun, and had the House completely under the spell of his humor and magnetism. Although Mr. Lincoln was speaking at the expense of the Democrats, they enjoyed it immensely. Members crowded around him to hear every word he said. He completely dominated the situation. Mr. Hamlin never forgot this scene, which was a unique illustration of Mr. Lincoln's power over his audiences. When Mr. Hamlin entered the House, the future President was saying in his quaint, droll way : —

" By the way, Mr. Speaker, did you know that I am a military hero? Yes, sir, in the days of the Black Hawk war, I fought, bled, and came away.

Speaking of General Cass's career reminds me of my own. I was not at Stillman's defeat, but I was about as near it as Cass was to Hull's surrender; and like him saw the place very soon afterwards. It is quite certain that I did not break my sword, for I had none to break; but I bent a musket pretty badly on one occasion. If Cass broke his sword, the idea is he broke it in desperation; I bent the musket by accident. If General Cass went in advance of me in picking whortleberries, I guess I surpassed him in charges upon the wild onions. If he saw any live, fighting Indians, it was more than I did, but I had a good many bloody struggles with the mosquitoes; and although I never fainted from loss of blood, I can truly say I was often very hungry. Mr. Speaker, if I should ever conclude to doff whatever our Democratic friends may suppose there is of black cockade federalism about me, and thereupon they shall take me up as their candidate for the presidency, I protest they shall not make fun of me as they have of General Cass by attempting to write me into a military hero."

Mr. Hamlin and Mr. Lincoln did not meet until after the presidential campaign of 1860. Almost the first thing Mr. Lincoln said was in reference to the speech Mr. Hamlin made on the Oregon Compromise Bill.

CHAPTER XIX

When General Zachary Taylor was inaugurated President on March 4, 1849, the opponents and supporters of slavery knew that a great crisis was imminent, and prepared themselves for the struggle. The contest was over the disposition of the territory acquired from Mexico. The interests involved were immense, for they included the region that now mostly comprises California, New Mexico, Arizona, and other territory. Texas, which had also been a part of Mexico, was already in the Union as a slave State. Now, as the slave power had planned and fought the war with Mexico, its leaders were naturally anxious to obtain the results of their scheming. In the waning hours of the Polk administration Mr. Calhoun attempted to rush a bill through Congress, attached to the general appropriation bill "extending the Constitution to the ceded territory." Once again, Mr. Calhoun enunciated his peculiar doctrine that "the flag carries slavery wherever it floats." This was trying to steal a march on the incoming administration. Daniel Webster exposed the flaw in Calhoun's argument as applied to the territories by showing that the Constitution was for the States, not for the territories, and that the latter to enjoy its benefits must organize themselves into States. Courtesy and fairness to the new administration should have deterred Mr. Calhoun from this course; but he was the genius of the slave power, and pressed the issue to a vote. Smarting under defeat, Mr. Calhoun called the famous secret meeting of the Southern congressmen, and issued his inflammatory address to the South, advising disunion, as plainly as he dared, in case the anti-slavery party should succeed in saving the new territory from the peculiar institution, under General Taylor's administration.

This was the situation that confronted General Taylor when he became President, and very few people knew what he would do. Probably no man ever came to the presidency with so little known about him as Zachary Taylor. When he was nominated by the Whigs for President, they were not sure that he was a good party man. Webster denounced the nomination as one "unfit to be made," and Clay at first refused to take part in the campaign. He was believed by the general public to be a gallant officer, and an honest, rough-and-ready kind of a man, and the popular opinion was that he would eventually serve as the figurehead to an administration that would be conducted by other men. But the leaders of the Whigs who suggested General Taylor as their party candidate were not mistaken in their estimate of him. Although he had lived most of his life on the frontier, and had never even voted, he was nevertheless well informed about public men and measures, and had his own ideas about conducting his administration. Removed from the scene of excitement at the national capital, General Taylor had clearly perceived the rock towards which the ship of state was drifting. When he took the helm he displayed the same sagacity, coolness, judgment, and patriotism that had distinguished him as a commander on the battlefield.

When Congress convened, in December, 1849, for the first time under President Taylor's administration, the situation was complicated by unexpected happenings in California. The discovery of gold on the Pacific slope, late in the previous year, had drawn an immense army of men thither from the free States and elsewhere. Within a marvelously short time, California had more than enough citizens within her borders to fulfill the requirements of admission to the Union. The presence of lawless adventurers from all parts of the world made it necessary to organize a state government at once to preserve life and property. A constitutional convention was called; Thomas Butler King, of Georgia, who was in California, and was acting as the agent of the slave power, endeavored to induce the convention to adopt a constitution permitting slavery to be established in the new State. But the free-soil element triumphed, and California asked Congress to admit her as a free State. Yet, in spite of the fact that the vast majority of the people in California had voted against the introduction of the peculiar institution, Mr. Calhoun and his followers boldly conspired to plant slavery on their soil. Their action was all the more indefensible in view of their loud professions to be the champions of the old-fashioned Democratic doctrine of personal liberty. But while the leaders of the slave power at first proclaimed their intention of making California a slave State, they finally admitted among themselves their inability to accomplish their entire purpose, and planned to take California by the throat in order to effect a compromise from which they could gain some advantage. In brief, their ultimate hope was to force the anti-slavery party into an agreement whereby the Missouri Compromise line would be extended across the country to the Pacific slope. This would greatly increase the area of slavedom, though taking only a part of California.

President Taylor's action was therefore awaited with great anxiety by the entire nation, for the initiative lay with him. He promptly acted, and in his first and only annual message to Congress he dealt both the slave power and Mr. Calhoun a heavy blow by recommending the immediate admission of California as a free State, and the keeping of New Mexico under military government until it should be sufficiently populated to become a State. These were the chief features of the message; the other suggestions it contained need not be detailed. A circumstance that increased the anger of the slave party was that the President was himself a Southerner and a slaveholder. An incident that gave the message a bitter personal flavor was General Taylor's contemptuous treatment of Mr. Calhoun. It leaked out that the Great Nullifier had requested the President-elect, through the Secretary of State, Mr. Clayton, to make no references in his message to the fears he entertained for the safety of the Union. General Taylor's reply was to add a paragraph, in which he emphasized his apprehensions, and announced his intention of doing all within his power to maintain the integrity of the Union. When the slave party took in the full significance of the President's message, Congress became a volcano of wrath, and a veritable battle between giants was begun over the direct issue of the restriction or extension of slavery, when Henry Clay came forward with his famous compromise measures, and changed the course of events.

Clay was profoundly alarmed over the fierce struggle that was raging in Congress, and he returned to the Senate with the hope that he might prevent a crisis by effecting a compromise over the questions at issue. He came in the rôle of a peacemaker, and his knowledge of the fact that his own end was not far distant gave unwonted solemnity and earnestness to his efforts. He knew that he was engaged in his last great life's work, and that personally he had no material reward to hope for. His mission was honorable, disinterested, and eminently patriotic. He sincerely believed that he could divert the danger of disunion, and perhaps settle the slavery question on a basis where it might work out a peaceful solution. But the salvation of the Union was his paramount object, and it was in this spirit that he offered his compromise measures. These, in brief, provided for the admission of California; the organization of government in the remaining territory acquired from Mexico; adjustment of the disputed boundary of Texas, and the allowance of $10,000,000 to that State for the payment of her debt; the abolition of the slave trade in the District of Columbia; more effectual provisions for the recovery of fugitive slaves. Mr. Clay's measures of compromise not only at first provoked a heated controversy, but also caused a serious breach in his own party. President Taylor vehemently opposed Mr. Clay's plan and the Southern extremists. Mr. Calhoun's last speech, which was read for him in the Senate, rejected the Clay compromise proposition, and predicted the coming of disunion. Benton threw his powerful weight against Clay ; Webster was for compromise. The President remained firm, and a deadlock between Congress and the Executive now seemed imminent.

As the debate waxed fiercer, the radical side of Mr. Hamlin's nature became more noticeable, and the causes are of personal and historical interest. During the five years Mr. Hamlin had been in Congress, he had steadily opposed the encroachments of the slave power, and with great mortification he had seen it increase the area of slavedom through alliances with Northern congressmen. He repudiated the Clay compromise bill, because he was unwilling to compromise his principles, and also because he believed that the time had come when the anti-slavery people should make a supreme effort to drive the slave party away from free soil, even if the disunion element should attempt ultimate measures. On general principles, Mr. Hamlin had little faith in "the glue of compromise ;" the Clay compromise measures he regarded as bad and dangerous ; the proposed fugitive slave law [1] was to him an atrocious thing, and he would have opposed the omnibus bill on that account alone. But the main consideration with Mr. Hamlin now was the necessity of making a final stand against the enemy, even if it provoked a crisis.

There is a glimpse revealed of his heart-felt grievances in the following letter he wrote William P. Haines on May 4, 1849 : —

"I thank you most truly for your kind appreciation of my course during the brief time I have held a place in the Senate. I feel the importance of the position, and it shall be my anxious effort to pursue that course which shall be neither *rash* nor *diffident* upon the slavery question. I can only say that my course is taken and will be adhered to, come weal or woe to me. . . . I will resist firmly but not factiously the extension of human slavery into regions where it does not now exist. Your generous approval is cheering, and the more so because I have at times felt a terrible pressure upon me in my official position. . . .

"This troublesome question might have been settled long ago if the North had honestly and firmly represented, through the press and public servants, the sentiment of her people. *The South was ready to acquiesce.* But, alas ! the patronage of the government was thrown into the contest. . . . Many Northern men surrendered the right in order to 'stand well at headquarters.' . . . But I still look to the future, with faith and confidence that the right will triumph over the wrong, and that we and those who come after us shall rejoice in the consummation of correct principles. So may God in his mercy order it.

[1] Mr. Hamlin, John P. Hale, William H. Seward, and other anti-slavery senators did not vote on this measure. Mr. Hamlin was paired, and undoubtedly the others were. The *Congressional Globe* did not record pairs at that time. Mr. Hamlin's opposition to the Fugitive Slave Law was known through his speeches, and his pair was understood.

" We have had rich times here.   Moral treason, blustering, and gasconade
have been the Southern staple.   Within the past week some severe rebukes
have been given in the Senate by Clay and by some men in the House.   A
different temper is plainly manifest.   The result will be that the North will
not be frightened by the utterance of such stuff, and those who talk of disunion as flippantly as schoolgirls will regret and repent of their course.
We have had one dissolution convention [1] at the North, and those who engaged in it acquired an infamy that still clings to them.   Those at the South
who pursue the same course will meet with the same fate.

" Well, I like Henry Clay!   He is a bold man.   I like him for that.   He
is an honest man in my opinion.   The rebukes which he gave Foote were
well timed.   He is an anti-slavery man at heart, and really I believe he
would be an Abolitionist at the North.   He goes as far as he can now. . . .
California will come in and no mistake! . . . On the admission of California I rather think you may hear from me."

Although Senator Hamlin was politically opposed to President
Taylor, and favored an aggressive anti-slavery policy, nevertheless
circumstances brought him close to the President, and enabled him to
gauge " Old Rough-and-Ready" at his true worth.   Mr. Hamlin was
first called to the White House on executive business connected with
the Senate, and it appears that President Taylor and he liked each
other's prompt way of transacting business.   It would also appear
that the President in these interviews revealed to Mr. Hamlin a more
intimate knowledge of public men and affairs than it was supposed
he possessed.   After Mr. Hamlin had had several conferences with
President Taylor, he was surprised one day by receiving a peremptory summons to come to the White House.   When Mr. Hamlin
presented himself, the President, without any preliminary remarks,
proceeded to address him in his blunt, characteristic way as follows : —

" Senator Hamlin, I know you to be an honest man.   You and I
don't belong to the same party, but I know you well enough now to
believe that you will give your President your honest advice for his
own good when he asks it.   Now the Whigs in Maine are disputing
over the patronage, and I want you to tell me who are the best men
to appoint."

" Yes, sir, you are my President," replied Mr. Hamlin laughingly,
"and as a good citizen of this republic I will cheerfully and gladly
obey your orders, even in assisting you to settle family quarrels in
your party."

" Good!" said " Old Rough-and-Ready" with a laugh, and then
clasping his hands behind his back, and tilting his head to one side,
he began to pace up and down the room, discussing the various candidates for office in Maine who had been presented to him.   President
Taylor would discuss the candidates like this : —

[1] The Hartford convention.

"What do you think of this man? Isn't honest? Then I won't appoint him. What do you think of that man? Isn't a good Whig? Then I won't appoint him. These men you say are honest and competent? Then I will send their names to the Senate."

This occurred within a short time after Congress had convened, in December, 1849, when the debate over California was beginning. Not long afterwards, and before Mr. Hamlin had made a public declaration of his opinions on the Clay compromises, he received another imperative summons from the President. Then a dramatic incident occurred that suggests what might have happened if General Taylor had lived out his term, and also explains why Union men like Mr. Hamlin had supreme faith in him. As Mr. Hamlin was entering the White House he almost ran into Robert Toombs, Alexander H. Stephens, and Thomas L. Clingman, who were still leaders in the House, and were now high priests in the inner councils of the slave power. They came hurriedly out of the President's room with angry looks on their faces and talking in loud voices. They had every appearance of being thoroughly enraged, and they were so engrossed in denouncing some one that they did not see Mr. Hamlin at first. When they looked up and recognized him they started, and one of them said sharply: "What are you doing here?"

Mr. Hamlin was surprised, but his feelings were turned to amazement when he was forthwith admitted to the President's room and saw the chief magistrate of the nation apparently unable to control himself. "General Taylor," to quote Mr. Hamlin's words, "was rushing around the room like a caged lion;" his face was almost livid with anger; he was fiercely muttering to himself and shaking his fist at imaginary foes. He was so completely carried away by his feelings that he passed Mr. Hamlin three or four times without noticing him. But when President Taylor saw Mr. Hamlin he stopped with a start, and then rushing up to him, asked, —

"Did you see those damned traitors? They have been making demands concerning my administration, and threatened that unless they were acceded to the South would secede. But if there are any such treasonable demonstrations on the part of the Southern leaders, I will hang them; —— —— them, I will hang them as high as I hung spies in Mexico, and I will put down any treasonable movement with the whole power of the government, if I have to put myself at the head of the army to do it."

"Mr. Hamlin, what are you doing in the Senate with the omnibus bill?"

"Mr. President," replied Mr. Hamlin, "I believe the bill wrong in principle, and am doing what I can to defeat it."

"That is right," rejoined President Taylor, his excitement breaking

out again; "stand firm; don't yield; it means disunion, and I am
pained to learn that we have disunion men among us. Disunion is
treason; and if the disunionists attempt to carry out their schemes
while I am President, I will hang them." [1]

Taylor was in no mood to transact the business for which he
had sent for Mr. Hamlin, and the latter, perceiving it, quickly withdrew, after warmly commending the President for his firmness, and
expressing his own opinion of the actions of the disunionists. As
Mr. Hamlin was coming out of the White House, he met Thurlow
Weed, of New York,[2] one of the powers of the Whig party. Mr.
Weed was close to General Taylor, and Mr. Hamlin, knowing that,
stopped long enough to tell him that he would find him greatly
agitated. Mr. Weed at once hurried to the President's room and
found him still excited. He repeated to Mr. Weed what he had
told Mr. Hamlin, in almost the same language, assuring Mr. Weed
of his intention to check any disunion movement that might be set
on foot while he was President. Then President Taylor added some

---

[1] Condensed accounts of this incident are published in Wilson's *Rise and Fall
of the Slave Power*, vol. ii. p. 529, and Thurlow Weed's *Memoirs*, vol. ii. p. 178.

[2] Thurlow Weed wrote Mr. Hamlin as follows: —

NEW YORK, Aug. 8th, 1876.

DEAR MR. HAMLIN, — You will have seen, I suppose, that Messrs. Stephens
and Toombs deny that there was a stormy interview between themselves and General Taylor on the occasion to which I referred in a letter to the *Herald*. In my
reply to Mr. Stephens (which I hope you saw), I found evidence that both gentlemen made disunion speeches on the subject and the occasion in question. And in
reply to Mr. Stephens's statement that he and his colleague (Mr. Toombs) "favored the admission of California," I proved by the record that Mr. Toombs
voted against such admission, and that Mr. Stephens was absent or did not vote.

I think that Mr. Stephens and Toombs base their denial on the ground that
they did not require General Taylor to veto a bill that had not passed. Mr.
Toombs says that he and Mr. Stephens had "earnest" conversations with General Taylor about the policy of his administration. That policy, you will remember, had been enunciated in an executive message.

You met Messrs. Stephens, Toombs, and Clingman coming out of the White
House. I met them passing from the house to the avenue. You saw General
Taylor before I did. Will you favor me with your recollection of what General
Taylor said to you on that occasion, that I may make your letter a part of my
response to Mr. Stephens.

The struggle between freedom and slavery during that session of Congress was
the "beginning of the end." Had General Taylor lived, the "Compromise Measures," including the atrocious Fugitive Slave Law, would have encountered a veto.
That might have precipitated the rebellion. You and I know with what devoted
courage and patriotism General Taylor would have stood by the Union.

The presidential ticket unites all phases and shades of opposition to bogus
Democracy in this State, supplemented by a good state ticket. New York may
be "scored" for Hayes and Wheeler.

Very truly yours,

THURLOW WEED.

information that was of peculiar interest in the light of subsequent events.[1] He said that the ultra members of Congress from the Southern States had presumed on his acquiescence in their views because he was a Southern man and a slaveholder; that before he had been placed in a position that made it his duty to examine both sides of the question, he had entertained and expressed views differing widely from his then sentiments. Relying on the assurances of distinguished Southern statesmen that the North was "aggressive," and that the compromises of the Constitution were in danger, he had written a letter to his son-in-law, Jefferson Davis, saying that he was ready to stand with the South in maintaining all the guarantees of the Constitution; but that since it had become his duty to look carefully into the merits of the controversy, he had satisfied himself that the exactions and purposes of the South were intolerant and revolutionary. He added that he regarded Davis as the chief conspirator· in the scheme which Toombs, Clingman, and Stephens had enunciated.

In a letter to Mr. Weed, General A. Pleasanton presented some significant testimony that throws further light on President Taylor's feelings about the disunion element and the measures he proposed to adopt to check it. General Pleasanton served under General Taylor in the Mexican war, and when ordered, in June, 1850, to rejoin his command in New Mexico called on the President, who said to him, —

"I am glad you are going to New Mexico. I want officers of judgment and experience there. These Southern men in Congress are trying to bring on a civil war. They are now organizing a military force in Texas for the purpose of taking possession of New Mexico and annexing it to Texas, and I have ordered the troops in New Mexico to be reinforced, and directed that no armed force from Texas be permitted to go into that territory. Tell Colonel Monroe" (commanding in New Mexico) "that he has my entire confidence, and if he has not force enough to support him" (and then his features assumed the firmest and most determined expression) "I will be with you myself; but I will be there before those people shall go into that country to have a foot of that territory. The whole business is infamous and must be put down."

Mr. Hamlin paid as close attention as he could to the California question, from its inception in the previous session of Congress until its settlement in this session. He took no part in the debate, however, until it was prolonged into March, when he arose to speak, chiefly for the purpose of exposing the tortuous line of argument the Southern senators had pursued, and the glaring inconsistency of their course. It must be admitted that although the Southern senators were on the

[1] See *History of the United States from the Compromise of 1850*, by James Ford Rhodes, vol. i. p. 134.

wrong side of the California question, they nevertheless made the
most of a poor case. The debate from day to day was a brilliant
contest between brilliant men, but in its entirety the Southern argument against the admission of California was an extraordinary record
of inconsistency and bold quibbling. The slave power tore California
from Mexico to make a new slave State, and when her people organized a free state government, the slave party would have denied California admission for the alleged reasons that it would not be lawful
to admit California, because Congress had not granted her permission
to form a constitution ; that aliens had voted at the election when
the people of California proposed to organize a state government ;
that there was not a sufficiently large population to warrant Congress
to give California statehood, and also that the territory of California
was too large for a State.

These claims Mr. Hamlin answered by the facts of history. Up to
the time of the debate more States had been admitted to the Union
without an enabling act of Congress, and it was also shown that no
objection had been raised to the admission of Texas and other States
on the score of an alleged insufficient population, or undue extent of
territory, or voting of aliens. But whenever beaten on these lines,
the Southern senators would return with greater vehemence to the
general plea that slavery should be extended to California, to "preserve the equality of the States," and also to "maintain the principle
of non-intervention." Now, while the senators who were fighting the
slave party undoubtedly had the better of the argument, it nevertheless appears from a careful reading of their speeches that they failed
to see the fundamental flaw in the slave party's attitude towards California ; if they did see it, they did not take advantage of their opportunity to place their opponents in an embarrassing position. Mr.
Hamlin observed this flaw, and on March 5, 1850, the day after Mr.
Calhoun's last speech was heard in the Senate, he took the floor to
show the slave party that it had forgotten one important fact, that
California was applying for admission into the Union under precisely
the very conditions the slavery leaders, including Mr. Calhoun, had
laid down the year before.

Mr. Hamlin's speech was widely commented on in the newspaper
press, and in several New England publications little pictures of the
scene that was presented form an interesting preface to Mr. Hamlin's remarks. His style and manner of speech-making had consid-
erably changed from the time he entered the House at thirty-three,
fresh from the farm and country courts, with defects in style pardonable in one who had had an incomplete education. He spoke in a
plainly worded way with the evident purpose of making a very complicated problem clear to the average understanding. One corre-

spondent, commenting on Mr. Hamlin's simple method of speech-making, wrote : " The argument was clear and luminous throughout, and showed that Mr. Hamlin was not only a master of the subject, but had authentic facts and evidence to prove his position. It was decidedly the most logical and forcible argument that I have heard or read on this side of the question, and amounted to a demonstration that California ought to be admitted without unnecessary delay. These manly and patriotic sentiments, though unsavory to some of the ultra Southern members, were pronounced in such a spirit of courtesy and good taste as to conciliate rather than to offend, cannot fail to have a good effect in settling the great question amicably for the best interests of the country. . . . Mr. Hamlin was listened to with profound attention from all parts of the House. This speech will place him on lofty ground as a statesman of enlarged and comprehensive views, worthy of the confidence of the nation."

Another correspondent wrote : " The Southern members were unusually restive under his remarks, and with their accustomed courtesy interrupted Mr. Hamlin with interrogatories, until, finding him armed at all points and a little too caustic for their comfort, they concluded to submit to their chastisement with as good a grace as they could. . . . Mr. Hamlin's friends are jubilant. I understand they at once subscribed for five thousand copies for public circulation."

In opening his remarks, Mr. Hamlin maintained that there should be only one subject before the Senate in the current debate, and that was the admission of California into the Union. He commented, in passing, on the unparalleled opposition which had been offered to California, and enumerated the irrelevant subjects that had been brought into discussion, — slavery, the formation of territorial governments, and the boundary of Texas. He said these questions should be legitimately submitted to the Senate for action in their proper places, and that they should not be permitted to delay the admission of California into the Union. He reminded the Senate that the people of California had rights, and they asked no entangling alliances. Mr. Hamlin was therefore opposed to submitting all these questions to the special committee appointed at Mr. Clay's request, and favored referring the California question to the proper committee in accordance with Colonel Benton's plan, with instructions to disconnect all unrelated subjects, that the Senate might then act only on the admission of California.

But while Mr. Hamlin desired to pursue the main theme of his argument, he paused to rebuke the cry of disunion which had been raised during the debate, and to charge point-blank that the purpose was to frighten the country into a state of alarm wherein the conspirators hoped they might accomplish their objects. " There need be no alarm," said Mr. Hamlin; "this Union will stand as a monument of grandeur, glory, and greatness long after every senator here shall have crumbled into dust. The affections of our people will cling to it and sustain it in spite of the madness of party and politicians."

Mr. Hamlin then proceeded to the real question, "whether a new sister State should be added to the Union." He examined first the rights of the people of California to form a constitution, and next the duty of Congress, in order to answer the quibbles of the slave party that the people of California had no right to erect a state government without a preliminary permission from Congress. Mr. Hamlin asserted that the people of California had proceeded in the right way, and he showed that they had acted in accordance with precedent, and had not violated the Constitution. He demonstrated, moreover, that the initiative in organizing a state government resided in the people of a territory, and that it was only within the jurisdiction of Congress to act upon the admission of a State. Article four, section three, of the Constitution says: "New States may be .admitted by the Congress into this Union," which means that Congress cannot "create" a State. Mr. Hamlin pursued this line farther to show that the Constitution was not only silent as to the power of creating a State, but that the constitutional convention did not even consider such a question. Madison, in the forty-third number of the " Federalist," wrote, " The eventual establishment of new States seems to have been overlooked by the framers of the instrument (the Constitution)."

In connection with this, and before citing his precedents in support of California's action, Mr. Hamlin embarrassed the pro-slavery senators by reading them their own opinions on the power of Congress in the matter of "creating States," as expressed by the Judiciary Committee at the previous session of the Senate, when the question of admitting California first arose. This opinion was delivered by Senator Berrien, of Georgia, who was now opposing the admission of California, and it was in part as follows: " The power conferred by the Constitution on Congress is to admit new States, not to create them. According to the theory of our government, the creation of a State is an act of popular sovereignty, not by ordinary legislation. It is by the will of the people of whom the State is composed, assembled in convention, that it is created." Mr. Hamlin emphasized his advantage by expressing his belief that this opinion was a doctrine to which he subscribed, because it was the doctrine of the Constitution.

The fact must be borne in mind that the year before the anti-slavery senators proposed to authorize California to erect a state government, and the pro-slavery senators checkmated them by asserting, through the Judiciary Committee, that the people of California

should take the lead.   Their private reason was that the slave power
was making desperate efforts to carry the territorial election in California and put a pro-slavery clause in her constitution.   But now
that this effort had been defeated and the situation changed, Judge
Berrien and his friends did not enjoy the grim irony of fate.   To
admit that the opinion of the Judiciary Committee was good doctrine
now was to admit that California had fulfilled all requirements for
admission, and that those who were opposing her admission stulti-
fied themselves by so doing.   Judge Berrien was in the worst plight
of all the pro-slavery senators, because he was responsible for the
advantage Mr. Hamlin had.   He interrupted Mr. Hamlin precipi-
tately, and propounded an evasive question which "ran up a squirrel
track."

"Is it the purpose of the senator," he asked, "to deduce from that
report the inference that it was the opinion of the Judiciary Committee
that it belonged to the territories, without the sanction of Congress, to
erect themselves into States ?   If so, he misunderstands that report.   The
sovereignties, in the view of that committee, only become incipient with
the authorization of Congress to form a constitution.   When that authorization is obtained, then, and not until then, the territory can proceed to act in
the erection of a State and the formation of a government and constitution."

Mr. Hamlin replied : "I do not think that there was any necessity for the
honorable senator from Georgia to interrupt me.   I speak in all kindness.
I was not speaking of the power of the territory to erect a territorial or a
state government, whether authorized by Congress or not, but of the power
of Congress to create a state government.   I quoted the report made by
the senator from Georgia for that and no other purpose ; but, taking the
language of that report, I must be permitted to declare that I find in it no
such explanation as that which the senator has just now seen fit to give us.
It is undoubtedly right for the senator from Georgia to make any explanation he may now deem fit ; but the report itself nowhere affirms or denies
the power of the people of the territories to erect themselves into a State
without the previous assent of Congress ; nor does it claim that such
assent must be given.   That belongs to the explanation of the senator from
Georgia."

Senator Berrien replied : "That was not the question before the committee.   It was, whether an unauthorized body could erect a State."

This was a palpable evasion of the point at issue, and Mr. Hamlin
answered : —

"That report has been quoted for the purpose I have already stated ;
but I propose to inquire into the very point which the senator from Georgia
has suggested in his interruption.

"My first proposition is that Congress has not the power to create a
State.   My second, that the people of this territory of California have.
Congress having failed to make a territorial government for the people of

California, it is clearly within the power of the people inhabiting that territory to create a state government, as they have already done, to present their constitution here and ask to be admitted as one of the sovereign States. They are the persons to act, not we; they are the persons more directly interested, and who have the power. California has acted from right as well as from necessity. . . . We have been told in these halls that we have no power to create a territorial government. That is one doctrine. Another is, now, that the people of the territory have no power to erect themselves into a State. Taking both propositions, and presenting them to the people of a territory, we may ask in what manner can they institute a state government? Or in what manner can they become a part of this Union? We speak, sir, in just praise of the character of our country, — its influence upon other nations and other people; but to my mind there is no single feature in all our government better calculated to spread abroad its true character, — there is no incident in the history of our people, our government, of which we may be more justly proud, — than the institution of this government in California among a people assembled there from every State of the Union, virtually without law.

" And when it was declared that the bowie knife and the revolver would be the common law of the land, they, in obedience to the . . . lessons of civil government, and the rights of which they had learned while citizens of the States, — they assembled themselves together, and from the existing necessity erected themselves into a State. . . . No other people on the face of this globe thus brought together, save those who have been educated in our States, . . . would have thus formed themselves into a State. . . . Without that education and training they received in the States, the bowie knife and the revolver would have been the common law of their land. It is, indeed, a sublime spectacle to witness the order and deportment of these people. It should excite a just pride in every breast, and create a living faith in the capacity of man for self-government.

" Now, sir, I hold that the people of that territory have by the law of nature, by that law which God gave to man, a right to form themselves into a government for the protection of life, liberty, and the pursuit of happiness. Our government is based upon that right; its foundations are laid deep and broad upon that principle. It was the assertion of that principle, — the right of the people to self-government, the right to institute a government to suit themselves, a government to protect their lives, liberty, and property, — it was in recognition of that principle that the first blood of the Revolution fertilized the soil of Lexington. It was in recognition of that principle that the declaration of 1776 was signed. It was in recognition of that principle that this government was reared . . . and is this day sustained. . . .

" Sir, allow me to read from the Declaration of Independence: ' We hold these truths to be self-evident : that all men are created equal ; that they are endowed by their Creator with certain inalienable rights; that among these are life, liberty, and the pursuit of happiness; that to secure these rights governments are instituted among men, deriving their just powers from the consent of the governed; that whenever any form of government becomes destructive of these ends, it is the right of the people to alter or abolish it, and to institute a new government.' . . .

" It is too late to controvert these doctrines. . . . They have been incorporated as the fundamental principle of the State. The senator from Alabama (Clement C. Clay, Jr.), if I understood him the other day, controverted and denied these propositions. Allow me to read from the Constitution of Alabama: ' All political power is inherent in the people, and all free governments are founded on their authority and instituted for their benefit; and, therefore, they have at all times an inalienable and indefeasible right to alter, reform, or *abolish* their form of government in such manner as they may think expedient' (Mr. Hamlin emphasized the word ' abolish' in order to show Southern authority for the course the people of California had in abolishing the military government that had been established in their territory in order to form a state government).

"I will also read from the Constitutions of Arkansas and Maine: ' All power is inherent in the people. . . . They have at all times an unqualified right to alter, reform, or abolish their governments in such manner as they think proper' — Constitution of Arkansas. ' All power is inherent in the people. . . . They have, therefore, an unalienable and indefeasible right to institute government, to alter, reform, or totally change the same, when their safety and happiness require it,' — Constitution of Maine.

" Massachusetts, New Hampshire, Vermont, Connecticut, Pennsylvania, Delaware, Maryland, Virginia, North Carolina, Kentucky, Tennessee, Ohio, Indiana, Mississippi, Illinois, Michigan, Florida, Wisconsin, Iowa, and other States affirm the same sovereign and unlimited capacity of the people to form their constitutions. Now, we are told that the people of California, having been denied by Congress any government, have no right to erect themselves into a State. The right of a people to form a State in such a case is a proposition which I do not see fit to argue. . . . I prefer rather to give authorities and precedents."

Mr. Hamlin next patiently reviewed the charge that President Taylor had interfered in the California election, and had inspired General Riley, the military governor of the territory, to take the lead in calling a state convention. This charge was trivial, almost frivolous, and the fact that the slave party should press it shows how it grasped at straws. The immense activity the people of California manifested in organizing a state government evidenced a spontaneous desire to make California a State. When Mr. Hamlin showed how vague and conflicting the evidence of executive interference was, Senator King, of Alabama, and Senator Downs, of Louisiana, interrupted to interpose their inferences and hearsay evidence — no facts. But Mr. Hamlin was armed at these points; he produced General Riley's proclamation, and the correspondence of Thomas Butler King, which proved that General Riley had issued his proclamation long after the people of California had called their primary meetings, and before Mr. King arrived in California, — the first man to go to that territory from Washington after General Taylor had become President, and himself an agent of the slave power! There were no more questions or interruptions from the Southern senators on this score, and Mr. Hamlin took up the next point.

This was the claim that the constitutional election in California was void on the grounds that aliens had voted. Mr. Hamlin not only demonstrated that, under the treaty with Mexico, Mexicans who chose to live in California were to be regarded as American citizens and therefore had a right to vote, but that it was the custom among the territories in forming state governments to allow alien citizens to cast their ballots. He produced voluminous evidence to establish this fact, mentioning the cases of Maine, Illinois, and Michigan, without comment or criticism; but he took occasion to say in passing, that this was a question which the territories should decide, and had decided, for themselves; it was the first time he had heard it raised in Congress, when objection was made to the custom.

Mr. Hamlin turned now to review the history of numerous States which had organized their respective governments without the permission of Congress, and had been admitted into the Union. There were nine, — Vermont, Kentucky, Tennessee, Maine, Arkansas, Michigan, Florida, Texas, and Iowa. Eight had been admitted with a previous act of Congress, and thus the rule up to the present sanctioned the act of California. Mr. Hamlin in connection with this briefly cited the facts in the case of the nine States; and his remarks on the action of Tennessee were of special interest. John C. Calhoun, in his speech the day before, had asserted that Tennessee had applied for admission to the Union without the permissory act of Congress, and for that reason had been remanded back to a territorial condition. Mr. Calhoun claimed that California afforded a parallel case, and argued that on this account Congress should deny her admission.

Mr. Hamlin took sharp issue with Mr. Calhoun, and by reciting the historical facts proved that Mr. Calhoun had made an egregious blunder. Mr. Hamlin stated that Tennessee was ceded to the United States by North Carolina, with the provision that she should be admitted to the Union when she had a population of sixty thousand inhabitants. That condition was fulfilled in 1796, and Tennessee, forming a constitution and fixing her own boundary without the consent of Congress, applied for admission into the Union. The Constitution was presented to the Senate accompanied by a message from the President. Both these circumstances occurred in the case of California. A committee from the Senate recommended that Tennessee be remanded back to a territorial condition inasmuch as there had been no census taken by the government in that territory, and also because Congress had not yet decided how many States should be made out of Tennessee. But the House refused to concur in this action, the Senate receded from its position, and Tennessee was brought into the Union.

The most interesting thrust Mr. Hamlin made at Mr. Calhoun was in reading the following extract from the latter's speech of February, 1849: " Sir, I hold it to be a fundamental principle of our political system, that the people have a right to establish what government they may think proper for themselves ; that every State about to become a member of this Union has a right to form its government as it pleases ; and that, in order to be admitted, there is but one quali- fication, and that is the government shall be republican.   There is no express provision to that effect, but it results from that important section which guarantees to every State in this Union a republican form of government."

In commenting on Mr. Calhoun's change of position, Mr. Hamlin said that he had encouraged the people to go to California to do the very thing they had done.   He added that he could continue to quote until the sun went down from Southern statesmen, orators, and newspapers, who professed their willingness to leave this question of slavery to the people of the territory.   After having encouraged the people of California to take this step, it was too late to resist the admission of their State.

One of the most transparent objections raised to California was that her territory was too large for one State.   Mr. Hamlin turned this objection to advantage by asking the Southern senators why they had not protested against the admission of Texas on the same score. No complaints or objections against Texas on account of her size were even heard, and yet if the boundaries of Texas, which were in dispute, should be compressed into their narrowest limits, Texas would yet remain larger than California, and be able to support a population ten times larger.   As to the charge that California had an insufficient population, Mr. Hamlin asked why Mr. Clay, of Alabama, had passed over the case of Florida, which had less than 50,000 inhabitants when she applied for admission ; and he also asked why objections were not made to Texas on the same score, when she sought entrance into the Union with a population of about 80,000.   California, from reliable information, had a population of from 110,000 to 120,000, and it was increasing with astonishing rapidity.

In closing, Mr. Hamlin briefly declared that the facts of the case warranted the immediate admission of California, and that he thought there was only one question to be determined, and that was whether the Constitution presented was republican.   He believed that it was, and that it was evidence of the character of her people, who were worthy and intelligent men who had gone to their new home to build up a republic and make it one of the marts of commerce which shall connect us with the distant East. " They have gone there and asserted their rights as citizens," Mr. Hamlin concluded, " and have come here asking us to admit them into this Union. That, sir, is the real question for our decision, and I have no doubt that California is to be welcomed into this Union, and that her star is to stud with other stars our national flag."

Of the numerous comments on Mr. Hamlin's speech, the following from the Washington correspondence of the " New York Evening Post," William Cullen Bryant, editor, is selected to show the effect of the speech on the anti-slavery press and people of the times : —

" Mr. Hamlin addressed the Senate at length, and made one of the most able and eloquent pleas for the immediate unconditional admission of California yet heard in either branch of Congress. Mr. Hamlin took an early occasion to correct Mr. Calhoun in his misstatement of facts yesterday, but Mr. Calhoun did not think it expedient to defend his own assertions, though they were not yet a day old ; and it was very remarkable that when Mr. Hamlin contradicted Mr. Calhoun's statement respecting the admission of Tennessee, neither of the senators from that State saw fit to sustain the South Carolina senator.

" Mr. Hamlin showed, by a mass of evidence that cannot be evaded or resisted, that neither the present nor the late administration had exerted any influence to prevent the adoption of the anti-slavery clause of the Constitution (of California), and he took the last plank from beneath the feet of his opponents by quoting from their own previous declarations to prove that California now presented herself for admission under the very conditions which they themselves prescribed a year ago.

" I own I was surprised to see him catch even Mr. Calhoun in this awkward predicament. Following Mr. Calhoun through his tortuous career on these territorial questions, he brought to the attention of the Senate a paragraph from a speech of his in February, 1849, in which he declared himself ready to receive California with open arms and clasp her to his heart, when her own people came here with institutions established by their own free will and congenial to their ideas and wishes, provided only her government was republican in form.

" Upon the whole, I consider this speech of the senator from Maine one of the most satisfactory refutations yet delivered of the special pleadings by which it is sought now to exclude California. As an argument it covers the whole ground, and seems to me unanswerable. Mr. Hamlin has established by his effort of to-day a reputation of one of the first debaters in the Senate."

William Pitt Fessenden, then preparing to enter public life, wrote to Mr. Hamlin : —

" I congratulate you on your speech, which is highly spoken of, and which I have read, so far as it has appeared in the 'Argus.' I like it very much. It gives much better satisfaction to men of all parties here than Mr. Webster's. If you have a copy to spare, I should like much to receive one."

The next speech the Senate heard was one of momentous interest. This was Webster's memorable 7th of March speech. The great expounder was filled with fear, and he launched his thunder not at the slavery propagandists, but at the abolitionists and the anti-slavery people ; he held them responsible for the agitation, and he supported the Clay compromise measures as the surest means of saving the Union from the danger that threatened it. Webster's speech fell on the opponents of slavery extension like a clap of thunder from the clear sky. They received it as a recantation of principle, the ruin of a noble career, and the turning back of the hands on the clock of time. In their sore grief they charged Webster with bidding for Southern support for the presidency. Old friends fell away from him ; and yet the effect of his speech was to turn Northern sentiment towards compromise. Webster's sun went down, and his defeat for the presidency in 1852 probably broke his heart.

This speech is of both historical and personal interest to these pages. It is to be noted that Webster, in the course of his remarks, took occasion to refer to Mr. Hamlin's speech on California, and also to compliment him on his opposition to the annexation of Texas. But there was little in common between the two men, and their relations were purely functionary. Then, again, Webster was a Whig, and had been long in public life, while Mr. Hamlin was comparatively a beginner. Yet Mr. Hamlin's opinions of Webster and his course at this juncture are interesting. In the main he coincided in the latter-day verdict that Webster was influenced almost wholly by patriotic motives. His passion was his overwhelming love for the Union, and his great mind clearly saw the conflict impending that broke only ten years later. He wished to avert it ; he feared strife ; he could not take the public entirely into his fears without incurring the danger of precipitating a crisis. He deliberately imperiled his great name and fame in what he sincerely believed to be a patriotic cause. His paramount object was the salvation of the nation ; all else, even his own career, was subsidiary.

But while Mr. Hamlin at the time of Webster's departure recognized his main motive, he nevertheless was of the opinion that he erred. He criticised Webster's lack of courage to meet the emergency with firmness, and place the responsibility where a Southern President and slaveholder said it belonged. Mr. Hamlin also criticised Webster's morals. He always severely reflected on his loose financial habits, and his notion that it was right for him to advocate private bills in the Senate for pay. "A man," said Mr. Hamlin, "who is careless about money matters cannot always be honest." But he rarely failed, out of his sense of justice, to mitigate his criticism of Webster by praising his great life's work in expounding the Constitution, which, as has been happily said, "had the force of constitutional amendments."

The sudden death of General Taylor and the accession of Millard Fillmore to the presidency secured the success of the Clay compromise bill. It will probably always be a fascinating subject of speculation among historians as to the results of President Taylor's policy, had he lived to enforce it. It seems reasonable to conclude that his ability, courage, and military experience would have made him master of the situation. It is easy to see that Mr. Fillmore did not possess the strength and alertness necessary to meet an emergency similar to that which threatened General Taylor. Mr. Fillmore signed the Fugitive Slave Law, although he had been identified with the anti-slavery wing of the Whig party, and for that reason was nominated for Vice-President. Later generations that can have no partisan feelings about this probably will extend to Mr. Fillmore the same consideration they extend to his counselor, Daniel Webster. This generous view of the case would at least incline them to believe that it was Mr. Fillmore's natural conservatism, timidity, and lack of strength which governed him in his course rather than personal ambition. But whatever were his motives, the facts remain that he was not called on to meet the crisis, and that the Fugitive Slave Law, for which he was partially responsible, became a great factor in educating the masses of the North against the iniquities and horrors of slavery. It was reserved for another man to appear when the hour of action arrived. Mr. Hamlin spoke of Mr. Fillmore personally as a clean, upright, dignified man, of an imposing presence and naturally genial disposition. His mental habits were somewhat sluggish, but he was a man of ability, and with the exception of his course towards the compromises of 1850 gave the country a good administration.

One more incident remains to be related in connection with Mr. Hamlin's work in this session of Congress, which closed his first term as a senator. A movement was in progress to abolish the brutal custom of flogging that still existed in the navy. John P. Hale was the foremost leader in Congress in this move, and Mr. Hamlin heartily coöperated with him. There was decided opposition. The general objection against abolishing flogging was the plea that the officers of the navy favored it. There were also senators who maintained that Congress had no right to interfere with the discipline of the navy. Mr. Hamlin rejected both these arguments. He favored the abolishment of flogging on humane principles, and also because he had obtained authoritative information that in the opinion of the most intelligent and efficient officers of the navy this mode of punishment was detrimental to the service. One of his authorities was the Rev. Walter Colton, who had been for many years a chaplain in the navy, and was a writer of considerable popularity in his day. Mr. Colton had served under Commodore R. H. Stockton, and these two were prime movers in this humane crusade against a barbarous cruelty.

Mr. Hamlin made a brief speech in answer to Yulee, of Florida, and other Southern senators who opposed the abolishment of flogging. The main points he made were that flogging belonged to another age, that its abolition was desired by men of all creeds, religions, and politics, for humane reasons, and that to abolish flogging would make the sailor more of a man. Senator Dawson, of Georgia, interrupted Mr. Hamlin to assert that there was little sentiment in favor of the bill before Congress. Mr. Hamlin replied in amazement : " Well, the bill passed the House by a majority of 130, and I should think that that represented a sentiment. If it does not, then I should like to have the gentleman explain what it does mean or represent."

Nevertheless, the bill did not pass the Senate. A year or two afterwards Commodore Stockton entered the Senate, and by tacking a bill to abolish flogging in the navy as a rider on another measure, secured its passage. Then he resigned from the Senate.

CHAPTER XX

THE tumult that the compromise measures of 1850 raised, subsided after their adoption. Congress was no longer an arena of wrath and wrangling, and a more moderate tone prevailed throughout the country. While the Fugitive Slave Law provoked indignation at the North, and served in itself to keep alive the agitation against slavery, yet, coming after the tempestuous times that accompanied the discussion and enactment of the Clay compromise plan, the period that followed, and preceded the breaking-down of the Missouri Compromise, was one of comparative quietude. But this was not strange. The North was governed by its commercial and manufacturing interests, and they were alarmed over the conflict the slavery question precipitated in Congress. Capital is proverbially timid. The moneyed interests of the North demanded a cessation of the strife. There were cotton Whigs and conscience Whigs, dough-face Democrats and anti-slavery Democrats. To use a common expression, money talked. The North might have lapsed into its former condition of cowardly indifference to slavery if the Fugitive Slave Law had not remained in force to prick its conscience. Both political parties professed their willingness to make a fair test of the compromise plan, and eventually the acceptance of the measures of 1850 became a test of party fealty in both great political organizations.

When it is borne in mind that the Missouri Compromise was repealed in 1854, through the efforts of conspirators, not through the movements of events, it is not strange that this comparatively peaceful interval misled some of the far-sighted statesmen of the day. It is easy to look back over the printed pages of history, and wonder, — but the infallible prophet had not yet arrived. While it may not be worth while to speculate on what would have happened if the slavery propagandists had let the Missouri Compromise alone, it is nevertheless interesting to note the attitude of some of the leading men of the country. The extreme hopeful view was expressed by Benton when he said to Charles Sumner : " You have come on the scene too late, sir. Not only have our great men passed away, but the great issues have been settled also. The last of these was the United States bank, and that has been overthrown forever. Nothing is left you, sir, but puny sectional questions and petty strifes about slavery and fugitive slave laws, involving no national interests." [1] Abraham Lincoln, who was already recognized as an anti-slavery leader of great prominence, said at this time that he was losing his interest in politics, and that it was not awakened until the attack on the Missouri Compromise was begun. John P. Hale, whose term in the Senate expired in 1853, left Washington, not to return to New Hampshire to resume his fight against slavery, but to go to New York to practice law in that metropolis.

Senator Hamlin did not subscribe to the optimistic view his friend Benton took, and more will be said on that point later ; but while he did not believe that the slavery question was settled by the compromise measures of 1850, he did not foresee or think the conflict would be so shortly renewed. His private letters, his words to his intimate friends and family, show that he was troubled in mind and brooded over the situation. His exact words on several occasions are recalled : " This thing of slavery will sooner or later try to subvert the government, but I do not expect it will happen in my day." In other words, while there were no clouds gathering on the political horizon, Mr. Hamlin yet felt that there were elements of a future storm brewing. He pointed out the conditions. Here was slavery ; it had proved itself to be a curse ; only evil had come out of it, and he held it to be a self-evident proposition that it would continue a source of trouble as long as it was allowed to exist. All the compromises in the world could not palliate its wickedness, and yet life was vouchsafed it by the Constitution. The Fugitive Slave Law was in his eyes an inhuman thing, and was certain to increase Northern repugnance to slavery. Two civilizations were growing up in the country and trending apart. How long could this go on ? This was the question that perplexed him.

The chief reason Senator Hamlin had for believing that the solution of the problem would not be reached in his day is another striking proof of his large faith in men and his strong belief in those whom he respected. He hoped that the slave party was now convinced that the North would not have the loathsome institution on its soil ; he trusted in the honor of Sam Houston, Jefferson Davis, Robert M. T. Hunter, Willie P. Mangum, John McPherson Berrien, George E. Badger, John Bell, John M. Clayton, Andrew P. Butler, Howell Cobb, and other Southern statesmen whom he respected, to abide by the law of the land and keep slavery a local institution. He did not believe in the fire-eaters, nor did he believe that they represented the South. Their threats of disunion were in his eyes the bluster and froth of vain, petulant, and overbearing men, and he ignored them.

[1] Ben : Perley Poore's *Reminiscences*, vol. i. p. 409.

While there were many red-hot speeches in Congress on the slavery question during this interval of three years, they were of an
intermittent nature, and Congress returned to its duty of attending
to the regular business of the nation. A business era of vast importance to the United States had set in, and the best energies of the
country were now enlisted to meet the requirements of the time.
The discovery of gold in California marked an epoch in the development of our Western domains. Cities, towns, and hamlets sprang up
on the Pacific slope as if by magic. Great plans were projected for
establishing rapid communication between the East and the West by
means of transcontinental railroad lines. Asa Whitney, of New York
city, who projected in 1846 a railroad across the country, now found
powerful supporters at Washington. Preparations for a war that broke
out in the Crimea in 1853 stimulated our foreign trade. There was
a tentative movement here and there to enlist the aid of the government in assisting the American manufacturers to find markets in
South America for his products. Domestic trade and subsidiary
interests were generally promoted. But it is designed only to outline the salient points in this era of development in order to give an
idea of the duties that were now pressed on Congress and their effect
on Mr. Hamlin. The story of his life now takes up a new phase of
his career, and gives the keynote to his course of action during the
remainder of his public life.

Mr. Hamlin became a business senator, and from choice. Personal
ambition dictated another course. He might have enhanced his
reputation by devoting himself to one or more subjects on which to
make himself a special authority — such as slavery, the tariff, or the
financial question. Many a senator or representative has achieved
national prominence by making a specialty of one subject, although
taking a low rank as a practical legislator. But Mr. Hamlin was indifferent about his fame. It may be repeated that he rarely wrote
out a speech, and seldom was known to revise one. He disliked to
talk about himself. In his later days his aversion for the newspaper
interviewer was notorious. The truth is Mr. Hamlin's governing idea
of life was that "one should do the duty that lies nearest." He was
also a man of action rather than words, and when this great era of
development began, he plunged into the business of the Senate, and
accomplished results that are a story by themselves and a monument
to his attention to his duties. This record in detail would prove dry
reading, but it represents work that had to be done, and required close
attention and an intimate knowledge of government and public affairs.
Several subjects in connection with this will present themselves elsewhere.

Mr. Hamlin's election to the chairmanship of the Committee on

Commerce was undoubtedly a circumstance that contributed in a large measure to his development into a business senator. He was not quite thirty-nine when he entered the Senate, and during his second year he was elected chairman of this committee. His habits of life, characteristics, and public course had not yet been fully matured, and his new duties tended to awaken and strengthen his natural preference for action. The scope of the work devolving upon the Committee on Commerce embraced a vast field, and it was a more important arm of business for the government than now. The nature of its work was more largely creative than now; the rapid growth of the country constantly created new conditions that the committee had to meet. In brief, this committee was required to give its attention to shipping interests, the customs and revenue marine services, river and harbor improvements, the life-saving department, and coast survey. The chairmanship involved the personal supervision of an immense amount of detail. The incumbent was also chosen with regard to his ability and experience as a political manager, because there was much patronage connected with the post.

In a year or two after Mr. Hamlin had been chairman of the Committee on Commerce, a marked change took place in him; he became not only a business senator, but also a silent senator. This at first puzzled his friends, who had expected him to play a conspicuous part in the Senate's debates and discussions. In the House and state legislature he had been regarded as one of the most promising and forcible debaters and speakers in the Democratic party. He was often selected by his party managers in the House in preference to older and more experienced men to champion measures. His associates urged him to study the graces of oratory, for they thought that he could develop oratorical ability of a high order. It is not known whether Mr. Hamlin ever went to the trouble of studying a model. It is doubtful if he did. He was original, and disposed to be sparing of his words. It was the talkative nature of the legislature and House and the partisanship of his youth that impelled him to speak in those bodies rather than a desire to hear himself talk. When he became a member of the Senate, he found its dignified tone and deliberate method of procedure more to his liking. As his predilection for work was encouraged by circumstances, he was soon more active in the committee room than in the forum.

The congressional habit of talk was another factor of this change in Mr. Hamlin. The long speech was still in vogue among the senators, and it was no uncommon thing for one to take the larger part of two daily sessions to deliver a speech. When a senator's arguments, ideas, and position were pretty well known, reiteration somewhat palled on his colleagues. But some of the senators of this period would have flowed on forever like Tennyson's brook if the transaction of public business had not held them in check. A reaction was setting in against the long-winded, ornate style of speech-making which had long prevailed. The death of Calhoun, Webster's entrance into the Cabinet, and the decline of Clay left few men in the Senate with the ability that justified the taking of a day of the Senate's time for the delivery of a speech. Mr. Hamlin grew impatient; his private letters and conversation resounded with an emphatic protest. "Congress talks too much" was the burden of his complaint, and he saw no reason to change his mind in the days of his retirement. Many amusing stories were related how Mr. Hamlin would retire from the Senate in great displeasure when a verbose senator took the floor to ramble for a couple of hours on his favorite theme, "His Majesty Myself," and check the transaction of public business.[1]

But while Senator Hamlin virtually withdrew from the political discussions in the Senate, he nevertheless participated in the debates on business affairs, and occasionally made set speeches when he thought that he ought to speak. He would sometimes rise to cut the knot of debate upon a question of order, for he was recognized as an authority on parliamentary procedure. There was a noticeable change in his style of speaking. His remarks on business matters were usually very brief, concise, exact, without a superfluous word; his speeches were modeled on the same plan, and presented facts marshaled in perfect order with little or no attempt to rise into flights of eloquence. His remarks in connection with the government reports, as they appear in the "Congressional Record," cover a wide range of topics; he dealt with these subjects as only a man could who was entitled to speak with authority and exact knowledge. Without going into detail now, it may be said that Professor Alexander D. Bache and Professor Joseph Henry regarded Mr. Hamlin as their most consistent and intelligent supporter in the Senate when they were engaged in developing the coast survey and lighthouse departments.

This general outline of Mr. Hamlin's work in the Senate and its effect on him would not be complete without the explanation of a seeming inconsistency in the narrative. While Mr. Hamlin was known

[1] Senator Hamlin once said that he agreed with the following sentiments which Bismarck expressed to his secretary, Dr. Busch, in 1871: "The gift of oratory has ruined much in parliamentary life. Time is wasted because every one who feels ability in that line must have his word, even if he has no new point to bring forward. Speaking is too much in the air, and too little to the point. Everything is already settled in committees; a man speaks, therefore, at length only for the public, to whom he wishes to show off as much as possible, and still more for the newspapers, who are to praise him. Oratory will, one day, come to be looked upon as a generally harmful quality, and a man will be punished who permits himself to be guilty of a long speech!"

to the end of his career at Washington as a silent senator, he yet became one of the most widely known campaign orators of his day. There is no contradiction or inconsistency. Mr. Hamlin early imbibed the idea that the Senate was a place for the transaction of public business. He also believed that a senator should give an account of himself to his constituents. Then, again, he was a born politician, and loved the excitement of a campaign. This overbore his natural modesty, which inclined him to remain in retirement, and for years he regularly took the stump in the service of his party when it needed him. The speeches that Mr. Hamlin made on the stump were simple in style, and always aimed at the level of popular understanding. He instinctively gauged that level, and that was one thing which gave him his hold on the masses of the people. He gave the rank and file of his party what they could carry, assimilate, and repeat, and no more. His ideas on this point are well expressed in Lincoln's advice to his partner, William H. Herndon: "Don't shoot too high; aim lower, and the common people will understand you. They are the ones you want to reach — at least the ones you ought to reach. The educated and refined people will understand you anyway. If you aim too high, your ideas will go over the heads of the masses, and only hit those who need no hitting."

It is clear that Mr. Hamlin was justified in pursuing this course. In Maine he always had the masses of the people with him, though his opponents might have the party machinery. He knew that it was one thing to deliver a finished speech, and that it was quite another to make one which would influence the masses. The necessity ·of keeping the slavery question, with its involved and rapidly changing phases, clear to the common people was a circumstance in itself that rendered it advisable for Mr. Hamlin, during his first years in the Senate, to speak to the twelfth man in the public jury. The result was that the voters of Maine always understood him, and kept him at Washington for over thirty years, without his expending one cent for other than legitimate purposes.

It is interesting now to note the kind of men with whom Mr. Hamlim was most intimately associated in the Senate during this period of work. They were preëminently workers. Prominent among them were Thomas H. Benton, Sam Houston, John Davis, Jefferson Davis, John Bell, Willie P. Mangum, George E. Badger, John McPherson Berrien, Solon Borland, of Arkansas, General Henry Dodge, of Wisconsin, and Alpheus Felch, of Michigan. The one with whom Senator Hamlin at this time sustained the closest personal and party relations was Benton, who was the father of the Senate and the most revered Jackson Democrat of the times. His noble and useful career in the Senate was now drawing to a close; yet, at no time in his long and distinguished life had Benton more clearly revealed his true qualities as a pure patriot and wise statesman. A Southern man by birth, a slaveholder, too, he combated the Calhoun party with all his great power and force. The slave party succeeded in preventing his reëlection to the Senate in 1850, after thirty years' service in that body ; but that was a Pyrrhic victory, and enhanced Benton's fame.

The measure of Benton's statesmanship is to be determined by the immense influence he exerted in the formative period of congressional legislation, by his honorable, wise, and aggressive leadership, his personal qualities of integrity, honor, moral courage, ample knowledge, and force. Thus, while Benton's name is not attached to specific acts of legislation as author, yet he was one of the great powers of his day. He was identified with many measures of vast importance, and through his management was entitled to a large share of credit for their success. He was Jackson's right-hand man in his fight against the United States bank ; he was probably more instrumental than any other man in inducing the government to adopt and maintain the double currency coin standard ; he promoted the homestead movement, which was to bestow government land on those who settled on it. He was at that time deeply interested in the development of the country's material resources, and in certain plans to promote its business welfare. One was the building of a Pacific railroad, and this he had taken up again about the time Mr. Hamlin entered the Senate.

An amusing story is told of the first meeting between Senator Hamlin and Colonel Benton. The day the former took the oath of senator, he sat down in a seat near Benton. Presently Mr. Hamlin saw "Old Bullion," as Benton was called, looking at him with a smile. Then, without any preliminary remark or introduction, Benton put out his hand to the new senator from Maine, and said in a jocose, rhythmical way : "Honorable Hannibal Hamlin, of Hampden, Maine. Why, sir, your name ought to make you President some day." Benton, it appears, had watched Mr. Hamlin's course in the House, and had picked him out as a rising man. After Mr. Hamlin entered the Senate, Benton displayed almost a paternal interest in his young associate. He selected Mr. Hamlin for the position of chairman of the Committee on Commerce, urged him to take a more prominent part in the inner councils of his party, and constantly invited him to his house. Although Benton had pompous ways, yet they were pure mannerisms. Mr. Hamlin said that Benton was one of the kindesthearted men he ever knew, and a most enjoyable and sociable entertainer. He ranked Benton, too, as one of the greatest and best men he knew among the leading statesmen of the country.

Mr. Hamlin's relations with Jefferson Davis throw some interesting light on the peculiar views Southern senators of a certain type held with regard to the relations between the government and the individual States. These men lived in communities where they saw comparatively little of business life, and, imbibing Calhoun's doctrines, they evolved ideas of their own. They not only sincerely believed that each State in the Union was a sovereign nation, but they were always on the alert to see that the government took no step which would be in their eyes an infringement on state rights. They evidently thought the fathers of the government attached no importance to the name, "The United States," which they gave to this nation. Sometimes these Southern statesmen were carried far beyond the bounds of common sense when they got astride of their hobby. One was Clement C. Clay, Jr., of Alabama, who was known as Copperhead Clay, after the snake by that name, on account of his venomous attacks on those whom he disliked. One of Clay's notions was that the government had no right to appropriate money to improve rivers and harbors. Once he got appointed to the Committee on Commerce, where he made no end of trouble. It became necessary on a certain occasion for the committee to recommend the appropriation of $50,000 to render navigation safe in a certain Southern harbor. Clay insisted that the State where the harbor existed should make the improvements, and all the precedents in the history of the government could not drive the idea out of his head. All the other members of the committee favored the appropriation, and after a stormy session Mr. Clay departed from the meeting in a state of high dudgeon, threatening to invoke the aid of his quixotic Southern brethren to defeat the bill.

At this juncture Senator Hamlin appealed to Jefferson Davis, who, although impregnated with the Calhoun idea, still believed that the government had a right to pass measures which were for the good of all the States. He listened to Mr. Hamlin's recital of facts, and when he saw that a refusal to improve the harbor in question might endanger life and property, he courteously interrupted Mr. Hamlin by saying: "No argument is necessary, Mr. Hamlin; the interests of humanity alone dictate that your appropriation bill should be passed, and I will promise you my support." Mr. Davis was as good as his word. He went among his Southern brethren, who were in a state of ferment over the matter, and labored with them to such good effect that Mr. Clay was able to muster just seven votes against Mr. Hamlin's bill.

On other occasions, Mr. Hamlin received cordial support from Mr. Davis, and they soon established very pleasant personal relations, which were not terminated until ten years later. The military education Mr. Davis had received at West Point, and his experience as an engineer, had taught him the need of placing the simple demands of civilization above the tenets of political creeds. But by nature he was more practical, sensible, and courteous than the other members of the extreme and aggressive school of Southern statesmen with whom he was associated. He had a high sense of personal honor and of national obligations. One incident will illustrate. At the outbreak of the Mexican war, the government advertised through the War Department for sappers and miners. As an inducement to enlist, it offered to give all who joined the sappers and miners corps an education as mining engineers. Some seventy young men enlisted. Some were from Maine. After the war the government not only failed to keep its promise, but also refused these men a discharge from the army. The reason is not known, but there was probably a red-tape complication at the bottom of the matter. The soldiers from Maine came to Mr. Hamlin in their trouble, and he offered a bill discharging them from the army. This was referred to the Military Committee, of which Jefferson Davis was chairman. It appears that he did not hear Mr. Hamlin's argument, and he caused the committee to report against the bill, on the ground that the Senate could not interfere with the executive management of the army. The Senate accepted the committee's report and rejected Mr. Hamlin's bill. But when Mr. Hamlin saw that Mr. Davis had not grasped the principle involved, he called Davis aside, and reviewing the case, said : —

"Davis, you do not see the point. It is this: the government gave its word to these young men that if they would enlist, it would educate them as mining engineers. Now it has not only broken its pledges, but it is even trying to coerce these men into remaining in the army. I know you do not believe that the government should be allowed to break its pledges."

Mr. Hamlin's explanation cleared up the misapprehensions Mr. Davis had been laboring under, and he exclaimed : "You are right, Hamlin. I had misunderstood the case. The evidence you present exhibits the case in another light. I agree with you ; the government must keep its promises, and I pledge you I will do what I can to induce the Senate to reverse its action." In a few days, largely through Mr. Davis's efforts, Congress released the soldiers, and the Maine men, to show their appreciation of Mr. Hamlin's labors in their behalf, presented him with a gold-headed cane made from the timber of "Old Ironsides."

Mr. Hamlin was pleasantly associated on the Committee on Commerce with John Davis, of Massachusetts ; General Dodge, of Wisconsin ; John Bell, of Tennessee ; and Pierre Soule, of Louisiana. Perhaps during his entire term of service in Congress, he liked no senator better than "Honest" John Davis. The senator from Massachusetts was noted for his upright character, sound, practical mind, and gracious, genial personality. He was Mr. Hamlin's most active cooperator during the first four years the latter was chairman of the Committee on Commerce. Together they devised and framed several important and salutary measures of legislation that are still in force. One was the well known act "to provide for the better security of the lives of passengers on board vessels propelled in whole or in part by steam."

The cause and enactment of this measure may be briefly traced, to give a concrete illustration of the nature of Mr. Hamlin's most important work at this time. Navigation on the waters of the United States had not been properly regulated, since the advent of the steamboat up to Mr. Hamlin's appointment as the head of the Committee on Commerce. An inadequate act was passed in 1838. With the opening up of the great West, followed by the discovery of gold in California, a feverish spirit prevailed in the West and Southwest. Travel was accomplished under great pressure; there was intense rivalry among the steamboat lines on the Mississippi, the Great Lakes, and the California route. Racing was frequent; the management was characterized by frightful recklessness. There was a long era of apalling accidents. Hundreds of steamboats were sunk on snags, or blown up, or burned with a terrible loss of life and property, where proper navigation laws would have averted these calamities. The Secretary of the Treasury transmitted to the Senate a report on June 30, 1851, which is a horrible record of casualties. Up to 1849, from the commencement of navigation by steam in the United States, there were 1865 steamers built in the Mississippi Valley and on the Gulf. Of that number 736 were destroyed, 419 by snags, 104 by fire, 82 by boiler explosions, and the rest by bursting of pipes, collapsing of flues, and collision. The selfishness of owners, reckless and incompetent management, lack of equipment, and inadequate navigation laws were the chief causes. In 1851 the steamer C. P. Griffith took fire on Lake Erie, and over two hundred people were lost, although the boat was only a short distance from shore. She had no lifeboats! The record presented is chiefly of local accidents, but enough has been given to show the conditions of travel on water in this period.

When Mr. Hamlin became chairman of the Committee on Commerce, steamboat travel was one of the first subjects to which he gave his attention. He set the machinery in motion as soon as possible to effect a radical and lasting reform. Mr. Davis coöperated with him. Together they personally consulted hundreds of navigators, steamship owners, scientists, and travelers, to seek the proper remedy. Together they framed a bill, but Senator Davis had the honor of taking charge of it, and of managing the measure on the floor of the Senate. He made the principal speech in favor of the bill, and Mr. Hamlin supported him. This bill struck the evils of steamship management their death-blow. It compelled all owners of public steamboats to license their crafts; established a board of supervising inspectors to examine applicants for the positions of pilot and engineer; appointed inspectors to examine hulls and boilers; required all passenger steamers to be provided with metallic lifeboats, force pumps, fire-buckets, axes; forbade the carrying of inflammable material as cargo without certain precautions; prescribed clear and inflexible rules for navigation, to avoid collisions; exacted the display of the inspector's certificate of examination in a conspicuous place, and after many other provisions fixed heavy penalties for disregarding the statute.

This was one of the most advanced reforms that the government effected before the civil war in the interests of civilization. The importance of the measure, the wide field of inquiry it covered, the selfishness of shipowners, the opposition of certain senators, and the usual delay between the Senate and the House in coming to an agreement, were obstacles to a speedy action by Congress. Mr. Hamlin and Mr. Davis worked on their bill the larger part of two years before they could act. Mr. Davis presented the bill on July 7, 1852. It was passed the following month with over one hundred amendments by the House, which Mr. Davis advised the Senate to accept, chiefly to avoid further delay. Stephen R. Mallory, of Florida, who was afterwards secretary of the Confederate navy, was one of the few senators who opposed the bill. The reason he gave was that the progress in the invention of machinery would in time obviate the dangers of navigation in the United States. When the bill was enacted a salutary effect was soon felt. In 1854 Mr. Hamlin had the act strengthened by further amendments. The certificate of inspection, that the traveler now finds in every public passenger steamboat in this country, is living testimony to the work Mr. Hamlin and John Davis accomplished many years ago to save life and property, and is a reminder of the era of terrible accidents and criminal negligence long happily past.

Mr. Hamlin was personally instrumental in placing on the statute books a reformatory act of great importance limiting the liabilities of shipowners. The old law bore heavily and unjustly in several respects on shipowners, and they made loud complaints to Congress. An illustration may be taken from Mr. Hamlin's speech, February 26, 1851. If a ship lying at a pier caught fire and communicated the flames to a neighboring ship, the owner of the second was held responsible for the cargo on his vessel, if it was consumed. Mr. Hamlin's bill was framed on the English law, and held an owner harmless in such a contingency, provided, of course, the loss did not happen through any fault or neglect on his part. Another section directed that all gold dust, silver bullion, jewelry, and other articles of value, when laden on a vessel, should be accompanied by a description in writing to be given to the master. The owner was thus apprised of the risks he assumed. A third section provided that the owner of a vessel should be liable only to the full extent of his ownership in the vessel. The fourth provided a remedy for those who might sustain a loss where the value of a vessel and her freight for the voyage should not be sufficient to pay the whole amount of the loss. A fifth prescribed that where A chartered his vessel to B, he should not be held responsible for B's debts. Another fixed a penalty of $1000 for the loading of inflammable materials, specified without informing the master of the vessel in writing. This is only an outline of the bill; the particulars need not be detailed. It is only necessary to say that it placed American shipping on a footing with English shipping. The merchants of New York city tendered Senator Hamlin a public banquet in recognition of his labors in behalf of American shipping interests, but he declined it.

An important act of legislation which Mr. Hamlin conceived, and the passage of which he secured, was one providing for the recording of the conveyances of vessels. It is an interesting fact that prior to the enactment of this law there was no national uniform system of recording the titles of vessels; it was subject to local laws. Much confusion of titles arose; worse than that, some sharpers took advantage of the condition of affairs to perpetrate outrageous swindles. There were many cases on record where a man sold a ship or vessel in one State, took the craft to another, and sold it again. Mr. Hamlin's long experience in maritime affairs, both as the chairman of the Committee on Commerce and as shipowner, were the means of his ascertaining the necessity of a reform. He drafted the bill without suggestion from any one, and procured its passage without opposition. It is recorded among the acts of Congress in the United States Statutes at Large, vol. ix. p. 440. It caused comparatively slight litigation, and was a great benefit to marine interests. It became a law on July 29, 1850.[1]

[1] William Shaw Lindsay, elected member of Parliament from Tynemouth in 1854, one of the largest shipowners in England, and a well-known writer on maritime subjects, was commissioned by the British government in 1856 to visit the United States in the interest of better maritime laws. He met Mr. Hamlin at Hampden, and in speeches before the Philadelphia Board of Trade, in 1856, asserted that he had met no man on either side of the Atlantic who understood the commercial relations between Great Britain and the United States, and the reformatory measures needed, as well as Governor Hamlin did. In 1860 Mr. Lindsay revisited the United States when Mr. Hamlin was candidate for Vice-President, and repeated his opinion in another speech.

Other bills, measures, and incidents with which Senator Hamlin was identified during this period as chairman of the Committee on Commerce may be briefly grouped. He made several short speeches in favor of improving certain rivers and harbors. He offered an amendment to the pension laws, which was adopted. He was instrumental in having the revenue laws codified. Congress passed a resolution which he introduced appropriating $10,000 for that purpose. He had charge of the bills making appropriations for the construction of numerous custom-houses, — at Cincinnati, Chicago, St. Louis, Philadelphia, New Orleans, Mobile, Wheeling, Bangor, Belfast, Bath, Portsmouth, Galveston, Georgetown, Milwaukee, Norfolk, and many other places. He was also a member of the Committee on Printing, and these duties increased the details of his work, a record of which it would hardly be worth while to present, though it was laborious and important.

There are several incidents to be recorded now of a larger and more general interest. Congress was still engaged with the problem of cheap postage when Mr. Hamlin entered the Senate. His interest was still strong in this subject. He made a few short, practical speeches on this needed reform, favoring a large reduction of rates. It is noticeable that he reiterated his opposition to the franking privilege in some remarks on January 19, 1849. His stated reason was that he believed that the Post-office Department should derive its support from its income, and that none should enjoy the benefit of the mail service without contributing to its maintenance. To the end of his life Mr. Hamlin opposed franking. A story is told that illustrates the scrupulous use he made of the franking privilege. Some senators had a rather loose idea of this right, and thought it proper for them to frank a friend's letter. They looked on the franking privilege as a sort of free pass which they might use for the benefit of their personal friends. One day a wealthy man, who believed in getting all that he could without paying for it, had a little business with Senator Hamlin. After this was settled, the man handed Mr. Hamlin a couple of letters, saying, —

"Senator, I want you to do me a little favor. Just put your name on these letters, will you?"

Mr. Hamlin pulled out his pocket book, and taking out some money, said, —

"I will give you the money, sir."

"Sir," replied the astonished man, "do you mean to insult me?"

"No, sir," said Senator Hamlin; "you ask me to insult the government by abusing a privilege which it extends to me as a senator."

One of the most practical and beneficial acts of legislation Mr.

Hamlin was identified with was the building of the Pacific Railroad. While he was not one of the conspicuous leaders in this enterprise, he was one of the strongest friends the project had in Congress, and accomplished a great deal of work to secure the necessary legislation. It will be recalled that in his first Oregon speech in the House, Mr. Hamlin predicted the construction of a transcontinental railway. In 1849 Senator Benton instituted the legislation to build the road. In 1853 Congress authorized surveys of the proposed routes. Senator Hamlin supported this legislation in speeches, newspaper articles, and by his vote. He urged that the road would bind the Union closer together, open up travel, develop the country, increase trade, and would also be a great safeguard to the nation as a means of military defense. The strict constructionists and advocates of the extreme doctrine of state rights opposed the granting a government subsidy to help build the Pacific Railroad. Mr. Hamlin believed that the government had the necessary power. The Constitution gave Congress the right to regulate commerce between the States. But the broad, general reasons he had were that the United States was a nation, and the welfare of the Union could be promoted by the construction of a transcontinental railroad; that as the enterprise was beyond the power of individuals to carry out, the government ought to act. The breaking out of the civil war opened the eyes of many conservative men who had not seen the necessity for calling on the government to lend its aid to this plan to unite the East and the West.

Another circumstance occurred at this time which shows the range of Mr. Hamlin's ideas in regard to national, commercial, and business interests. He reported a bill from the Committee on Commerce calling for certain appropriations. One section authorized the government to appropriate $5000 to send a commission to Paraguay to study the conditions of trade there in order to ascertain how the United States might obtain a market in that country. It should be explained that there were circumstances at this particular time that rendered it advisable for the government to operate first in Paraguay; Mr. Hamlin had in mind the desirability of opening up trade in South America, and selected Paraguay as the starting-point. But Mr. Hamlin's resolutions met with only good-natured ridicule. One senator declared that he had never heard of such a preposterous suggestion. Mr. Hamlin turned the tables on him by reading an extract from the last report of the Secretary of the Treasury favoring the extension of our trade with South America, and showing that England was rapidly getting control of the South American markets. But the Senate thought Mr. Hamlin's resolution chimerical, and, after the expenditure of considerable humor, rejected it. Nearly forty years later, when James G. Blaine proposed his plan of reciprocity, there was a large party that laughed at it at his expense. Yet England controls South American trade to-day, and possibly the British merchants have their own idea of American humor.

Frequent complaints were heard from time to time that American seamen who had been wrecked on the coast of Japan had been imprisoned and barbarously treated by the natives. Mr. Hamlin investigated these charges. At the same time his attention was drawn to the possibilities of trade which the United States might build up with Oriental nations. On February 21, 1850, he introduced a resolution calling on the Secretary of State for whatever information he might possess covering these points, and also requesting him to report on the advisability of appointing a commissioner or diplomatic agent to open up amicable relations and negotiate commercial treaties with these nations. These resolutions were adopted by the Senate on March 21, 1850. Negotiations were begun with Japan, and in 1854 Commodore M. C. Perry signed an amicable treaty with the Japanese government. The incident created great interest. These are only the dry facts.

In the summer of 1852 there was again trouble between American and Canadian fishermen along the coast of the British provinces. This time there was a war scare. The English government sent a fleet of a dozen or more men-of-war to the scene of contention. Commodore M. C. Perry was dispatched to the same place, and once more the question of our rights in the North American fisheries was under discussion. Senator Hamlin was peculiarly interested in this question, and he made, on August 3 and 5, 1852, the most extensive and comprehensive speech he had delivered after he became a working senator. It is of historical value since it deals minutely with a subject that has caused so much friction. While it need not be reviewed, the nature of Mr. Hamlin's argument may be indicated. He demonstrated that Great Britain had acknowledged by treaty and acts of acquiescence that American fishermen had the right to take fish within the three-mile limit along the coast of the British provinces. He urged the government to protect the fishermen in their rights, and showed how the fisheries had developed the American navy. His citation of facts left no room for doubt as to our rights, and his speech was accepted by the Senate as authoritative. Those who care to investigate the subject further will find this speech of historical authority, and also a striking example of Mr. Hamlin's peculiar powers of statement. He convinced the Senate, and at the same time provided the fishermen themselves with arguments that they could use with understanding. Pierre Soule, one of the most eloquent members of the Senate, pronounced this "a remarkable speech."

Nothing serious came from the dispute over the fisheries. Webster, who was still secretary of state, and dying, spent some of his last hours in smoothing over the trouble with Mr. Crampton, the British minister at Washington. The reciprocity treaty of 1854 was the outcome of this.

But this period of quietude was now drawing to a close; the slavery issue was beginning to loom up again. The adoption of the compromise measures had the effect of increasing the small anti-slavery party in the Senate by two important additions, — Charles Sumner, of Massachusetts, and Benjamin F. Wade, of Ohio. There could hardly be a greater contrast between two leaders. Sumner was the scholar in politics, and excelled as an orator. He represented the most enlightened State in the Union, and his supporters encouraged him to give all his time to the slavery issue. This was a great advantage to Mr. Sumner. He was practically excused from the routine duties of a senator, and was also relieved from the worry of managing his own campaigns in Massachusetts. He was the Bay State's selected champion in the anti-slavery fight. Wade, who was also a Massachusetts man by birth, was the antithesis of Sumner. He was self-made, raised up from the ranks, a bluff, emphatic, aggressively honest man of great but undisciplined powers. It is related that he once began a speech by saying : " Mr. President, them resolutions." But the tremendous blows which he dealt in debate made him feared by his better educated opponents. He was a " rough jewel." Mr. Hamlin enjoyed pleasant personal relations with Sumner at this time, but of Wade it may be said that few men were ever closer to Mr. Hamlin's heart than "bluff " Ben Wade, of Ohio, one of the bravest of men.

The Fugitive Slave Law was now beginning to make serious trouble, and the Senate had occasional reminders of the indignation the measure provoked at the North. Senator Hamlin early came to the conclusion that this law would eventually work out its own destruction. He realized as Grant did when the latter said, " The way to abolish a bad law is to enforce it." Yet Mr. Hamlin strongly favored action. With the Senate in the hands of the pro-slavery party, it was hopeless now to agitate a complete repeal. President Fillmore, Edward Everett, secretary of state, Rufus Choate, General Cass, Stephen A. Douglas, and scores of other prominent Northern statesmen were opposed to further agitation. But Mr. Hamlin hoped that Northern sentiment would eventually crystallize against this law, and compel its statesmen to change their course. In the mean time he thought the most practical step to be taken was to favor trial by jury. No more arbitrary or despotic law was ever placed on the statute books of a republic than the Fugitive Slave Law. It vested complete power in a United States commissioner to decide the liberty of a colored person. There was no appeal from his decision. He even received twice the fee for consigning a colored man to slavery than for dismissing his case. No one knows how many freed men and women were sworn into slavery by perjurers and kidnappers. This was why Mr. Hamlin favored trial by jury as the first act of remedial legislation.

During the first few years Sumner was in the Senate, prior to the repeal of the Missouri Compromise, he was rather quiet, while familiarizing himself with his position. But he made several moves at this time which were precursors of his notable course in subsequent years. One of the first things Sumner did of importance after entering the Senate was to offer, on May 26, 1852, a petition from the Society of Friends of New England praying for the repeal of the Fugitive Slave Law. The pro-slavery men were more tolerant and courteous than their predecessors were in the days of the gag-law. Mr. Mangum and Mr. Badger, for example, expressed the desire that the petition should be received, although announcing their intention of voting to table it. The petition was received by a unanimous vote, but it was promptly tabled by a vote of 40 to 10.[1] The ten who voted to take up the petition were Messrs. Hamlin, Sumner, Borland, Chase, Wade, Hale, Seward, Davis, of Massachusetts, and Walker and Dodge, of Wisconsin. But this vote did not entirely represent the anti-slavery sentiment in the Senate. Among the forty who opposed the petition were Hamilton Fish, of New York, whose public career is without a blot ; Alpheus Felch, a pure and able senator from Michigan, who was a decided opponent of slavery, and William Upham, an anti-slavery man from Vermont. The difference between these men and their anti-slavery colleagues was that between conservatism and radicalism, or, fairer still, a matter of judgment. They were averse to reopening the agitation. They did not think the time had come for that, and that is the whole story.

On July 27, 1852, Sumner introduced a bill calling on the Judiciary Committee to consider the expediency of reporting a bill to repeal the Fugitive Slave Law. This was rejected the next day, after a short debate, by a vote of 32 to 10.[2] Mr. Hamlin was one of the ten who supported Sumner's bill. But this was only fencing. The narrative now turns back to a marked epoch in the history of Maine, — the senatorial election of 1850. Many details have been omitted from this record of Mr. Hamlin's work, in order that the story of events might not be too long delayed. But it is well to close this chapter by adding the facts, that during the seven years Mr. Hamlin was chairman of the Committee on Commerce, he personally exam-

[1] *Congressional Globe*, May 26, 1852, p. 1475.
[2] *Ibid.*, July 28, p. 1953.

ined all bills and measures brought before it, answered all important communications to him in his own writing, while he was in the Senate, and finally made no distinction between his constituents on account of politics in discharging his duties as senator.   This was his conception of his duties as a business senator, although he was always a strong partisan.

CHAPTER XXI

THE fierce quarrel over the omnibus bill in Congress widened the split in both parties on the slavery issue ; at the same time, it nerved Mr. Hamlin's pro-slavery opponents in Maine to make a supreme effort to prevent his reëlection to the Senate in the summer of 1850. This was the severest struggle that Mr. Hamlin ever had with the slave party ; and there is no incident in his life which so clearly reveals the peculiarly perplexing and practical difficulties that beset him as an anti-slavery leader. Again Mr. Hamlin had the people of his party with him, and the politicians against him. Two thirds of the party favored Mr. Hamlin's return to the Senate ; in fact, he was renominated in the legislative caucus by two thirds of the Democratic members ; but by the accidents of politics, the balance of power in this election was held for two months by a small number of pro-slavery men, who did their utmost to defeat Mr. Hamlin. They did, however, make several offers of compromise, and promised to elect Mr. Hamlin if he would consent to the rescinding of resolutions he had caused the previous legislature to pass, instructing the Maine congressmen to oppose all measures extending slavery into free territory. This would have allowed Senator Hamlin to continue his opposition to slavery ; but it would have freed Senator Bradbury and two Hunker representatives, Thomas J. D. Fuller and Moses McDonald, from all restraint. Mr. Hamlin refused to listen to these terms ; he was contending for his principles and the honor of Maine. In the end, he was elected by the aid of a few Free-Soilers, who came to his help in a dramatic way at a critical moment. This was one of the hardest blows the pro-slavery machine in Maine received before it was wiped out of existence by the civil war.

Discouraging conditions existed at the outset. The pro-slavery machine was at the height of its power, and in consequence of the action of its leaders, the Democratic party was steadily losing ground in Maine. This machine had a leader in the governor's chair, Mr. Dana ; two men in Congress, Fuller and McDonald ; a quasi friend in Senator Bradbury ; half a dozen able men in the state Senate ; twenty-five in the House. It had adherents and henchmen by the score in minor state offices who were appointed by Governor

ANTE-BELLUM MAINE LEADERS.

Dana. Among its prominent leaders were Nathan Clifford, who had just retired from President Polk's Cabinet, and was anxiously seeking a return to official life ; George F. Shepley, who was afterwards judge of the United States Circuit Court, and was now recognized as one of the most brilliant lawyers in New England ; Bion Bradbury, who was the suavest and craftiest wire-puller the Democratic party of Maine ever produced ; Wyman B. S. Moor, who had been attorney-general of Maine four times ; Shepard Cary, who had been in Congress and was now in the state Senate ; Virgil D. Parris, another former congressman ; Benjamin Wiggin, who was in the governor's council ; George W. Stanley, a leading banker of the State, a power in Kennebec County ; and many others who were well known in their day.   They comprised a group of strong and resourceful politicians.

Mr. Hamlin and his friends had two things to do to secure his reëlection : one was to wrest the control of the party machine away from the pro-slavery wing, and the other was to carry the State for the Democracy.   It is interesting to observe the kind of men who were Mr. Hamlin's most active followers in this campaign.   There were few office-seekers among them, and not many practiced politicians.   They did not have a tithe of the titles the pro-slavery men enjoyed.   Outside of Mr. Hamlin's lieutenants, they were mostly plain men from the people.   The one on whom Mr. Hamlin depended most in this campaign was William P. Haines, of Saco, who at this time was one of the leading business men of Maine, and was largely instrumental in developing the textile manufacturing interests of his part of the State.   He was a strong, sagacious, upright, modest man, a gentleman, and a scholar.   Mr. Hamlin wanted Mr. Haines for his colleague in the Senate ; but he preferred private life, though he gave his time ungrudgingly for his party's good.   Ezra B. French, of Damariscotta, was another man whom Mr. Hamlin highly esteemed. He was Maine's secretary of state for four years, was one of the first Republicans Maine sent to Congress, and was appointed second auditor of the United States Treasury by President Lincoln, at Mr. Hamlin's request.   George P. Sewall, an able lawyer and wit, of Old Town, was the practical politician.   Judge R. D. Rice, of Augusta, who served nearly twelve years on the Supreme Bench of Maine with honor to the State and credit to himself ; General Samuel F. Hersey, a leading lumberman of Maine ; William T. Johnson, editor of the "Augusta Age ;" Joseph Bartlett, editor of the "Bangor Jeffersonian ;" Leander Valentine, of Westbrook ; Charles J. Talbot,[1] of Wil-

---

[1] One result of this contest was the cementing of a lifelong friendship between Mr. Hamlin and Mr. Talbot, who was a pure, unselfish, and large-minded man of uncommon ability and character.   He was probably closer to Mr. Hamlin than

ton; George H. Shirley, of Portland; John S. Chadwick, of Bangor; General John J. Perry and George F. Emery, of Oxford County; Samuel Peters Brown, of Bluehill; Isaac Dyer, of Baldwin; John Gardner, of Patten, and others, were also loyal supporters of Mr. Hamlin.

The first move Mr. Hamlin made was to select his candidate for governor. A man was needed who would unite both wings of the party, and bring back five thousand Democrats who had voted the Free-Soil ticket the year before. He decided on Dr. John Hubbard, an eminent physician of Hallowell, who was a man he regarded of "popular possibilities." Dr. Hubbard was bluff, honest, kind-hearted, sturdy, of considerable political ability, and had an immense practice. He was nominated after a sharp fight in a convention of over six hundred delegates, and elected over Elijah L. Hamlin, the Whig candidate, and the senator's brother, by a substantial majority. The Democrats also carried the legislature by a good vote, with Mr. Hamlin's friends largely in the ascendency; in fact, more than two thirds of the Democrats elected had been instructed by their constituents to vote for Mr. Hamlin's renomination. Thus, with the Hunkers beaten in the state convention and in the legislative caucus, and with the anti-slavery men in control of the state government and legislature, Mr. Hamlin's success seemed assured without further trouble.

But it is the unexpected that happens in politics. Shortly after the personnel of the legislature had been determined, the Hunkers discovered a desperate chance of blocking Mr. Hamlin's election. They hoped that they could create a peculiar contingency out of certain conditions that existed in the state Senate. The Senate was entitled to thirty-one members, and it appeared before its organization that there would be twenty-one Democrats and ten Whigs. The Hunker opportunity arose from the fact that there had been several failures to elect, and the legislature was required to fill the vacancies. Now the Hunkers figured that if they could elect a proslavery man to fill one of these vacancies, they might be able to hold up the Senate. Of the Democrats in that body, eleven were known to be warm friends of Mr. Hamlin's; five, who had been elected or were certain of getting their seats, were privately determined to bolt him; four more were very doubtful, though they were inclined to stand by the party nominee. The eleven senators who were Mr. Hamlin's friends were a majority of the Democrats; but although these were sufficient to give him a regular party nomination in the Senate, they could not elect him, sixteen votes being necessary for a choice. The

any other political associate in Maine. George H. Shirley, of the same pure type, is another brave anti-slavery fighter who was one of Mr. Hamlin's most devoted and affectionate friends for life. See Neal Dow's *Reminiscences*.

plan the Hunkers concocted involved an unscrupulous violation of party pledges and usages.   One feature included a secret bargain with the Whigs to elect George F. Shepley to fill one of the vacancies in the Senate ; another was a scheme to lead the doubtful senators off on a collateral issue.   If this plotting succeeded, Mr. Hamlin's election in the Senate would fail by one vote, unless the Free-Soil members came to his aid, and steps were taken to meet this contingency.

This conspiracy was set on foot soon after the fall election of 1849. As the legislature did not convene until the following May, the Hunkers had ample time to work every wire within their clutches. They were of course too adroit to give any hint of the purpose until they had carefully canvassed the situation, and sounded every pro-slavery Democrat of influence in Maine.   But all this time the Hunkers were asserting in public their intention of contesting Mr. Hamlin's renomination in the regular party caucus.   This was to divert attention from their underground scheming.   There was a comic side to the Hunkers' proceedings.   In public they demanded Mr. Hamlin's defeat, on the allegation that he was an "unsafe party man" and an "unsound Democrat;" yet in private they were preparing to violate the fundamental principle of the Democratic party, that the will of the majority should be respected.   They shut their eyes to the inconsistency of their course ; it was "anything to beat Hamlin."

But Mr. Hamlin's friends were not to be deceived.   They knew the temper and the disposition of their opponents, and they watched the Hunker camp day and night.   There were mysterious conferences in the governor's rooms at Augusta, between Mr. Dana and the leaders of the pro-slavery wing.   The Hunker rank and file were in a hubbub of excitement.   The real Wild-Cat element began to show its claws. This crowd was composed of men who, happily for Maine, were few in number, although they were cunning and reckless.   They would have been slaveholders had they lived in the South.   They instinctively opposed an honest man ; they could not understand such a man.   During the war of the rebellion, they were copperheads of the most virulent type.   They were perniciously alive in this contest, and their conduct reflected the actual hatred that the pro-slavery machine had for Senator Hamlin.   They waged a campaign of slander ; they sought to arouse racial prejudice.   A favorite trick was to coin catch phrases and pass them around the State.   One was, "The niggers love Hamlin ;" another was, "Hamlin loves the niggers."   One wretch whom his unsavory crowd managed to get into Congress for a short time capped the climax of slander against Mr. Hamlin, inventing a story which he told in a cunning way, so as to make it appear that Mr. Hamlin had negro blood in him.

A campaign of falsehood against an honest man never failed to react

on its authors.   In this instance, the tactics of the Wild-Cats made the
anti-slavery men all the more watchful.   They cherished Mr. Hamlin's
interests as they would their own.   Their devotion to him is the touching feature of this contest.   They might be outwitted in skirmishes
and be drawn into ambuscades, but in fighting in the open, when principle, courage, and honesty were the heaviest guns, they won.   Through
the alertness of his friends, Mr. Hamlin quickly ascertained the formation of a plot to cheat him out of a reëlection, even if he should be
renominated in his party's regular caucus.   It appears that the Hunkers overreached themselves in their desire to pledge a member of the
House to join in their contemplated bolt.   Secretary French had suspected that the Hunkers were brewing mischief at their mysterious
conferences with Governor Dana.   He obtained proof of his suspicions.
A representative named Small, of Newry, told Mr. French that Bion
Bradbury had informed him that the Hunkers would not support Mr.
Hamlin, and if necessary to defeat him would remain out of the party
caucus, so as to escape being bound by its action.   Mr. French warned
Mr. Hamlin in December, 1849, and added these prophetic words to his
letter : —

"Desperate and reckless, they (the pro-slavery men) will make a
push for power under Dana such has never been seen in this State. . . .
I have no hope in their prudence ; it is rather in their recklessness and
imprudence which will excite indignation, and justify bold retaliatory
measures, that I see hopes of health and success to the party."

Mr. French was right.   With all the zeal of a newly made convert,
Governor Dana lent the aid of his office to the schemes of his faction
to strengthen the pro-slavery machine in its tricky fight against Mr.
Hamlin.   Few men who have occupied the governor's chair in Maine
ever prostituted the power of their office to a baser purpose, or more
willfully violated the sentiment of the State, than Mr. Dana did in this
fight between the anti-slavery and pro-slavery Democracy.   This was
a great pity, for in his private life Mr. Dana was an upright man, of
whom better things had been expected.   But he worshiped the politician's god, — party action, — and fell.   In spite of his professed belief
in the rule of the majority, the rights of the States, the sentiment of
Maine, the warnings and protests of the majority of his party, Governor Dana's last important act before retiring from office was to
fill all the offices at his disposal, which were a large number and important, with bitter and avowed supporters of the doctrine of slavery
extension.

This act, in a strong anti-slavery State at this crisis, carries its own
condemnation.   The feelings of the anti-slavery Democracy may be
more easily imagined than described.   It infuriated them to see the
power of the state government employed to thwart the wishes of

the vast majority; they felt as if circumstances were conspiring to tie them hand and foot. But without going further into the details of Governor Dana's acts, their importance may be readily gathered from the following terse letter of comment that Senator Hamlin wrote Mr. Haines, January 11, 1850: —

"I have seen the appointments to which you allude. I did not doubt, nor do I now, that they are made mainly to injure me. . . . I know the desperation with which I am to be fought, and while I am not at all nervous, yet, of course, I have some anxiety. I fear the use of *money* against me. Yet with prudence and proper effort all will be well. The acts of Governor Dana will react with terrible force."

There were other reasons why Mr. Hamlin felt himself master of the situation. This involves a short explanation of his political methods. When he went into a political fight, in which his own fortunes were at stake, he usually formulated a plan of action and selected his lieutenants. He assigned to each a specific line of work, but always kept to himself the plan in its entirety. The reason of this is easily understood when it is remembered that it was Mr. Hamlin's nature to command and to adopt the simplest methods to obtain a result. He trusted and believed in his friends, but he feared accidents and confusion. Now, while Mr. Haines, Mr. French, Mr. Sewall, and other of Mr. Hamlin's lieutenants were each following up certain details, Mr. Hamlin had men, unknown to his chief supporters, at work in other parts of the State carrying out other directions. The business intrusted to Mr. Haines and his associates was to help Mr. Hamlin keep his forces intact; the task devolving on the second group of lieutenants was to assist Mr. Hamlin in dividing his opponents and upsetting their plans.

This programme was well carried out, and with results that were not without an amusing side. In the beginning of this campaign, the Hunkers had intended to make a fight in the caucus against Mr. Hamlin; and they thought of a bolt as a last desperate expedient. They encouraged Mr. Dana to enter the lists, hoping that by an energetic use of the patronage he might weaken Mr. Hamlin's forces and perhaps beat him. This was good Hunker argument. But as the campaign waxed hot, the Hunkers found their chance of defeating Mr. Hamlin in the caucus melting away; it was ascertained that Dana could not carry his own county, Oxford, and he was therefore dropped. At this juncture the pro-slavery leaders decided to bring forward Bion Bradbury as their candidate. He was willing, and forthwith began to travel all over Maine, organizing his own campaign. There was no secret about it; the Hunker leaders backed Bradbury, and his friends made great claims for him. This was the situation several months before the legislature convened.

Although Bradbury had small chance of success, he evinced, in so marked a degree, a talent for organization, and an ability for pulling wires, that Mr. Hamlin quickly recognized in him a dangerous opponent. If Bion Bradbury had lived in New York city, where his peculiarly adroit political ability would have found a suitable field, he doubtless might have attained great prominence as a political leader. He was a member of the National Executive Committee of the Democratic party for many years, and exercised no mean influence in its councils, though he was but little known outside of Maine. Mr. Hamlin took measures to head Bradbury off. It appears that in selecting Bradbury for their candidate, the Hunker leaders had omitted to consult their rank and file. Mr. Hamlin took advantage of this; Mr. Bradbury, who was still young in politics, overlooked the circumstance. While he was spending time and money in traveling over Maine, Mr. Hamlin was quietly laying plans to trip him up. For example, Mr. Hamlin intimated to a confidential friend in Cumberland County that he would like to have it suggested to the Hunkers there that John Anderson, of that county, ought to have the support of his own district. This pleased the friends of Mr. Anderson, who, by the way, was a popular and able man, and they brought him forward as their candidate, with results to be noted later. Mr. Hamlin introduced clever tactics in other counties, and before long the Hunkers had a very interesting contest in their own camp to settle, without dreaming how it originated.

Other incidents happened as the campaign progressed from stage to stage that showed Mr. Hamlin's knowledge of men and politics. During his long career he made very few mistakes in choosing friends. It is true, too, that he never forgot a friend who helped him, or an enemy who willfully harmed him. In this campaign, Mr. Hamlin's letters to his friends are proofs of his shrewd and clear estimates of the promises of men. There were over one hundred Democrats in the legislature; the canvass lasted more than ten months, and during a large part of that time Mr. Hamlin's own lieutenants disagreed as to the number of votes he would receive in the caucus. In December, 1849, Mr. Hamlin wrote George P. Sewall, who was to be his manager in the House, that the Hunkers would nominate John Anderson, and would cast not over twenty-five votes in the House. Mr. Sewall, a very clever politician, and on the ground, too, dissented from these predictions. He said Bion Bradbury would be the Hunker nominee, and would poll more votes than Mr. Hamlin had figured that he would. But Anderson was the Hunkers' man, and for two months his vote in the House averaged twenty-five. In March, 1850, Mr. Hamlin wrote Mr. Haines that on the lowest estimate he would have sixty-one votes in the House and eleven in the

Senate. Precisely the same time Bradbury claimed that he would have forty-seven votes in the House, and he boasted of this to Sewall, who reported it to Mr. Hamlin. Commenting on this, in a letter to Mr. Haines, Mr. Hamlin said: "The Dana clique know absolutely nothing about the senatorial question. They cannot beat me." Between March and May, when the caucus was held, Mr. Hamlin gained some votes. He then announced that he would have sixty-seven votes in the House and eleven in the Senate. This was the exact vote by which he was nominated. Mr. Hamlin's private correspondence shows that during the entire canvass he was in doubt about only two Democrats out of the one hundred or more in the legislature. After much promising and fair talk these men went against him.

When the legislature at last met, in May, 1850, it was proved that Mr. Hamlin's forces outnumbered the Hunkers nearly three to one. Men came forward and were counted. This was a crushing blow to the pro-slavery machine, after the bluster its leaders had made about beating Mr. Hamlin in the caucus. But the crowning humiliation the Hunker leaders suffered was when they discovered that their rank and file had got away from them, and would not accept Bion Bradbury as their candidate, even after his hard work in organizing the Hunker campaign against Mr. Hamlin. The leaders were greatly disgusted, Bradbury was very sore, while Mr. Hamlin was secretly much amused. The pro-slavery men were indeed so confused over this difficulty that they could not agree on a candidate for several days. All they could do at first was to decide on a bolt, and to stay out of the party caucus. The fact is the Hunkers never learned how Bion Bradbury was bowled out of the great senatorial contest of 1850 and John Anderson brought forward in his place. The story has never been told before. It is possible that this ruse saved Mr. Hamlin's reëlection. Bradbury was a member of the House, and had he been the Hunkers' nominee, it was among the possibilities that he might in that capacity have prevented the legislature from electing a senator. His cunning, adroitness, and gift for intrigue made him feared; his defeat lessened his prestige. Mr. Hamlin's efforts to pull Bradbury out of the field show that he was convinced there was a necessity for it. The incident evidences how hard Mr. Hamlin had to fight in ante-bellum days to remain in the Senate as an anti-slavery man.

The long looked for caucus took place on May 20; Mr. Hamlin was nominated in the House by a vote of 67 to 1 for Dana, and in the Senate by 11 to 1 for Nathan Clifford. The Hunkers carried out their threats, and refused to enter the caucus. They sent Shepard Cary, however, to the senate caucus to make their official declaration of war. Cary's speech was an effort to read Mr. Hamlin out of the Democratic party. It was an unscrupulous misrepresentation and a garbled version of Mr. Hamlin's relations with the Democracy; but it is of special interest as an exposition of the curious ideas men of Cary's stamp had of the anti-slavery Democratic leaders. He was a bold, energetic man, and had a considerable following among the rural Hunkers of Aroostook County; indeed, he entertained ambitions to succeed Senator Bradbury. The principal points in Cary's speech were summarized in the "Bangor Democrat," the pro-slavery organ of eastern Maine, as a serious indictment against Mr. Hamlin in the following language : —

"It was openly charged in the caucus against Mr. Hamlin, that he had been the ally of John P. Hale, of New Hampshire, in treasonable designs against the Democratic party; that he had been closely connected in sentiment, sympathy, and action with the Wilmots of Pennsylvania and the Van Burens of New York, who had successfully conspired against the Democratic party of the nation and defeated the election of General Cass; . . . that he was an opponent of the measures of the last Democratic administration, and had denounced James K. Polk as a ' weak man, a second edition of John Tyler, not much improved ; ' that he favored the bringing forward of Mr. Van Buren against General Cass as a candidate for President; that he had approved the action of the Buffalo convention, and though Mr. Hamlin was in this city (Augusta) at the time, he denied none of these charges or allegations except that relating to the Buffalo convention."

This indictment was a bold perversion of facts ; yet that is not surprising considering the fact that it was framed by men who believed both in human slavery and party servitude. It was simply a pretext ; it was drawn up by men who supported slavery to give their partisan-blinded followers formulated reasons for bolting Mr. Hamlin. He could be sacrificed on the altar of party fetich, — party action. It was a solemn indictment in the eyes of men who regarded slavery as a sacred institution and consecrated by the Constitution ; it stiffened the backbones of thirty odd Hunkers who voted against Mr. Hamlin for two months in this session of the legislature. But the fact was, Mr. Hamlin supported Cass, though against his wishes ; he supported the principal measures of the Polk administration, though not its pro-slavery policy ; he supported Levi Woodbury against Van Buren and Cass in the Democratic National Convention of 1848 ; he did not indorse the action of the Buffalo convention. This last story was pure invention ; the man who was responsible for it showed a telegram from E. S. Hamlin, a Whig of Ohio, to the Buffalo convention, and out of this concocted the story about Senator Hamlin. It seems incredible, in view of Mr. Hamlin's character, his public record,

and the palpable falsity of these charges, that they should have had
an effect against him ; but men who in their hearts upheld slavery
could not but take a perverted view of a man who opposed the institution.   That is all that need be said.

The Hunkers now claimed that they were the real Democracy and
that Mr. Hamlin was an " unsound Democrat." They ignored the
fact that their national party had not as yet authoritatively accepted
the doctrine of slavery extension in its national conventions ; they
repudiated the principle of state rights in the case of their own
State ; they denied the rule of the majority in their own local party.
After this inconsistency, it was not strange that in their blindness
they should dethrone their own god, — party action.   They rejected
the action of the regular party caucus, and then entered into a corrupt
bargain with the Whigs to defeat their own party.   This involved
even a further violation of party usages and personal pledges, and the
scheme, therefore, requires an explanation.   There were five vacancies in the Senate, owing to failures to elect.   The legislature was
compelled to fill these vacancies.   The long established custom was
for the senators and representatives from the county where a vacancy
existed to meet in a party caucus and nominate candidates from whom
the legislature made its choice.   The anti-slavery Democrats honor-
ably and loyally abided by this custom.   For example, there had been
a failure to elect in a district in Washington County.   George M.
Chase, a Hunker, who was the regular nominee on his party's ticket,
was duly nominated by the Democratic delegates from Washington
County, and elected by the votes of the anti-slavery Democrats over
the Whig nominee.   But the Hunkers broke faith in a Cumberland
County district.   There had been two Democratic candidates before
the people in this district : Charles Megquier, an anti-slavery man,
and George F. Shepley, a Hunker.   The Cumberland Democratic
senators and representatives nominated Mr. Megquier by a vote of
seven to two and made the nomination unanimous.   But the Hunkers, having elected Chase, now burned their last bridge ; they made
a combination with the Whigs and elected Shepley the day after the
senatorial caucus.

This was the most serious blow Mr. Hamlin had yet received.   By
electing Shepley the coalition had proved that it could control the
legislature, and no man could foresee how long it would hang together.
Truly, " politics makes strange bedfellows." Here were the anti-
slavery Whigs working with pro-slavery Democrats to punish a statesman for fighting the slave power.   Yet it was the politics of the day.
The Whigs justified their course by claiming that it would help them to
elect a Whig to succeed Senator Bradbury the next year.[1]   The anti-

[1] It is an interesting fact that in 1851 the pro-slavery Democrats bolted Lot

slavery Democrats were naturally much alarmed over this turn of affairs, and at once summoned Mr. Hamlin from Washington.

When he arrived at Augusta, he found the situation more complicated than when the coalition was first formed. The Hunkers were leaving no stone unturned to accomplish his defeat, and were now concentrating their efforts on the Senate. Mr. Hamlin had eleven supporters there, but sixteen votes were necessary to elect him in a full vote, — thirty-one. If the four doubtful senators voted for Mr. Hamlin, that would give him fifteen votes, or within one of an election. In that event there was danger of the Free-Soilers coming to Mr. Hamlin's rescue. They were having mysterious conferences by themselves, and no one outside of their councils could say what they would do. The Hunkers laid plans to get control of the Senate, and also to lead the doubtful senators off on a collateral issue. They tried to elect Shepard Cary president of the Senate, and attempted to bribe a senator to vote for him on the promise that Cary would resign, and he should be promoted to the presiding chair. This was the Chase-Dunn trick that beat Mr. Hamlin in 1846 ; the important difference was that the senator approached this time was an honest man. But the other scheme was more dangerous. This was to make it an issue with Mr. Hamlin to consent to the rescinding of the resolutions he had induced the previous legislature to pass instructing the Maine senators and representatives in Congress to oppose all measures favoring the extension of slavery into free soil. The Hunkers argued with some plausibility that these resolutions of instruction infringed on the liberty of the individual congressmen. Senator Bradbury upheld this view by journeying from Washington to Augusta to urge the repeal of the resolutions. This made an impression on the doubtful senators ; they listened, and, listening, they were led away too, to remain with the Hunkers to the end. The inevitable result was the sickening cry of compromise !

The councils of the anti-slavery men were divided, and feeling was running high when Mr. Hamlin took charge of his campaign. Judge R. D. Rice, who was at Augusta, wrote : "I saw Mr. Hamlin to-day. He is calm, smiling, confident, and surrounded by friends wherever he goes." Almost the first thing Mr. Hamlin did was to gather his supporters together, encourage them, repeat a rule he always laid down on entering a party contest, and outline the plan of action. He talked to men this time, who always treasured up in their hearts recollections of moments like this with the leader they loved so well. What Mr. Hamlin said was substantially as follows : —

"My friends, we are going to have a long and hot fight. Now, I

M. Morrill, an anti-slavery man, and, uniting with the Whigs, elected William Pitt Fessenden, a strong anti-slavery man, to the United States Senate.

want you to keep cool and keep up your courage. Don't abuse my opponents; let them do all the abusing and trading. I am going to win, and I want as little hard feeling as possible after it is all over. Don't listen to any offers of compromise. We are standing up for our principles. 'Sink or swim, live or die,' I am in this fight to the end to keep that accursed thing of slavery out of free soil and the Democratic party." Mr. Hamlin's words inspired his followers with new zeal and courage, and thereafter he often said of his active supporters in this campaign, "No man ever had more devoted friends." Among the group who stood close to him now were a number of men who were known in their day as faithful and creditable legislators. In the Senate was Paulinus M. Foster, of North Anson, the president; Noah Prince, of Buckfield; Robert A. Chapman, of Bethel; Sheldon Hobbs, of North Berwick; Thomas M. Morrow, of Searsport; William Milliken, of Burnham; James Lancaster, of Northport; Benjamin Rhea, of Brooksville; Amos Pickard, of Hampden; William R. Hersey, of Lincoln, and Nehemiah Bartlett, of Garland. In the House were Samuel Belcher, of Farmington, the speaker; George P. Sewall, of Old Town; Samuel Jordan, of Westbrook; John Goodell, of Hampden; Ebenezer Knowlton, of Montville; Daniel Rogers, of Windham; Daniel Chamberlain, of Bristol; Jeremiah Tolman, of Rockland; Wyer G. Sargent, of Sedgwick; Josiah Harmon, of Thorndyke; Lorin D. Hayes, then of Garland, and General William S. Cochran, of Waldoboro. These men with those already mentioned formed a veritable body-guard in this fight, and Mr. Hamlin never forgot them. The majority followed him into the Republican party.

The coalition, having control of the situation, forced a resolution through the legislature by a narrow majority, postponing the election of senator for a month — until June 25. This gave the Hunkers more time to make trouble, and they improved their opportunity. The day Mr. Hamlin left Augusta to return to Washington, he met Charles Stackpole, the editor of a Portland Free-Soil newspaper, who asked him his views about the scheme that Stephen A. Douglas was advocating to annex Cuba to the United States. Douglas's object was to strengthen himself with the slave power; but while Mr. Hamlin did not entertain a high opinion of Douglas and his policy, he nevertheless refrained from discussing this matter, for the reason that he did not wish to introduce any more issues in his senatorial campaign. Mr. Hamlin contented himself with alluding to his attitude towards slavery. His exact words were: "My course towards slavery is well known. I have taken that course and I will adhere to it, 'sink or swim, live or die.'" Mr. Stackpole published a correct report of the interview, and the incident should have ended there. But the

Hunkers saw an advantage offered them, and although the course of procedure involved was unscrupulous and dishonorable in the extreme, they seized the opportunity presented. At this time the public mind was easily inflamed against the Abolitionists; they were bitterly denounced as disunionists and marplots. While they were animated by the purest of motives, it is nevertheless a question for the philosophical historians to decide whether the Abolitionists were a help or a hindrance to the men who actually exterminated slavery, however much their agitation contributed to forcing the issue. To charge an anti-slavery leader of Mr. Hamlin's status at this time with sympathizing with the Abolitionists, who advocated disunion, and called the Constitution "a covenant with death and an agreement with hell,"[1] was a gross libel on him and an insult to the thousands of men who supported anti-slavery leaders. But this is what the pro-slavery Democrats in their desperation did charge against Mr. Hamlin. The fact that Mr. Hamlin had given an interview to a Free-Soil newspaper was proof to the blind that he was an Abolitionist; they could not see that the incident served the pro-slavery leaders as a pretext to malign Mr. Hamlin. So a wave of passion swept over the pro-slavery party; their newspapers shrieked in leaded type that Hamlin was an Abolitionist! Even two months after this crusade was started the "Bangor Democrat," in common with newspapers of its kind, kept up the charge. Here is one extract from its issue of July 23, 1850, which shows how willfully Mr. Hamlin was misrepresented in consequence of the Stackpole interview: —

"Mr. Hamlin has for years been engaged in the unholy work of agitation, and in bringing the Union into danger; if nine tenths of the people are ready to say, Never again introduce into our conventions resolutions touching the question of slavery, they must also be prepared to say, Do not elect Mr. Hamlin senator, for he is one of the chief agitators and false friends of the Union. . . . He has trifled with the Union and the Democratic party too much to be rewarded with an important office for six years. To elect him would be to offer a large bounty to those who would imperil the Union."

The balloting for senator began on June 20, with the House leading off; the Senate followed five days later. The Hunkers, still in a quandary over their candidate, made an audacious move to seduce Governor Hubbard into accepting their nomination by voting for him. On the first ballot 149 votes were cast; 75 were necessary for a choice. Mr. Hamlin received 67, eight less than was needed for an election. The Hunkers threw 20 votes for Hubbard; the Whigs, 42 for George Evans; the Free-Soilers or Abolitionists, 15 for General Fessenden; and the rest were scattering. The next day Governor

[1] William Lloyd Garrison.

Hubbard wrote a letter forbidding the use of his name, and urging the Democrats to support the regular nominee. The Hunkers then concentrated on John Anderson, the man Mr. Hamlin predicted they would have to take up. The Senate balloted five times on June 25. Mr. Hamlin received 13 votes, or three short of a majority ; Mr. Evans had seven ; Mr. Anderson six, General Fessenden four and five. The first test demonstrated, therefore, that ten Hunkers had the balance of power, if the contest continued a straight party fight. If ten Hunkers would vote for Mr. Hamlin they could elect him. The pro-slavery men made a point of this, as will appear later.

A week's balloting followed without a result. The Senate made eleven attempts to break the deadlock, the House ten. It would be tedious reading if the details of the voting were recorded. It is sufficient to say that with a single exception, when Mr. Hamlin came within four votes of an election in the House, the situation remained unchanged. At the end of the week, when the coalition found that Mr. Hamlin's forces could not be broken, the election was again postponed for a month, after another sharp fight and close vote. The Hunkers' object this time was to renew their struggle to rescind Mr. Hamlin's resolutions of instructions. But their Whig allies deserted them on this move, and the legislature by an overwhelming vote reaffirmed the principle laid down by Mr. Hamlin. Still the Hunkers persevered. They tried a trick. Some of their Bangor friends drew up resolutions that pretended to reaffirm Mr. Hamlin's resolutions, but which stopped short of actual instructions. The plan was to rush this bogus affair through the legislature, if they could catch it napping. John S. Chadwick got hold of a copy of the resolutions before they were set in type in the office of the " Bangor Democrat." When the printed articles arrived at Augusta, there was a roar of laughter from Mr. Hamlin's friends.

And now the Hunkers began to talk once more of compromise ; they sang of harmony ; [1] they said Mr. Hamlin could be elected if he would give up his resolutions of instructions ; all he needed was ten votes ! But the die was cast ; the end of the long fight was near. Mr. Hamlin had made a strong fight for reëlection as a strict party man, and for two months his forces had worked according to party usages. He was the choice of the majority of his party, and his reelection had been prevented by a minority that had adopted irregular and unscrupulous methods. He had won a moral victory, and was now justified in accepting help outside of party lines. He did this.

[1] Mr. Hamlin wrote Mr. Haines on July 4, 1850 : " When I was at Augusta, I was sounded on rescinding the resolutions of last year." He replied : " I will obey your instructions, or resign." He added to Haines : " You must not consent to place me in a position which will demand of me an acquiescence in the extension of slavery."

There were about twenty Free-Soilers or Abolitionists in the legislature. The majority would have voted for Mr. Hamlin at any time if they were certain their votes could elect him. But they were good enough politicians to know that their open support of Mr. Hamlin might repel strict party Democrats, who were voting for him because he was their regular nominee. Then again, while there were enough Free-Soilers in the House to elect Mr. Hamlin in that body, it was doubtful whether three of the Free-Soilers in the Senate, or just the number needed, would vote for him. Two were certain of helping; one was uncertain, and all depended on this man. He was a cautious old man by the name of Ozias Blanchard, of the town of Blanchard. At this juncture General Samuel Fessenden, Mr. Hamlin's former law preceptor, Joshua R. Giddings, and Neal Dow came to Mr. Hamlin's aid.[1] Another who aided Mr. Hamlin at this time was Isaac Dyer, of Baldwin, long a powerful leader in the politics of Maine. He was then an anti-slavery Whig, and afterwards a Republican. Mr. Hamlin spoke of Mr. Dyer as one of the ablest politicians he ever knew, and a friend as true as steel. General Fessenden was the nominee of the Free-Soil party, and it is not necessary to say that he was loyal to it; but he had no hope of an election, and it angered him to see the pro-slavery Democrats persecute Senator Hamlin for fighting slavery. Fessenden corresponded with Giddings and brought their joint influence to bear on Blanchard. They convinced him that it was his duty to help Mr. Hamlin, and finally he consented.

Mr. Hamlin's success seemed now assured. But something happened that threatened shipwreck at the last moment. The legislature had voted to resume balloting for senator on July 25, and in the time that elapsed after the trial in June, one of Mr. Hamlin's friends in the House, Lorin D. Hayes, of Garland, was seized with a bad attack of typhoid fever, and was now dangerously ill. But Hayes was one of those simple, faithful men willing to trust all to a leader who their hearts tell them is true. Hayes sent word to his friends in the House: "Any time my vote will elect Hannibal Hamlin to the United States Senate, I will come to the House, if you have to carry me on my dying bed."

On July 25 the House prepared to take a ballot. When the result was announced, Mr. Hamlin had received 75 votes out of 150, or one short of an election. A score or more of men dashed out of the House in an instant, and bolted into Hayes's room. Picking him up, bed and

---

[1] The author is indebted to General Dow for a personal account of this incident. Neal Dow was already a leader at this early period, and was noted for his immense will power and devotion to principle. He was an influential factor in this battle, and his friendship with Mr. Hamlin was never broken. See his *Reminiscences*.

all, they moved as rapidly as it was safe to the House. When they appeared with the sick man on his bed, pandemonium reigned for a moment among the anti-slavery Democrats. The next ballot was taken amidst breathless excitement, and when it was announced that Mr. Hamlin was elected, having received 77 votes, his friends were wild with joy. Then there was a rush to the senate chamber just as that body was preparing to ballot.

The situation in the Senate at this juncture was very delicate. Of the thirteen senators who voted for Mr. Hamlin, two had been led away from him once on the issue raised over the instructions to congressmen. They were conservative on the slavery question, but voted for Mr. Hamlin as the regular nominee. There was grave danger that they might bolt him if they had learned the Free-Soilers were going to vote for him. It was indeed suspected that one of them would have opposed Mr. Hamlin, if his constituents had not remonstrated with him over his course in voting with the coalition to postpone the election.

Blanchard was the leader of the Free-Soil men, and they agreed to look to him for instructions and signals. The Senate prepared to ballot, when the cheers from the House announced that Mr. Hamlin had won in that body. Blanchard looked at his coadjutors on the other side of the chamber, and, placing his left hand in his side coat pocket, pulled out a ballot. This was the signal, though of course the Hunkers did not suspect it. Blanchard and Newman T. Allen,[1] of Industry, cast their votes for Mr. Hamlin, while a third Free-Soiler threw a blank vote, and two did not vote at all. Thus, 29 votes were cast, and Mr. Hamlin, having 15, or a majority, was elected. This was accomplished and announced so quickly that the Hunkers sat as if in a dream. They had not suspected that the Free-Soilers would come over this time. They sat sullen and dejected, while the happy, exultant Hamlin men made the senate chamber ring with their cheers.

There was great jubilation among the anti-slavery people of Maine, irrespective of party, over Mr. Hamlin's triumph. The Democrats rang bells, and lighted fires along the hilltops. The anti-slavery press throughout the country generally rejoiced over Mr. Hamlin's reëlection. Perhaps the most interesting comment made at the time was one that appeared in the "New York Evening Post," edited by William Cullen Bryant, which was then the leading organ of the Wright Democracy of the Empire State. Mr. Hamlin met Bryant soon after he entered Congress. Though not meeting frequently, their relations were very cordial. The editorial was as follows : —

[1] Charles J. Talbot and George W. Whitney arranged a private Free-Soil meeting at Farmington, to which Mr. Allen was invited. Mr. Talbot read Mr. Hamlin's anti-slavery speeches, and this won Mr. Allen's vote for Mr. Hamlin.

"With examples of treachery and faltering around him for the past three years, Mr. Hamlin has not swerved a hair's breadth from the rectitude of his course as an opponent of slavery extension in every shape in which the scheme has presented itself. His reëlection was resisted by the Hunker Democrats upon this ground alone. He had been true to his professions and to the principles of the party before the propagandism of this institution was foisted and intruded into its success. He might have trimmed and temporized and secured success without effort, but he chose to make no concessions. He was nobly sustained by his friends, and notwithstanding the open and continued defection and desertion of the Hunkers, has triumphed over them by just the requisite number of votes. He is a safe, rational, and comprehensive statesman." [1]

But the result of this contest in Maine had more than a personal or local significance, which is readily recognized when the contemporary happenings of the day are considered. Mr. Hamlin's return to the United States Senate, by a union of anti-slavery Democrats and Free-Soilers, was accomplished about the same time as Thomas H. Benton's defeat in Missouri for reëlection to the Senate, after thirty years' service in that body, by a combination of pro-slavery Democrats and Whigs; and these events were followed by Charles Sumner's first election to the Senate, in the succeeding January, by the united votes of Free-Soil Whigs and anti-slavery Democrats. The anti-slavery people of the North were coming together; the pro-slavery people of the South were joining forces. The Republican party of the North and the aggressive pro-slavery Democracy of the South were forming.

Finally, Mr. Hamlin's vindication furnished evidence of the disposition and ability of the Northern masses to support leaders who were right on the slavery issue, in the face of great obstacles and inducements to act against them. It must be remembered that every national administration since 1840, except that of General Taylor, had favored the extension of slavery into free soil, or had yielded in part to the demands of the slave power; the fact must not be forgotten that great Northern statesmen and powerful party leaders, such as Webster, Cass, and Douglas, counseled compromise or surrender on the slavery issue; it must also be borne in mind that the Democratic party was now a great machine in the hands of the slavery propagandists, and was bribing the press and politicians with patronage to support its policy; it is necessary, also, to consider the influence of the conservative element at the North, that feared a change and protested against the agitation of the slavery issue; yet, when it would

[1] It may be said, on the authority of Parke Godwin, that Bryant wrote this editorial.

have been easier to compromise, when Webster's courage failed him, and Cass and Douglas tried to obscure the issue with their sophistries, when great commercial interests allied themselves with the slave oligarchy, the Northern masses saw their duty clearly, and followed the right leaders to the end.   The slavery question at this period was peculiarly complicated.   The intelligent and sympathetic coöperation that anti-slavery leaders such as Mr. Hamlin received from the rank and file of their party at this time is in itself a striking proof of the ability of a people reared under the influence of free institutions to govern themselves, and decide civic and moral problems of vital importance to the State and untold generations to come.

CHAPTER XXII

THE approach of the presidential campaign of 1852 made the Democratic party anxious for harmony, and the leaders began to work to this end soon after the compromise measures of 1850 had an effect of quietude on the country. While it may never be known what the leaders in the inner circles of the slave oligarchy plotted and planned in advance of the Democratic National Convention of 1852, it is certain that, with the possible exception of these marplots, the Democratic party was desirous of a reconciliation on the basis of the compromise plan. The sincerity of the party in this respect cannot be doubted. The leaders of the wing to which Colonel Benton and Senator Hamlin belonged accepted the situation in good faith, and initiated a movement to nominate Levi Woodbury, of New Hampshire, for President. Woodbury's untimely death in September, 1851, nine months before the convention, renders speculation futile as to his chances of the nomination; yet the incident may be reviewed with profit, since the Woodbury movement assumed formidable proportions, and seemed to promise success. There is also a little history connected with it that has never before been published, and which throws some light behind the scenes on the Democratic party.

Mr. Hamlin was both a practical statesman and politician. The situation that was presented and his duty were equally clear to him. He decided to remain with his party and strive for the nomination of a man for President who in his opinion possessed the requisite ability, training, honesty, and firmness to maintain the existing balance of conditions in regard to slavery that had been established under the Constitution and the Clay compromises. He made a reservation in the case of the Fugitive Slave Law that has already been explained. He thought that Woodbury fulfilled the necessary qualifications, and he had a high personal regard for the distinguished jurist. The consideration of availability also influenced Mr. Hamlin to favor Woodbury. He had peculiar qualifications in this respect. He came down from the Jacksonian era; he had been a senator, a cabinet officer; he was now an able member of the United States Supreme Court; he occupied middle ground on the slavery question, and finally was a

New England man.   Then, again, the candidacies of Cass, Buchanan, and Douglas would make Woodbury the best man in Mr. Hamlin's opinion, by the simple process of exclusion.   He once voted for Cass under protest, and he never favored Buchanan or Douglas for the presidency.   Some men, who appeared to know more about Mr. Hamlin's affairs than he did, asserted that he favored Douglas at this time.   This story, indeed, was published in the Portland "Argus." The truth is that while Mr. Hamlin might prefer pleasant rather than unpleasant personal relations with Douglas as a brother senator and party colleague, he regarded the "Little Giant" as a tricky and insincere politician, whose success in hoodwinking upright and able men he always regretted.

The story of Woodbury's campaign begins with the spring of 1851. After Benton's retirement from the Senate he was elected to the House, and he and Mr. Hamlin maintained their close personal and party relations.   It was understood that Colonel Benton was to promote Woodbury's interests throughout the West and South, while Senator Hamlin was to direct the campaign in New England; at the same time Benton arranged to supervise the editorial conduct of the canvass.   He gave the key to Woodbury's followers by apostrophizing the jurist as the "rock of New England Democracy."   The New Hampshire Democrats formally opened the campaign by presenting Judge Woodbury as New England's candidate.   The plan was to have other States follow.   Correspondence between Benton and Hamlin throws some light on the inside situation.   Benton wrote to Mr. Hamlin from Washington, June 16: "I suppose you see from the papers that I am here and what I am about, namely, making a history of the workings of the government for the thirty years I was in the Senate, being a selection of my speeches, with historical notes and illustrations.   But this does not interfere with other works — the redemption of the State of Missouri from the Whigs and nullifiers — and the presidential election.   It is on the latter point I now write to you.   The State of New Hampshire has given through her Democracy a unanimous nomination to Woodbury.   This is a good start.   I can draw up an article for the papers which will back it, and be understood and felt by the people.   I spoke of him (Woodbury) to all my friends in the West, and always with the best effect.   The time has fully come to act.   A paper here is essential.   You know all my views on that point, and I wish to know what are its prospects.   Of course Mr. Woodbury can have nothing to do with it.   His friends must act.   I shall be here for a month or so, and can give some attention to the matter.   I shall draw up an article anyhow.   Where do you think it had best be published?   My mind vibrates between Maine and Missouri.   Which say you?   If Maine, I would send it to you to convey to a paper. I feel like I could make a pretty strong article."

There was a strong sentiment in favor of Judge Woodbury among the Democrats of Maine who followed Mr. Hamlin; but at the same time some of his old friends were greatly desirous of supporting a movement for Sam Houston. Mr. Hamlin believed in Houston [1] and liked him as a man, but he saw that Houston was not available. In his letters to Judge R. D. Rice, William P. Haines, and others, he pointed out that the very qualities and acts of Houston which had evoked admiration at the North — his opposition to the extension of slavery, his attitude towards the Calhoun party — would be arguments used against him in the South. On the other hand, he dwelt on the Hunker opposition in Maine to Woodbury as a point in his favor. He believed that Woodbury would veto any measure extending slavery. Mr. Hamlin's arguments prevailed, and his friends all went for Woodbury.

In the mean time, Senator Hamlin became anxious about the New York Democracy, and in June, 1851, he wrote Benton. The latter replied the 26th of that month as follows : —

"In answer to your inquiry respecting the disposition of our friends in New York, I feel myself justified in answering affirmatively; but to give you a kind of assurance which will leave no doubt, you will soon receive a communication from our friend Blair, who will go on to New York.

"I have sketched an article, and as it amplifies, under one of its heads, the claim of New England mentioned in the New Hampshire nomination, I deem it best to let it appear as a New England article, and therefore will send it to you for one of your papers.

"I am fixed in my opinion about the necessity of a paper here. Unless we have an organ here to collect and distribute intelligence, we will hardly be able to make Mr. W. accepted as a candidate at all. Be assured he has nothing to expect from any paper here but viperous attacks from the Republicans, and no defense from the ' Union,' or worse than none. It should not be set up as an opposition paper to the ' Union,' but a helper. The Whigs have two, and they are supported by the whole power of the administration; and the Democracy should have two. That is a public reason to be given. Another public reason for its open advocacy of Mr. W. should be the venomous attacks upon him here, repeated in all the administration papers throughout the United States, and which the ' Union ' would not undertake to answer without seeming to become the advocate of one of the candidates — which it professes not to become. Submission to the majority of a national convention should be a point maintained in the paper. Not only not a word against other candidates, but a defense of them ; the harmony and reconciliation of the party to be made a leading point. The article

[1] Senator Hamlin wrote to A. M. Robinson, "How I would like to go for old Sam!"

which I shall send you touches these and other points; and in my opinion chalks out a good line for the new paper.

"Without such a paper I do not see that we can do anything. A daily attack upon a man, from the centre to the circumference, and no defense, and he must be overwhelmed."

Benton wrote Mr. Hamlin another letter the same day : —

"I send you the article mentioned. It is deemed by friends, as well as by myself, best that it should appear in a New England paper, and it is drawn up as a New England article. The paper that contains it should be published in numbers, and a copy sent to every Democratic paper in the Union. Besides sending it direct to the papers from the office with the article marked, it should be sent to friends in different States to see to the publication of it. Send some to me.

"From further advices I adhere to my declaration that our friends in New York will come in. I have also spoken with friends in the South with good prospects."

Benton's editorial was a brilliant presentation of Woodbury's qualifications for the presidency, but it is of noteworthy interest in only one respect, aside from its general merits, and this may be mentioned. Mr. Hamlin had it published in several newspapers in Maine. One was the "Bangor Jeffersonian," his organ. Benton claimed that the slavery question was settled. In commenting on this, the "Jeffersonian" reflected Mr. Hamlin's views by dissenting from Colonel Benton's conclusions, though indorsing his support of Woodbury.

But, alas! for the plans of men. When it appeared morally certain that Woodbury would go into the Democratic convention with the support of New England, and with the good prospect of uniting all factions on himself, he was seized with a fatal illness that terminated in a week. Mr. Hamlin always spoke of Woodbury's death as a great blow to the Democracy at a critical period. True, Woodbury voted for the annexation of Texas, but he believed that slavery was a sectional institution, and while he would not interfere with it where it existed, he was opposed to the Calhoun doctrine. Knowing Mr. Woodbury as well as he did, Mr. Hamlin spoke with authority when he said Judge Woodbury would oppose any scheme to extend or disturb slavery in the event of his election to the presidency. Thus if Levi Woodbury had been President instead of Franklin Pierce, his firmness, honesty, and loyalty would have been unconquerable obstacles to the conspirators who broke down the Missouri Compromise. But those who see the hand of fate in the affairs of men believe that Pierce was but an instrument in bringing on the crisis which rid the country of a loathsome institution it could throw off only through a gigantic convulsion.

Woodbury's death set the New England Democracy at sea. A

little talk was heard about Franklin Pierce, but that was at first believed to mean that he was thinking of becoming a candidate for Vice-President. For several months, General William O. Butler, of Kentucky, was seriously considered by Benton, Hamlin, and their associates as the most available man of the hour. Butler was a man of decided ability, forceful character, picturesque personality, and natural qualities of leadership. He also had a record that might have made him a popular candidate. He distinguished himself by his gallantry at the battle of New Orleans, where he was one of Andrew Jackson's right-hand men; he had served in the House with credit ; he was ranked as one of the leaders at the Kentucky bar, and he had demonstrated his personal strength among the masses of his State in 1844 by reducing the Whig majority from 20,000 to 5000, as the Democratic candidate for governor, the year Henry Clay made his strongest run for the presidency. Butler was believed to be opposed to the extension of slavery. His refusal of the governorship of Nebraska in 1855 under the Pierce administration was convincing evidence of this. In short, while Butler was not regarded as a great statesman, he was thought to possess the ability and character requisite for the presidency and certain possibilities of popularity with the masses. Finally, it was believed that he could keep the peace on the slavery question.

Colonel Benton wrote Mr. Hamlin the following interesting letter about Butler on October 12, 1851 : —

"I have thought over what you say in relation to Butler, and felt no objection to him on that score. I have but a poor opinion of what is called talents in the United States, and by which is generally understood some capacity for speaking and writing without much regard to the judgment and moral qualities, without which speaking and writing are empty or pernicious. Moral qualities are the first thing with me in a public man ; common sense and common judgment will do the rest. I could name thousands I would be willing to take for President ; but they have not the national name which would carry them before the people. It was the remark of Dean Swift, himself a man of genius and the friend of the two greatest political geniuses of the day, and in relation to their miscarriages, that genius was not necessary in administering government, and was often hurtful ; and that common sense, honesty of purpose, were all that were necessary. This is my opinion, and Butler under that aspect is fully qualified. But there is another consideration which was a pretty controlling one, when I came into Congress, in the minds of the old Democracy, and that was the soundness of his (a statesman's) associates. He must not only be sound himself, but have sound associates ; as every President must be more or less in the hands of his friends. Under this aspect Butler is safe. He has no connection with any clique, fragment, or faction, and was voted for by all without a word as Vice-President (in the convention of '48, that nominated Cass and Butler). Most of them want him for V. P. now. But the overruling idea at present with all our friends is a new man, one that has had nothing to do with late events, and, therefore, has no section arrayed against him. That idea brought out for Woodbury was doing an immensity for him, and Butler, who was to have been V. P. on his ticket, now falls heir to it. He is a *new* man, and has nothing against him, and has great personal popularity. It is believed that he can unite every Democratic State, and carry the two Whig States of Kentucky and Tennessee. Who can you name in N. E. for V. P. if he is taken up ? I go to Missouri in three weeks, and will be glad to hear from you again."

About this time a number of Judge Woodbury's former leading supporters in New England held several conferences at Boston to further General Butler's candidacy. Charles Levi Woodbury, son of the jurist, was already coming forward as a leader in the Boston Democracy. He was Mr. Hamlin's lifelong friend. Mr. Hamlin on several occasions found Mr. Woodbury a safe and sound adviser. In the fisheries incident, for example, Mr. Woodbury furnished Senator Hamlin with valuable data and information. Mr. Woodbury took part in the Butler movement, and in a personal letter to the author, under date of August 4, 1896, gave some interesting facts concerning the chief conference at Boston. An understanding was reached to favor the nominations of General Butler for President and General Franklin Pierce, of New Hampshire, for Vice-President. Mr. Woodbury also noted that for the next few months the New Hampshire Democracy continued to support Butler and Pierce in such a way that Pierce might be placed at the head of the ticket or the foot. They had the idea that Pierce instead of Butler should fall heir to the Woodbury movement, and they worked to this end.

But the Butler movement was destined to failure. The reasons may not be detailed. The incident is noticed for the purpose of emphasizing the course that Senator Hamlin, Colonel Benton, and men of their kind pursued in the hope of saving the Democracy from falling completely into the hands of the slavery propagandists. It may be said, briefly, that Butler was not the kind of man the Southern Democracy wanted. There was now a new Southern Democracy; but that fact was not fully grasped by the anti-Calhoun wing. Its leaders were aggressive ; undoubtedly they had a secret understanding among themselves to force the nomination of a man who would do their bidding, — break down the Missouri Compromise. This was of course not even suspected at the time, and will be more fully alluded to in the proper place. These leaders were determined to reject the Democracy of Jefferson, Macon, Pinckney, and Jackson. They therefore likewise rejected the followers of the apostle of the true Democracy, which would uphold the Constitution, and give slavery only the rights granted it by that instrument. The memory of Jackson was growing hateful to them. Did not Old Hickory say in his dying hours that posterity would never forgive him for not hanging John C. Calhoun when he attempted to withdraw South Carolina from the Union when Jackson was President? Why, then, should they listen to Benton, and make Butler President,— a man who was one of the last of the iron Jackson stock?

Although there were many Butler delegates elected to the Democratic National Convention, it was apparent a few months before the convention assembled in June, 1852, that Butler lacked support in the South, and he practically retired from the contest. Nevertheless, some of Butler's friends decided to keep him in reserve, so to speak, in the hope that if the convention came to a deadlock over the more prominent candidates, it might unite on Butler. Senator Hamlin was one of these men. He was a delegate from Maine. He was as strongly opposed as ever to the nomination of Cass, Buchanan, Douglas, Marcy, or Jefferson Davis, who were most conspicuously before the convention until the last ballot, — the forty-ninth. Charles Levi Woodbury, who was present with Mr. Hamlin, afterward recalled the fact that the Maine delegation was divided, but that Senator Hamlin, Lot M. Morrill, who was later his colleague in the Senate, and Colonel A. W. H. Clapp, of Portland, all acted together.

After the convention had struggled several days to make a choice, it became apparent that it would be necessary to take a new man. When the convention was in a mood to recognize the situation, the current beneath the surface turned in favor of Franklin Pierce. There were several factors that were instrumental in causing this result. The futility of continuing the deadlock was obvious; the necessity of selecting a new man was clear. The New England Democracy was clamorous to have a New England man chosen, and preferred Pierce. Their claims appeared to be the final consideration that tipped the scales in Pierce's favor; but in reality they were surface evidence, though astute observers of political affairs were deceived by them. The probable truth is, Pierce owed his nomination to a secret understanding between himself and the Calhoun Democracy, which was guarded so carefully that only the subsequent acts of Pierce as President exposed and at the same time proved its existence. His managers in the convention carefully held him back until the last moment, when they rushed him into nomination amidst great enthusiasm, and he was chosen practically by acclamation. William R. King, an amiable and well-liked senator of Alabama, was chosen for Vice-President, the compromise measures of 1850 were indorsed, and the Democracy, united for the last time in ante-bellum days, went forth to do battle against the Whigs.

The Whig party was now at the end of its career. Signs of approaching dissolution were manifested in its presidential convention, which was the scene of a bitter struggle between various factions. President Fillmore desired the nomination, and so did Webster, his secretary of state. But a large element favored General Winfield Scott, and he was finally chosen. The chances of success seemed well divided at the opening of the campaign. But the Whigs were doomed. The people, having made up their minds to try the compromise measures of 1850, saw that the Democracy, which had enacted them, should be intrusted with their enforcement. The Whig temple was also badly shaken by the fall of its two great pillars, Webster and Clay, who both died during the campaign. The final cause of General Scott's defeat was his persistence in making vain and pompous speeches. The hero of Lundy's Lane and Buena Vista was out of his element. Ridicule was turned on him and his defeat was overwhelming. He carried only four States. Mr. Hamlin earnestly supported Pierce as a party man, though he afterwards regretted this as one of the mistakes of his life, and said so.

CHAPTER XXIII

FEW men have come to the presidency under apparently brighter auspices and with a larger measure of good-will from the American public than Franklin Pierce. The general impression was that with General Pierce's inauguration an era of peace had been ushered in, and that the new President would be the last to disturb it. In his letter of acceptance, Mr. Pierce had pledged himself to abide by the compromise measures ; in his inaugural address on March 4, 1853, he reaffirmed these pledges, and in his first message to Congress, December 5, 1853, he reverted to his promise, and speaking of the repose the nation enjoyed, declared that it should suffer no shock from any act of his, if he had the power to avert it. These words naturally created greater confidence in President Pierce, and greater interest in him personally. He seemed to fill the public ideal in some respects as to what the President of a young nation should be. He was the youngest chief magistrate the country had yet chosen, and he was brilliant, eloquent, magnetic, handsome, and democratic. He seemed to be the personification of Young America, and even when the blackest pages of his administration were being written, Mr. Pierce maintained a strong popularity among those who knew him and fell under the charm of his personality.

But with all his gifts, and in spite of his opportunities, Franklin Pierce was the greatest failure and disappointment in the presidency the country had experienced. Yet he was President nearly a year before his weak nature was fully understood. This was a year, though, of comparative calm. Mr. Hamlin became well acquainted with General Pierce, and at first liked him. He was slow to change his opinion of the President. That was his nature. Then again it is to be said that President Pierce took great pains to make himself agreeable to Mr. Hamlin in order to win his support and friendship. But this is a story for another page. While Mr. Hamlin gave President Pierce his friendship, it is certain that he, in common with the Democrats of his school, regretted to find Pierce surrounded by a cabinet of the strongest pro-slavery sympathies, and also that the President was still inclined to pursue John P. Hale with oldtime vindictiveness. Yet the anti-Calhoun wing were fair to the young President and gave him full credit for sincerity in professing a desire to preserve peace on the slavery question.

Franklin Pierce's betrayal of his solemnly plighted words was due to his pliant, fickle nature and environments. He was dazzled by the pomp and splendor of his great office, and received the tributes paid to him as due him as an individual. He seems to have had a fatuous idea of his power, for he allowed himself to be carried into scandalous convivial excesses. He soon learned to listen only to the voice of the sycophant, who spoke the truth to him. Mr. Pierce easily fell into the hands of those who wanted to use him. They sang his praises and painted the possibilities of his reëlection with consummate art. Always a strong partisan, Mr. Pierce was soon inflated with inordinate ambition, and lent himself to the plans of his unscrupulous advisers. He saw only one side, and in the end gave the slave oligarchy all that a President could. Yet he had strong men in his Cabinet, who advised against the repeal of the Missouri Compromise. One was Mr. Marcy, the secretary of state, and he had always been a Hunker. Another conservative member was James Guthrie, of Kentucky, the secretary of the treasury, who was a true Union man, and whose ability and upright character were conceded and recognized by all who knew him. Robert McClelland, of Michigan, the secretary of the interior, was one of the few Democrats in the House who supported the Wilmot Proviso, and James Campbell, of Pennsylvania, the postmaster-general, was another highly respected member. But the men who eventually were closest to Mr. Pierce were Jefferson Davis, secretary of war, and Caleb Cushing, of Massachusetts, the attorney-general. Davis was the *deus ex machina* of the ill-fated Pierce administration, and Cushing its tool.

But this was the man who was as yet behind the scenes, and it was not until the machinery of the slavery propagandists was set in motion that he was placed on the stage of action in the light of publicity. To carry the simile further, it must be said that the plot to break down the Missouri Compromise unfolded like a Sardou drama. The first schemes of the conspirators that were presented in Congress were not understood in their actual purpose. It was not until the plot had been fully developed in debate that the full purport was grasped. Even to this day all the details of this conspiracy in its inception, the concoction of the secret bargain between Pierce and the Calhoun Democracy before his nomination, the development of the plan of action from day to day, and its termination in the wholesale purchase of Northern senators and representatives by patronage, will never be learned. But it is enough for this narrative to say that the chief odium of this act rests equally on the shoulders of Franklin Pierce and Stephen A. Douglas.

It has been well said that Pierce and Douglas ran a race for the presidency. This is a terse description of their conduct and an explanation of their motives for doing the work of the slave oligarchy. With Pierce in the presidency, and Douglas chairman of the Senate Committee on Territories, the slave power knew that it had two men who would do its bidding in return for the great reward it promised, — the presidency. What the slave party wanted was the abrogation of the Missouri Compromise, that it might seize more territory for slavedom. The most important result of the Mexican war was the addition of a large free State to the Union, — California. This was the irony of fate. The free States now not only exceeded the slave States in number, population, territory, and wealth, but promised in the near future to exercise the political power of government. The slave party laid longing eyes on the territory that now comprises the States of Kansas and Nebraska, and, to quote Mr. Hamlin, the plot of "infinite mischief" was conceived.

In the waning hours of the Fillmore administration a bill was introduced in the Senate to organize a government in Nebraska. Senator Douglas reported it, but it was killed by the votes of the pro-slavery senators under different pleas. This did not attract much attention, and the matter did not come up again until Congress met for the first time under Mr. Pierce's administration, December, 1853. It was afterwards recalled that the first bill Mr. Douglas presented recognized the Missouri Compromise; it was also remembered that in 1850 Douglas said in a speech to his Illinois constituents, "I am prepared to stand or fall by our American Union, clinging with the tenacity of life to all its glorious memories of the past; . . . and among the memories of the past I pronounce the Missouri Compromise of 1820 to be one." After the beginning of the Pierce administration Douglas experienced a change of mind: he resolved that the Missouri Compromise should in fact be a memory of the past.

There was quick work. On January 4, 1854, Senator Douglas reported the Nebraska bill again, with the significant declaration that the question of slavery, according to the compromises of 1850, should be left to the people of the territories to decide. This declaration was untrue, but it was a step towards the new ground on which Mr. Douglas meant to plant himself. On January 16, Archibald Dixon, who by a strange fate had succeeded Henry Clay, the peacemaker, as a senator from Kentucky, moved that the bill be made a special order for the following Monday, giving notice of his intention to move that "the Missouri Compromise be repealed, and that the citizens of the several States be at liberty to take and hold their slaves within any of the territories." Mr. Dixon added that on "this question of slavery I know no Whig party, no Democratic party. I am a pro-slavery man, and represent pro-slavery constituents. I intend to promote slavery interests as far as I can. This bill, if adopted, will carry out these principles."

Dixon's declaration was at first regarded as the expression of individuals rather than of a party, but events rapidly dissipated this mistaken idea. Senator Dixon's proposition to repeal the honored landmark of 1820 was the logical outcome of Calhoun's theories and teachings. When Mr. Dixon said that on the question of slavery he knew no Whig party, no Democratic party, he spoke for the vast majority of the people south of the Mason and Dixon line. In the great Democratic landslide of the presidential election many Southern Whigs had renounced their allegiance to their party and taken their place in the Calhoun wing of the Democracy. Mr. Dixon was simply stating the situation, but the facts were a revelation to the slow North. Douglas recognized the state of affairs, and took advantage of it in a characteristic manner. He had no scruples; success was his standard; the presidency his aim. He had no sincerity; politics was to him a game, and slavery at this juncture was the football that was being kicked about. The South was the master, and he hastened to curry its favor. He made his greatest bid for the presidency on January 23, when he reported his territorial bill in its perfected form. This provided for the division of the territory in question into two parts, to be known as Kansas and Nebraska, with the declaration that the Missouri Compromise was null and void, and suspended by the compromise measures of 1850.

Mr. Douglas spent a part of the preceding Saturday and Sunday with President Pierce in consultation over the Kansas-Nebraska bill, and together they developed the measure into the shape in which it was presented in the Senate. There was sharp fencing between them; each was afraid that the other would get ahead of him in the race both were making for Southern favor. More details will be presented in another place; it is enough to state the brief facts now. It would appear that President Pierce was doubtful about the step he was taking; he urged Mr. Douglas to consult with Secretary Marcy. It happened that Mr. Marcy was not at home when Douglas called, and therefore did not probably know that the conspiracy had been planned out until it was too late to arrest it. When Fenton, of New York, saw Mr. Marcy he indicated by his dejected manner and brief speech that he believed a terrible mistake had been made, and that nothing could be done to prevent it. This all happened while Congress was considering the Nebraska bill. The anti-slavery members considered that a bad measure; but they little dreamed that while they were preparing to resist it, the President of the United States and a great leader of the Democracy were plotting to launch a thunderbolt out of the clear sky, as it were.

The repeal of the Missouri Compromise was accomplished partially through the unscrupulous use of patronage by the administration. The men who were instrumental in forcing this corrupt job through Congress believed that "every man has his price." If they applied their false measure to honest men, it was their own mistake. They certainly made a mistake in the case of Senator Hamlin, and their efforts to approach him reacted on them. The plan of influencing Mr. Hamlin to give his support to the Douglas bill was a deep-laid scheme, and was probably the counterpart of others that succeeded with several Northern senators and representatives. President Pierce was directly connected with this plot, and was probably the author. It is referred to now because it was undoubtedly conceived before the Douglas bill was presented in the Senate, before Mr. Hamlin even suspected the deviltry Mr. Pierce was engaged in behind the scenes. There is direct evidence of President Pierce's part in this job and moral evidence that he tried to take advantage of the condition of affairs in Maine to force Mr. Hamlin into line with the miserable creatures who betrayed their States in this disgraceful affair. It was a thumbscrew business.

There was a changed condition of affairs in Maine, and Mr. Hamlin's oldtime enemies, the pro-slavery Democrats, were the cause of it. They had failed to rule, and now they were trying to ruin the Democratic party in their State. They bolted Governor Hubbard in the fall of 1851, when he was a candidate for reëlection, because he was instrumental in procuring the enactment of the famous Maine Prohibitory Liquor Law. It was said that the Hunkers wanted "free rum as well as free slave trade." They succeeded in preventing an election by the people, and when the legislature was called on to act, the Hunkers combined with the Whigs, and elected William G. Crosby governor over Dr. Hubbard, and although the latter had a large plurality in the total number of votes thrown by the people. The Hunkers hoped that they could effect a coalition with the Whigs whereby they could elect one of their own men to the Senate to succeed Mr. Bradbury in 1853. They were ready to do business with Franklin Pierce. This was the situation in Maine when the Missouri plot began to develop at Washington.

Mr. Hamlin seems to have had some suspicions at this juncture that President Pierce was not sincere ; but he was disposed to be just and generous. His letter to Mr. Haines is good evidence of this. He wrote, among other things : —

"The President is kind and cordial, but I think I can see a fear in his mind that he may yield too much to me ; in other words, while he is disposed to give me his confidence, he is still induced, perhaps insensibly, to withhold much of it in consequence of the continued assaults on me by a class of men in Maine. . . . I mean that the President shall understand that I am entitled to his confidence. He has not treated me right, but no matter. It is our administration, and I say, let us give it a generous support. We have brought it into power, let us take care of it. It is too small business for a man to allow his little disappointments to control his public action. I fear we have too many who do so."

This was December 16, about the time when it is definitely known that President Pierce and Senator Douglas were beginning to consult over the scheme to abrogate the Missouri Compromise. Mr. Hamlin quickly learned why the President was listening to the Hunkers of Maine. On January 23, 1854, Douglas took Congress by surprise by presenting his bill that proposed the repeal of the Missouri Compromise. The anti-slavery senators had had no intimation of what was coming when Douglas took the floor. They were simply aghast when they heard his proposition. Mr. Hamlin could hardly believe the evidence of his senses. Repeal the Missouri Compromise! What next? Would the Calhoun party lay hands on the Constitution itself? The anti-slavery men were sickened and angered; the pro-slavery men were jubilant. Congress was at once in a roar of angry debate. The excitement over the Wilmot Proviso was slight in comparison with that which now agitated the country. The North's amazement turned to indignation, and a storm of wrath arose that was a precursor of the fury which was to burst forth only six years later when the government was assaulted.

When Douglas had finished his memorable speech introducing his bill and urging its adoption on the ground that it would vindicate the principle of "non-intervention," and allow the people of the territories to decide for themselves on the question of slavery, Mr. Hamlin at once sought opportunity to speak with him. He said : —

"Douglas, your bill is a gross moral wrong. In my judgment it would be a bad party measure. It is vicious in principle, and, if enacted, will produce infinite mischief. I shall oppose it. That is all I have to say." [1]

Men who were associated with Mr. Hamlin, and were familiar with his record of consistent opposition to the extension of slavery, knew that he meant precisely what he said. None at Washington but the blind President and his miserable tools supposed for a moment that Mr. Hamlin would support the Douglas bill. Douglas knew that he would oppose it, and, suave politician as he was, accepted Mr. Hamlin's announcement good-naturedly, and said no more at that time. The exciting debate then opened, but Mr. Hamlin, having stated his position authoritatively, turned to other affairs for the present.

[1] Mr. Hamlin characterized the Douglas bill in similar terms in a letter which was published at this time in the *Boston Commonwealth*.

Having announced in public his intention of opposing the Douglas bill, Mr. Hamlin thought that he had said enough. The proposition to repeal the time-honored bulwark between freedom and slavery was an act of unparalleled perfidy. His position was clearly understood. Two dramatic incidents that happened later reflect Mr. Hamlin's feelings. The debate was to him words, words, and nothing but words. His attitude was one of cold contempt towards this conspiracy against national and party honor. Silence best expressed his feelings. The words of the Roman are recalled : " I have spoken." Then, again, there was work to be done. Mr. Hamlin's laborious duties as chairman of the Committee on Commerce, as well as the peculiar situation in Maine, now claimed his attention.

At this juncture, the State was in a political ferment, and the outcome was in the dark. It is easy now to see that the anti-slavery elements were then coalescing to form the Republican party. This process was going on throughout the North, and Maine, then as now, was always among the first States in the Union to feel and register a moral uprising. At the South the pro-slavery men were uniting. While conditions at the North were in a state of flux, and far-sighted men realized that national questions would sooner or later readjust the American people in new political relations, the anti-slavery Democrats of the Pine Tree State gave their attention to the pressing need of the hour, which was to prevent the Hunkers from electing one of their own men to the Senate. Mr. Hamlin feared this, although it was a remote contingency. The Hunkers and the Whigs had combined to defeat him ; they had also combined to elect Mr. Crosby governor. Some of the Whig leaders had persistently misrepresented Mr. Hamlin's position on the Texas question. He was not disposed to trust them. What bargain was to be made between the Whigs and the Hunkers, to reward the latter for electing Mr. Crosby ? Nathan Clifford and ex-Governor Dana were active candidates for the Senate to succeed Mr. Bradbury.

Mr. Hamlin accordingly joined with the anti-slavery Democracy in an effort to control the party in 1853. It is interesting to note the kind of a man he favored as his colleague in this crisis. This was William P. Haines, of Biddeford, as has been intimated before. From 1850 to the winter of 1854, Mr. Hamlin strove to induce Mr. Haines to become a candidate for the Senate. In that time Mr. Haines had grown into a leader of recognized ability, judgment, and character. He was entirely in sympathy with Mr. Hamlin on the slavery issue, he was also a strong party man ; in fact, he never left the Democracy. He was fine-looking ; he had an attractive personality. While Mr. Haines was active in politics, he never sought office. In short, he was one of those strong, upright, unselfish men, who dominate the

inner circles of parties and seek to direct their party in the right
course. Mr. Haines was also a scholar of large attainments. A
graduate of Dartmouth, he was for many years one of the leading
trustees of that institution. His taste inclined him to his home and
books. The following extract from a letter that Mr. Haines wrote
Mr. Hamlin, in July, 1854, commending his course in the Senate,
gives an idea of the man and his relations with Mr. Hamlin : —

" I have very happy reflections when I call to mind how worthily our
friend Hamlin fulfills all his friends predicted when he was elected to the
Senate. In fact, my dear friend, you have demonstrated how well a man
may stand even at Washington, who will respect himself and represent *truly*
the will of a *Northern* constituency. I thank God for this ! But enough —
May God bless you, and return you in safety to the beloved family circle."

Mr. Hamlin felt that Mr. Haines had the qualities and peculiar
party qualifications which would rally the Democracy around him. He
had few enemies ; even the Hunkers thought well of him. But Mr.
Haines withstood all pressure, and the Democracy eventually nominated Lot M. Morrill, who had already achieved an honorable status
in his party as an anti-slavery man and clear-headed parliamentarian.
Again there was no election for governor by the people, although the
Democrats controlled the legislature. The situation had too many
complications to be described in detail, but a few phrases and results
may be presented to illustrate the peculiarities of politics. The year
before, the Hunkers, it will be remembered, bolted Governor Hubbard,
and by combining with the Whigs made Mr. Crosby governor. This
time a group of anti-slavery Democrats [1] bolted their party, and, joining with the Whigs in the legislature, reëlected Mr. Crosby and chose
William Pitt Fessenden United States senator, although he was a
Whig. This bolt was no aspersion on Mr. Morrill's principles. He
was defeated by a curious accident of politics. Mr. Hamlin cordially
supported Mr. Morrill, and regretted his defeat. The incident has
been presented only to show that Mr. Hamlin stuck to his party in
its hour of need, and exerted himself to strengthen the anti-slavery
party in the Senate. He believed that the election of a good, sound,
anti-slavery Democrat to the Senate, — such as Mr. Morrill, — in the
midst of the struggle over the Douglas bill, would be a rebuke to the
Democratic leaders who were plotting to betray their party. He went
to Maine several times before and during the contest at Augusta, to
help Morrill. This is one reason why he did not speak during the
debate. He was looking for votes. One more Democratic vote
against the repeal of the Missouri Compromise would have been worth
tomes of speech to him.

[1] These were Know-Nothing men. That party had just begun its brief career
in Maine.

But however unkind fate seemed to be to the anti-slavery Democracy of Maine, Fessenden's election proved opportune. He was the leader of the Whigs in the legislature and a member of the House when chosen to the Senate. In shifting his scene of action he remained a leader. When Fessenden delivered his maiden speech in the Senate, — against the repeal of the Missouri Compromise, — he stepped into the front ranks of the debaters in Congress. To quote another writer: "The friends of freedom knew that a new champion had arrived." This was the beginning of a career that reflects lustre and honor on the man and his State. Mr. Hamlin and Mr. Fessenden did not maintain close relationship at first; each continued for a few years to act nominally with his old party, but eventually they coöperated in forming the Republican party, in which they remained as leaders to the end of their lives.

When the debate over the Douglas bill in the Senate began to near its close, there were two kinds of Northern Democrats who gave unmistakable evidence of their intention to support Douglas. One was the kind which worshiped the god of party action. The other was the venial sort. General Cass, of Michigan, represented the former. On the adoption of the Kansas-Nebraska bill, he declared that his doctrine of "squatter sovereignty" was vindicated. Another was John Pettit, of Indiana. He once said, in defending the extension of slavery, that the Declaration of Independence was a self-evident lie. A third was Moses Norris, of New Hampshire. Once he upbraided Ben Wade for opposing the Fugitive Slave Law. Wade coolly inquired of Norris whether he would help catch a "nigger" if summoned to do so by an officer of the law. Norris replied in some confusion that he would. Wade turned to Archibald Dixon, and asked him the same question. "No; I would be damned if I would," was the frank reply. "Then," rejoined Wade, "I don't see why you Southern gentlemen should catch niggers, when you can find Northern men to do your dirty work for you."

The other kind of men who betrayed their constituency were soon forgotten, though the memory of their deed lived long after them, This narrative is concerned only with the chief figures in the mercenary job that carried the Douglas bill through to success. President Pierce employed the vast patronage at his disposal to force the repeal of the Missouri Compromise. The following extract from an editorial that appeared in the "New York Evening Post," at this period, gives a good idea of the situation as it was revealed to the anti-slavery press by their friends in Congress: "All the methods of influence and intimidation which organization, numbers, and patronage can supply are used without stint at the seat of government to silence those who disapprove of the bill, and engage the wavering to give it support. Those who have visited Washington speak of a leaden tyranny which is felt everywhere, weighing upon men's minds, coercing them into a sad, helpless acquiescence in the measure." But this told only a fractional part of the story.

When the Douglas bill was fairly under discussion, the "Little Giant" one day, in a burst of confidence, told Mr. Hamlin what he had suspected, — that the bill was an administration measure. Mr. Douglas said at the same time that he purposed to get something in black and white from President Pierce to hold him fast to the bill. A day or two afterwards, Mr. Douglas showed Senator Hamlin the original draft of the final amendment to the Kansas-Nebraska bill. This contained the clause repealing the Missouri Compromise, and was written by Franklin Pierce himself.[1] Jefferson Davis, in his account[2] of the interview between Mr. Douglas, President Pierce, and others regarding the fateful amendment, denied that the measure originated with the President or any member of the Cabinet. It would also appear from Senator Dixon's story that he took Douglas by surprise when he proposed to repeal the compromise of 1820. No doubt Mr. Davis and Mr. Dixon were correct. Senator Douglas was quick to catch the drift of things political. Probably he got an idea from Mr. Dixon's proposition as to what was the intention among the Southern senators, and acted on it. Then Mr. Pierce entered the race with Mr. Douglas.

The responsibility for inventing the scheme of abrogating the Missouri act need not be detailed; the story deals with the results. It cannot be proved that there was a secret understanding established between General Pierce and the Southern leaders prior to his nomination for the presidency; and it is not contended that there was an agreement, whereby Mr. Pierce pledged himself in terms to favor the annullment of the compromise of 1820; on the other hand, it is asserted that the leaders of the slave oligarchy, in their search for a Northern man with Southern principles, were satisfied by pledges of a convincing nature that Franklin Pierce was the one they wanted and would do what they desired. Three times he broke his solemn vow to the country to maintain the compromise measures of 1850. A man who would do that would hardly hesitate to make secret ante-convention promises to gain the great office of the presidency. The promptness with which Robert Toombs, Alexander H. Stephens, Thomas L. Clingman, Judah P. Benjamin, and other leading Whigs deserted their party to support Pierce for President; the conferences at Concord between General Pierce and Southern leaders before his nomination, and his subsequent conduct as President, admit of no other conclusion

---

[1] *Life of Lincoln*, by Nicolay and Hay, vol. i. p. 350.
[2] *Rise and Fall of the Confederacy*, vol. i. p. 28.

than that Mr. Pierce bound himself to advance the interests of the slaveholding South.   This was Senator Hamlin's belief.

A few days before the Senate came to a vote on the Douglas bill, Mr. Hamlin received direct proof that the administration was resorting to venality to accomplish its object.   This was one of the two occasions during the quarter of a century Mr. Hamlin sat in the Senate when he was approached by corrupt men.   The first who approached him was Caleb Cushing, attorney-general of the United States.   He was a singular character.   A man of great ability, yet without sincerity, though his adroitness blinded many as to the real man.   He threaded his way from one party to another on thin pretenses that entitled him to be called the political Blondin of his day.   He had but one rival as a political prestidigitateur, and that was his associate, Benjamin F. Butler, of Massachusetts.   The two were once aptly characterized as "the Siamese Twins in chicanery and intrigue." Butler was the more mischievous of the two.   His sophisms were not wholly confined to politics, but filled the court-room, and influenced young men in forming their ideas of the standards and actions of life.   These two men were active in arranging the terms of Pierce's nomination, — whatever they were, — and now Cushing came to Senator Hamlin to complete his record of jobbery.

The interview took place in Mr. Hamlin's rooms at the St. Charles Hotel.   Cushing in his adroit way presented the Kansas-Nebraska bill to Mr. Hamlin as an administrative measure, and urged him to support it as a party bill.   Gradually he unfolded the obstacles that had already been overcome, and then when he came to those that remained, Cushing, in direct terms on behalf of the administration, offered Mr. Hamlin control of all the patronage in New England, or Maine, that he might ask for.   This was to be his reward for voting in favor of the Douglas bill.   Senator Hamlin cut the interview short by rising to his feet and saying, with considerable grimness of manner: "Cushing, I am forty-four years old.   I have never done anything for which I am ashamed, and with God's help I don't propose to either." Mr. Cushing and his oily manner evaporated at once.

But this was not all.   The next day President Pierce resolved to sound Mr. Hamlin, and accordingly sent for him.   Mr. Hamlin called at the White House, and was received in the President's private room. Mr. Pierce almost immediately came to the point.   He asked Mr. Hamlin what the Senate was going to do about the Douglas bill. Mr. Hamlin was at once on his guard, and replied that there was apparently not a majority in favor of it.

"Well," continued the President, "suppose, now, that it should become a party measure, what would you do in regard to it?"

"As to that," said Hamlin quietly, "it is only necessary for me to say at this time that I do not regard the measure as a wise one."

"Still," urged the President, "you could not stand up against your party; even Calhoun and White, of Tennessee, failed to do that."

"And yet," said the Maine senator, "I shall, if necessary, take the responsibility of standing up against my party. I have my constituents to serve, and they shall be served to the best of my ability, irrespective of any party. At the same time, let us understand each other. Did you ask me to come here expecting to get me to aid you in repealing the compromise?"

"Yes," replied Mr. Pierce, after a moment's consideration, "I did."

"Then, sir, I must say to you," replied Mr. Hamlin earnestly, "that during the more than forty years I have lived, I have doubtless made many mistakes, but I have never lost self-respect. I would do so should I vote for the repeal of the Missouri Compromise. It is needless to say more, and I shall bid you good-morning."[1]

This was the last time Mr. Hamlin spoke with Franklin Pierce. When he withdrew from the White House on this occasion, he resolved never to return while Mr. Pierce was its occupant. It is also of interest to note that this was the last time Mr. Hamlin entered the White House as a member of the Democratic party. A few days later, March 4, at five o'clock in the morning, after an exhausting struggle, just a year after Mr. Pierce had been installed in the presidency, the Senate voted to repeal the Missouri Compromise. The iron pressure of the administration proved too much for certain senators, and the hopes Mr. Hamlin and others had were disappointed. With the two honorable exceptions of John Bell, of Tennessee, and Sam Houston, of Texas, the Southern senators were a unit, and, with their Northern allies, threw thirty-seven votes for the destruction of the nation's solemn pledges of 1820. Houston's protest was moving and eloquent, and the more patriotic since he knew that it would ruin whatever chances he had for the presidency. Bell's course was equally honorable, and his fame would have been enviable in all respects had he remained as consistent to the end as Houston did.

Fourteen Northern senators voted for the abrogation of the Missouri Compromise, and several more were not in their seats when the final roll was called. The fourteen were General Lewis Cass and Charles E. Stuart of Michigan; Moses Norris and Jared W. Williams, of New Hampshire; Augustus C. Dodge and George W. Jones, of Iowa; Stephen A. Douglas and James Shields, of Illinois; William M. Gwin and John R. Weller, of California; Richard Brodhead, of Pennsylvania; John Pettit, of Indiana; John R. Thompson, of New

[1] Carroll's *Twelve Americans*, p. 137.

Jersey, and Isaac Toucey, of Connecticut. Jesse D. Bright, of Indiana, and Robert Toombs, of Georgia, were both absent when the vote was taken, but sent word that they favored the passage of the Douglas bill. Philip Allen, of Rhode Island, was called away from Washington on account of sickness in his family, but authorized his colleague to announce that he was opposed to the Douglas bill. Edward Everett, of Massachusetts, did not vote, on account of illness. He was opposed to the repeal. Pairs were not announced in the "Congressional Globe" at that time.

In the following May, the House passed a bill to repeal the Missouri Compromise by a vote of 113 to 100. There were forty-four Northern men among the majority, and they were distributed among a dozen different States, as the list will show. They were : Moses Macdonald, of Maine ; Harry Hibbard, of New Hampshire; Collin M. Ingersoll, of Connecticut; Thomas W. Cumming, Francis B. Cutting, Peter Rowe, John J. Taylor, William M. Tweed, Hiram Walbridge, William A. Walker, Mike Walsh, Theodoric R. Westbrook, of New York ; Samuel Lilly and George Vail, of New Jersey ; Samuel A. Bridges, John L. Dawson, Thomas B. Florence, J. Glancey Jones, William H. Kurtz, John McNair, Asa Packer, John W. Robbins, Christian M. Straub, William W. Witte, and Hendrick B. Wright, of Pennsylvania ; David T. Disney, Frederick W. Green, Edson B. Olds, Wilson Shannon, of Ohio ; Samuel Clark and David Stuart, of Michigan ; James C. Allen, Willis Allen, and William A. Richardson, of Illinois ; Bernhart Henn, of Iowa ; John G. Davis, Norman Eddy, William H. English,[1] Thomas A. Hendricks,[2] James H. Lane, Cyrus L. Dunham, and Smith Miller, of Indiana ; Milton S. Latham and James A. McDougall, of California.

There were nine Southern men in the House who resisted the cry of their section of the country for the wiping out of the Missouri Compromise. They were Thomas H. Benton, of Missouri ; Robert M. Bugg, William Cullom, Emerson Etheridge, and Nathaniel G. Taylor, of Tennessee ; Theodore G. Hunt, of Louisiana ; John S. Millson, of Virginia ; Richard C. Puryea and Sion H. Rogers, of North Carolina. The rest of the one hundred were : Israel Washburn, Samuel P. Benson, Samuel Mayall, E. Wilder Farley, and T. J. D. Fuller, of Maine ; Nathaniel P. Banks, Samuel L. Crocker, Alexander DeWitt, Edward Dickinson, J. Wiley Edmands, Thomas D. Eliot, John Z. Goodrich, Charles W. Upham, Samuel H. Walley, and Tappan Wentworth, of Massachusetts; George W. Kittredge, George W. Morrison, of New Hampshire ; James Meacham, Alvah Sabin, and Andrew Tracy, of Vermont ; Thomas Davis and Benjamin B.

[1] Democratic candidate for Vice-President in 1880.
[2] Elected Vice-President on the Democratic ticket in 1884.

Thurston, of Rhode Island; Nathan Belcher, James T. Pratt, and Origen S. Seymour, of Connecticut; Henry Bennett, Davis Carpenter, Gilbert Dean, Reuben E. Fenton, Thomas T. Flagler, George Hastings, Solomon G. Haven, Charles Hughes, Daniel T. Jones, Caleb Lyon, Orasamus B. Matteson, Edwin B. Morgan, William Murray, Andrew Oliver, Jared V. Peck, Rufus W. Peckham, Bishop Perkins, Benjamin Pringle, Russell Sage, George A. Simmons, Gerrit Smith, and John Wheeler, of New York; Alexander C. M. Pennington, Charles Skelton, and Nathan T. Stratton, of New Jersey; Joseph R. Chandler, Carlton B. Curtis, John Dick, Augustus Drum, William Everhart, James Gamble, Galusha A. Grow, Isaac E. Hiester, Thomas H. Home, John McCulloch, Ner Middleswarth, David Ritchie, Samuel Russell, and Michael C. Trout, of Pennsylvania; Edward Ball, Lewis D. Campbell, Alfred P. Edgerton, Andrew Ellison, Joshua R. Giddings, Aaron Harlan, Andrew J. Harlan, Scott Harrison, Harvey H. Johnson, William D. Lindsley, Matthias H. Nichols, Thomas Ritchey, William R. Sapp, Andrew Stuart, John L. Taylor, and Edward Wade, of Ohio; David A. Noble and Hestor L. Stevens, of Michigan; James Knox, Jesse O. Norton, Elihu B. Washburne, John Wentworth, and Richard Yates, of Illinois; Andrew J. Harlan, Daniel Mace, and Samuel W. Parker, of Indiana; Benjamin C. Eastman and Daniel Wells, of Wisconsin.

It is not easy to separate the sheep from the goats in this instance. It is probable that partisanship and patronage were equally responsible for the disastrous step Congress took. Macdonald, of Maine, one of the three representatives who falsified the sentiment of New England, was instructed by an almost unanimous vote of the legislature of Maine to oppose the repeal of the Missouri Compromise. In an extreme speech in the House, Macdonald denied the right of the legislature to instruct him, and claimed that that body did not correctly represent the sentiment of the State. He had long been one of Mr. Hamlin's most active opponents. He was now retired from Congress for misrepresenting the people of his district.

It was not clear what the slavery propagandists would do after they had succeeded in tearing down the bulwark of 1820. Their plan to colonize Kansas and Nebraska with slaveholders was carefully concealed at first. It was apparent, of course, that their onslaught on the Missouri Compromise meant "infinite mischief." There was nothing to do but wait and see what the conspirators would do next. Shortly after the Missouri Compromise was repealed, and before the Calhoun party had given a hint of the programme its leaders were plotting, Senator Hamlin stated his position to Douglas, Hunter, and other pro-slavery leaders of his party with whom he had sustained personal and party relations. He said to them: —

"If the Democratic party indorses the doctrine of non-intervention in its next presidential convention I will leave it."

With this Mr. Hamlin rested his case, awaiting official action of the party two years later. He voted with the Democratic senators on questions affecting the true principles of Democracy, but always opposed them on the slavery issue, and also squarely antagonized President Pierce on any measure that he favored in the interests of the slave power. Mr. Hamlin, therefore, virtually held the position of a Republican during the rest of the Pierce administration; but he was not the man to give up the ship while there was hope of keeping her afloat, and he did not officially sever his relations with the Democratic party until by its own act it was about to sink itself in the maelstrom in which the unhappy Pierce administration was wrecked.

One more incident of a personal nature, that reflects the rotten and reckless character of this unhappy political period, remains to be recorded. When the representatives of Texas were trying to induce the government to assume the heavy debt of their State, there was more than one member of Congress who profited financially through unscrupulous lobbyists who offered them Texas bonds at a low figure. One prominent Democrat, who was identified with the scheme to bribe Kansas to adopt a pro-slavery constitution by offering her land, and who was afterwards an unsuccessful candidate for Vice-President, laid the basis for his private fortune by buying up Texas scrip at this time. A certain senator, whose name Mr. Hamlin would not divulge out of consideration for his family, approached him at this time, and made him the only corrupt offer of money that was ever made to him in all his career. Mr. Hamlin had only a speaking acquaintance with this senator, and he was angered when the latter said to him in a mysterious way, "Senator, I know where Texas bonds can be obtained for fifty cents on the dollar."

"Indeed," replied Mr. Hamlin with a sharp look that was intended to preclude any suggestion of a dishonorable nature.

The senator, not understanding, proceeded eagerly, "Yes; I know where they can be bought for twenty-five cents on the dollar. What do you say?"

"I have this to say," replied Senator Hamlin, turning on the lobbyist, "I am forty-four years old to-day. I may have made mistakes, but I have never done anything of which I am ashamed, and with God's help I never will. Damn you and damn your bonds!"

Printed by BoD˝in Norderstedt, Germany